NEIL WILSON
MARK BAKER

PRAGUE
CITY GUIDE

INTRODUCING PRAGUE

Interior of the Estates Theatre (p103), where Mozart's Don Giovanni *premiered in 1787*

CHRISTER FREDRIKS

Prague can be all things to all people. It's the equal of Paris in terms of beauty. The history goes back a millennium. And the beer? The best in Europe.

The 1989 Velvet Revolution that freed the Czechs from communism bequeathed to Europe a gem of a city to stand beside stalwarts like Rome, Amsterdam and London. Not surprisingly, visitors from around the world have come in droves, and on a hot summer day it can feel like you're sharing Charles Bridge with the rest of humanity. But even the crowds can't take away from the spectacle of a 14th-century stone bridge, a hilltop castle and a lovely, lazy river – the Vltava – that inspired one of the most hauntingly beautiful pieces of 19th-century classical music, Smetana's 'Moldau'.

Modern-history buffs will be riveted by the ups and the downs of the 20th century here, from the country's founding in 1918 to the tragic Nazi occupation of WWII, the communist coup in 1948, the Warsaw Pact invasion of 1968, and finally the triumph of 1989 that brought hundreds of thousands of peaceful protesters onto the streets and sent playwright Václav Havel to Prague Castle.

Since 1989 it seems the changes have only become more frenetic. The city's arts and music scenes are thriving once again; the cultural calendar is packed with events and festivals, including the internationally renowned Prague Spring in May and early June. The standards of restaurants and hotels are much improved and unrecognisable from just a decade ago.

And if that's not enough to pique your interest, the beer is pretty good, too.

PRAGUE LIFE

The summer of 2010 finds Prague in the midst of a hectic, multi-million-euro makeover that promises to finally deliver the city from a once-sleepy Eastern bloc capital into the modern age. The biggest individual project – in terms of impact and euros – is the construction of the Blanka highway tunnel just north of the city centre between Letná park and the Hradčanská metro station. The tunnel will eventually stretch several kilometres underground and form a crucial link in Prague's ring-road motorway system. But for the time being (through 2012 at least) the result is absolute chaos. The area around Hradčanská bears more than a passing resemblance to Berlin at the end of WWII. The warren of tram lines that normally snake through the area have been completely re-routed and re-routed again, leaving even hardened transport veterans wondering from day to day which line goes where.

A second major reconstruction project involves something even closer to the hearts of most travellers: the renovation of the main train station (Praha hlavní nádraží). At the time of research, work was continuing apace to clean up and modernise the building, which just a couple of years ago could easily have taken top honours as Central Europe's sleaziest train station. The first phases have been encouraging: the main hall is filled with new shops, the information and ticketing areas have been vastly improved and the platforms are cleaner and better signposted. The work is expected to continue for a couple more years and is hoped to spur the revitalisation of the entire neighbourhood, which adjoins the top of Wenceslas Square and has been quite run down for a number of years.

While Czechs grumble about the inconveniences, there's a shared sense that the modernisation efforts were long overdue. Both the city's dilapidated road system and its derelict train station were legacies of the communist era. If Prague is ever hoped to take its rightful place among Europe's leading metropolises, it's generally agreed that these were necessary steps and that, anyway, it won't be that long before the tram lines are restored to their traditional routes.

Old Town Square (p89) bustles at dusk (as well as most other times of the day)   IZZET KERIBAR

HIGHLIGHTS

HISTORY & ARCHITECTURE

In Prague you can soak up a thousand years of European history, laid out in a giant smorgasbord of architectural styles that ranges from soaring Gothic and voluptuous baroque to elegant art nouveau and that uniquely Czech take on architecture, cubist.

RICHARD NEBESKY

WILMAR PHOTOGRAPHY/ALAMY

JOHN ELK III

RICHARD NEBESKY

❶ Prague Castle
Follow Havel 'na hrad!' – 'to the castle!' (p61).

❷ Charles Bridge
At its best on a misty summer's morning (p76).

❸ Vyšehrad
Escape the crowds at Prague's other castle (p119).

❹ Prague Jewish Museum
A sombre reminder of a darker side of
Prague's history (p98).

❺ Vinohrady
The district that brings on bouts of
apartment-envy (p124).

❻ Municipal House
Art nouveau for breakfast, lunch and dinner
(p102).

1 **Letná**
Praguers and visitors alike love the views from this hilltop park (p136).

2 **Wallenstein Garden**
Now, *this* is what you call a *real* garden…(p81)

3 **Vltava River**
Take a paddle on a hired boat from Slav Island (p116).

DOUG MCKINLAY

OUTDOOR PRAGUE

When the sun comes out, Prague's countless parks and gardens – not to mention the Vltava and its islands – come into their own. Whether it's skating in Stromovka, hiking up Petřín or just lounging with a beer in Letná, don't forget to pack shades and sunscreen.

RICHARD NEBESKY

RICHARD NEBESK

DRINKING

Prague is a drinker's town par excellence – the Czechs did invent lager, after all. From traditional pubs full of froth-tipped moustaches to cool cocktail bars where the staff are even more stylish than the clientele, Prague has the lot.

RICHARD NEBESKY

❶ U zlatého tygra
Where Havel took Bill Clinton to experience a real Prague pub (p186).

❷ U vystřeleného oka
Classic Žižkov pub, probably the most authentic in town (p190).

❸ Letenský zámeček
(Letná beer garden)
Just the place to spend a lazy Sunday afternoon (p191).

RICHARD NEBESKY

RICHARD NEBESKY

ART & LITERATURE

From Kafka to Kundera, the Czechs have made a major contribution to 20th-century European literature. In the art world, 'artist-provocateur' David Černý keeps up the Czech tradition of creating challenging and controversial art that makes us smile at the same time.

1

RICHARD NEBESKY

18

2

RICHARD NEBESKY

3

RICHARD NEBESKY

① Veletržní Palace
Four floors of modern art in a magnificent functionalist building (p139).

② Franz Kafka Museum
Explore the claustrophobic and paranoid world of Kafka's novels (p80).

③ Kafka's Grave
True Kafka fans can make a pilgrimage out to the Jewish Cemetery (p129).

④ David Černý
Černý's witty works pop up all over Prague (p142).

⑤ Franz Kafka Monument
Based on one of his stories, Kafka rides on an empty suit's shoulders (Map p90).

RICHARD NEBESKY

SCULPTURE BY JAROSLAV RÓNA/PHOTO BY RICHARD NEBESKY

MUSIC

Music is everywhere in Prague: from the great classical concert halls to the basement jazz joints; from the buskers lining Charles Bridge to the sounds of piano practice tinkling from an open window in a Malá Strana backstreet.

① Rudolfinum
Play 'spot the famous composer' among the statues lining the roof (p99).

② Dvořák's Tomb
The most famous Czech composer is buried at Vyšehrad Cemetery (p120).

③ Buskers on Charles Bridge
A few coins in the hat gets you an open-air jazz gig (p76).

④ Smetana Monument
Some consider Smetana superior to Dvořák – follow the debate at the Smetana museum (p103).

⑤ Chapel of Mirrors
One of the prettiest concert venues in the city (p101).

⑥ Smetana Hall, Municipal House
Stages the first performance of the annual Prague Spring festival (p102).

RICHARD NEBESKY

RICHARD NEBESKY

RICHARD NEBESKY

RICHARD NEBESKY

① Bunkr Parukářka
Beer and industrial music in the depths of a nuclear bunker (p198).

② Ecotechnical Museum
Who could resist a museum dedicated to sewage disposal? (p135)

③ Žižkov TV Tower
Futurist landmark covered in…David Černý's crawling babies? (p133)

④ Cubist lamppost
Where else in the world has a cubist lamppost? (p123)

OFFBEAT PRAGUE

One of the best bits about visiting Prague is wandering off the main streets to discover the sort of weird and wonderful stuff that you don't find back home.

RICHARD NEBESKY

DOUG MCKINL

CONTENTS

THE AUTHORS

Neil Wilson

Neil first succumbed to the pleasures of Prague back in 1995, beguiled, like everyone else, by its ethereal beauty, but also drawn to the darker side of its hidden history. He has returned regularly for a fix of the world's finest beers, and the chance to track down yet another obscure monument. He has now worked on six consecutive editions of Lonely Planet's *Prague* guide. A full-time freelance writer since 1988, Neil has travelled in five continents and written more than 50 travel and walking guides for various publishers. He is based in Edinburgh, Scotland. For more information see www.neil -wilson.com.

Neil was the coordinating author and wrote the Introducing Prague, Getting Started, Excursions, Transport and Directory chapters. He also cowrote the Neighbourhoods, Shopping, Eating, Drinking, Entertainment, Sports & Activities and Sleeping chapters.

NEIL'S TOP PRAGUE DAY

I'd start the day at Krásný Ztráty (p185), relaxing with the papers over a cappuccino. Then, after wandering through the backstreets of Staré Město, perhaps stopping to browse the bookshelves at Anagram (p152) and Big Ben (p152), I'd cross the river and spend the rest of the morning strolling through the gardens of Malá Strana (p86), stopping to read for a while on a park bench in either the Wallenstein Garden (p81) or the Palace Gardens Beneath Prague Castle (p81).

For lunch I'd grab a riverside table at Hergetova Cihelna (p164) and then take the funicular railway up Petřín (p85) for a stroll through the gardens to Strahov Monastery (p69), followed by a visit to the Story of Prague Castle (p66) exhibit in the castle grounds. By this time I'd be more than ready for a beer, so I'd walk east through Letná park to the beer garden (Letenský Zámeček; p191) and enjoy a Gambrinus or two with a view over the city.

Finally, I'd round off the day with dinner on the terrace at Terasa U zlaté studně (p164) – so that I could continue to enjoy that city view as the sun sets – followed by live jazz (and more beer) at U malého Glena (p201).

Mark Baker

Mark first visited Prague in the 1980s as a journalist for the Economist Group. Those were the dark days of the dying communist regime, yet even then he was hooked by the city's beauty, mysticism and roast pork. He moved to Prague in the early '90s shortly after the Velvet Revolution, and following a stint as a co-founder-owner of the Globe Bookstore & Coffeehouse and a journalist for Radio Free Europe/Radio Liberty, he's found permanent employment as a freelance travel writer. In addition to Lonely Planet's *Prague,* Mark is co-author of *Romania.*

Mark wrote the Background and Architecture chapters for this book, and cowrote the Neighbourhoods, Shopping, Eating, Drinking, Entertainment, Sports & Activities and Sleeping chapters.

WHEN TO GO

Prague caters for visitors year-round, so there's really no such thing as a bad time to visit. The city is at its prettiest in spring, when the many parks begin to bloom with flowers and the budding leaves on the trees are a glowing green.

The tourist crush is especially oppressive during Easter and Christmas through New Year, as well as in May (during the Prague Spring festival), June and September. Many Czechs go on holiday in July and August, when the weather can be uncomfortably hot – you'll probably want a hotel with air-con at this time of year. If you can put up with the cold and the periodic smog alerts, hotel space is plentiful in winter (outside Christmas to New Year), and the city looks gorgeous and mysterious under a mantle of snow.

FESTIVALS

Spring and autumn are the main festival seasons in Prague, and are when the big classical music events take place. Other minor festivals and events are scattered throughout the year – for a fuller listing check out www.pis.cz/en/prague/events and click on Preliminary Outline of Cultural Events in Prague.

January
THREE KINGS' DAY (SVÁTEK TŘÍ KRÁLŮ)
6 Jan

Three Kings' Day, also known as Twelfth Night, marks the formal end of the Christmas season on 6 January. The Czechs celebrate it with carol-singing, bell-ringing and gifts to the poor.

ANNIVERSARY OF JAN PALACH'S DEATH
19 Jan

A gathering in Wenceslas Square commemorates the Charles University student who burned himself to death in 1969 in protest against the Soviet occupation (see the boxed text, p29).

February
MASOPUST
www.carnevale.cz

Street parties, fireworks, concerts and revelry mark the Czech version of carnival. Banned by the communists, this tradition was first revived in Žižkov in 1993, and the rest of the city is now joining in. Celebrations start on the Friday before Shrove Tuesday (aka Mardi Gras), and end with a masked parade.

March
ST MATTHEW FAIR (MATĚJSKÁ POUŤ)

From the Feast of St Matthew (24 February) up to and including Easter weekend, the Výstaviště exhibition grounds (p134) fill with roller coasters, fair rides, ghost trains, shooting galleries and stalls selling candy floss and traditional heart-shaped cookies. The fair is open 2pm to 10pm Tuesday to Friday and 10am to 10pm Saturday and Sunday.

BIRTHDAY OF TOMÁŠ GARRIGUE MASARYK
7 Mar

The father figure and first president of Czechoslovakia is commemorated in a ceremony at Prague Castle.

ADVANCE PLANNING

Apart from booking flights and hotels well in advance in high season, Prague is not a city that asks you to do a great deal of forward planning.

If your main reason for visiting is to attend a major festival such as Prague Spring, check the festival website at least a month in advance, and book tickets for any performances you don't want to miss. If all you want to do is see some opera, listen to live jazz or catch a rock gig, take a look at websites such as www.prague.tv a week or two ahead to see what's on. Most opera and classical concert tickets are sold on the day or so before the performance.

We've mentioned in individual reviews where you might want to book a table at a particular restaurant. However, if you want somewhere special for, say, Valentine's Day, it's best to reserve a table a couple of weeks ahead.

Be aware that the economic downturn might result in some of our listings not lasting the lifetime of the book.

EASTER MONDAY (PONDĚLÍ VELIKONOČNÍ)

In this mirthful rite of spring, Czech boys chase their favourite girls and swat them on the legs with willow switches decked with ribbons (you'll see them on sale everywhere); the girls respond with gifts of hand-painted eggs (likewise on sale), then everyone gets down to some serious partying. It's the culmination of several days of spring-cleaning, cooking and visiting family and friends.

ONE WORLD (JEDEN SVĚT)

www.oneworld.cz

This week-long film festival is dedicated to documentaries on the subject of human rights. Screenings are held at some of the smaller cinemas around town, including Kino Světozor (p205).

FEBIOFEST

www.febiofest.cz

This international festival of film, TV and video features new works by international film-makers. Continues throughout the Czech Republic following the Prague festival.

April

BURNING OF THE WITCHES (PÁLENÍ ČARODĚJNIC)   30 Apr

This Czech pre-Christian (pagan) festival for warding off evil features the burning of brooms at Výstaviště (p134) and all-night, end-of-winter bonfire parties on Kampa island (p81) and in suburban backyards.

SPERM FESTIVAL

www.sperm.cz

A festival of contemporary art, music and 'visual culture' based at David Černý's avant-garde Meet Factory (p142).

May

BOOKWORLD PRAGUE (SVĚT KNIHY)

www.bookworld.cz

This major international book festival is held at the Výstaviště exhibition grounds (p134). Though primarily an industry event, it's open to the general public and has author readings, book launches, exhibits, seminars and lectures, mostly in English.

LABOUR DAY (SVÁTEK PRÁCE)   1 May

Once sacred to the communists, the 1 May holiday is now just an opportunity for a pic-

nic. To celebrate the arrival of spring, many couples lay flowers at the statue of the 19th-century romantic poet Karel Hynek Mácha (Map p78), author of *Máj* (May), a poem about unrequited love. Former president Václav Havel has been known to pay homage here.

PRAGUE SPRING (PRAŽSKÉ JARO)

Running from 12 May to 3 June, this international music festival is Prague's most prestigious event, with classical music concerts held in theatres, churches and historic buildings. For details, see the boxed text, p206.

PRAGUE FOOD FESTIVAL

www.praguefoodfestival.com

A Friday-to-Sunday celebration of all that is best in Czech and international cuisine, with cooking demonstrations, food stalls, beer- and wine-tastings and children's events spread throughout the gardens on the south side of Prague Castle.

KHAMORO

www.khamoro.cz

This festival of Roma culture, with performances of traditional music and dance, exhibitions of art and photography, and a parade through Staré Město, is usually held in late May.

June

PRAGUE FRINGE FESTIVAL

www.praguefringe.com

This nine-day binge of international theatre, dance, comedy and music, inspired by the innovative Edinburgh Fringe, takes place in late May/early June. Hugely popular with visitors, now pulling in more and more locals.

PRAGUE WRITERS' FESTIVAL

www.pwf.cz

An international meeting of writers from around the world, with public readings, lectures, discussions and bookshop events.

DANCE PRAGUE (TANEC PRAHA)

www.tanecpraha.cz

International festival of modern dance held at theatres around Prague throughout June.

July

JAN HUS DAY (DEN JANA HUSA)   6 Jul

Celebrations are held to remember the burning at the stake of Bohemian religious reformer Jan Hus in 1415. They're kicked off with low-key gatherings and bell-ringing at Bethlehem Chapel (p104) the evening before.

August

FESTIVAL OF ITALIAN OPERA

www.opera.cz

Beginning sometime in late August and extending into September, this festival features the works of Verdi and other Italian composers performed at the Prague State Opera (p205) – your chance to see quality productions outside of the main opera season.

September-November

STRINGS OF AUTUMN (STRUNY PODZIMU)

www.strunypodzimu.cz

Stepping into the gap left by the demise of the Prague Autumn festival, Strings is an eclectic program of musical performances from classical and baroque to avant-garde jazz, Sardinian vocal polyphony and contemporary Swiss yodelling. It runs for eight weeks (mid-September to mid-November).

December

CHRISTMAS-NEW YEAR (VÁNOCE-NOVÝ ROK)

From 24 December to 1 January many Czechs celebrate an extended family holiday. Revelling tourists engulf Prague, and a Christmas market is held in Old Town Square beneath a huge Christmas tree.

COSTS & MONEY

Gone are the days when Prague was a cheap destination. A rapidly growing tourism industry and an increasingly strong currency mean that the Czech capital now ranks alongside most Western European cities when it comes to quality hotels and restaurants.

In high season you can expect to pay around €160 (US$200) a night for a double room in a midrange hotel, while luxury and boutique hotel rooms can be in the €260 (US$325) range. Backpacker hostels typically charge around €15 (US$21) for a dorm bed. Dinner for two in a good Malá Strana restaurant can easily be €38 (US$52) per head with a bottle of wine, and the famously 'cheap' beer is now at least €2 (US$2.75) per 0.5L in tourist bars.

The good news is that you can still find relatively inexpensive food and drink if you're

HOW MUCH?

1L of petrol 31Kč

Bottled water (1.5L) 18Kč

Guardian newspaper 95Kč

Beer (0.5L) in tourist/nontourist pub 60Kč and up/30Kč

Pork & dumplings 100Kč to 150Kč

'Prague Drinking Team' T-shirt 200Kč to 400Kč (plus any remaining shreds of personal dignity)

Ticket to Laterna Magika 250Kč to 650Kč

Tour of Municipal House 270Kč

Cinema ticket 100Kč to 170Kč

Vintage car tour 1200Kč (per car)

prepared to venture off the beaten tourist trail – just a few blocks away from Old Town Square there are places where you can eat for under €11 (US$15) per person, and get that same beer for under €1 (US$1.30).

As for accommodation, oversupply in the hotel sector has seen room rates fall back to reasonable levels, and it's once again possible to snag a bargain. Search the internet for deals – many hotel websites offer special rates or weekend packages. Or consider visiting out of season: hotel rates can fall by up to 40% in winter.

INTERNET RESOURCES

All Praha (www.allpraha.com) Info for tourists and expats, with local listings (restaurants, bars, etc) reviewed by users.

Expats.cz (www.expats.cz) Community site for expats in Prague: listings, articles, forums, bar and restaurant reviews.

Living Prague (www.livingprague.com) Insider guide to the city by a British expat who has lived there for more than a decade.

Prague City Hall (http://magistrat.praha-mesto.cz) Official website of the city council, with lots of useful background information.

Prague Daily Monitor (www.praguemonitor.com) News site with English translations of what's making headlines in Czech newspapers.

Prague information service (www.pis.cz) Official tourist information website.

Prague Public Transport (www.dpp.cz) Everything you ever wanted to know about Prague's metro, tram and bus services.

PragueTV (www.prague.tv) Useful listings site covering nightlife, cinema, restaurants etc.

HISTORY
AN UNFAMILIAR STORY

The great irony of a trip to Prague is that though the city is steeped in history, it's a history that is unfamiliar to many visitors. London, Paris and Rome can feel instantly recognisable because their stories and myths have played such an important part in the way that Western culture has traditionally been taught. Prague is not like that. A tour of Prague Castle, for example, reveals a bewildering array of Sigismunds, Bořislavs, Boleslavs and, especially, Václavs. If you're not a grad student in European history, you're not likely to recognise many of the names or grasp much of their significance. That's a shame. Not just because Czech history is filled with gripping characters and stories, but also because it's an integral part of European history as a whole.

Visitors may be surprised to learn, for example, that Prague, under Charles IV and subsequent rulers, was once the seat of the Holy Roman Empire. Not Nero's empire in Rome, of course, but the patchwork of Christian kingdoms and principalities stretching across Europe that had evolved by the 14th and 15th centuries. In the late 16th century Prague, under Rudolf II, was also for a time the seat of the sprawling Habsburg empire, with territories as far flung as modern-day Italy and Poland.

Indeed, the city was once so tied into what we now consider to be Western Europe that all it took was for two Catholic councillors and a secretary to be flung out of a window at Prague Castle in the 17th century to ignite a war – the Thirty Years' War – that would subsume the entire continent.

All this, of course, won't help you get through the Boleslavs and Václavs, but it should be enough to persuade you to look past those unpronounceable names and see the connections. A little knowledge can make a big difference and help make that slog through Prague Castle much more rewarding. For a list of books that can take you deeper into Czech history, see the boxed text, p20).

THE RECEIVED WISDOM

Before getting started, a few words are in order regarding how history has traditionally been taught and told in the Czech Republic. For decades now, under the communists and in the years since the Velvet Revolution, an orthodox version of history has held sway that tends to see the Czechs as victims in their own national drama. Czech history, in this view, is a straightforward narrative of a small but just nation struggling to emerge from under the thumb of much bigger and more powerful adversaries. These included, over the years, the hierarchy of the Catholic Church in Rome, the Habsburgs in Vienna, the Germans in more modern times and, most recently, the Russians. This theme still permeates popular attitudes and forms the subtext behind descriptive information presented at museums and exhibitions. It also forms the fodder for guidebooks and newspaper and magazine articles.

500 BC–AD 400	AD 500	Early 600s
Celtic tribes thrive in the territory of the modern-day Czech Republic, building settlements whose remains will later be discovered in and around Prague.	Slavic tribes enter Central Europe during the period of the Great Migration, forming settlements along the Vltava River. Recent excavations indicate that the largest of these may have been near Roztoky, northwest of Prague.	Princess Libuše, the fabled founder of the Přemysl dynasty, looks out over the Vltava valley and predicts that a great city will emerge there someday.

READING UP ON CZECH HISTORY

Prague and the Czech Republic are not lacking in well-written historical accounts in English. The selection is particularly strong on books about the Nazi occupation and somewhat weaker about life under communism. British professor Timothy Garton Ash's *The Magic Lantern* remains the gold standard for accounts in English of the Velvet Revolution (as well as the 1989 anticommunist revolutions across Eastern Europe).

- *Magic Prague* (Angelo Maria Ripellino, 1973) – Italian professor Ripellino breathes new life into historical figures in this inventive and highly entertaining blend of fact and fiction. With characters like Rudolf II, the Golem and Franz Kafka to work with, it's hard to see how he could miss. Out of print but still possible to find secondhand.
- *Prague: A Cultural History* (Richard Burton, 2003) – A beautifully written cultural history by an English professor obviously in love with Prague and its myths. The first chapter, 'How to Read Prague', is especially helpful for visitors. The chapters are arranged around stories and characters – both real and fictional – that have shaped the city.
- *Prague in Black and Gold* (Peter Demetz, 1998) – The first of two books by émigré Czech literary historian Peter Demetz. This volume is a sweeping history of Demetz's hometown, with a keen eye for the absurd. It's a challenging read if you don't have a background in Czech or Central European history, but those who do will find it enriching.
- *Prague in Danger* (Peter Demetz, 2008) – Demetz's second (and more accessible) work is partly a classic history and partly a lively and moving chronicle of his own family – Demetz's mother was Jewish and died at Terezín. These personal remembrances are especially strong and give a firsthand feel for what life in Prague was like during the Nazi occupation. It's also a good general primer for historical markers like Reinhard Heydrich's assassination in 1942.
- *Prague in the Shadow of the Swastika* (Callum MacDonald and Jan Kaplan, 1995) – Part serious history and part powerful picture book focusing on Prague during the Nazi occupation. Hard to find, but usually stocked by English booksellers in Prague, such as Big Ben (p152).

That's not to say it's false. In fact, there's much truth in it. The Czechs have endured long periods of war and hardship, suffering foreign invasions that were not of their choosing. It's true that remarkable personalities, such as the religious reformer Jan Hus (see the boxed text, p22), were ultimately betrayed outside the country; indeed Czechoslovakia itself was in a sense betrayed by the West at Munich before WWII. The Czechs also suffered greatly under both Nazism and a repressive, Soviet-style communism.

But this view of history tells only part of the story. The Czechs have always been closer to the centre of their own history – both in good ways and bad – than some of their history books would like to believe. Just as the communists could not have ruled so long without the active engagement of some Czechs (and the quiet acquiescence of many), so too did the Germans, Austrians, Catholics and others over the years find willing locals to do their bidding. This is part of 'Czech history', too.

It would also be misleading to characterise foreign influences as invariably negative. Prague, to its great benefit, has always been a cosmopolitan place – we need only look at a handful of architectural masterpieces to make the point. The Charles Bridge (p76) and parts of St Vitus Cathedral (p65) were designed by a German, Peter Parler. Many statues that line the bridge were sculpted by Austrians. The baroque masterpiece of St Nicholas Church (p77) in Malá Strana was the work of a father-and-son team from Bavaria; much of the rest of Malá Strana's baroque splendour was built by Italians.

870s	26 August 1278	4 August 1306
Prince Bořivoj begins construction of Prague Castle on Hradčany to serve as the seat of his Přemysl dynasty – as it will for kings, emperors and presidents for centuries to come.	King Otakar II is thrashed by the Habsburgs at the Battle of Marchfeld (Moravské Pole in Czech) at the height of the Přemysl dynasty's influence.	The last Přemysl king, Wenceslas III, is murdered, leaving no male heir. The dynasty passes to John of Luxembourg, who will give Bohemia its greatest ruler, his son Charles IV.

- *So Many Heroes* (Alan Levy, 1980) – Gripping account of the 1968 Warsaw Pact invasion and the immediate aftermath through the eyes of an American journalist who witnessed it. Levy was eventually banned by the communists from living here and was allowed to return only in 1990. He served as editor-in-chief of the *Prague Post* until his death in 2004. Originally published under the title *Rowboat to Prague*.
- *The Coast of Bohemia* (Derek Sayer, 2000) – This broad historical treatment follows the rise of Czech national consciousness in the 19th century, through independence, the First Republic, WWII and the communist period. The title alludes to an oft-quoted line from Shakespeare's *The Winter's Tale*: 'Thou art perfect then, our ship hath touch'd upon the deserts of Bohemia?' – either proof of the Bard's appalling geography or a poetic reference to Bohemia's mythical sea coast.
- *The Killing of Reinhard Heydrich* (Callum MacDonald, 2007) – Absorbing account of the killing of Nazi Reichsprotektor Reinhard Heydrich in 1942 by Czech patriots who had parachuted in from Britain. The act remains highly controversial. The assassination helped burst the myth of Nazi invincibility, but resulted in reprisal attacks that cost thousands of lives.
- *The Magic Lantern: The Revolution of 1989 Witnessed in Warsaw, Budapest, Berlin, and Prague* (Timothy Garton Ash, 1993) – Some historians just seem to live right. Oxford professor Garton Ash had the professional and linguistic skills to interpret history as it was unfolding during the tumultuous months of 1989 – and the presence of mind to write it all down. Looks at the major anticommunist revolutions in Central Europe but is strongest on the Velvet Revolution.
- *Under a Cruel Star: A Life in Prague 1941–1968* (Heda Margolius Kovály, 1997) – One of the few books to forge a link between the Nazi and communist periods. The author, Jewish and born in Prague, had the double misfortune of being sent to Terezín and Auschwitz during WWII, only to survive the war and marry an up-and-coming communist who was executed in the 1950s show trials. This remarkable book is unfortunately out of print and hard to find, but worth the effort.

When President Tomáš Garrigue Masaryk commissioned the renovation of Prague Castle (p61) in the 1920s, he selected a Slovenian, Jože Plečnik, as chief architect. The list could go on and on.

There are encouraging signs that this orthodox view is starting to give way to a more nuanced perspective. One of the catalysts has been a change in generations at universities as professors who rose up through the ranks under the former communist regime gradually retire and give way to academics with more varied interests. One of the fastest-growing areas of scholarship these days is Jewish history and Prague's former position as a Central European centre for Jewish scholarship – something that would have been ignored or greatly diminished just a decade or two ago.

THE EARLY YEARS

There's been human habitation in and around Prague for some 600,000 years and permanent communities since around 4000 BC, but it's the Celts, who came to the area around 500 BC, who have aroused the most interest. The name 'Bohemia' for the western province of the Czech Republic derives from one of the most successful of the Celtic tribes, the Boii. Traces of Boii culture have been found as far away as southern Germany, leading some archaeologists to posit a relation between local Celts and those in France and possibly even further afield to the British Isles. It's also spurred playful speculation – more wishful thinking than historical fact – that the Czechs are actually the modern-day offspring of these historic warriors.

26 August 1346	6 July 1415	30 July 1419
Charles IV becomes Bohemian king on the death of his father; later, he adds the honorific Holy Roman Emperor to his list of titles. Prague booms as the seat of the empire.	Religious reformer Jan Hus is burned at the stake at Konstanz, Germany, for refusing to recant his criticisms of the Catholic Church. His death enrages supporters and enflames decades of religious strife.	Angry Hussite supporters rush into the New Town Hall and toss several Catholic councillors out the window, introducing the word 'defenestration' to the world.

JAN HUS

Jan Hus was the Czech lands' foremost – and one of Europe's earliest – Christian reformers, anticipating Martin Luther and the Lutheran reformation by more than a century.

Hus was born into a poor family in southern Bohemia in 1372. He studied at the Karolinum (Charles University) and eventually became dean of the philosophy faculty. Like many of his colleagues, Hus was inspired by the English philosopher and radical reformist theologian John Wycliffe. The latter's ideas on reforming the Roman Catholic priesthood meshed nicely with growing Czech resentment at the wealth and corruption of the clergy.

In 1391 Prague reformers founded the Bethlehem Chapel (p104), where sermons were given in Czech rather than Latin. Hus preached there for about 10 years while continuing his duties at the university. Hus' criticisms of the Catholic Church, particularly the practice of selling indulgences, endeared him to his followers but put him squarely in the pope's black book. The pope had Hus excommunicated in 1410, but he continued to preach. In 1415 he was invited to the Council of Constance to recant his views. He refused and was burned at the stake on 6 July 1415. An enormous statue of Hus stands in Old Town Square (p89).

Celtic settlements have been unearthed in several parts of Prague. During the construction of metro line B in the 1980s, a large Celtic burial ground was discovered at Nové Butovice, and evidence of early iron furnaces has been found not far away in Jinonice. Some even think there was an early Celtic settlement where Prague Castle now stands, but there's no physical evidence to support the claim.

THE ARRIVAL OF THE SLAVS

It's not clear even today what prompted the great migration of peoples in the 6th and 7th centuries, but during this time large populations of ethnic Slavs began arriving in Central Europe from the east, driving out the Celts and pushing the Germanic tribes further to the west. The newcomers established several settlements along the Vltava, including one near the present site of Prague Castle and another upriver at Vyšehrad (p119).

Archaeologists working near the town of Roztoky, northwest of Prague, recently unearthed what may be the largest and oldest of these settlements, dating from the first decades of the 6th century.

THE MYTH OF LIBUŠE

Fittingly for a city that embraces so much mystery, the origins of Prague are shrouded in a fairy tale. Princess Libuše, the daughter of early ruler Krok, is said to have stood on a hill one day at the start of the 7th century and foretold of a glorious city that would one day become Prague. According to legend, Libuše needed a strong suitor who would yield sturdy heirs to the throne. Passing over a field of eligible bachelors, including some sickly looking royals, she selected a simple ploughman, Přemysl. She chose well. The Přemysl dynasty would go on to rule for several hundred years.

In the 9th century, the Přemysl prince, Bořivoj, selected an outcropping on Hradčany to build Prague Castle, the dynasty's seat and the locus of power in this part of the world ever since.

Christianity became the state religion under the rule of the pious Wenceslas (Václav in Czech), Duke of Bohemia (r c 925–29), now the chief patron saint of the Czech people. Wenc-

Early 15th century	1583	23 May 1618
The Hussite Wars – pitting radical reformers against Catholics and, ultimately, different Hussite factions against each other – rage throughout Bohemia, laying waste to the country.	Habsburg Emperor Rudolf II moves the dynasty's seat from Vienna to Prague, ushering in a second golden age. It lasts only until Rudolf dies three decades later, when tensions between Protestants and Catholics start boiling over.	A Protestant mob pushes two Catholic councillors and their secretary from a window at Prague Castle. This 'second defenestration' pushes the Habsburgs into starting the Thirty Years' War.

eslas was the 'Good King Wenceslas' of the well-known Christmas carol, written in 1853 by English clergyman John Mason Neale. Neale, a scholar of European church history, had read about St Wenceslas's legendary piety, and based his carol on the story of the duke's page finding strength by following in the footsteps of his master. Wenceslas' conversion to Christianity is said to have angered his mother and his brother, Boleslav, who ended up killing the young duke in a fit of jealousy.

In spite of the occasional fratricide, the Přemysls proved to be effective rulers, forging a genuine Slav alliance and governing Bohemia until the 14th century. Until the early 13th century, the Přemysl rulers were considered dukes or princes, but in 1212, the pope granted Otakar I the right to rule as a king. At one point, Přemysl lands stretched from modern-day Silesia (near the Czechoslovakia and Poland border) to the Mediterranean Sea.

THE HOLY ROMAN EMPIRE

It's hard to imagine that Prague will ever exceed the position it had in the 14th century, when for a time it became the seat of the Holy Roman Empire under King and later Emperor Charles IV (Karel IV).

The path to glory began predictably enough with the 1306 murder of Přemysl ruler Wenceslas III, leaving no male successor to the throne. Eventually, John of Luxembourg (Jan Lucemburský to the Czechs) assumed the Czech throne through his marriage to Wenceslas III's daughter Elyška, in 1310.

Under the enlightened rule of John's son, Charles IV, Prague grew into one of the continent's largest and most prosperous cities. It was at this time that the city assumed its handsome Gothic look. Charles commissioned both the bridge that now bears his name and St Vitus Cathedral, among other projects. He also established Charles University as the first university in Central Europe.

CZECH VERSION OF 'THE TROUBLES'

In contrast to the 14th century, the 15th century brought mostly hardship and war; much of the good of preceding years was undone in an orgy of religion-inspired violence and intolerance. This period saw the rise of the Church reformation movement led by Jan Hus (see the boxed text, p22). Hus' intentions were admirable, but his movement ended up polarising the country.

In 1419, supporters of Hussite preacher Jan Želivský stormed Prague's New Town Hall on Wenceslas Square and tossed several Catholic councillors out of the windows. This act not only hardened attitudes on both sides but also introduced the word 'defenestration' (tossing someone from a window in order to do bodily harm) into the political lexicon.

The Hussites assumed control of Prague after the death of Holy Roman Emperor Wenceslas IV in 1419. This sparked the first anti-Hussite crusade, launched in 1420 by Holy Roman Emperor Sigismund. Hussite commander Jan Žižka successfully defended the city in the Battle of Vítkov Hill, but religious strife spilled into the countryside. The Hussites themselves were torn into warring factions: those wanting to make peace with the emperor and others wanting to fight to the end. The more radical Hussite faction, the Taborites, were ultimately defeated in battle at Lipany in 1434.

Following Sigismund's death, George of Poděbrady (Jiří z Poděbrad) ruled as Bohemia's one and only Hussite king, from 1452 to 1471, with the backing of the moderate Hussites known

8 November 1620	21 June 1621	29 October 1787
Czech soldiers, united under Protestant leader Frederick V, Elector Palatine, lose a crucial battle at Bílá Hora, west of Prague, to Austrian Habsburg troops. The loss brings in 300 years of Austrian rule.	Twenty-seven Czech noblemen are executed in Old Town Square for their part in instigating the anti-Habsburg revolt. Their severed heads are hung from the Old Town Tower on Charles Bridge.	Wolfgang Amadeus Mozart, already far more popular in Prague than in Vienna, serves as conductor at the premiere of his opera *Don Giovanni*, staged at the Estates Theatre near Old Town Square.

as the Utraquists. The damage, however, had been done, and once-prosperous Bohemia lay in ruin. The rest of the century was spent in an uneasy balance between the Protestant Czech citizenry and the Catholic nobility.

ENTER THE AUSTRIANS

Though it took time for the country to recover from the Hussite Wars, the latter part of the 16th century is generally viewed as a second 'golden age' under Habsburg Emperor Rudolf II (the first being the reign of Charles IV in the 14th century). Austria's Habsburg dynasty generally gets a bad rap in Czech history books, largely because of the repressive means, including public executions, that the Habsburgs used to enforce their rule after the Czech defeat at Bílá Hora (White Mountain) in 1620 (see p147). But it's generally forgotten that it was the Czech nobility, in 1526, who invited the Habsburgs – in the person of Ferdinand I – to rule in the first place. Ferdinand endeared himself to the mostly Catholic nobility, but alienated large sections of Czech society.

Ferdinand's grandson Rudolf, however, was a far more popular figure. He preferred Prague to Vienna and moved the seat of the Habsburg empire here for the duration of his reign (r 1575–1611). Today Rudolf is generally viewed as something of a loveable kook. It is true that he used his patronage to support serious artists and scientists, including noted astronomers Tycho Brahe and Johannes Kepler, but he also had a soft spot for some more esoteric pursuits, including soothsaying and alchemy. The English mathematician and occultist John Dee and his less well-regarded countryman Edward Kelly were just two of the noted mystics that Rudolf retained at the castle in an eternal quest to turn base metals into gold. Rudolf was also a friend to Prague's large Jewish population, who enjoyed a rare period of prosperity during his reign, despite being crowded into a tiny ghetto just north of the Old Town (see the boxed text, opposite).

The end of Rudolf's reign in the early 17th century was marked by renewed strife between Protestants and Catholics, culminating in 1618 in what became known as the 'second defenestration of Prague'. A group of Protestant noblemen stormed into a chamber at Prague Castle and hurled two Catholic councillors and their secretary out the window. The men survived – legend has it they fell onto a dung heap that softened the blow. But the damage was done. The act sparked a decades-long war – the Thirty Years' War – that eventually consumed the whole of Europe and left Bohemia once again in tatters.

For the Czechs it was to get even worse. Following the second defenestration, the Czech nobility elected a German Protestant – Frederick V, Elector Palatine – to be their leader in a looming battle with the Catholic Habsburgs. Frederick's rule was dogged by poor morale, and most of the European powers sided with the Habsburgs. In the end, the Czechs were routed by the Habsburgs at the Battle of Bílá Hora on the western edge of Prague, on 8 November 1620. The fighting lasted less than two hours. Frederick, the 'Winter King' (so called because he ruled Bohemia for just one winter), fled and in 1621, the 27 nobles who had instigated the revolt were executed in Old Town Square.

The defeat at Bílá Hora slammed the door on Czech independence for three centuries. Czechs lost their privileges, rights and property, and almost even their national identity through enforced Catholicisation and Germanisation as part of the wider Counter-Reformation movement. During the Thirty Years' War, Saxons occupied Prague from 1631 to 1632, and the Swedes seized

3 July 1883	28 October 1918	1920s
German-Jewish writer Franz Kafka is born just off Old Town Square. He'll go on to lead a double life: mild-mannered insurance clerk by day, harried father of the modern novel by night.	A newly independent Czechoslovakia is proclaimed at the Municipal House (Obecní dům) in the final days of WWI. Crowds throng Wenceslas Square in jubilation.	The heyday of the First Republic, now seen as another golden age. Prague intellectuals are heavily influenced by modern movements in art, architecture, literature and photography.

THE JEWS OF PRAGUE

Prague's Jews first moved into a walled ghetto in about the 13th century, in response to directives from Rome that Jews and Christians should live separately. Subsequent centuries of repression and pogroms culminated in a threat from Ferdinand I (r 1526–64) to throw all the Jews out of Bohemia.

Official attitudes changed under Rudolf II at the end of the 16th century. Rudolf bestowed honour on the Jews and encouraged a flowering of Jewish intellectual life. Mordechai Maisel, the mayor of the ghetto at the time, became Rudolf's finance minister and the city's wealthiest citizen. Another major figure was Judah Loew ben Bezalel (Rabbi Loew), a prominent theologian, chief rabbi, student of the mystical teachings of the kabbalah and nowadays best known as the creator of the mystical creature, the Golem – a kind of proto-robot made from the mud of the Vltava River.

When they helped to repel the Swedes on Charles Bridge in 1648, the Jews won the favour of Ferdinand III to the extent that he had the ghetto enlarged. But a century later they were driven out of the city, only to be welcomed back when city residents missed their business.

In the 1780s Habsburg emperor Joseph II (r 1780–90) outlawed many forms of discrimination, and in the 19th century the Jews won the right to live where they wanted. Many chose to leave the ghetto for nicer parts of the city. At the end of the 19th century the city decided to clear the ghetto, which had become a slum. In place of the ancient buildings they built the beautiful art nouveau apartment houses found there today.

The ghetto, renamed Josefov in Joseph's honour, remained the spiritual heart of Prague's Jewish community, but that came to a brutal end with the Nazi occupation during WWII. Today the entire city is home to roughly 5000 Jews, a fraction of the community's former size.

Hradčany and Malá Strana in 1648. Staré Město, though unconquered, suffered months of bombardment (the Old Town Tower on Charles Bridge still shows the scars of battle). Prague's population declined from 60,000 in 1620 to 24,600 in 1648. The Habsburgs moved their throne back to Vienna, reducing Prague to a provincial backwater.

REVIVAL OF THE CZECH NATION

Remarkably, Czech language and culture managed to hold on through the years of the Austrian occupation. As the Habsburgs eased their grip in the 19th century, Prague became the centre of the Czech National Revival. The revival found its initial expression not in politics – outright political activity was forbidden – but in Czech-language literature and drama. Important figures included linguists Josef Jungmann and Josef Dobrovský, and František Palacký, author of *Dějiny národu českého* (The History of the Czech Nation).

While many of the countries in post-Napoleonic Europe were swept up in similar nationalist sentiments, social and economic factors gave the Czech revival particular strength. Educational reforms by Empress Maria Theresa (r 1740–80) had given even the poorest Czechs access to schooling, and a vocal middle class was emerging through the Industrial Revolution.

Prague joined in the 1848 democratic revolutions that swept Europe, and the city was first in line in the Austrian empire to rise in favour of reform. Yet like most of the others, Prague's revolution was soon crushed. In 1863, however, Czech speakers defeated the German speakers in Prague council elections and edged them out of power, though the shrinking German-language minority still wielded considerable power until the end of the century.

30 September 1938	15 March 1939	27 May 1942
European powers, meeting in Munich, agree to Hitler's demand to annex Czechoslovakia's Sudetenland region. British PM Neville Chamberlain declares they have achieved 'peace in our time'.	German soldiers cross the Czechoslovak frontier and occupy Bohemia and Moravia. Czechoslovak soldiers, ordered in advance not to resist, allow the Germans to enter without firing a shot.	Czechoslovak patriots succeed in assassinating German Reichsprotektor Reinhard Heydrich. The men are later found hiding in a church in Nové Město. Trapped by Nazi soldiers, some take their own lives; the others are killed.

INDEPENDENCE AT LAST

For Czechs, WWI had a silver lining. The 1918 defeat of the Axis powers, including the Austro-Hungarian empire, left the empire too weak to fight for its far-flung holdings. Czech patriots Tomáš Garrigue Masaryk and Edvard Beneš had spent much of the war years in the United States, where they lobbied ceaselessly with Czech and Slovak émigré communities for a joint Czech and Slovak state. The plea appealed especially to the idealistic American president, Woodrow Wilson, and his belief in the self-determination of peoples. The most workable solution appeared to be a single federal state of two equal republics, and this was spelled out in agreements signed in Cleveland, Ohio, in 1915 and Pittsburgh, Pennsylvania, in 1918 (both cities having large populations of Czechs and Slovaks).

As WWI drew to a close, Czechoslovakia declared its independence, with Allied support, on 28 October 1918. Prague became the capital, and the popular Masaryk, a writer and political philosopher, the republic's first president.

THE FIRST REPUBLIC & WORLD WAR II

Czechoslovakia in the two decades between independence and the 1939 Nazi invasion was a remarkably successful state. Even now Czechs consider the 'First Republic' another golden age of immense cultural and economic achievement.

Czechoslovakia's proximity to Nazi Germany and its sizeable German minority in the border region with Germany, known as the Sudetenland, however, made it a tempting target for Adolf Hitler. Hitler correctly judged that neither Britain nor France had an appetite for war – and certainly not for a small country like Czechoslovakia. At a conference in Munich in 1938, Hitler demanded that Germany be allowed to annex the Sudetenland. British Prime Minister Neville Chamberlain acquiesced, famously calling Germany's designs on Czechoslovakia a 'quarrel in a faraway country between people of whom we know nothing'.

On 15 March 1939 Germany occupied all of Bohemia and Moravia, declaring the region a 'protectorate', while Slovakia was permitted to declare independence as a Nazi puppet state. During the war, Prague was spared significant physical damage, though the Nazis destroyed the Czech resistance – and killed thousands of innocent Czechs in retaliation for the assassination in Prague of SS general and Reichsprotektor Reinhard Heydrich by Czech patriots in 1942 (see the boxed text, p118).

Prague's pre-WWII Jewish community of around 40,000 was all but wiped out by the Nazis. Almost three-quarters of them, and 90% of all the Jews in Bohemia and Moravia, died of disease or starvation or were killed in Nazi extermination camps from 1941 to 1944.

On 5 May 1945, with the war drawing to a close, the citizens of Prague staged an uprising against the Germans. The Red Army was advancing from the east and US troops had made it as far as Plzeň (80km west of Prague), but were holding back from liberating the city in deference to their Soviet allies. The only help for Prague's lightly armed citizens came from Russian soldiers of the so-called Vlasov units, former POWs who had defected to the German side and now defected in turn to the Czech cause. Many people died in the uprising before the Germans pulled out on 8 May, having been granted free passage out in return for an agreement not to destroy more bridges and buildings. Most of Prague was thus liberated by its own citizens before the Red Army arrived on 9 May. Liberation Day is now celebrated on 8 May; under communism it was 9 May.

5 May 1945	9 May 1945	25 February 1948
Prague residents begin an armed uprising against the Germans and liberate the city after three days of fighting. The Germans are given free passage out in exchange for agreeing not to destroy the city.	The Soviet Army formally liberates the city, though most of the German soldiers are already defeated or gone. Under the communists, this will be recognised as the official day of liberation.	Communists stage a bloodless coup. Party leader Klement Gottwald proclaims the news on Old Town Square. Crowds cheer, but the coup ultimately leads to four decades of oppressive communist rule.

In 1945 Czechoslovakia was reconstituted as an independent state. One of its first acts was the expulsion of the remaining Sudeten Germans from the borderlands. By 1947, some 2.5 million ethnic Germans had been stripped of their Czechoslovak citizenship and forcibly expelled to Germany and Austria. Thousands died during the forced marches.

Despite a 1997 mutual apology for wartime misdeeds by the Czech Republic and Germany, the issue of the postwar German expulsions still brings emotions to the boil. Many ethnic-German survivors feel their citizenship and property were taken illegally. Many Czechs, on the other hand, remain convinced that the Sudeten Germans forfeited their rights when they initially sought help from Nazi Germany, and that a formal apology by President Václav Havel in 1990 for the expulsions was unwarranted.

FROM THE NAZIS TO THE COMMUNISTS

For many Czechs, WWII had tarnished the image of the Western democracies for sanctioning Hitler's rise to power and the dismemberment of Czechoslovakia. Communist appeals for world peace and economic justice found a receptive ear in a war-torn country. In the first elections after the war, in 1946, the Communist Party of Czechoslovakia (KSČ) became the republic's dominant party, winning 36% of the popular vote.

As relations between wartime allies the US and the Soviet Union deteriorated, Soviet leader Josef Stalin tightened his grip on Eastern and Central Europe. In February 1948, with Stalin's blessing, Czechoslovak communists staged a bloodless coup, proclaiming a workers' state, with the government and economy to be organised along Soviet lines. KSČ leader Klement Gottwald announced the coup to euphoric crowds from the balcony of the Goltz-Kinský Palace (p94) on Old Town Square.

PLAYWRIGHT-PRESIDENT VÁCLAV HAVEL

The Velvet Revolution produced at least one great name known around the world. Václav Havel – playwright, dissident and the country's first postcommunist president – was born on 5 October 1936, the son of a wealthy Prague businessman. His family's property was confiscated in the communist coup of 1948, and because of his bourgeois background, he was denied easy access to education. He nevertheless finished high school and studied for a time at university before landing a job as a stagehand at the Theatre on the Balustrade (p207). Nine years later he was its resident playwright.

His enthusiasm for the liberal reforms of the 'Prague Spring' and his signature on the Charter 77 declaration made him an enemy of the communist government. His works, which typically focused on the absurdities and dehumanisation of totalitarian bureaucracy, were banned and his passport seized. Altogether he spent some four years in jail for his activities on behalf of human rights.

The massive demonstrations of November 1989 thrust Havel into the limelight as a leading organiser of the noncommunist Civic Forum movement, which ultimately negotiated a peaceful transfer of power. Havel was swept into office as president shortly after, propelled by a wave of thousands of cheering demonstrators holding signs saying *Havel na hrad!* (Havel to the castle!)

In 2003, after two terms as president, Havel was replaced by former prime minister Václav Klaus. Since leaving office, Havel has finished at least two memoirs and in 2008 returned to the stage as the author of a new and highly acclaimed play, *Odcházení* (Leaving).

20 November 1952	20–21 August 1968	16 January 1969
In a Soviet-style purge, communists accuse several of their own party functionaries, including General Secretary Rudolf Slánský, of treason. The prisoners are executed at Prague's Pankrác prison.	Warsaw Pact forces, led by the Soviet Union, invade Czechoslovakia to put an end to reforms known as the Prague Spring. Reforming communist leader Alexander Dubček is replaced by hard-liner Gustáv Husák.	Student Jan Palach immolates himself at the top of Wenceslas Square to protest the Warsaw Pact invasion. Thousands come to the square in the following days to mark his memory and attend his funeral.

By the 1950s the initial enthusiasm had faded as communist economic policies nearly bankrupted the country and a wave of repression sent thousands to labour camps. In a series of Stalin-style purges staged by the KSČ in the early '50s, many people, including top members of the party, were executed.

In the 1960s, Czechoslovakia enjoyed a gradual liberalisation under reformist party leader Alexander Dubček. The reforms reflected a popular desire for full democracy and an end to censorship – 'Socialism with a Human Face', as the party called it.

But Soviet leaders grew alarmed at the prospect of a democratic society within the Eastern bloc and the potential domino effect on Poland and Hungary. The brief 'Prague Spring' was crushed by a Soviet-led military invasion on the night of 20–21 August 1968. Prague was the major objective; Soviet forces, with the help of the Czechoslovak secret police, secured the airport for Soviet transport planes. At the end of the first day, 58 were dead. Much of the fighting took place near the top of Wenceslas Square; the facade of the National Museum still bears bullet scars.

In 1969 Dubček was replaced by the hard-line Gustáv Husák and exiled to the Slovak forestry department. About 14,000 party functionaries and another 280,000 members who refused to renounce their belief in 'Socialism with a Human Face' were expelled from the party and lost their jobs. Many other educated professionals became manual labourers and street cleaners.

In January 1977 a group of 243 writers, artists and other intellectuals signed a public demand for basic human rights, Charter 77, which became a focus for opponents of the regime. Prominent among them was the poet and playwright Václav Havel (see the boxed text, p27).

VELVET REVOLUTION & DIVORCE

The year 1989 was a momentous one throughout Central and Eastern Europe. Czechoslovak communist officials watched nervously as one by one the neighbouring regimes toppled, culminating in the breaching of the Berlin Wall in early November. There was a growing sense of excitement within the population that the leadership would not be able to cling to power, but there was also palpable fear over how the transfer of power would take place.

On 17 November Prague's communist youth movement organised an officially sanctioned demonstration in memory of the students who were executed by the Nazis in 1939 (see the boxed text, opposite). But the peaceful crowd of 50,000 was cornered on Národní třída. Hundreds were beaten by police, and around 100 were arrested.

Czechs were electrified by the violence, and demonstrations were held by students, artists and then most of the population, peaking at a rally of 750,000 people in Letná (p136). Leading dissidents, with Havel at the forefront, formed an anticommunist coalition, which negotiated the government's resignation on 3 December. A 'government of national understanding' was formed with the communists as a minority. Havel was elected president by the Federal Assembly on 29 December. These events became known as the Velvet Revolution because of their nonviolent nature.

Almost immediately after the revolution, problems arose between Czechs and Slovaks. The Slovaks had for a long time harboured grievances against the dominant Czechs, and many Slovaks dreamed of having their own state. The Czech side was deeply divided: some wanted to keep Czechoslovakia intact while others were willing to see the economically weaker Slovaks go their own way.

On 1 January 1993, amid much hand wringing on both sides – especially from Havel, who refused to preside over the splitting up of the country – the Czechs and Slovaks peacefully divided into independent states.

1977	17 November 1989	1 January 1993
Life in Prague after 'normalisation' reaches a political and cultural nadir. Václav Havel and other dissidents sign Charter 77, a petition calling on Czechoslovakia to meet its international obligations on human rights.	Police use violence to halt a student demonstration along Národní třída. The action shocks the nation, sparking days of demonstrations that culminate in the communists relinquishing power – soon to be called the Velvet Revolution.	The Czech and Slovak republics agree peacefully to split into independent countries, formally bringing an end to Czechoslovakia. The split later becomes known as the 'Velvet Divorce'.

STUDENT SACRIFICES

Throughout Czech history, from the time of Jan Hus to the Velvet Revolution, Prague's university students have not been afraid to stand up for what they believe. Many of them have even sacrificed their lives. Two student names that have gone down in 20th-century Czech history are Jan Opletal and Jan Palach.

On 28 October 1939, shortly after the start of WWII and on the 21st anniversary of Czechoslovak independence, Jan Opletal, a medical student, was shot and fatally wounded by police who were trying to break up an anti-Nazi rally. After his funeral, on 15 November, students took to the streets, defacing German street signs, chanting anti-German slogans, and taunting the police. The Nazi response was swift and brutal.

In the early hours of 17 November that year, now known as the 'Day of Students' Fight for Freedom and Democracy', the Nazis raided Prague's university dormitories and arrested around 1200 students before carting them off to various prisoner camps. Some were executed and others died. Prague's universities were closed for the duration of WWII.

Thirty years after Opletal's death, on 16 January 1969, university student Jan Palach set himself on fire on the steps of the National Museum (p115) in protest of another foreign occupation, this one the Warsaw Pact invasion of the country the previous August. He staggered down the steps in flames and collapsed on the pavement at the foot of the stairs. The following day around 200,000 people gathered in the square in his honour.

It was three days before he died, and his body was buried in the Olšany Cemetery (p132) in Žižkov. His grave became a focus for demonstrations and in 1974 his remains were exhumed and moved to his home village. By popular demand he was re-interred in Olšany Cemetery in 1990. A cross-shaped monument set into the pavement in front of the National Museum marks the spot where he fell.

The street in Staré Město called 17.listopadu (17 November; Map p90) was named in honour of the students who suffered on 17 November 1939. Exactly 50 years later, on 17 November 1989, students marching along Národní třída in memory of that day were attacked and clubbed by police (there's a bronze memorial at the spot; see p114). The national outrage triggered by this event pushed the communist government towards its final collapse a couple of weeks later.

POST-'89 PRAGUE

It would be impossible to summarise in a few paragraphs the changes that have taken place in the 20 years since the Velvet Revolution. The big-picture view is largely positive, though. The Czech Republic achieved its two major long-term foreign policy goals, joining the NATO military alliance in 1999 and the EU in 2004.

When it comes to local politics, the country continues to ride a knife-edge. Neither major centrist party, the right-leaning Civic Democratic Party (ODS) or the left-leaning Social Democratic Party (ČSSD), has been able to cobble together a lasting consensus. In 2009 and early 2010, wrangling between the major parties left the country without an elected government for the second time in three years, leading local wags to declare the Czech Republic to be the world's largest nongovernmental organisation. The parliamentary elections in May 2010 appear to have solved the country's governing difficulties, at least for the time being. The vote brought a centre-right coalition to power with a stable majority, giving rise to hope that the country may finally be on the road to political maturity.

Havel finished 13 years as president in 2003 and was replaced by his rival, conservative Václav Klaus (formerly the prime minister). Klaus was re-elected to a second five-year term in 2008, though the president remains largely a figurehead.

12 March 1999	14 August 2002	1 May 2004
The Czech Republic enters the NATO military alliance along with Poland and Hungary. The move angers Russia in spite of assurances from NATO that the alliance is purely defensive.	Several city districts and the metro tunnels are inundated as the flooded Vltava River reaches its highest level in modern times. The damages cost several billion euros and spark redevelopment in hard-hit areas.	The Czech Republic achieves its biggest foreign policy objective since the Velvet Revolution and joins the European Union, along with several other former communist countries from Central and Eastern Europe.

WHEN 'BIG BROTHER' WAS REAL LIFE

More than 20 years on from the Velvet Revolution, it seems as if communism never happened. Prague has taken its place among Europe's colourful capitals, and on a sunny day it can feel like all is right with the world. But memories of a darker period still run deep. Anna Siskova, a Czechoslovak by birth, was a high-school student in Bratislava in 1989 when communism fell. She now lives in Prague, where she works in communications for an international hotel chain. She told us a little bit about life with 'Big Brother'.

What's your strongest memory when you think back to communist times? Everything suddenly turns grey: grey streets, grey houses, shops that had identical goods all over Czechoslovakia no matter what city you lived in. I think about our family trips to the Black Sea. We went to Bulgaria, the only country easily accessible to citizens of the communist camp. To get to Yugoslavia, you needed a special grey passport. The Bulgarian coast was full of Hungarians, East Germans, Slovaks, Czechs and Poles. You could tell where someone was from by his or her swimsuit!

Do you remember where you were when you first heard about the Velvet Revolution? I remember exactly. It was 16 November, the day before. We were sent home from school early (normal procedure if there was a demonstration planned). We were told to go straight home and not to go to the centre. There was a student protest at the Ministry of Education and, surprisingly, state TV reported the students' complaints. On 17 November, when news came in from Prague, it was very surprising. I was excited. Older people kept saying we shouldn't be too enthusiastic – remember what happened with the Prague Spring? But I didn't care. I stood on the square every day. It was amazing.

Give us a feeling for how it was back then to live. How was it buying food or clothes? One of the best jobs was to work in a vegetable or meat shop. If you knew someone from a *zelovoc* (fruit and veg shop), you could at least get bananas and tangerines. And clothes – everyone was wearing the same. There was no choice, and if the shops got something special – I remember once [there were] clothes from Greece – there was an enormous line in front. There was always some kind of shortage, though. When the paper factory burned down, there was no toilet paper in the whole country.

Is there anything from that period you really miss? What is worse now than it was then? People used to read more. They loved going to the theatre as they could always find some political hints in the plays. It was a strange atmosphere. I don't miss it, but it brings back nostalgic memories. As kids we were motivated to learn German and English, just so we could understand Austrian TV and radio, and English songs.

In terms of the economy, Prague has prospered since the Velvet Revolution, becoming one of the biggest tourist draws on the continent. Unemployment is minimal, the shops are full and the facades that were crumbling a decade ago have been given facelifts.

It would be a stretch to say the economic transformation from communism to capitalism has been easy. The complex process of selling off state-owned assets to private buyers was rife with corruption. And even now there's a lingering sense that wealth is concentrated in far too few hands and that while the communists may have lost the political game, they have prospered through their former positions and connections. The global economic downturn in 2009 and 2010 didn't help matters, reminding Czechs as well as people from across Europe that whereas capitalism has significant power to create wealth, it can also occasionally deliver unexpected hardship.

15 February 2008	1 January 2009	28–29 May 2010
By a narrow margin, the Czech parliament re-elects conservative economist Václav Klaus to his second five-year term as President of the Czech Republic.	Czech Republic formally assumes the rotating six-month EU presidency. The period will be marked by gaffes and errors, punctuated by the collapse of the Czech government in a confidence vote in March 2009. It will be hailed as the most chaotic EU presidency ever.	In landmark elections, Czechs vote in a new centre-right coalition, ending nearly a year without an elected government.

ARTS

Ask anyone outside the Czech Republic to name a famous Czech artist, musician or writer, and odds are he or she will come up with Alfons Mucha, Antonín Dvořák or Franz Kafka. But to the generation of Czechs who have grown up in the 20 years since the Velvet Revolution, these are names from the very distant past. Even relatively recent cultural icons like writers Milan Kundera or Ivan Klíma (both still alive and writing, by the way) seem out of touch with new realities. Václav Havel was only recently able to salvage his ageing reputation as a playwright with a hit play in 2008 – his first since 1989.

Enthused by romantic notions of the Czech National Revival, art nouveau or outdated notions of the noble dissident struggling against an oppressive communist regime, visitors to Prague all too often overlook the vibrant arts scene that has arisen here since 1989. Prague's major art galleries are complemented by dozens of small, independent and commercial galleries, where you can begin to appreciate the artistic energy that bubbles away beneath the city. And the many concert venues, jazz clubs and rock bars are fun, affordable and easily accessible.

MUSIC

Praguers have eclectic tastes, ranging from the ever-popular Mozart, who conducted the premier of *Don Giovanni* here in 1787, to Tom Waits, who sold out the Kongresové Centrum (Congress Centre) in a matter of hours for two concerts in July 2008.

The rock and pop scene has evolved greatly since 1989, when it was dominated by dissident-era rock bands and highly influential (but well past their prime) international acts like the Velvet Underground and the Rolling Stones. Those bands were soon drowned out by a flood of international acts and newer trends like electronic music, trance, techno, hip hop, rap, world and indie. One of the surprise bands to emerge in recent years has been Čechomor, which combines harmonies and Czech folk traditions in songs that are simple and yet hauntingly beautiful.

At the classical end of the musical spectrum, mezzo-soprano Magdalena Kožená (b 1973) is a leading light in the younger generation of opera singers. She has carved out a career as a major concert and recital artist – performing at the Salzburg, Glyndebourne and Edinburgh festivals, among others – and has recorded best-selling albums of Mozart arias, French opera and Bach's *St Matthew Passion*.

Classical

Classical music is hugely popular in Prague, and not only with the crowds of international aficionados who flock to the renowned Prague Spring music festival every May – the Czechs themselves have always been keen fans. Under the Austro-Hungarian monarchy, Czechs were considered to have discriminating tastes and even embraced Mozart's music long before the composer achieved any measure of respect in Vienna.

Distinctly Czech classical music first blossomed in the mid-19th century, when the National Revival saw the emergence of several great composers who drew inspiration for their work from traditional Czech folk music. Bedřich Smetana (1824–84) incorporated folk motifs into his classic compositions. His best-known works are *Prodaná nevěsta* (The Bartered Bride), *Dalibor a Libuše* (Dalibor and Libuše), and the six-part symphonic poem *Má vlast* (My Homeland), which contains arguably the most famous Czech classical composition, *Vltava* (The Moldau).

Antonín Dvořák (1841–1904) is probably the best-known Czech composer internationally. He spent four years in the US, where he lectured on music and composed his famous *Symphony No 9, From the New World,* a copy of which was taken to the moon by Neil Armstrong in 1969. Among his other well-known works are two *Slavonic Dances* (1878 and 1881), the operas *Rusalka* and *Čert a Káča* (The Devil and Kate), and his religious masterpiece *Stabat Mater* (a 13th-century Latin hymn; the title means 'The Mother was Standing').

Moravian-born Leoš Janáček (1854–1928) is widely considered the leading Czech composer of the early modern period, though he was never as popular as Smetana and Dvořák in his native country. His discordant violin pieces are hard to listen to at first but mellow with familiarity. His better-known compositions include the tricky-to-pronounce-fast *The Cunning Little Vixen* and *Káťa Kabanová,* as well as the *Glagolská mše* (Glagolitic Mass) and *Taras Bulba,* based on

TEN CZECH TUNES FOR YOUR MP3 PLAYER

Czechs tend to be pretty patriotic when it comes to their own music. While everyone listens to the latest bands from the UK or the US, the party only really starts once the DJ begins spinning Czech songs. Pop songs from the 1960s and '70s are beloved because they're sappy and inflected with nostalgia for simpler times under communism. Songs from the '90s and '00s tend to sound less synthetic, with a harder edge. All are great in their own way and form the perfect soundtrack when streaming from your iPod or MP3 player as you stroll around town.

- 'Želva' (Turtle; 1967) by Olympic – The Czech 'Beatles' of their day had the moves, the tunes and the hair.
- 'Stín Katedrál' (1968) by Helena Vondráčková – One of the simplest and sweetest pop songs to emerge out of the 1960s.
- 'Modlitba pro Martu' (Prayer for Marta; 1969) by Marta Kubišová – A sad song that for many still instantly recalls the 1968 Warsaw Pact invasion. Later became the unofficial anthem of the 1989 Velvet Revolution.
- 'Bratříčku, zavírej vrátka' (Oh Brother, Close the Door; 1969) by Karel Kryl – Another wistful tune from the late '60s. The 'close the door' part echoes the hopelessness many felt after the Warsaw Pact invasion and the sterile decade of normalisation that followed under communism.
- 'Je jaká je' (She Is As She Is; 1975) by Karel Gott – Czech crooner-extraordinaire Gott is still going strong today, well into his 70s. This was one of his biggest hits at the height of his powers.
- 'Medvídek' (Teddy Bear; 1998) or 'Černí Andělé' (Black Angels; 1991) by Lucie – Critics' choice for the best rock band of the 1990s. Hypnotic 'Medvídek' could serve as an anthem for Czechs who came of age in the decade after the Velvet Revolution.
- 'Láska je láska' (Love Is Love; 1995) by Lucie Bílá – One of the biggest hits of the '90s, from a woman with a raspy voice you won't soon forget.
- 'Lolita' (2001) by Kryštof – The current king of the Czech pop world has recorded a string of instantly likeable, addictive hits over the last decade.
- 'Pohoda' (Ease; 2002) by Kabát – Abrasive, abusive tune from arguably the country's biggest band throughout most of the '00s.
- 'Proměny' (2006) by Čechomor – Hauntingly beautiful music from a group that almost single-handedly made folk music hip again.

Gogol's short story of the same name. Other well-known Czech composers include Josef Suk (1874–1935), Dvořák's son-in-law and author of the *Serenade for Strings* and the *Asrael Symphony;* and Bohuslav Martinů (1890–1959), famed for his opera *Julietta* and his *Symphony No 6.*

Among contemporary composers, the most widely known is probably Milan Slavický (b 1947), who teaches at the Prague Academy of Performing Arts. His most famous piece, *Requiem,* premiered in Prague in 2005. Other modern composers worth looking out for include Petr Eben (1929–2007), a survivor of the Buchenwald concentration camp during WWII who is known for his choral and organ music, and Marek Kopelent (b 1932), who made his name with avant-garde compositions in the 1950s and '60s.

Both locals and visitors can choose from a rich program of concerts performed by Prague's three main resident orchestras: the Prague Symphony Orchestra (Symfonický orchestr hlavního města prahy; www.fok .cz); the Czech Philharmonic Orchestra (Česká filharmonie; www.czechphilharmonic.cz); and the Czech National Symphony Orchestra (Český národní symfonický orchestr; www.cnso.cz).

Jazz

Jazz was already being played in Prague in the 1930s and retains a strong grip on the city. Czech musicians remained at the forefront of the European jazz scene until the communist takeover in 1948, when controls were imposed on performing and publishing jazz. Even so, in the late 1950s Prague Radio still had a permanent jazz orchestra, led by saxophonist Karel Krautgartner (1922–82).

Restrictions were gradually lifted in the 1960s. One of the top bands of this period was SH Quartet, which played for three years at Reduta, the city's first professional jazz club and still going strong (though no longer the centre of the jazz scene). Another leading band was Junior Trio, with Jan Hamr and brothers Miroslav and Allan Vitouš, all of whom left for the US after 1968. Hamr became prominent in American music circles as Jan Hammer and even composed the *Miami Vice* soundtrack (which sold some 4 million copies in the US alone).

Today, the scene is not quite as vibrant, but on any given night you can still catch a number of decent shows. One of the most outstanding musicians is Jiří Stivín, who produced two excellent albums in the 1970s with the band System Tandem and is regarded as one of the most innovative jazz musicians in Europe. Two others to watch for are Emil Viklický and Milan Svoboda.

Rock & Pop

The rock scene in Prague today is deeply divided into genres and subgenres, each with its own distinct fan base, groups and clubs. Electronic music, including techno and drum 'n' bass, is standard fare in many dance clubs. Other popular styles include indie rock (a catch-all for bands who don't fit a label), classic rock, revival, pop, folk rock, and even a budding Czech hip hop scene.

Rock, in the form of American-style rock 'n' roll, took the country by storm in the 1950s. It was officially frowned upon but more or less tolerated. Even today, Czechs retain a fondness for '50s rockers like Elvis, Chuck Berry and Little Richard, and Czechs of all ages can still cut a rug much more skilfully than their American or Western European counterparts. Czech dancers like Roman Kolb regularly win world rock 'n' roll dance championships.

Popular music blossomed during the political thaw of the mid-1960s and Western influences from acts like the Beatles, Beach Boys and Rolling Stones were strongly felt. The 1967 hit single 'Želva' (Turtle) by the band Olympic bears the unmistakable traces of mid-decade Beatles. One of the biggest stars of that time was pop singer Marta Kubišová (b 1942). Banned by the communists for two decades after the 1968 Warsaw Pact invasion, she still occasionally performs in Prague; for many Czechs, her voice still captures something of the ill-fated optimism of the '68 period.

The 1968 Warsaw Pact invasion silenced the rock revolution. Many bands were prohibited from openly performing or recording. In their place, the authorities encouraged singers like Helena Vondráčková (b 1947) and Karel Gott (b 1939), who admittedly had beautiful voices but whose recordings lacked any originality. Many popular songs from those days, like Gott's classic 'Je jaká je' (She Is As She Is), are simply Czech covers of the most innocuous Western music of the day (in this case the Italian song 'Sereno è'). Vondráčková and Gott are still recording and remain highly popular. Most Czechs by now have forgiven them their collaboration during the 1970s and '80s, and their songs today invoke powerful feelings of nostalgia for what many now see as a simpler time.

Rock became heavily politicised during the 1980s and the run-up to the Velvet Revolution. Even the 'Velvet' part of the name owes a partial debt to rock music, in this case the American band the Velvet Underground, one of Havel's favourites and a strong influence on underground Czech bands at the time. Hardcore experimental bands like the Plastic People of the Universe were forced underground and developed huge cult followings. Another banned performer, Karel Kryl (1944–94), became an unofficial bard of the people, singing from his West German exile. His album *Bratříčku, Zavírej Vrátka* (Oh Brother, Close the Door) came to symbolise the hopelessness that the Czechs felt during the Soviet invasion and the decades that followed.

The Velvet Revolution opened the door to a flood of influences from around the world. In the early days of Havel's presidency, rock icons who had inspired the revolution, like Frank Zappa, Mick Jagger and Lou Reed, were frequent visitors to the castle. Zappa was even referred to as the unofficial 'Culture Minister'. Early-'90s Czech bands like rockers Lucie and Žlutý Pes soon gave way to a variety of sounds from the Nina Hagen–like screeching of early Lucie Bílá to the avant-garde chirping of Iva Bittová, in addition to a flood of mainstream Czech acts. The best of these included Psí Vojáci, Buty, Mňága a Žďorp, Laura a Její Tygři, Už Jsme Doma, Support Lesbiens, and many more. Currently, the most popular acts include hard rockers Kabát, pop heartthrobs Kryštof, and the folk, world-music band Čechomor. For more on these and other Czech tunes, see the boxed text, opposite.

Prague has also become a more important concert venue for touring Western acts. In the first years after the Velvet Revolution, big names were few and far between, but did include the Rolling Stones (on several occasions), Pink Floyd, REM, U2, Bruce Springsteen and Guns N' Roses. Axl Rose legendarily opened his 1992 concert at Strahov stadium with the words, 'OK, you ex-commie bastards, it's time to rock and roll!' In recent years, everybody from Madonna to Radiohead to Tom Waits has paid a visit, and every summer seems to bring a richer concert schedule.

LITERATURE

There's no shortage of new Czech literary talent. Names like Jáchym Topol, Petra Hůlová, Michal Viewegh, Magdaléna Platzová, Emil Hakl, Miloš Urban and Hana Androniková are already taking their places among the country's leading authors. They are pushing out the old-guard figures like Milan Kundera and Ivan Klíma, who are now seen as chroniclers of a very different age.

Increasingly, though, younger writers are looking outside the Czech Republic for themes and ideas. In the past, writers like Kundera or Klíma could ruminate for whole books on a character's internal motivations, but many newer writers are setting their novels further afield to win over readers hungry for adventure. One of the best recent titles, Hůlová's *Paměť mojí babičce* (Memories of My Grandmother; 2002), is set in Mongolia and tells of three generations of Mongolian women. Similarly, Platzová's *Sul, ovce a kamení* (Salt, Sheep and Stones; 2003) alternates between the Czech Republic and the Dalmatian coast. Another younger writer, Iva Pekárková, seems at home anywhere except the Czech Republic, placing stories in locations like New York, Thailand and India.

Until a couple of years ago, however, very few of these new writers had found English publishers. With the notable exceptions of Pekárková's *Truck Stop Rainbows*, Topol's stream-of-consciousness epic *City Sister Silver*, and two titles by Michal Viewegh, there wasn't much contemporary Czech literature to sample if one couldn't read Czech. The good news is that, slowly, that's starting to change. Topol's most recent book, *Kloktat dehet* (Gargling with Tar), about life at an orphanage during the 1968 Soviet invasion, has finally found an English publisher, Portobello Books. Similarly, the English translation of Miloš Urban's dark thriller *Sedmikosteli* (Seven Churches, by PeterOwenPublishers) has also hit the bookshelves.

Even if this much-anticipated miniwave of new translations doesn't pan out in the long term, there's still a decent canon of older Czech literature published during the Cold War and immediately after that's held up remarkably well and still provides insights into Czech culture.

Kundera remains the undisputed champ of Czech literature and was even – grudgingly – awarded the Czech state prize for literature in 2007 for a new translation of his classic *The*

BOOKS TO BRING ALONG

You can find many of the titles listed here at large bookshops and all are available over the internet through online booksellers:

- *Bringing Up Girls in Bohemia* (Michal Viewegh, 1996) – Humorously captures the early years of newly capitalist Prague. The movie of the same name stars Czech actress Anna Geislerová and opens with Geislerová relaxing at the old Globe Bookstore & Coffeehouse (now the Ouky Douky) in Holešovice – a classic intersection of art and real life.

- *Closely Watched Trains* (Bohumil Hrabal, 1965) – Hrabal's novella tells the story of a young railway worker finding his manhood during WWII, and by extension his country finding its courage. The screen adaptation won the Oscar for best foreign film in 1967.

- *City Sister Silver* (Jáchym Topol, 1994) – Translator Alex Zucker modestly describes this rambling, words-on-speed novel as 'the story of a young man trying to find his way in the messy landscape of postcommunist Czechoslovakia'. Dense, deeply meaningful, and probably hard as hell to translate.

- *Daylight in the Nightclub Inferno* (edited by Elena Lappin, 1997) – Decent anthology of the best young Czech writers working in the years immediately after the Velvet Revolution. Includes selections from Jáchym Topol, Michal Viewegh, Daniela Fischerová and Michal Ajvaz, among others.

- *I Served the King of England* (Bohumil Hrabal, 1990) – Czechoslovakia's tortured history provided fodder for some brilliantly funny novels in Hrabal's capable hands. In this one, a vertically challenged waiter named Ditie rises, Švejk-like, to wealth and prominence under the German occupation, only to lose it all after the war.

- *Life with a Star* (Jiří Weil, 1949) – Jewish writer Weil survived the Nazi occupation by faking his own death and hiding out for the duration of the war. This highly moving account from that period tells the story of an ordinary bank clerk whose life is turned upside down when he's forced to wear the yellow star.

- *Mendelssohn is on the Roof* (Jiří Weil, 1960) – This classic from the Nazi occupation opens with an absurd account of SS workers ordered to remove a statue of the 'Jew composer' Mendelssohn from the Rudolfinum's roof. They can't figure out which one is him, so they pull down the statue with the biggest nose – which turns out to be Hitler's favourite: Richard Wagner.

Unbearable Lightness of Being. The word 'grudgingly' is in order because Czechs, perhaps unfairly, have never forgiven him for leaving his homeland in the mid-'70s just as they were suffering under the Russian occupation. For visitors to Prague, this book, along with *The Joke* and *The Book of Laughter and Forgetting,* remains the most rewarding (see the boxed text, p34, for recommended titles). Kundera's later works, including 2007's *The Curtain,* tend towards drier, more clinical divinations of the novel and are best left to hardcore fans and grad students.

Other giants who came of age during the period from the Soviet-led invasion in 1968 to the Velvet Revolution include Ivan Klíma, Bohumil Hrabal, Josef Škvorecký and Václav Havel (as an essayist and playwright; see the boxed text, p27). Klíma, who survived the Terezín camp as a child and who still lives in Prague, is probably best known for his collections of bittersweet short stories of life in Prague in the 1970s and '80s like *My First Loves* and *My Merry Mornings.* He also wrote a series of very good novels after 1989 exploring the conflicting moral climate of post–Velvet Prague, including *Waiting for the Dark, Waiting for the Light* and *No Saints or Angels.*

Ask any Czech who their favourite author is: chances are the answer will be Bohumil Hrabal, and it's not hard to see why. Hrabal's writing captures what Czechs like best about their society and culture, including a keen wit, a sense of the absurd and a fondness for beer. He's also a great storyteller, and novels like *I Served the King of England* (which was made into a movie in 2006) and *The Little Town Where Time Stood Still* are both entertaining and insightful. Hrabal died in 1997 in classic Czech fashion – by falling from a window.

Josef Škvorecký emigrated to Canada shortly after the 1968 invasion and, like Kundera, his writing is dominated by themes of exile and memory. Look for *The Cowards, The Swell Season* and *The Engineer of Human Souls.*

No discussion of Czech literature would be complete without Franz Kafka, easily the best-known writer to have ever lived in Prague and author of the modern classics *The Trial* and *The Castle.* Though Kafka was German-speaking and Jewish, he's as thoroughly connected to the city as any Czech writer could be. Kafka was born just a stone's throw from the Old Town Square and rarely strayed more than a couple of hundred metres in any direction during the course of his short life (see the boxed text, p84). The Nazi occupation 15 years later wiped out

- *My Merry Mornings* (Ivan Klíma, 1986) – Klíma is a quietly powerful writer with an impressive collection of books from both the pre- and post-1989 period. Collections such as *My Merry Mornings* and *My First Loves* capture the kind of quirky magic the city had before it was inundated with 'Prague Drinking Team' T-shirts.
- *Prague: A Traveler's Literary Companion* (edited by Paul Wilson, 1994) – Indispensable collection of excerpts and short stories from a range of Czech writers through the ages and conveniently organised according to districts of the city.
- *The Book of Laughter and Forgetting* (Milan Kundera, 1979) – Kundera wrote this poignant and very funny collection of thematically related short stories from his Paris exile in the 1970s. It immediately established his reputation as Central Europe's leading writer.
- *The Castle* (Franz Kafka, 1926) – Though Kafka was a quintessential Prague writer, very few of his books actually mention the city by name. *The Castle* is no exception. Poor K never makes it inside, and the novel ends 280 pages later in midsentence. A work of genius or simply frustrating? You decide.
- *The Good Soldier Švejk* (Jaroslav Hašek, 1923) – Hašek's WWI novel about an amiable Czech oaf who manages to avoid military service has fallen out of favour – Czechs resent the portrayal and foreigners don't get the humour. Still, for anyone with a fondness for the Austro-Hungarian monarchy, it's a must-read.
- *The Joke* (Milan Kundera, 1967) – Kundera's first novel was published in Czechoslovakia in 1967 in the brief thaw that preceded the Soviet invasion. It's a tragicomic love story of what happens when a spurned lover sends a dumb joke to his ideologically blinkered girlfriend.
- *The Trial* (Franz Kafka, 1925) – 'Someone must have been telling lies about Josef K, for without having done anything wrong he was arrested one fine morning.' Kafka wrote these words in 1914, but they were eerily prophetic of the arrests of Czechs and Jews to come during WWII or of communist show trials after the war.
- *The Unbearable Lightness of Being* (Milan Kundera, 1984) – Kundera's best-known novel because of the 1988 movie starring Daniel Day-Lewis and Juliette Binoche. The novel's elixir of Prague during the 1968 invasion and a highly likeable womanising character named Tomáš combined to cement Kundera's genius rep in the 1980s. It's still highly readable.

THE EXPAT LITERARY CONTRIBUTION

Expat writers have had it rough in Prague. It's hard enough to be a successful writer, but thanks to the late American editor Alan Levy, expat scribes in Prague have laboured under almost unbearable levels of expectation. It was Levy who, writing in the debut issue of the *Prague Post* in October 1991, coined the phrase that Prague was the 'Left Bank of the '90s'. He went on to write that future Isherwoods and Audens were already hard at work chronicling the course. Yeah, right.

In the first decade after Levy's pronouncement, it was easy enough to dismiss it all as self-serving hype. It's true that Prague at the time was crawling with wannabe writers, but the actual combined published opus was thin indeed. With 20 years' hindsight, though, it's now possible to say the critics were maybe too quick to pounce. The Prague expat pond has actually spawned more than its fair share of decent writers. A partial list would include the following:

- Gary Shteyngart, a student at Charles University in the early 1990s and author of *The Russian Debutante's Handbook* (2003) and *Absurdistan* (2006), the former set partially in Prague in the aftermath of the Velvet Revolution.
- Jonathan Ledgard, a long-time Prague correspondent for the *Economist,* is the author of the acclaimed novel *Giraffe* (2006), based on the story of the slaughter of Central Europe's largest giraffe herd by the Czechoslovak secret police in 1975.
- Maarten Troost was a reporter in the early days of the *Prague Post* and the subsequent author of two hilarious titles: *The Sex Lives of Cannibals* (2004) and *Getting Stoned with the Savages* (2006) – books that could have been written about Prague but are actually about his later adventures in the South Pacific.
- Olen Steinhauer spent time here in the mid-'90s before decamping to Budapest to write five acclaimed Cold War spy thrillers. The fourth book, *Liberation Movements* (2006), opens in the Czech Republic, and shades of Prague can be seen throughout the series.
- Robert Eversz has lived off and on in Prague since 1992, and his 1998 novel *Gypsy Hearts* is set here. He's written several popular noir thrillers, including *Shooting Elvis* (1997), which explores America's obsession with celebrity culture.
- Brendan McNally for years was a reporter for the *Prague Post* with a keen sense of humour and a strong interest in German history. After returning to the US, he put it all together in *Germania* (2009), the wackiest, most surreal book on Nazi Germany you're ever likely to read.
- Arthur Phillips apparently never lived in Prague but still managed to write the best-known expat novel to come out of Eastern Europe, called simply *Prague* (2002) – though confusingly set in Budapest. Phillips does have a legit Prague connection, though: his short story 'Wenceslas Square' was printed in the 2003 anthology *Wild East: Stories from the Last Frontier.*
- In 2010 Prague-based editor Louis Armand assembled and published samples of what he considered to be the best expat writing since 1989. The anthology *The Return of Kral Majales* runs to more than 900 pages and is available at bookstores around town.

No discussion of expats would be complete without mentioning the growing genre of 'I Lived Here and This Is How It Was' books. Gene Deitch's *For the Love of Prague* is one of the most enjoyable. Deitch is a former Hollywood animator who moved to Prague in the late 1950s and worked on cartoons like *Tom and Jerry*, *Popeye* and *Krazy Kat* from behind the Iron Curtain. Douglas Lytle's *Pink Tanks and Velvet Hangovers* was written not long after the expat 'golden age' (from 1991 to 1995) and recounts the major events of the day filtered through the eyes of a young American journalist. One of the newest entries in the genre is Rachael Weiss' wide-eyed *Me, Myself & Prague*, the well-crafted story of an Australian woman who leaves the modern comforts of Sydney in 2005 to move to cold and cranky Prague. Not to spoil the ending, but she winds up loving it.

any vestiges of Kafka's circle of German writers, which included his friend and publicist Max Brod and journalist Egon Erwin Kisch.

Kafka's Czech contemporary and easily his polar opposite was the pub scribe Jaroslav Hašek, author of the – in equal measures – loved and reviled *The Good Soldier Švejk*. For those who get the jokes, the book is a comic masterpiece of a bumbling, good-natured Czech named Švejk and his (intentional or not) efforts to avoid military service for Austria-Hungary during WWI. Czechs tend to bridle at the assertion that an idiot like Švejk could somehow embody any national characteristic. Admirers of the book, on the other hand, feel in this instance that perhaps the Czechs doth protest too much.

The Czech language is highly inflected, giving grammatically gifted writers ample ammo to build layers of meaning simply by playing with tenses and endings. The undisputed master of this is the interwar writer Karel Čapek, an essayist and author of several novels, including the science fiction *RUR (Rossum's Universal Robots)*, from where the English word 'robot' (from the Czech for 'labour') derives.

Czech contributions to literature are not limited to fiction. Czech poet Jaroslav Seifert (1901–86) won the Nobel Prize for Literature in 1984. The American publisher Catbird Press has come out with an excellent collection of his work in English, *The Poetry of Jaroslav Seifert*. The irony is that Seifert is not universally considered by Czechs to be their best poet. Depending on whom you ask, that distinction often belongs to poet-scientist Miroslav Holub (1923–98).

VISUAL ARTS

Ask about visual arts in Prague and many visitors will probably draw a blank, perhaps conjuring up some art nouveau images by Alfons Mucha (see the boxed text, p39). But the city has much more to offer than Mucha's sultry maidens. Prague has both a long tradition of avant-garde photography and a rich heritage of public sculpture, ranging from the baroque period to the present day. There is always something new and fascinating to see at the Veletržní Palace (p139). or in one of the private galleries around town.

Photography

Czech photographers have always been at the forefront of the medium. The earliest photographers, in the late 19th and early 20th centuries, worked in the pictorialist style, which viewed photography as a kind of extension of painting. Photographers were encouraged to use various shooting and printing techniques to introduce imprecision, much like an Impressionist painting.

It was after independence in 1918 and during the 1920s and '30s that early modern styles captured the Czech imagination. Local photographers seized on trends like cubism, functionalism, Dadaism and surrealism, turning out jarring abstracts that still look fresh today. Two of the best photographers from that time are František Drtikol and Jaroslav Rössler. Drtikol was a society portraitist who mainly shot nudes poised against dramatic, angular backdrops. Rössler spent several years in Paris, refining a style of powerful abstract imagery that draws on constructivist trends.

During communism, photography was enlisted in the service of promoting the workers' state. Picture books from that time are comically filled with images of tractors, factories, housing projects and beaming peasants. Serious photographers turned inward and intentionally chose subjects – like landscapes and still-lifes – that were, at least superficially, devoid of political content.

Arguably the best Czech photographer from this period was Josef Sudek. During a career that spanned five decades until his death in the mid-'70s, Sudek turned his lens on the city of Prague to absolutely stunning effect. Sudek exhibitions are relatively rare, but collections of his photography are widely available at antiquarian bookshops around town.

Current Czech bad-boy photographer Jan Saudek (b 1935) continues to delight his fans (or appal his critics) with his dreamlike, hand-tinted prints that evoke images of utopia or dystopia – usually involving a nude or seminude woman or child. Saudek is unquestionably the best-known contemporary Czech photographer and his works are frequently on display, but the jury is still out on whether the pictures – especially those involving kids – don't transgress the boundaries of good taste or decency.

Sculpture

Public sculpture has always played a prominent role in Prague, from the baroque saints that line the parapets of Charles Bridge to the monumental statue of Stalin that once faced the Old Town from atop Letná Hill (see the boxed texts, p82 and p94). More often than not, that role has been a political one.

In the baroque era, religious sculptures sprouted in public places; they included 'Marian columns' erected in gratitude to the Virgin Mary for protection against the plague or victory over anti-Catholic enemies. One such Marian column stood in Old Town Square from 1650 until 1918. The placing of the statue of St John of Nepomuk on Charles Bridge in 1683 was a conscious act of Habsburg propaganda designed to create a new – and Catholic – Czech national hero who would displace the Protestant reformer Jan Hus. As such it was successful. John of Nepomuk was canonised in 1729, and the Nepomuk legend, invented by the Jesuits, has passed into the collective memory.

DAVID ČERNÝ: ARTIST-PROVOCATEUR

Czech artist David Černý (b 1967) first made international headlines in 1991 when he painted Prague's memorial to the WWII Soviet tank crews bright pink (see the boxed text, p94). Since then he has become internationally famous, cultivating a reputation as the enfant terrible of the Prague art scene.

His works often turn into major media events, notably in 2009 when his sculpture *Entropa* – commissioned to celebrate the Czech Republic's presidency of the EU – resulted in a major diplomatic storm. The sculpture, which pokes fun at national stereotypes, captured news headlines all over Europe and offended the Bulgarians so much that the depiction of Bulgaria (as a series of squat toilets) had to be covered with a black cloth. At the time of research, *Entropa* was on display at the DOX Centre for Contemporary Art (p135), but had not yet found a permanent home.

Černý lived for a time in the US, and his art has been exhibited in New York, Chicago, Dresden, Berlin, Stockholm and London, among other places. Many of his works are on display in Prague (see the boxed text, p142). Like others of his generation, he is virulently anticommunist – when the Rolling Stones played Prague in 2003, Keith Richards wore a Černý-designed T-shirt with the words 'Fuck the KSČM' (the initials of the Communist Party of Bohemia and Moravia).

He's also heavily involved in promoting cross-cultural links with artists abroad through his sprawling 'Meet Factory' (p142) artist-in-residency project in Smíchov. You can find more details on Černý's work and the Meet Factory on his website at www.davidcerny.cz.

The period of the Czech National Revival saw Prague sculpture take a different tack: to raise public awareness of Czech traditions and culture. One of the most prolific sculptors of this period was Josef Václav Myslbek, whose famous statue of St Wenceslas, the Czech patron saint, dominates the upper end of Wenceslas Square (p113). He also created the four huge statues of the historic Czech characters Libuše, Přemysl, Šárka and Ctirad that grace the gardens in Vyšehrad fortress (p121).

The art nouveau sculptor Ladislav Šaloun was responsible for one of Prague's most iconic sculptures, the monument to Jan Hus that was unveiled in the Old Town Square (p89) in 1915 to commemorate the 500th anniversary of Hus being burned at the stake. The figure of Hus – standing firm and unmoving, while the events of history swirl around him – symbolised the Czech nation, which, three years later, would be fully independent for the first time in history. For three short years Hus stared defiantly across the square at the statue of the Virgin Mary – symbol of the Habsburg victory over the Czechs – until a mob toppled her soon after independence was declared in 1918. Šaloun's works also grace the facade of the Municipal House (p102), the Grand Hotel Evropa (p115) and Prague City Hall (one block west of the Old Town Square on Mariánské náměstí). He created the bust of Antonín Dvořák that adorns the composer's tomb in Vyšehrad Cemetery (p120).

Probably the most imposing and visible sculpture in Prague is the huge, mounted figure of Hussite hero Jan Žižka – reputedly the biggest equestrian statue in the world – that dominates the skyline above Žižkov, the city district named after him. Created by sculptor Bohumil Kafka (no relation to writer Franz) in 1950, it was originally intended to form part of the National Monument (p132) in memory of the Czechoslovak legions who had fought in WWI. It was instead hijacked by the communist government and made to serve as a political symbol of Czech workers and peasants.

The city's long tradition of politically charged sculpture continues today with the controversial and often wryly amusing works of David Černý (see the boxed texts, above and p142).

Painting

The luminously realistic 14th-century paintings of Magister Theodoricus, whose work hangs in the Chapel of the Holy Cross at Karlštejn Castle (p236) and in the Chapel of St Wenceslas in St Vitus Cathedral (p65), influenced art throughout Central Europe.

Another gem of Czech Gothic art is a late-14th-century altar panel by an artist known only as the Master of the Třeboň Altar; what remains of it is at the Convent of St Agnes (p97) in Prague's Old Town.

The Czech National Revival in the late 18th and 19th centuries witnessed the revival of a Czech style of realism, in particular by Mikuláš Aleš and father and son Antonín and Josef Mánes. Alfons Mucha is well known for his late-19th- and early-20th-century art nouveau posters, paintings and stained glass (see the boxed text, below). Czech landscape painting developed in the works of Adolf Kosárek, followed by a wave of Impressionism and symbolism in the hands of Antonín Slavíček, Max Švabinský and others.

In the early 20th century, Prague developed as a centre of avant-garde art, concentrated in a group of artists called Osma (the Eight). Prague was also a focus for cubist painters, including Josef Čapek and the aptly named Bohumil Kubišta. The functionalist movement flourished between WWI and WWII in a group called Devětsíl, led by the critic and editor Karel Teige. Surrealists followed, including Zdeněk Rykr and Josef Šima.

Visual arts were driven underground during the Nazi occupation, and in the early years of the communist period painters were forced to work in the official socialist realist style, usually depicting workers and peasants building the workers' state. Underground painters included Mikuláš Medek (whose abstract, surrealist art was exhibited in out-of-the-way galleries) and Jiří Kolář, an outstanding graphic artist and poet whose name when pronounced sounds something like 'collage' – one of his favourite art forms.

Cinema

For a small country with a minuscule box office, the Czech Republic has an active film industry, producing 15 to 20 features a year. Nearly all features receive some monetary support from the state and sponsors such as Czech TV, but it helps that Czechs are avid moviegoers. Hollywood films account for the majority of movie receipts, but Czech features still bring in around a quarter of the total box office.

Czechs were some of the earliest pioneers in movie-making, with the first Czech films – silent, American-style slapstick comedies – arriving at the end of the 19th century. Movie-making took off during the interwar First Republic. American westerns were popular and even responsible for kicking off a Czech obsession with living in nature and the 'Wild West' that endures to this day. The first film ever to show full-frontal nudity was Gustav Machatý's *Exstace* (Ecstasy; 1932). Revealing it all was one Hedvige Kiesler, who went on to later stardom in Hollywood as Hedy Lamarr.

THE UNDERAPPRECIATED ALFONS MUCHA

Alfons Mucha (1860–1939) is probably the most famous visual artist to come out of the Czech lands, though his reputation within the Czech Republic is less exalted than it is abroad.

Mucha's life and career changed almost overnight after a chance meeting in a print shop led him to design a poster for famous actress Sarah Bernhardt, promoting her new play *Giselda;* you can see the original lithograph in the Mucha Museum (p107). The poster, with its tall, narrow format, muted colours, rich decoration and sensual beauty, created a sensation.

Mucha quickly became the most talked-about artist in Paris. He signed a six-year contract with Bernhardt during which he created nine superb posters in what became known as *le style Mucha*. He also designed jewellery, costumes and stage sets, and went on to produce many more posters promoting, among other things, Job cigarette papers, Moët & Chandon champagne and tourism in Monaco and Monte Carlo.

Although firmly associated with art nouveau, Mucha himself claimed he did not belong to any one artistic movement, and saw his work as part of a natural evolution of Czech art. His commitment to the culture and tradition of his native land was expressed in the second half of his career, when he worked on the decoration of the Lord Mayor's Hall in Prague's Municipal House (p102), designed new stamps and banknotes and created a superb stained-glass window for St Vitus Cathedral (p65).

He devoted 18 years of his life (1910–28) to creating his *Slovanské epopej* (Slavic Epic), which he later donated to the Czech nation. The 20 monumental canvasses encompass a total area of around 0.5 sq km and depict events from Slavic history and myth. Although very different in style from his Paris posters, they retain the same mythic, romanticised quality, full of wild-eyed priests, medieval pageantry and battlefield carnage, all rendered in symbolic tints. In the artist's own words, 'black is the colour of bondage; blue is the past; yellow, the joyous present; orange, the glorious future'. (The *Slavic Epic* is on display in the town of Moravský Krumlov, near Brno, about 200km southeast of Prague.)

When the Nazis occupied Czechoslovakia in 1939, Mucha was one of the first to be arrested by the Gestapo. He was released but died a few days later, shortly before his 79th birthday. He is buried in the Slavín at Vyšehrad Cemetery (p120).

Mucha's granddaughter, Jarmila Plocková, uses elements of his paintings in her own works. Those interested can check out Art Décoratif (p152).

A LIST OF GREAT CZECH FILMS

- *Amadeus* (1985) – Until the Velvet Revolution, the biggest Hollywood production to be filmed here. Director Miloš Forman chose Prague for his Oscar-winning tale of composer Wolfgang Amadeus Mozart because it looked more like '18th-century Vienna' than Vienna – he even got to film inside the Estates Theatre, where *Don Giovanni* premiered in 1787.
- *Beauty in Trouble* (Kráska v nesnázích; 2006) – By acclaimed director Jan Hřebejk, who holds a mirror up to Czech society, showing it warts and all. Czech actress Anna Geislerová plays a woman whose life collapses after the 2002 Prague floods and who takes up a hesitant relationship with a wealthy Czech émigré living in Italy.
- *Black Peter* (Černý Petr; 1963) – This early Miloš Forman film wowed the New York critics on its debut with its cinematic illusions to the French New Wave and its slow but mesmerising teenage-boy-comes-of-age storyline. Also called *Peter and Pavla*.
- *Bony a Klíd* (1987) – Vít Olmer's communist-era classic looks at Prague in the pre–Velvet Revolution years, when a corrupt secret police and organised crime were one and the same. Banned on release, it was widely circulated underground on video and features arguably the best-ever use of a Frankie Goes to Hollywood soundtrack.
- *Closely Watched Trains* (Ostre sledované vlaky; 1966) – Jiří Menzel's adaptation of Bohumil Hrabal's comic WWII classic won an Oscar in 1967 and put the Czech New Wave on the international radar screen. Watch for young Miloš delicately broaching the subject of premature ejaculation with an older woman as she lovingly strokes a goose's neck.
- *Cosy Dens* (Pelíšky; 1999) – The story of two neighbours on the eve of the 1968 Warsaw Pact invasion with radically differing political views. Czech directors have yet to make the definitive film about communism, but this attempt – sad and funny in equal measures – comes close.
- *Czech Dream* (Český sen; 2004) – Arguably the finest Czech documentary in recent years. Two locals fake the opening of a new hypermarket, handing out flyers promising the lowest prices ever, and then film the result. The ending is both predictable and sad, an allegory of the newly capitalist Czech Republic.

American films retained their popularity until the US entered WWII at the end of 1941 and the Nazis banned them. Even during the difficult years of the war, Czechs continued to go to the cinema, substituting American dramas and comedies with German ones. The communist coup in 1948 shifted the focus of movie-making from entertainment to education, and films were placed in the service of the state to foster the class consciousness of the workers. The result was predictable mediocrity that didn't end until the political thaw of the 1960s, when a younger generation from the Prague film academy, FAMU, crafted tragicomic films that slyly criticised the communists and garnered rave reviews around the world.

These 'New Wave' films, as they became known, took the world by storm. Czechoslovak films won the Oscar for Best Foreign Film twice in the 1960s, for Ján Kadár and Elmar Klos' *Little Shop on Main Street* (Obchod na korze) in 1965 and Jiří Menzel's *Closely Watched Trains* (Ostre sledované vlaky) in 1967. Miloš Forman was the acknowledged master of the New Wave, kicking off with the spare but absorbing *Black Peter* (Černý Petr) in 1963, and then creating classics like *Loves of a Blonde* (Lásky jedné plavovlásky; 1966) – which was nominated for an Oscar but didn't win – and *The Fireman's Ball* (Hoří, má panenko; 1967) before moving to the US after the Warsaw Pact invasion. Forman went on to win Oscars for Best Picture for *One Flew Over the Cuckoo's Nest* and *Amadeus*. Other prominent directors to emerge during the Czech New Wave included Ivan Passer, Věra Chytilová and Jan Němec, among others. Many of these directors' films are now available on DVD with English subtitles (for an admittedly opinionated list of the best Czech films through the ages, see the boxed text, above).

Since the Velvet Revolution, Czech directors have struggled to make meaningful films, given their tiny budgets and a constant flood of movies from the US. At the same time, they've had to endure nearly nonstop critical demands that their output meet the high standards for Czech films set during the 1960s. Given the high expectations, the newer Czech directors have largely succeeded, settling for smaller, ensemble-driven films that focus on the hardships and moral ambiguities of life in a society rapidly transiting from communism to capitalism. If the Czech New Wave was mostly about making light of a bad situation, it wouldn't be a stretch to say today's films strive to make bad out of a comparatively light situation.

Films like David Ondříček's *Loners* (Samotáři), Jan Hřebejk's *Up and Down* (Horem pádem), Sasha Gedeon's *Return of the Idiot* (Návrat idiota), Bohdan Sláma's *Something Like Happiness*

- *Divided We Fall* (Musíme si pomáhat; 2000) – Jan Hřebejk and Petr Jarchovský's comic but unsparing view of the German occupation and the Czechs who collaborated. A couple hides a Jewish refugee in their house and must take convoluted steps to conceal their actions – including publicly embracing the Nazis.
- *Kolya* (Kolja; 1996) – Jan Svěrák's Oscar-winning tale of an ageing Czech bachelor and a cute Russian kid was originally cheered for helping salvage Czech films' international reputation. It hasn't worn well with time and is now considered syrupy. Still worth a look for the sumptuous shots of what was intended to be prerevolutionary Prague.
- *Loners* (Samotáři; 2000) – David Ondříček's hugely influential film set the standard for the ensemble-driven, life-of-a-20-something chronicles that have become the staple of post–Velvet Revolution Czech cinema.
- *Loves of a Blonde* (Lásky jedné plavovlásky; 1965) – Miloš Forman's bittersweet love story of a naive girl from a small factory town and her more sophisticated Prague beau. Arguably Forman's finest film, effortlessly capturing both the innocence and the hopelessness of those grey days of the mid-1960s.
- *Panel Story* (Panelstory; 1979) – Věra Chytilová's classic from communist times about young families who buy apartments in the new high-rise apartment blocks going up all over town, only to discover how bad they are. It's mesmerising from the opening shot on.
- *Something Like Happiness* (Štěstí; 2005) – Bohdan Sláma's bleak film is similar in tone to *Beauty in Trouble* and also stars Geislerová, but this time around she plays an emotionally disturbed mother on the verge of a breakdown in the northern city of Most. The movie is redeemed by level-headed Monika, played by Czech actress Tatiana Vilhelmová.
- *The Ride* (Jízda; 1994) – Hugely influential Czech road movie starring a young Geislerová, who hitchhikes her way to hopeful freedom. Captured something of the optimism and spirit of those early postrevolutionary years.
- *Up and Down* (Horem pádem; 2004) – Director Jan Hřebejk's highly regarded film is one of several in recent years that takes a hard look at the new realities of post–Velvet Revolution Prague, where money talks and age-old hatreds are given more-or-less free rein.

(Štěstí) and Petr Zelenka's *Wrong Way Up* (Příběhy obyčejného šílenství) are all very different, yet each explores the same familiar dark terrain of money, marital problems and shifting moral sands. Running against this grain has been director Jan Svěrák, who continues to make big-budget films that have attracted more international attention; he even took home the country's first Oscar since the 1960s, for the film *Kolja* in 1996.

In addition to Czech films, the country has managed to position itself as a lower-cost production centre for Hollywood films. Part of the pitch has been the excellent production facilities at Barrandov Studios, to the south of Smíchov. The effort has paid off, and dozens of big budget films – including *Mission: Impossible,* the James Bond film *Casino Royale* and the first two *Chronicles of Narnia* movies – have all been filmed here. Whether Prague can continue to lure big-time productions remains in doubt, however, as the Czech crown has appreciated and cheaper facilities in Hungary and Romania have opened up.

Animation & Fantasy

It's not surprising for a country with such a long tradition of puppetry that Czechs would also excel at animation. The centre for much of this activity was Prague's famed Krátký Film studios.

Czechs are especially well known in Central and Eastern Europe for animated films and shorts aimed at kids; the most popular character is doubtless 'Krtek', the little mole, created by animator Zdeněk Miler in the 1950s. You'll recognise Krtek puppets in shops by his big white eyes, red nose, and three strands of hair on his head. Krtek has starred in dozens of films over the years, starting with the 1957 classic *How the Mole Got His Trousers* (Jak krtek ke kalhotkám přišel).

Czech painter and illustrator Jiří Trnka won worldwide recognition for his evocative puppet animation films, beginning in 1946 with *The Czech Year* and continuing until his death in 1969. His best works include a parody of American westerns called *Song of the Prairie, The Emperor's Nightingale* (narrated by Boris Karloff in a 1951 American version), *The Good Soldier Švejk* and, finally, 1965's *The Hand* – a highly politicised work illustrating the struggle of the artist against totalitarian authority, portrayed by a simple, white-gloved hand. That film was initially tolerated by the government but banned from theatres shortly after Trnka's death. It wasn't rereleased until after 1989.

Czech Jan Švankmajer is celebrated for his bizarre, surrealist animation work and stop-motion feature films, including his 1988 version of *Alice in Wonderland*, called *Alice* (Něco z Alenky), and the 1994 classic, *Faust* (Lekce Faust). His 1996 *Conspirators of Pleasure* (Spiklenci slasti) is an over-the-top take on fetishism and self-gratification. There's no dialogue, making it accessible (if that's the right word) in any language.

THEATRE

Theatre in Prague remains a popular and vital art form, in spite of rising competition from the internet, film and TV. Openings for key performances, such as Tom Stoppard's riveting play *Rock 'n' Roll* at the National Theatre (Národní divadlo; p205) in 2007 or Václav Havel's acclaimed *Odcházení* (Leaving) at Divadlo Archa in 2008, are often sold out months in advance and duly debated in the papers and by the public for weeks after.

In addition to the main venues, including the National Theatre and the Estates Theatre (Stavovské divadlo; p204), there are dozens of smaller theatres scattered around the centre and in nearly every one of the city's neighbourhoods and districts. Unfortunately for non-Czech speakers, much of the action remains inaccessible. Occasionally, big theatrical events will be supertitled in English, but the bread and butter of Czech drama is performed in Czech only. Two theatres, Archa (p206) and the Švandovo divadlo in Smíchov (p207), are committed to English-friendly performances and occasionally host English drama in the original language. Additionally, the annual Fringe Festival, held at the end of May and early June, brings a week of nonstop drama, comedy and sketch performances, much of it in English.

Theatre has always played a strong role in the Czechs' national consciousness, both as a way of promoting linguistic development and defending the fledgling culture against the dominant Habsburg, German and, later, communist influences. Czech-language (as opposed to German) drama found an early home in the late 18th century at the Nostitz Theatre, now the Estates Theatre. Historical plays with a nationalist subtext flourished during the 19th century as part of the Czech National Revival. The decade-long construction of the National Theatre and its opening in 1881 was considered a watershed in Czech history. Tragically, the theatre burned down shortly after opening but was completely rebuilt following a public outcry just two years later.

Drama flourished in the early years of independent Czechoslovakia, but suffered under the Nazi occupation, when many Czech-language theatres were closed or converted into German theatres. Under communism, classical performances were of a high quality, but the modern scene was stifled. Exceptions included the pantomime of the Cerné divadlo (Black Theatre) and the ultramodern Laterna Magika (Magic Lantern), founded by Alfréd Radok and still going strong.

Many fine plays during this period, including those by Havel, were not performed locally because of their antigovernment tone, but appeared in the West. In the mid-1960s, free expression was briefly explored in Prague's Theatre on the Balustrade (p207), with works by Havel, Ladislav Fialka and Milan Uhde, and performances by the comedy duo of Jiří Suchý and Jiří Šlitr. The centrality of theatre to Czech life was confirmed in 1989 during the Velvet Revolution, when Havel and his Civic Forum movement chose to base themselves at the Laterna Magika for their epic negotiations to push the communists from power.

While theatre remains a vital art form and is well attended, there are concerns for its future as prices for performances rise and cultural budgets remain under pressure. One of the main issues facing the city government is how to finance cultural establishments, and many in City Hall are calling for substantial cuts to subsidies. Former president and playwright Václav Havel took the controversial step recently of calling on Prague residents not to support the right-of-centre Civic Democratic Party (ODS) because of the party's position on cultural funding.

Havel's play *Odcházení*, his first major dramatic work since 1989, opened to nearly universal acclaim in May 2008. It's a parody of life in postcommunist Prague, involving a compromised politician, Vlastík Klein, who bears at least a superficial resemblance to Havel's political rival, President Václav Klaus (even having the same initials). Havel wrote the female lead for his second and current wife Daša, but she fell ill shortly before the play's premiere and was not able to perform.

In addition to traditional drama, Czechs have a long history of puppet and marionette theatre going back to the Middle Ages. A major figure of this art form was Matej Kopecký (1775–1847). Marionette theatres opened in Prague and Plzeň in the early 20th century. Josef

Skupa's legendary Spejbl and Hurvínek (a Czech version of 'Punch and Judy') attracted large crowds then, and still does.

ENVIRONMENT & PLANNING

Prague has gone a long way towards improving the quality of its air: restricting coal burning within the city, capping factory emissions, and pulling ageing trucks, coaches and cars off the streets. Still, much of this good work has been undercut by a massive increase in automobiles on roadways. The authorities are now in the midst of building an ambitious ring-road system to reroute long-haul traffic around the city, and are even considering introducing a London-style congestion fee to limit the number of drivers in the centre.

Sprawl remains a potentially more vexing problem. The Velvet Revolution sparked a 20-year building boom that shows no sign of letting up. Every year sees thousands of acres of orchards and farmland paved over to make way for new housing developments and shopping centres. These in turn create new traffic patterns and problems of their own. Attempts by the city to limit or plan development have so far had only limited success.

THE LAND

Prague's Old Town (Staré Město) and Malá Strana – along with the districts of Smíchov to the south and Karlín and Holešovice to the east and north – sit along a low-lying bend of the Vltava River, the longest river in the Czech Republic. The position leaves the districts prone to flooding, and over the years the city has seen a series of serious floods, beginning with the deluge of 1342, which wiped out Judith Bridge, precursor to Charles Bridge.

Until relatively recently, the flood of 1890, which broke away part of Charles Bridge, was considered an insuperable deluge, but the devastating flood of 2002 was even worse. Heavy rains swelled the Vltava's tributaries and caused officials to make the fateful error of opening levees upriver to release the pressure. The result was a wall of water that cascaded into the city on 13 August 2002, inundating Malá Strana as well as Smíchov, Karlín, Holešovice and the Prague Zoo at Troja.

The surface of the Old Town was spared destruction by last-minute metal barriers that were erected along the banks, though the groundwater rose to nearly street level, flooding out the old Gothic cellars. Some 19 people were killed and many of the zoo's animals were drowned or intentionally destroyed to put them out of their misery. The damage was estimated at €2.4 billion. The flood had a silver lining for formerly industrial districts like Smíchov, Karlín and Holešovice, though – hundreds of millions of crowns in flood relief and development money were channelled into those districts, transforming them from borderline slums into highly desirable residential neighbourhoods.

The city centre is surrounded on three sides by high hills: Petřín and Hradčany to the west, Letná to the north and the Žižkov bluff to the east. This creates some lovely vistas, but in practical terms restricts the number of roads and access ways that can be built and forces traffic onto a few very heavily congested trunk roads. It has also hampered efforts to promote cycling. While much of the Old Town is flat, the hills present considerable obstacles for potential bicycle commuters coming in from the western, northern and eastern sides.

GREEN PRAGUE

When it comes to large-scale recycling, sustainable energy and organic farming, the Czech Republic still lags far behind Germany, the UK and Scandinavia. All the same, Czech industry has cleaned up its act considerably since the fall of communism, with the annual production of greenhouse gases falling to a fraction of pre-1989 levels.

Czechs have been recycling waste for a long time; you'll find large bins for glass, plastics and papers all over Prague. Most glass bottles are recyclable, and the prices of many bottled drinks – beer, too – include a deposit refundable at supermarkets.

Property developers are finally seeing the economic and marketing potential in making sustainable buildings, and several new projects now tout their 'greenness'. Two developments on opposite sides of the city – the Park, next to the Chodov metro station in the south, and the River City-Amazon Court development in Karlín – are being touted as pioneers in 'green' architecture.

One intractable problem that bedevils green planners is what to do about the *paneláky* – the high-rise public-housing projects that ring the city and are home to a majority of Prague's population. The projects are notoriously environmentally unfriendly, allowing residents to bake in the summer while leaking valuable heat in the winter. Many of them are now being fixed up with the help of public funding and mortgage financing, though the global economic contraction has slowed the amount of money available for these rehabs.

URBAN PLANNING & DEVELOPMENT

Since the 1989 Velvet Revolution, city authorities have tried to strike a balance between promoting economic growth while preserving green areas that surround the city and contribute greatly to the quality of life.

The jury is still out as to whether they've succeeded, but the consensus is they've not done enough. Critics point to the recent explosion in hypermarket shopping complexes that ring the outskirts in all directions. The pattern has been the same nearly everywhere, with developers buying up large tracts of land – usually near metro terminuses – and then constructing mixed-use commercial and residential zones, drawing shoppers and commuters to areas that just a few years ago were farmers' fields. The full impact is not yet clear, but there's concern that the new developments are siphoning off money and vitality from the centre.

To be sure, city authorities inherited a highly dysfunctional planning system from the previous communist government. The roadways and retail spaces were woefully inadequate. One need only look at the city's main highway, the *magistrála,* that ploughs through the heart of the city and severs the National Museum (p115) from the rest of Wenceslas Square, to see how poor the planning was during those times.

Along with this boom in private development, the city has embarked on the largest public-works build-up in its history, the centrepiece of which will be an enormous ring-road system of roads, bridges and tunnels that will allow traffic to bypass the city centre. In 2008, crews broke ground on the Blanka Tunnel (Prague's 'Big Ditch'), which will eventually run from the district of Břevnov in Prague 6 all the way to near the Prague Zoo in Troja, including stretches below Letná and Stromovka parks. At a cost of €800 million, it's one of the most expensive construction projects in the EU. In addition, authorities have announced plans to build a rail link between the centre and Prague Airport and have committed themselves to a massive expansion of the metro system until the year 2100, including starting construction of a new D line in the coming years. The year 2008 also saw the opening of three new metro stations along the northern portion of the C line, which now runs all the way to – what else? – a major shopping centre at Letňany.

Plans by Czech Rail, the public railway authority, to upgrade stations and improve services have languished, though. Major renovations under way at both the main station, Praha hlavní nádraží, and the chief station servicing key destinations like Budapest, Vienna and Berlin, at Nádraží Holešovice, are proceeding only slowly, and while at least the main station looks a bit better, both are likely to remain eyesores for years to come. In an apparent literary in-joke, the wags at Czech Rail have formally renamed Nádraží Holešovice as 'Nádraží Franze Kafky' (Franz Kafka Station), unfortunately linking Kafka's name to one of the most decrepit train stations in the country. (Thanks, guys!)

Meanwhile, work is continuing on long-overdue repairs to Charles Bridge. Sections of the bridge are likely to remain closed to visitors through 2010, though the span itself remains open across its length.

GOVERNMENT & POLITICS

As capital of the Czech Republic, Prague is the seat of the government, parliament and the presidency. The city itself is governed separately. The mayor is Pavel Bém (b 1963), a trained medical doctor and the local head of the right-leaning Civic Democratic Party (ODS). Bém has a decidedly mixed record. Though many policies have resulted in some positive outcomes for the city under his tenure, his name has been associated with more than one kickback scandal

(Continued on page 53)

ARCHITECTURE

The towering spires of St Vitus Cathedral (p65), Prague Castle

ARCHITECTURE

Prague is a living textbook of a thousand years of European architecture. The city's historic core escaped significant damage in WWII, so it records a millennium of continuous urban development, with baroque facades encasing Gothic houses perched on top of Romanesque cellars – all following a street plan that emerged in the 11th century. Much of it is protected as a Unesco World Heritage Site.

ROMANESQUE

The oldest surviving buildings in Prague date back to the Přemysl dynasty. In the crypt of St Vitus Cathedral (p65) are the remains of the Rotunda of St Vitus, built for Duke Wenceslas (the 'Good King Wenceslas' of Christmas-carol fame) in the early 10th century.

Several stone Romanesque rotundas (circular churches from the 10th to 12th centuries) survive intact in Prague, though most have been incorporated into larger churches. Examples include the Rotunda of St Longinus (early 12th century; p117) in Nové Město, the Rotunda of the Holy Cross (mid-12th century; p105) in Staré Město, and the Rotunda of St Martin (late 11th century; p120) at Vyšehrad. Prague's finest Romanesque structure is the Basilica of St George (p66) at Prague Castle. Although its exterior is hidden behind an elaborate 17th-century baroque facade, the interior exhibits the heavy walls, plain columns and barrel-vaulted ceilings that typify Romanesque.

GOTHIC

Gothic style flourished in Prague from the 13th to the 16th centuries. It represented not just a new aesthetic but also a design revolution that allowed architects to build thinner walls and higher vaults. Gothic architecture is characterised by tall, pointed arches, ribbed vaults and columns, external flying buttresses and tall, narrow windows with intricate tracery supporting great expanses of stained glass.

RICHARD NEBESKY
Romanesque Basilica of St George (p66), Prague Castle

RICHARD NEBESKY
Gothic interior of St Vitus Cathedral (p65), Prague Castle

Detail of the fountain at the Renaissance Summer Palace (64), Royal Garden, Prague Castle RICHARD NEBESKY

Czech Gothic architecture flourished during the rule of Charles IV, especially in the hands of German architect Peter Parler (Petr Parléř), best known for the eastern part of St Vitus Cathedral (p65) at Prague Castle. Begun by Matthias of Arras (Matyáš z Arrasu) in 1344, work on the cathedral continued under Parler until his death in 1399. Parler was also responsible for the Gothic design of the Charles Bridge (p76), the Old Town Bridge Tower (p101), the Church of Our Lady of the Snows (p113) and the Cathedral of St Barbara (p244) in Kutná Hora.

Another master builder was Benedikt Rejt, whose finest legacy is the petal-shaped vaulting of Vladislav Hall (1487–1500; p64) in the Old Royal Palace at Prague Castle. Its flowing, intertwined ribs are a beautiful example of late Gothic craftsmanship.

RENAISSANCE

When the Habsburgs assumed the Bohemian throne in the early 16th century, they invited Italian architects to Prague to help create a royal city worthy of their status. The Italians brought a new enthusiasm for classical forms, an obsession with grace and symmetry and a taste for exuberant decoration.

The mix of local and Italian styles gave rise to a distinctive 'Bohemian Renaissance', featuring heavy, ornamental stucco decoration and paintings of historical or mythical scenes. The technique of *sgraffito* – from the Italian word 'to scrape' – was often used, creating patterns and pictures by scraping through an outer layer of pale plaster to reveal a darker surface underneath.

The Summer Palace (1538–60; p64), or Belvedere, found in the gardens to the north of Prague Castle, was built for Queen Anna, the consort of Prague's first Habsburg ruler Ferdinand I. It is almost pure Italian Renaissance, with features that will remind some of Brunelleschi's work in Florence.

Other examples of Renaissance buildings are the Ball-Game House (1569; p63) in Prague Castle; the Schwarzenberg Palace (1546–67; p68) in Hradčany, with its striking Venetian-style *sgraffito* decoration; the House at the Minute (1546–1610; p96) in Staré Město; and the Star Summer Palace (1556; p147) to the west of the centre near White Mountain (Bílá Hora).

BAROQUE

In the aftermath of the Thirty Years' War (1618–48), the triumphant Habsburg empire embarked on a campaign to rebuild and re-Catholicise the Czech lands. The ornate baroque style, with its marble columns, florid sculpture, frescoed ceilings and rich ornamentation, was consciously used by the Catholic Church as an instrument of persuasion. By the 18th century a distinctly Czech baroque style had emerged. Its best-known practitioners were the Bavarian father and son Kristof and Kilian Ignatz Dientzenhofer and the Italian Giovanni Santini.

The most impressive example of Prague baroque is the Dientzenhofers' St Nicholas Church (1704–55; p77) in Malá Strana. Its massive green dome dominates Malá Strana in a fitting symbol of the Catholic Church's dominance over 18th-century Prague. Visitors enter through the western door at the foot of an undulating, tripartite facade decorated with the figures of saints, into a fantasy palace of pale pink, green and gold, where a profusion of pilasters, arches and saintly statues leads your eye upward to the luminous gleam of the dome. The magnificent fresco that adorns

St Nicholas Church (p77), Malá Strana

RICHARD NEBESKY

the ceiling of the nave depicts the apotheosis of St Nicholas, and portrays the saint performing acts such as rescuing shipwrecked sailors, saving three unjustly condemned men, and saving women from prostitution by throwing them bags of gold.

The final flourish of late baroque was rococo, a sort of 'baroque on steroids' featuring even more-elaborate decoration. The Goltz-Kinský Palace (1755–65; p94), overlooking Old Town Square, has a rococo facade.

NEOCLASSICAL & OTHER 'NEO'S'

After the exuberance of the 17th and 18th centuries, the architecture of the 19th century was comparatively dull. There was a feeling among architects that baroque and rococo had taken pure decoration as far as it could go and there was a need to simplify styles. They looked to classical Greece and Rome, where the buildings were prized for their restraint, symmetry and formal elegance. In practice, that meant stern facades, heavy columns and the conscious use of classical elements like triangular pediments above doors and windows.

Prague at the time was under the thumb of Habsburg Vienna, where neoclassical was perfectly in tune with the conservative tastes of Emperor Franz Josef I. It survives in hundreds of buildings across the city. As you walk around and admire the architecture, don't be fooled by appearances. If a building has lots of faux columns and rows of identical windows – and looks a little, well, boring – chances are that it's 19th-century neoclassical.

Neoclassical and other 'historicist' styles are closely associated with the 19th-century Czech National Revival. The National Theatre (1888; p114) and National Museum (1891; p115) were both built in neo-Renaissance style. The buildings are noteworthy not so much for the quality of the architecture – many critics would call them ponderous – but for what they represented: the chance for Czechs to show they were the equals of their Viennese overlords.

The 19th-century neo-Gothic revival, another 'neo', may have been the most successful style ever adopted here. In the 1880s and '90s, officials ordered the construction of dozens of faux neo-Gothic spires – including those atop the Powder Gate (p102) and the Jindřišská Tower (p107) – lending Prague the nickname 'City of a Hundred Spires'.

ART NOUVEAU

As the 19th century drew to a close, Czech architects began to tire of the relentlessly linear neoclassical facades and the pompous, retrograde style of imperial Vienna. They were looking for something new and found inspiration in Paris with art nouveau and its flowing lines and emphasis on beauty.

Art nouveau was frequently applied to upmarket hotels, including the Hotel Central (1899–1901; Map p108) on Hybernská in Nové Město, whose facade is decorated with stuccoed foliage, ornate lamps and a concrete cornice beneath a decorated gable. The more-famous Grand Hotel Evropa (1906; see the boxed text, p115) on Wenceslas Square is even grander and more ornate (on the outside at least; the accommodation inside leaves a lot to be desired), while the Hotel Pařiž (1904; Map p90) on U Obecního Domu in Staré Město has retained its interior as well as exterior splendour.

The city's finest expression of art nouveau is the magnificent Municipal House (1906–12; p102). Every aspect of the building's decoration was designed by leading Czech artists of the time, most famously Alfons Mucha (see the boxed text, p39), who decorated the Lord Mayor's Hall.

CUBIST

In just one decade (1910–20), barely half a dozen architects bequeathed to Prague a unique legacy of buildings – mostly private homes and apartment blocks – that were influenced by the cubist art movement. The Cubist style spurned the regular lines of traditional architecture and the sinuous forms of art nouveau in favour of triangular, polygonal and pyramidal forms, emphasising diagonals rather than horizontals and verticals and achieving a jagged, almost crystalline effect.

Some of Prague's finest Cubist houses (Map p120) were designed by Josef Chochol in 1912–14 and can be seen in the neighbourhood below the Vyšehrad fortress: check out Villa Libušina at the corner of Vnislavova and Rašínovo nábřeží, the houses at Rašínovo nábřeží 6-10 and the

Cubist house (Map p120) on Rašínovo nábřeží, Vyšehrad

RICHARD NEBESKY
Art nouveau detail, Municipal House (p102), Staré Město

top picks

ROMANESQUE
- Basilica of St George (p66)
- Rotunda of St Martin (p120)
- Rotunda of St Longinus (p117)

GOTHIC
- St Vitus Cathedral (p65)
- Vladislav Hall (p64)
- Charles Bridge (p76)

RENAISSANCE
- Summer Palace (p64)
- Schwarzenberg Palace (p68)
- House at the Minute (p96)

BAROQUE
- St Nicholas Church, Malá Strana (p77)
- Loreta (p69)
- Goltz-Kinský Palace (p94)

NEOCLASSICAL
- National Theatre (p114)
- National Museum (p115)
- Rudolfinum (p99)

ART NOUVEAU
- Municipal House (p102)
- Grand Hotel Evropa (p115)
- Hotel Paříž (p49)

CUBIST
- Houses below Vyšehrad Castle (p49)
- House of the Black Madonna (p102)
- Bank of Czechoslovak Legions (p51)

FUNCTIONALIST
- Baťa shoe store (p155)
- Villa Müller (p51)
- Veletržní Palace (p139)

COMMUNIST
- Hotel Crowne Plaza (p135)
- Kotva department store (p51)
- TV Tower (p133)

POST-1989
- Dancing Building (p116)
- Former Holešovice brewery (p52)
- Nový Smíchov shopping centre & adjoining office complexes (p157)

apartment block at Neklanova 30. Other appealing examples include the House of the Black Madonna (1912; p102) in Staré Město (which houses the Museum of Czech Cubism) and the twin houses (Map p70) at Tychonova 4-6 in Hradčany, all by Josef Gočár, and a 1921 apartment block (Map p90) created by Otakar Novotný at Elišky Krásnohorské 10-14 in Staré Město.

After WWI, cubism evolved into another unique Prague style as architects such as Pavel Janák and Josef Gočár added colour and decorative elements to their angular facades in another attempt to define a Czech national style. The more rounded forms that characterise these buildings led to the name 'rondocubism'. This short-lived style is seen in Janák's monumental Adria Palace (1922–25; p114) on Národní třída and in the tall, narrow apartment building at Jungmannovo náměstí 4, but its finest expression is seen in Gočár's Bank of Czechoslovak Legions (Legiobank; 1921–23; Map p51) at Na Poříčí 24, with its hypnotic alternation of rounded and right-angled features.

During this period, cubist designs were extended into both the field of decorative arts – examples of cubist furniture, ceramics and glassware can be seen in the Museum of Decorative Arts (p97) and the Museum of Czech Cubism (p102) – and the more mundane domain of street fixtures. Prague must be the only city in the world with a Cubist lamppost (1915; Map p110). Even Franz Kafka's tombstone (see p129), designed by Leopold Ehrmann in 1924, evokes the Cubist style in its crystalline prismatic pillar.

FUNCTIONALIST

The early modern mantra that 'form follows function' found a receptive following in the generation of architects that came of age in the 1920s and '30s. Functionalism – similar to Germany's Bauhaus school – appealed to architects precisely because it rejected everything that came before it. Cubism, and especially rondocubism, suddenly seemed overly decorative and more concerned with a building's aesthetics than its function.

In Czechoslovakia, Brno emerged as the centre of functionalist architecture; still, Prague has its share of smart-looking modern boxes, easily identified by their horizontal windowpane fronts and flat roofs. At their best, functionalist buildings enjoy the virtues of simplicity and symmetry.

Functionalism works best on a smaller scale in villas and small apartment blocks, but one successful functionalist building in the centre is the Baťa shoe store (1929; p155) on Wenceslas Square. Its seven-storey facade consists almost entirely of glass and still radiates a kind of infectious, flappers-and-Great-Gatsby modernism.

Functionalist fans will want to see Adolf Loos' Villa Müller (1930; p51) in the western suburb of Střešovice. Loos built the house in 1930 for industrialist František Müller and his wife, choosing a spare minimalist design and then filling the interior with sumptuous travertine marble and exotic hardwoods.

COMMUNIST

Ask your average Czech if the communist period produced anything of architectural value, and you'll get a belly laugh. The communists are uniformly derided for building hideous housing projects (called *paneláky* because they were built from prefab panels) and hundreds of schools, hospitals and institutes from a handful of cookie-cutter designs that are indistinguishable from one another, down to the same cheap, pale-green linoleum.

With the passage of time, though, some critics are starting to soften their views, and slowly an appreciation for the period is beginning to take root. It's not that the buildings are good, but at least they're bad in an interesting way.

In the early years after WWII, Czechoslovak architects were forced to design in the bombastic Stalinist, socialist realist style. The best of these is the former Hotel International (now the Hotel Crowne Plaza; 1954; p135) in Dejvice.

The mid-'70s apparently spurred a contest to see who could build the most dysfunctional department store. Both the Máj building (now Tesco; 1975; p163), in Nové Město, and Kotva (1975; Map p90), on the edge of Staré Město, opened the same year, and exhibited different tendencies of the then-popular 'brutalist' style. Tesco faintly resembles a mini Centre Pompidou, with its metal-and-glass facade consciously exposing the building's pipes and ducts. Kotva, built from giant hexagons perched on rough-hewn concrete posts, is closer to Prince Charles' brutalist

The Dancing Building (p116), Nové Město

RICHARD NEBESKY

'carbuncles' and wouldn't look amiss in a British Midlands town centre from the 1970s. Tellingly, both buildings have been granted protected landmark status.

The TV Tower (p133) in Žižkov dates from the end of the communist period. Its sheer scale dwarfs everything around – a metaphor for a communist system totally out of sync with the city. Surprisingly, it's worn well and locals point with some pride to a structure that pushes the extremes of ugliness to achieve something close to beauty.

POST-1989

Architectural purists are aghast by what has been designed and built since 1989. They point to hundreds of shopping-centre complexes, hypermarkets and McMansions that have sprung up on the outskirts of the city in all directions.

That said, it hasn't been a total loss. Arguably the most interesting structure of the post–Velvet Revolution period has been the so-called Dancing Building (1992–96; p116) on Rašínovo nábřeží in Nové Město, designed by Czech-based Croatian architect Vlado Milunić and American architect Frank Gehry. Built on a gap site created by a stray Allied bomb in WWII, it's a bold work whose curves seem tailor-made for guidebooks and tourist brochures. The building's resemblance to a pair of dancers saw it acquire the nickname 'Fred and Ginger', after the legendary dancing duo of Astaire and Rogers.

Some of the best new commercial architecture is going up in former industrial districts of the city, such as Smíchov, Karlín and Holešovice. One of the most innovative of these 'lifestyle' office-and-residential complexes is in the Holešovice district, where developers are rehabbing the former Holešovice brewery (Map p136).

The future of architecture came to Prague a couple of years ago in the form of a proposal by the late Czech-émigré architect Jan Kaplický to build a new national library near Letná park. Kaplický and his London-based firm, Future Systems, were renowned for their wavy-lined, organic, 'blob'-style architecture. The nine-storey building had been described as a 'biomorphic sea creature' (local wags called it 'the octopus'). Plans to actually build the building, however, came to a tragic end in 2009 when Kaplický suffered a sudden, fatal heart attack.

in recent years and as of mid-2010 Bém fatigue had settled in among many voters. His political star certainly doesn't look as bright as it did a couple of years ago.

The national government is plagued by near constant instability, resulting from the fact that neither of the large centrist parties, the centre-right Civic Democratic Party or the centre-left Social Democrats (ČSSD), will agree (out of principle) to form a government with the Communist party, the KSČM. In practice, that means fragile coalitions have to be stitched together with the remaining smaller parties: the Christian Democrats (KDU-ČSL), the Greens (SZ) and Top 09, a new right-leaning party comprised mostly of former ODS dissidents. The landmark parliamentary elections held in May 2010 hopefully have put this instability to rest, at least for a while. The result gave a right-leaning coalition of ODS and Top 09 a relatively stable majority, ending a period of more than a year during which the country lacked an elected government.

President Václav Klaus won re-election to a second five-year term in February 2008. Klaus, a noted sceptic of the EU and vocal critic of efforts to slow global warming, remains a highly polarising figure. His high-profile critiques of environmental efforts to cap greenhouse gases have made him the darling of the conservative think-tank crowd but have embarrassed many Czechs who see climate change as a serious issue.

MEDIA

Czechs are newspaper junkies, and you'll see people with their noses buried in the latest rag in bars, on trams, on park benches, and even walking on the street. Sadly, the overall standard of newspaper journalism today is low compared with the interwar years, any lingering tradition of quality investigative reporting having been thoroughly stamped out during the communist era.

There is a handful of major national dailies; most are now in the hands of German and Swiss media magnates. The biggest seller is the tabloid *Blesk,* controlled by the Swiss Ringier group. Also popular are the centre-right *Mladá fronta DNES* and the former communist paper, the left-leaning *Právo. Lidové noviny,* often shortened to *Lidovky,* has a smaller circulation though it's widely considered the 'quality' paper owing to its excellent reputation during the 1920s and '30s. It was closed down under communism and revised as a *samizdat* (underground press) publication shortly before the Velvet Revolution. It tends to lean centre-right in its opinions.

TOP MEDIA WEBSITES

Leading Czech dailies:
- *Blesk* (www.blesk.cz, in Czech)
- *Lidové noviny* (www.lidovky.cz, in Czech)
- *Mladá fronta DNES* (http://zpravy.idnes.cz/mfdnes.asp, in Czech)
- *Právo* (http://pravo.novinky.cz, in Czech)

English-language media:
- *aktuálně.cz* (http://aktualne.centrum.cz/czechnews) – Overview of politics and economics published in conjunction with the Czech online newspaper.
- *Czech Happenings* (www.ceskenoviny.cz/news) – English-language news magazine operated by the Czech News Agency, CTK.
- the *New Presence* (www.new-presence.cz)
- *Prague Post* (www.praguepost.com)
- *Prague Daily Monitor* (www.praguemonitor.com)
- *Provokátor* (http://provokator.org) – Online 'zine, strong on the club scene, music and lifestyle. Excellent online timetable for club bookings.
- Radio Prague (www.radio.cz) – Useful translations of news and cultural features broadcast by the international service of Czech radio.

CZECH TONGUE-TWISTERS

Forget Sally's seashells or Peter Piper's pickled peppers. With a language in which vowels appear to be optional, Czechs have a tradition of world-beating tongue-twisters. Practise these a few times if you want to impress your Czech hosts:

- Strč prst skrz krk (literally, 'Put your finger through your throat')
- Třistatřicettři stříbrných stříkaček stříkalo přes třistatřicettři stříbrných střech (Three-hundred-thirty-three silver sprinklers were spraying over 333 silver roofs)
- Šel pštros s pštrosáčaty pštrosí ulicí (The ostrich went with its baby ostriches through Ostrich Street)
- If you're really good, try this one (courtesy of Wikipedia – though we've never heard anyone actually attempt it): Prd krt skrz drn, zprv zhlt hrst zrn (A mole farted through the grass, having swallowed a handful of grain)

As far as English-language media go, the venerable *Prague Post* (now in its 19th year) continues to publish in spite of persistent rumours that it's on its last legs. The quality of the writing ebbs and flows depending on the staff, but the tabloid insert *Night and Day* remains an excellent weekly guide to restaurants, movies, happenings, concerts and galleries. Competing with the *Prague Post* in the internet space is the *Prague Daily Monitor,* a lively mix of original stories, supplemented by translations from Czech papers, wire-service pick-ups, and links to other news sources, including local blogs. The *New Presence* is a quarterly English translation of the Czech *Nová přítomnost,* with features on current affairs, politics and business. For a list of the leading media websites, see the boxed text, p53).

The situation is bleaker when it comes to 'zines. Over the years, Prague has supported dozens of English-language start-ups, alternative weeklies and general rant rags, but their number has dwindled in recent years. This probably reflects the shift in the expat community from slackers to older professionals and the influence of the internet, which makes printing on dead trees seem increasingly old-fashioned. One that's still holding on is the cheeky *Provokátor,* occasionally available around town in bars and coffee shops.

LANGUAGE

The Czech language is strongly bound up with the country's cultural and ethnic identity. Czech was squelched for centuries in favour of German during the Habsburg occupation and re-emerged as a literary language only in the 19th century. By the end of that century the number of Czech speakers in the city exceeded German speakers, and by 1939, when the Nazis rolled in, German speakers were a distinct minority (though Prague was still technically bilingual). During the war the Nazis attempted to reinstall German as the leading language, and after WWII, the Russians took their turn at cultural hegemony, making classes in learning Russian compulsory in schools.

Against this backdrop of struggle for linguistic supremacy, it's not surprising that Czechs sometimes appear unwilling to simply chuck it all in and just speak English. That said, you're unlikely to have any major problem in central Prague, where residents are accustomed to fielding basic queries in English. The situation changes outside the centre and in the rest of the country. In general, younger people can muster a bit of English. Older people usually know some German.

Czechs take a perverse pride in the difficulty of their tongue. Even compared with other Slavic languages like Polish and Russian, Czech is usually considered a notch harder. To give you an idea, nouns have four genders (masculine inanimate, masculine animate, feminine and neuter) and each is declined differently depending on its position in a sentence. If you assume around a dozen different noun types and at least half a dozen possible endings for each, you've got over 70 possible spellings – and that's just nouns. It's no wonder that even the most well-meaning visitor eventually shrugs his or her shoulders and falls back on the standard *Mluvíte anglicky?* (Do you speak English?) For a sample of Czech tongue-twisters, see the boxed text, above).

For more information, see the Language chapter, p265.

NEIGHBOURHOODS

top picks

What's your recommendation? www.lonelyplanet.com/prague

NEIGHBOURHOODS

The Vltava River sidles through the centre of Prague like a giant question mark, with the city centre straddling its lower half. There is little method in Prague's haphazard sprawl – it's a city that has grown organically from its medieval roots, snagging villages and swallowing suburbs as it spread out into the wooded hills of Central Bohemia.

The oldest parts of Prague cluster tightly just south of the river bend – Charles Bridge, the original crossing point on the Vltava, is the seed from which the city spread. At its western end is Malá Strana (Little Quarter), Prague's Left Bank: a banquet of beautiful baroque buildings interlaced with hidden gardens, its cobbled streets and squares lined with appealing bars, restaurants and cafes. The main sights here are the historic delights of St Nicholas Church and the Wallenstein Gardens, and more modern spots like the Franz Kafka Museum and John Lennon Wall.

Nerudova street leads uphill from Malá Strana's main square to Hradčany, the medieval castle district, dominated by the spires of St Vitus Cathedral, a landmark visible from most parts of the city. Visitors crowd the castle precincts and jostle for position at the midday changing of the guard, but elsewhere this is rather a peaceful part of town, with many quiet lanes to explore.

From the eastern end of Charles Bridge, tourist-thronged Karlova street leads to Old Town Square, the heart of medieval Staré Město (Old Town). Bounded by the river on one side and the line of the old city walls (along Revoluční, Na Příkopě and Národní třída) on the other, Staré Město is where you'll

> **'the city has grown organically, snagging villages and swallowing suburbs as it spread out into the wooded hills of Central Bohemia'**

find many of Prague's most popular attractions, including the Old Town Hall, Astronomical Clock, Municipal House and Prague Jewish Museum, as well as major concert and opera venues like the Rudolfinum and Estates Theatre.

Wrapped around Staré Město to the south and east, and bounded by the busy traffic artery of Wilsonova, is Nové Město (New Town) – this being Prague, 'new' means 14th-century. Its focal point is the kilometre-long boulevard of Wenceslas Square, and it's where you'll find the Mucha Museum, the National Museum, the National Theatre and many of Prague's more modern hotels and restaurants. At its southern end is the ancient citadel of Vyšehrad, perched on a crag high above the eastern bank of the river.

Beyond the centre lie mostly 19th- and 20th-century suburbs, just a five- or 10-minute tram or metro ride away. To the east lies elegant Vinohrady, with its leafy avenues and cool cafes, which are beginning to spill further east into Vršovice. To their north are grungy Žižkov, famed for its prominent TV Tower and down-to-earth pubs and clubs, and rapidly redeveloping Karlín. The latter two are separated by Žižkov Hill, another prominent landmark, topped by the boxy National Monument and the giant equestrian statue of Jan Žižka.

Back on the west side of the river, to the north of Hradčany, lie the up-and-coming suburbs of Holešovice, Bubeneč and Dejvice. Apart from the Veletržní Palace art gallery and the open green spaces of Letná and Stromovka there are not too many sights here, but there are plenty of worthwhile restaurants, bars and clubs. The same can be said of the formerly industrial district Smíchov, to the south of Malá Strana.

Finally, we have gathered together a grab-bag of outlying attractions under the heading Outer Neighbourhoods, taking in districts such as Troja, home to Prague Zoo and Střešovice, with its Public Transport Museum.

0 ──────────── 1 km
0 ──────────── 0.5 miles

**HOLEŠOVICE,
BUBENEČ & DEJVICE
(p134)**

**PRAGUE CASTLE
(p61)**

**HRADČANY
(p68)**

**ŽIŽKOV
& KARLIN
(p129)**

**STARÉ
MĚSTO
(p89)**

**MALÁ
STRANA
(p76)**

**VINOHRADY
& VRŠOVICE
(p124)**

**NOVÉ MĚSTO &
VYŠEHRAD
(p107)**

**SMÍCHOV
(p142)**

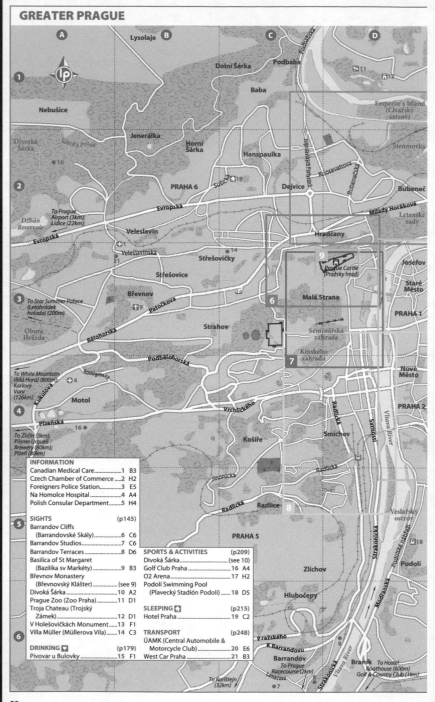

INFORMATION
Canadian Medical Care.................1 B3
Czech Chamber of Commerce 2 H2
Foreigners Police Station.............3 E5
Na Homolce Hospital 4 A4
Polish Consular Department........5 H4

SIGHTS (p145)
Barrandov Cliffs
(Barrandovské Skály).................6 C6
Barrandov Studios.........................7 C6
Barrandov Terraces.......................8 D6
Basilica of St Margaret
(Bazilika sv Markéty)................9 B3
Břevnov Monastery
(Břevnovský Klášter) ....(see 9)
Divoká Šárka..................................10 A2
Prague Zoo (Zoo Praha).............11 D1
Troja Chateau (Trojský
Zámek).......................................12 D1
V Holešovičkách Monument.....13 F1
Villa Müller (Müllerova Vila).......14 C3

DRINKING (p179)
Pivovar u Bulovky.........................15 F1

SPORTS & ACTIVITIES (p209)
Divoká Šárka............................(see 10)
Golf Club Praha 16 A4
O2 Arena...17 H2
Podolí Swimming Pool
(Plavecký Stadión Podolí) 18 D5

SLEEPING (p215)
Hotel Praha 19 C2

TRANSPORT (p248)
ÚAMK (Central Automobile &
Motorcycle Club) 20 E6
West Car Praha 21 B3

0 ━━━━ 1 km
0 ━━━━ 0.5 miles

Ve Višničkách

To Kobylisy Anti-Fascist Memorial (1.5km)

Vychovatelna Tram Stop

To Mělník (47km); Terezín (61km); Litoměřice (70km)

To Kbely Aircraft Museum (3km)

Trojská

Pelc-Tyrolka

V Holešovičkách

Bulovka

Prosecká

Troja

Vltava River

Praha-Holešovice

Vrchlického II Brána

Argentinská

Holešovice

PRAHA 8

Libeň

Palmovka

Palmovká

Praha-Vysočany Train Station

Vysočanská

Freyova

Českomoravská

Ocelářská

Českomoravská

To Kutná Hora (80km)

Karlín

Sokolovská

Pod Balkánem

Na Balkáně

Na Krejčárku

Koněvova

Křižíkova

Pražčka

PRAHA 3

Prokopova

Seifertova

Žižkov

Ondříčkova

Husitská

Olšanské náměstí

Olšany Cemetery (Olšanské hřbitovy)

Jewish Cemetery (Židovské hřbitovy)

Počernická

V Zahliní

Vinohradská

Žitná

Slezská

Korunní

Strašnice

Strašnická

Vinohrady

Ruská

Ruská

V Olšinách

Vršovická

Vršovice

Jaromírova

Vyšehrad

Vršovická

Na Slatinách

Zahradní Město

Nusle

Na Bohdalci

Bohdalecká

Pražského Povstání

Tyršův Vrch

Pankrác

Pankrác

5. května

Michle

Budějovická

Jeremenkova

Budějovická

Kačerov

Kačerov

Olbrachtova

Na Dobešce

PRAHA 4

Spořilov

5. května

Chodovec

To Velké Popovice Brewery (16km); Konopiště (49km); České Budějovice Brewery (160km); Brno (200km)

Turkova

Jižní spojka

Roztyly

Rytavého

Michelský les

Horní Roztyly

Chodov

Chodov

ITINERARY BUILDER

The table below allows you to plan a day's worth of activities in any area of the city. Simply select which area you wish to explore, and then mix and match from the corresponding listings to build your day. The first item in each cell represents a well-known highlight of the area, while the other items are more off-the-beaten-track gems.

	Sightseeing	Eating	Drinking & Entertainment
Prague Castle & Hradčany	St Vitus Cathedral (p65) Story of Prague Castle (p66) Strahov Library (p69)	Vikárka (p163) Malý Buddha (p164) U zlaté hrušky (p163)	Lobkowicz Palace Café (p183) Pivnice U Černého vola (p183) U zavěšenýho kafé (p183)
Malá Strana	Charles Bridge (p76) Wallenstein Garden (p81) Franz Kafka Museum (p80)	Hergetová Cihelná (p164) Noi (p165) U Malé Velryby (p165)	U malého Glena (p201) Malostranská Beseda (p202) Klub Újezd (p183)
Staré Město	Old Town Square (p89) Municipal House (p102) Prague Jewish Museum (p98)	Lokál (p168) Maitrea (p168) Allegro (p166)	U Zlatého Tygra (p186) Kozička (p184) Čili Bar (p185)
Nové Město & Vyšehrad	Wenceslas Square (p113) Mucha Museum (p107) Vyšehrad (p119)	Kogo (p169) Karavanseráj (p171) Oliva (p169)	Bokovka (p186) Pivovarský Dům (p183) Lucerna Music Bar (p202)
Eastern Suburbs	TV Tower (p133) National Monument (p132) Vinohrady & Vršovice Walking Tour (p124)	Ambiente (p172) Mozaika (p172) Café FX (p173)	Caffé Kaaba (p187) Blatouch (p187) Palác Akropolis (p202)
Northern Suburbs	Veletržní Paláce (p139) National Technical Museum (p137) Stromovka (p138)	Da Emanuel (p175) La Crêperie (p177) SaSaZu (p200)	Cross Club (p198) Fraktal (p190) Andaluský Pes (p192)

Drinking p183; Eating p163

Prague Castle – Pražský hrad, or just *hrad* to Czechs – is Prague's most popular attraction. According to *Guinness World Records*, it's the largest ancient castle in the world: 570m long, an average of 128m wide and covering a total area bigger than seven football fields.

Its history begins in the 9th century when Prince Bořivoj founded a fortified settlement here. It grew haphazardly as rulers made their own additions, creating an eclectic mixture of architectural styles. The castle has always been the seat of Czech rulers as well as the official residence of the head of state, although the Czech Republic's first president, Václav Havel, chose to live in his own house on the outskirts of the city.

Prague Castle has seen four major reconstructions, from that of Prince Soběslav in the 12th century to a classical facelift under Empress Maria Theresa (r 1740–80). In the 1920s President Masaryk hired a Slovene architect, Jože Plečnik, to renovate the castle; his changes created some of its most memorable features and made the complex more tourist-friendly.

We've organised this section starting with the castle's main entrance at the western end, then moving through the various courtyards and sights before exiting at the eastern end. You'll need at least two hours to see the main sights, and all day if you want to visit everything.

The following areas are wheelchair-accessible: the main entrance to St Vitus Cathedral, the Old Royal Palace, Vladislav Hall, the Basilica of St George, Ball-Game House, Prague Castle Gallery and the castle gardens. There's a wheelchair-accessible toilet to the right of the cathedral entrance.

Tickets & Opening Hours

You can wander freely through the castle grounds (⊙ 5am-midnight Apr-Oct, 6am-11pm Nov-Mar), the castle gardens (⊙ 10am-6pm Apr & Oct, to 7pm May & Sep, to 9pm Jun & Jul, to 8pm Aug, closed Nov-Mar) and St Vitus Cathedral (⊙ 9am-5pm Mon-Sat & noon-5pm Sun Mar-Oct, 9am-4pm Mon-Sat & noon-4pm Sun Nov-Feb) without a ticket, but you'll need one for all the main historic buildings (⊙ 9am-6pm Apr-Oct, to 4pm Nov-Mar).

There are six different tickets (each valid for two days), which allow entry to various combinations of sights (see the boxed text, p64); you can buy tickets at either of two information centres (Map p62; ☎ 224 372 419, 224 372 423; www.hrad.cz; ⊙ 9am-6pm Apr-Oct, to 4pm Nov-Mar) in the Second and Third Courtyards, or from ticket offices at the entrances to Golden Lane, the Old Royal Palace and the Story of Prague Castle exhibition.

Concession prices are for those aged six to 16 or over 65, students and visitors with disabilities; children aged five or under get in free. The family ticket is valid for one or two adults and up to five children aged under 16. Taking photographs indoors will cost you an extra 50Kč, and the use of a flash or tripod is not allowed.

Tickets listed here do not include admission to other art galleries and museums within the castle grounds; those admission costs are listed in the individual reviews.

One-hour guided tours are available in Czech (200Kč for up to four people, plus 50Kč per additional person), and in English, French, German, Italian, Russian and Spanish (400Kč, plus 100Kč per additional person) Tuesday to Sunday. Alternatively you can rent an audio guide (150Kč for two hours) from the information centres.

There's a post office (⊙ 8am-7pm Mon-Fri, 10am-7pm Sat), currency exchange (⊙ 8.10am-6.10pm) and ATM next to the information centre in the Third Courtyard, and another ATM and currency exchange inside the information centre in the Second Courtyard. You can buy tickets for concerts and other special events at the ticket office (☎ 224 373 483; ⊙ 9am-5pm Apr-Oct, to 4pm Nov-Mar) in the Chapel of the Holy Cross in the Second Courtyard.

TRANSPORT: PRAGUE CASTLE

Metro The nearest metro station is Malostranská, but from here it's a stiff climb up the Old Castle Steps to the eastern end of the castle. Hradčanská station is about 10 minutes' walk north of the castle, but it's an easy, level walk.

Tram Take line 22 from Národní třída on the southern edge of Staré Město, Malostranská náměstí in Malá Strana, or Malostranská metro station to the Pražský hrad stop. If you want to explore Hradčany first, stay on the tram until Pohořelec, the second stop after this one.

PRAGUE CASTLE

0   100 m
0   0.05 miles

See Hradčany Map (p70)

Riding School (Jízdárna)

To Summer Palace (270m)

Ball-Game House (Míčovna)

Royal Garden (Královská zahrada)

Stag Moat (Jelení příkop)

U Prašného mostu

Powder Bridge (Prašný most)

Tunnel

Gate

Passage

Second Courtyard

Fountain

First Courtyard

Hradčany Square (Hradčanské náměstí)

Archbishop's Palace

Prague Castle (Pražský hrad)

St George Square (Jiřské náměstí)

Golden Lane (Zlatá ulička)

Garden on the Ramparts (Zahrada na valech)

Third Courtyard

Castle Steps (Zámecké schody)

Thunovská

Eastern Gate

Palace Gardens Beneath Prague Castle

Old Castle Steps (Staré Zámecké schody)

Brusnice

Wallenstein Palace (Valdštejnský palác)

Wallenstein Garden (Valdštejnská zahrada)

Wallenstein Square (Valdštejnské náměstí)

Valdštejnská

Tomášská

Sněmovní

See Malá Strana Map (p78)

PRAGUE CASTLE

FIRST COURTYARD

The First Courtyard lies beyond the castle's main gate on Hradčany Square (Hradčanské náměstí), flanked by huge, baroque statues of battling Titans (1767–70) that dwarf the castle guards standing beneath them. After the fall of communism in 1989 then-president Václav Havel hired his old pal Theodor Pistek, the costume designer on the film *Amadeus* (1984), to replace their communist-era khaki uniforms with the stylish pale-blue kit they now wear, which harks back to the army of the first Czechoslovak Republic of 1918–38.

The changing of the guard takes place every hour on the hour, but the longest and most impressive display is at noon, when banners are exchanged while a brass band plays a fanfare from the windows of the Plečnik Hall (Plečnikova síň), which overlooks the First Courtyard.

This impressive hall, which opens off the left side of the baroque Matthias Gate (Matyášova brána; 1614), was created by Slovenian architect Jože Plečnik as part of the 1920s restoration of the castle; the pointy flagpoles in the First Courtyard are also Plečnik's. As you pass through the gate, note the contrast between the gilded baroque staircase to your right and the Doric simplicity of Plečnik's stair to the left.

SECOND COURTYARD

You pass through the Matthias Gate into the Second Courtyard, centred on a baroque fountain and a 17th-century well with lovely Renaissance latticework. On the right, the Chapel of the Holy Cross (kaple sv Kříže; 1763) was once the treasury of St Vitus Cathedral; today it houses the castle's box office and souvenir shop.

The magnificent Spanish Hall (Španělský sál) and Rudolph Gallery (Rudolfova galerie) in the northern wing of the courtyard are reserved for state receptions and special concerts; they are open to the public just two days a year, usually on the first Saturdays after Liberation Day (8 May) and Republic Day (28 October).

PRAGUE CASTLE PICTURE GALLERY
Map p62

Obrazárna pražského hradu; ☎ 224 373 531; www .obrazarna-hradu.cz; Pražský hrad, II. nádvoří; adult/concession 150/80Kč, 4-6pm Mon free; ☯ 9am-6pm Apr-Oct, to 4pm Nov-Mar; ☒ 22; ☒ The same Swedish army that looted the famous bronzes in the Wallenstein Garden (p81) in 1648 also nicked Rudolf II's art treasures. This exhibition of 16th- to 18th-century European art, housed in the beautiful Renaissance stables at the northern end of the Second Courtyard, is based on the Habsburg collection that was begun in 1650 to replace the lost paintings; it includes works by Cranach, Holbein, Rubens, Tintoretto and Titian.

ROYAL GARDEN Map p62

The gate on the northern side of the Second Courtyard leads to the Powder Bridge (Prašný most; 1540), which spans the Stag Moat (Jelení příkop) and leads to the Royal Garden (Královská zahrada), which started life as a Renaissance garden built by Ferdinand I in 1534. The most beautiful of the garden's buildings is the Ball-Game House (Míčovna; 1569; Map p70), a masterpiece of Renaissance *sgraffito* where the Habsburgs once played a primitive version of badminton. To the east

PRAGUE CASTLE TICKETS

Prague Castle – long tour (adult/concession/family 350/175/500Kč) Includes Old Royal Palace, Story of Prague Castle, Basilica of St George, Convent of St George, Powder Tower, Golden Lane and Daliborka, Prague Castle Gallery.

Prague Castle – short tour (adult/concession/family 250/125/300Kč) Includes Old Royal Palace, Story of Prague Castle, Basilica of St George, Golden Lane and Daliborka.

Story of Prague Castle (adult/concession/family 140/70/200Kč) Admission to Story of Prague Castle exhibition only.

Prague Castle Gallery (adult/concession/family 150/80/200Kč) Admission to Prague Castle Gallery only.

Convent of St George (adult/concession/family 150/80/200Kč) Admission to Convent of St George only.

Powder Tower (adult/concession/family 70/40/110Kč) Admission to Powder Tower only.

is the Summer Palace (Letohrádek; 1538–60; Map p70), or Belvedere, the most authentic Italian Renaissance building outside Italy, and to the west the former Riding School (Jízdárna; 1695; Map p70). All three are used as venues for temporary exhibitions of modern art.

A footpath to the west of the Powder Bridge (on the castle side) leads down into the Stag Moat, and doubles back through a modern (and rather Freudian) red-brick tunnel beneath the bridge. If you follow the path east along the moat you'll end up at a busy road that leads down to Malostranská metro station. A gate on the outer wall of the castle, overlooking the moat, leads to a nuclear shelter started by the communists in the 1950s but never completed; its tunnels run beneath most of the castle.

THIRD COURTYARD

As you pass through the passage on the eastern side of the Second Courtyard, the huge western facade of St Vitus Cathedral soars directly above you; to its south (to the right as you enter) lies the Third Courtyard. At its entrance you'll see a 16m-tall granite monolith dedicated to the victims of WWI, designed by Jože Plečnik in 1928, and a copy of a 14th-century bronze figure of St George slaying the dragon; the original is on display in the Story of Prague Castle exhibition.

The courtyard is dominated by the southern facade of St Vitus Cathedral, with its grand centrepiece the Golden Gate (Zlatá brána), an elegant, triple-arched Gothic porch designed by Peter Parler. Above it is a mosaic of the Last Judgment (1370–71) – on the left, the godly rise from their tombs and are raised into Heaven by angels; on the right, sinners are cast down into Hell by demons; and in the centre, Christ reigns in glory with six Czech saints – Procopius, Sigismund, Vitus, Wenceslas, Lud-

mila and Adalbert – below. Beneath them, on either side of the central arch, Charles IV and his wife kneel in prayer.

To the left of the gate is the Great Tower, which was left unfinished by Parler's sons in the 15th century; its soaring Gothic lines are capped by a Renaissance gallery added in the late 16th century and a bulging spire that dates from the 1770s.

OLD ROYAL PALACE Map p62

Starý královský palác; admission with Prague Castle tour ticket only; ⊗ 9am-6pm Apr-Oct, to 4pm Nov-Mar; ♿

The Old Royal Palace at the courtyard's eastern end is one of the oldest parts of the castle, dating from 1135. It was originally used only by Czech princesses, but from the 13th to the 16th centuries it was the king's own palace.

At its heart is the Vladislav Hall (Vladislavský sál), famous for its beautiful, late-Gothic vaulted ceiling (1493–1502) designed by Benedikt Rejt. Though around 500 years old, the flowing, interwoven lines of the vaults have an almost art nouveau feel, in contrast to the rectilinear form of the Renaissance windows. The vast hall was used for banquets, councils and coronations, and for indoor jousting tournaments – hence the Riders' Staircase (Jezdecké schody) on the northern side, designed to admit a knight on horseback. All the presidents of the republic have been sworn in here.

A door in the hall's southwestern corner leads to the former offices of the Bohemian Chancellery (České kanceláře). On 23 May 1618, in the second room, Protestant nobles rebelling against the Bohemian estates and the Habsburg emperor threw two of his councillors and their secretary out of the window. They survived, as their fall was broken by the dung-filled moat, but this

Second Defenestration of Prague sparked off the Thirty Years' War (see p24).

At the eastern end of the Vladislav Hall, steps lead up to a balcony that overlooks All Saints' Chapel (kaple Všech svatých); a door to the right leads you to a terrace with great views of the city. To the right of the Riders' Staircase you'll spot an unusual Renaissance doorway framed by twisted columns, which leads to the Diet (Sněmovna), or Assembly Hall, which displays another beautifully vaulted ceiling. To the left, a spiral staircase leads you to the New Land Rolls Room (Říšská dvorská kancelář), the old repository for land titles, where the walls are covered with the clerks' coats of arms.

ST VITUS CATHEDRAL Map p62

Katedrála sv Víta; ☎ 257 531 622; Pražský hrad, III. nádvoří; admission free; �YF 9am-5pm Mon-Sat & noon-5pm Sun Mar-Oct, 9am-4pm Mon-Sat & noon-4pm Nov-Feb; Ⓜ Malostranská; ☒

At first glance the western facade of St Vitus Cathedral, which looms above the entrance to the Third Courtyard, appears impressively Gothic, but in fact the triple doorway dates only from 1953, one of the last parts of the church to be completed. The cathedral's foundation stone was laid in 1344 by Emperor Charles IV, on the site of a 10th-century Romanesque rotunda built by Duke Wenceslas.

Charles' original architect, Matthias of Arras (Matyáš z Arrasu), began work in 1344 on the choir in the French Gothic style, but died eight years later. His German successor, Peter Parler – a veteran of Cologne's cathedral – completed most of the eastern part of the cathedral in a freer, late-Gothic style before he died in 1399. Renaissance and baroque details were added over the following centuries, but it was only in 1861 during the Czech National Revival that a concerted effort was made to finish the cathedral – everything between the western door and the crossing was built during the late 19th and early 20th centuries. It was finally consecrated in 1929.

Inside, the nave is flooded with colour from stained-glass windows created by eminent Czech artists of the early 20th century – note the one by art nouveau artist Alfons Mucha (see the boxed text, p39) in the third chapel on the northern side, to the left as you enter, which depicts the lives of Sts Cyril and Methodius (1909). Nearby is a wooden sculpture of the crucifixion (1899) by František Bílek.

Walk up to the crossing, where the nave and transept meet, which is dominated by the huge and colourful south window (1938) by Max Švabinský, depicting the Last Judgment – note the fires of Hell burning brightly in the lower right-hand corner. In the north transept, beneath the baroque organ, are three carved wooden doors decorated with reliefs of Bohemian saints, with smaller panels beneath each saint depicting their martyrdom – look on the left-hand door for St Vitus being tortured in a cauldron of boiling oil. Next to him is the martyrdom of St Wenceslas; he is down on one knee, clinging to a lion's-head door handle, while his treacherous brother Boleslav drives a spear into his back. You can see that very door handle on the other side of the church – it's now the door to the Chapel of St Wenceslas.

Just to the right of the south transept is the entrance to the 96m-tall Great Tower (�YF last entry 4.15pm Apr-Oct, closed during bad weather). You can climb the 297 slightly claustrophobic steps to the top for excellent views, and you also get a close look at the clockworks (1597). The tower's Sigismund Bell, made by Tomáš Jaroš in 1549, is the largest bell in the Czech Republic.

The eastern end of the cathedral is capped with graceful late-Gothic vaulting dating from the 14th century. In the centre lies the ornate Royal Mausoleum (1571–89) with its cold marble effigies of Ferdinand I, his wife Anna Jagellonská and their son Maximilián II. On the ambulatory's northern side, just beyond the old sacristy and the confessional booths, a wooden relief (1630) by Caspar Bechterle shows Protestant Frederick of the Palatinate (in his horse-drawn coach) legging it out of Prague after the Catholic victory at the Battle of Bílá Hora.

As you round the far end of the ambulatory you pass the tomb of St Vitus – as well as being a patron saint of Bohemia, Vitus is a patron of actors, entertainers and dancers, and is said to protect against lightning, dog bites and oversleeping. The brass crosiers set in the floor nearby mark the tombs of bishops. Further round you reach the spectacular, baroque silver tomb of St John of Nepomuk, its draped canopy supported by a squadron of silver angels (the tomb contains two tonnes of silver in all).

The nearby Chapel of St Mary Magdalene contains the grave slabs of Matthias of Arras and Peter Parler. Beyond is the ornate, late-Gothic Royal Oratory, a fancy balcony with ribbed vaulting carved to look like tree branches.

In the corner of the neighbouring Chapel of the Holy Rood, stairs lead down to the crypt, where you can see the remains of earlier churches that stood on the site of the cathedral, including an 11th-century Romanesque basilica. Beyond, you can crowd around the entrance to the Royal Crypt to see the marble sarcophagi (dating only from the 1930s), which contain the remains of Czech rulers including Charles IV, Wenceslas IV, George of Poděbrady (Jiří z Poděbrad) and Rudolf II.

The biggest and most beautiful of the cathedral's numerous side chapels is Parler's Chapel of St Wenceslas. Its walls are adorned with gilded panels containing polished slabs of semiprecious stones. Wall paintings from the early 16th century depict scenes from the life of the Czechs' patron saint, while even older frescoes show scenes from the life of Christ. On the southern side of the chapel a small door – locked with seven locks – hides a staircase leading to the Coronation Chamber above the Golden Gate, where the Bohemian crown jewels are kept (you can see replicas in the Story of Prague Castle exhibition; see below).

STORY OF PRAGUE CASTLE Map p62
☎ 224 373 102; www.pribeh-hradu.cz; admission with Prague Castle tour ticket, or adult/child 140/70Kč; ☯ 9am-6pm Apr-Oct, to 4pm Nov-Mar

Housed in the Gothic vaults beneath the Old Royal Palace, this huge and impressive collection of artefacts ranks alongside the Lobkowicz Palace as one of the most interesting exhibits in the entire castle. It traces 1000 years of the castle's history, from the building of the first wooden palisade to the present day – illustrated by large models of the castle at various stages in its development – and exhibits precious items such as the helmet and chain mail worn by St Wenceslas, illuminated manuscripts, and replicas of the Bohemian crown jewels, including the gold crown of St Wenceslas, which was made for Charles IV in 1346 from the gold of the original Přemysl crown.

Anyone with a serious interest in Prague Castle should visit here first, as orientation. If you don't have a Prague Castle tour ticket, you can buy individual tickets at the entrance to the exhibit (cash only).

ST GEORGE SQUARE
St George Square (Jiřské náměstí), the plaza to the east of the cathedral, lies at the heart of the castle complex.

BASILICA OF ST GEORGE Map p62
Bazilika sv Jiří; Jiřské náměstí; admission with Prague Castle tour ticket; ☯ 9am-6pm Apr-Oct, to 4pm Nov-Mar; ♿

The striking, brick-red, early-baroque facade that dominates the square conceals the Czech Republic's best-preserved Romanesque church, established in the 10th century by Vratislav I (the father of St Wenceslas). What you see today is mostly the result of restorations made between 1887 and 1908.

The austerity of the Romanesque nave is relieved by a baroque double staircase leading to the apse, where fragments of 12th-century frescoes survive. In front of the stairs lie the tombs of Prince Boleslav II (d 997; on the left) and Prince Vratislav I (d 921), the church's founder. The arch beneath the stairs allows a glimpse of the 12th-century crypt; Přemysl kings are buried here and in the nave.

The tiny baroque chapel beside the entrance is dedicated to St John of Nepomuk (his tomb lies in St Vitus Cathedral; see p65).

CONVENT OF ST GEORGE Map p62
Klášter sv Jiří; ☎ 257 531 644; www.ngprague.cz; Jiřské náměstí 33; admission with Prague Castle long tour ticket, or adult/concession 150/80Kč; ☯ 10am-6pm Tue-Sun

The very ordinary-looking building to the left of the basilica was Bohemia's first convent, established in 973 by Boleslav II. Closed and converted to an army barracks in 1782, it now houses a branch of the National Gallery, featuring a collection of 19th-century Bohemian art. Highlights include the art nouveau sculpture of Josef Myslbek, Stanislav Sucharda and Bohumil Kafka; the glowing portraits by Josef Mánes; and the atmospheric forest landscapes by Július Mařák.

POWDER TOWER Map p62
Prašná věž; admission with Prague Castle long tour ticket; ☯ 9am-6pm Apr-Oct, to 4pm Nov-Mar

A passage to the north of St Vitus Cathedral leads to the Powder Tower (also called Mihulka), which was built at the end of the 15th century as part of the castle's defences.

Later it became the workshop of cannon- and bell-maker Tomáš Jaroš, who cast the bells for St Vitus Cathedral. Alchemists employed by Rudolf II also worked here. Today the 1st floor houses a rather dull exhibition about the castle's military history.

GEORGE STREET

George St (Jiřská) runs from the Basilica of St George to the castle's eastern gate.

GOLDEN LANE Map p62

Zlatá ulička; admission with Prague Castle tour ticket; 🕙 9am-6pm Apr-Oct, to 4pm Nov-Mar
This picturesque, cobbled alley runs along the northern wall of the castle. Its tiny, colourful cottages were built in the 16th century for the sharpshooters of the castle guard, but were later used by goldsmiths. In the 18th and 19th centuries they were occupied by squatters, and then artists, including the writer Franz Kafka (who stayed at his sister's house at No 22 from 1916 to 1917) and the Nobel-laureate poet Jaroslav Seifert. Today, the lane is an overcrowded tourist trap lined with craft and souvenir shops; it's closed for renovations until May 2011.

At its eastern end is the Daliborka, a round tower named after the knight Dalibor of Kozojedy, imprisoned here in 1498 for supporting a peasant rebellion, and later executed. During his imprisonment, according to an old tale, he played a violin that could be heard throughout the castle. Composer Bedřich Smetana (see p31) based his 1868 opera *Dalibor* on the tale. More interesting than the small display of torture instruments in the tower is the modern bronze sculpture *Parable with a Skull*, by Jaroslav Róna (who also created the Franz Kafka Monument in Josefov; Map p90). Supposedly inspired by one of Kafka's characters, it shows a prostrate human figure bearing a giant skull on its back (you can still see homeless people in Prague begging in this traditional but submissive and rather despairing posture).

LOBKOWICZ PALACE Map p62

Lobkovický palác; ☎ 233 312 925; www.lobkowicz events.cz/palace; Jiřská 3; adult/concession/family 275/175/690Kč; 🕙 10.30am-6pm
Built in the 16th century, this palace has been home to the aristocratic Lobkowicz family for around 400 years. Confiscated by the Nazis in WWII, and again by the communists in 1948, it was finally returned in

2002 to William Lobkowicz, an American property developer and grandson of Maximilian, the 10th Prince Lobkowicz, who fled to the USA in 1939. It was opened to the public as a private museum in 2007.

You tour the main exhibition, known as the Princely Collections, with an audio guide dictated by William and his family – this personal connection really brings the displays to life, and makes the palace one of the castle's most interesting attractions. Highlights include paintings by Cranach, Breughel the Elder, Canaletto and Piranesi, original musical scores annotated by Mozart, Beethoven and Haydn (the 7th prince was a great patron of music – Beethoven dedicated three symphonies to him), and an impressive collection of musical instruments. But it's the personal touches that make an impression, like the 16th-century portrait of a Lobkowicz ancestor wearing a ring that William's mother still wears today, and an old photo album with a picture of a favourite family dog smoking a pipe.

The palace has an excellent cafe (p183), and stages concerts of classical music at 1pm each day (390Kč to 490Kč; www.matinee.cz).

TOY MUSEUM Map p62

Muzeum hraček; ☎ 224 372 294; Jiřská 6; adult/ concession/family 60/30/120Kč; 🕙 9.30am-5.30pm
In the tower of the Burgrave's Palace (Nejvyšší Purkrabství), across the street from the Lobkowicz Palace, is the second-largest toy museum in the world. It's an amazing collection – with some artefacts dating back to ancient Greece – but a bit frustrating for the kids as most displays are hands-off. Toys range from model trains and teddy bears to Victorian dolls, Action Men and the definitive Barbie collection.

GARDEN ON THE RAMPARTS

At the castle's eastern gate, you can either descend the Old Castle Steps to Malostranská metro station (Map p70) or turn sharp right and wander back to Hradčanské náměstí through the Garden on the Ramparts (Zahrada na valech; 🕙 Apr-Oct only). The terrace garden offers superb views across the rooftops of Malá Strana and permits a peek into the back garden of the British embassy.

Alternatively, you can descend to Malá Strana through the terraced Palace Gardens Beneath Prague Castle (p81).

HRADČANY

Drinking p183; Eating p163; Shopping p151; Sleeping p217

Hradčany is the attractive and peaceful residential area stretching west from Prague Castle to Strahov Monastery. It became a town in its own right in 1320, and twice suffered heavy damage – once in the Hussite Wars and again in the Great Fire of 1541 – before becoming a borough of Prague in 1598. After this, the Habsburg nobility built many palaces here in the hope of cementing their influence with the rulers in Prague Castle.

HRADČANY SQUARE

Hradčany Square (Hradčanské náměstí), facing the castle entrance, has retained its shape since the Middle Ages, with a central plague column by Ferdinand Brokoff (1726) and several former canons' residences (Nos 6 to 12) with richly decorated facades. At No 16 is the rococo Archbishop's Palace (Arcibiskupský palác), bought by Archbishop Antonín Brus of Mohelnice in 1562, and the seat of archbishops ever since; the exterior was given a rococo makeover between 1763 and 1765 (it's open to the public only on the day before Good Friday).

A statue of Tomáš Garrigue Masaryk, first president of the Czechoslovak Republic, watches over the entrance to the castle.

SCHWARZENBERG PALACE Map p70

Schwarzenberský palác; ☎ 224 810 758; www .ngprague.cz; Hradčanské náměstí 2; adult/child 150/80Kč; ⌚ 10am-6pm Tue-Sun; 🚋 22

Sporting a beautifully preserved facade of black-and-white Renaissance *sgraffito*, the newly renovated Schwarzenberg Palace houses the National Gallery's collection of baroque art. Sadly, a lot of the paintings are poorly lit and suffer from reflections from nearby windows – a shame, as the inside of the palace itself is far less impressive than the outside, and the collection is really only of interest to art aficionados.

The ground floor is given over to two masters of baroque sculpture, Matthias Braun and Maximilian Brokof, whose overwrought figures appear to have been caught in a hurricane, such is the liveliness of their billowing robes. The highlights of

the 1st floor are the moody 16th-century portraits by Petr Brandl and Jan Kupecký, while the top floor boasts a display of engravings by Albrecht Dürer.

STERNBERG PALACE Map p70

Šternberský palác; ☎ 233 090 570; www .ngprague.cz; Hradčanské náměstí 15; adult/child 150/80Kč; ⌚ 10am-6pm Tue-Sun; 🚋 22

Tucked behind the Archbishop's Palace is the baroque Sternberg Palace, home to the National Gallery's collection of 14th- to 18th-century European art, including works by Goya and Rembrandt. Fans of medieval altarpieces will be in heaven; there are also several Rubens, some Rembrandt and Breughel, and a large collection of Bohemian miniatures. Pride of the gallery is the glowing *Feast of the Rosary* by Albrecht Dürer, an artist better known for his engravings. Painted in Venice in 1505 as an altarpiece for the church of San Bartolomeo, it was brought to Prague by Rudolf II; in the background, beneath the tree on the right, is the figure of the artist himself. For a bit of grotesque, snot-nosed realism, it's worth a trip to the back of the 1st floor to see the 16th-century Dutch painting *The Tearful Bride*.

LORETA SQUARE

From Hradčany Square it's a short walk west to Loreta Square (Loretánské náměstí), created early in the 18th century when the imposing Černín Palace was built. At the northern end of the square is the Capuchin Monastery (1600–02), which is Bohemia's oldest working monastery.

ČERNÍN PALACE Map p70

Černínský palác; Loretánské náměstí; ⌚ closed to the public; 🚋 22 to Pohořelec

The late-17th-century early-baroque palace facing the Loreta boasts Prague's largest monumental facade. This imposing building has housed the foreign ministry since

---

TRANSPORT: HRADČANY

Tram Line 22 stops at Pohořelec, at the western end of Hradčany.

Metro Hradčanská station on line A lies at the northern edge of the neighbourhood.

the creation of Czechoslovakia in 1918, except during WWII when it served as the headquarters of the Nazi Reichsprotektor, and is where the documents that dissolved the Warsaw Pact were signed in 1991.

In 1948, Jan Masaryk – son of the Czechoslovak Republic's founding father, Tomáš Garrigue Masaryk, and the only noncommunist in the new Soviet-backed government – fell to his death from one of the upper windows. Did he fall, or was he pushed?

LORETA Map p70

☎ 220 516 740; Loretánské náměstí 7; adult/concession 110/90Kč; ☿ 9am-12.15pm & 1-4.30pm; ⓡ 22
The square's main attraction is the Loreta, a baroque place of pilgrimage founded by Benigna Kateřina Lobkowicz in 1626, and designed as a replica of the supposed Santa Casa (Sacred House; the home of the Virgin Mary). Above the entrance 27 bells, made in Amsterdam in the 17th century, play 'We Greet Thee a Thousand Times' on the hour. Legend says that the original Santa Casa was carried by angels to the Italian town of Loreto as the Turks were advancing on Nazareth. The duplicate Santa Casa, with fragments of its original frescoes, is in the centre of the courtyard.

Behind the Santa Casa is the Church of the Nativity of Our Lord (kostel Narození Páně), built in 1737 to a design by Kristof Dientzenhofer (see p48). The claustrophobic interior includes two skeletons – of the Spanish saints Felicissima and Marcia – dressed in aristocratic clothing with wax masks concealing their skulls.

At the corner of the courtyard is the unusual Chapel of Our Lady of Sorrows (kaple Panny Marie Bolestné), featuring a crucified bearded lady. She was St Starosta, pious daughter of a Portuguese king who promised her to the king of Sicily against her wishes. After a night of tearful prayers she awoke with a beard, the wedding was called off, and her father had her crucified. She was later made patron saint of the needy and the godforsaken.

The church's treasury (1st floor) has been ransacked several times over the centuries, but it remains a bastion of over-the-top religious bling centred on the 90cm-tall Prague Sun (Pražské slunce), made of solid silver and gold and studded with 6222 diamonds.

Photography is not allowed, and the rule is enforced with a 1000Kč fine.

top picks

IT'S FREE

- Charles Bridge (p76)
- National Museum (p115) – on the first Monday of the month
- Prague Castle (p61) – grounds and gardens
- St Vitus Cathedral (p65)
- Letná (p136) and Stromovka (p138)

STRAHOV MONASTERY

In 1140 Vladislav II founded Strahov Monastery (Strahovský klášter; Map p70) for the Premonstratensian order. The present monastery buildings, completed in the 17th and 18th centuries, functioned until the communist government closed them down and imprisoned most of the monks; they returned in 1990.

Inside the main gate is the 1612 Church of St Roch (kostel sv Rocha), which is now an art gallery, and the Church of the Assumption of Our Lady (kostel Nanebevzetí Panny Marie), built in 1143 and heavily decorated in the 18th century in the baroque style; Mozart is said to have played the organ here.

MINIATURE MUSEUM Map p70

Muzeum miniatur; ☎ 233 352 371; www.muzeum miniatur.com; Strahovské II.nádvoří; adult/child 70/50Kč; ☿ 9am-5pm; ⓡ 22
The 'write your name on a grain of rice' movement may have undermined the respectability of miniature artists, but Siberian technician Anatoly Konyenko will restore your faith with his microscopic creations. Konyenko once used to manufacture tools for eye microsurgery, but these days he'd rather spend 7½ years crafting a pair of golden horseshoes for a flea. See those, as well as the world's smallest book and strangely beautiful silhouettes of cars on the leg of a mosquito. Weird but fascinating.

STRAHOV LIBRARY Map p70

Strahovská knihovna; ☎ 233 107 718; www .strahovskyklaster.cz; Strahovské I.nádvoří; adult/concession 80/50Kč; ☿ 9am-noon & 1-5pm; ⓡ 22
The biggest attraction of Strahov Monastery is the Strahov Library, the largest monastic library in the country, with two magnificent baroque halls. You can peek through the doors but, sadly, you can't go

HRADČANY

Střešovice

Svatovítská

Pod Hradbami

Tram 2, 8, 20, 26, 51

U Prašného mostu

Cukrovarnická

13

Patočkova Tram 1, 2, 8, 15, 18, 25, 56, 57

Keplerova Tram 22

Černínská

32

Nový Svět

24

U Brusnice

6

Nový Svět

16

11

1

4

Kanovnická

U Kasáren

10

Hradčany Square
(Hradčanské náměstí)

5

Loreta Square
(Loretánské
náměstí)

15

Loretánská

Ke Hradu

28 31

29

27

Úvoz

22

23

Pohořelec

Strahovská
zahrada

Šporkova

33

21 12

30

26

7

17

Strahovská

19

18

Vlašská

Schönborská
zahrada

Lobkovická
zahrada

See Malá Strana
Map (p78)

0 — 200 Meters
0 — 0.1 miles

E Václavkova
Praha-Dejvice

Open Air Market **F**

Hradčanská **M**

Tram 1, 8, 15, 25, 26, 51, 56, 57 **G**

H

Na valech

Tram 18, 57

Letná Gardens (Letenské sady)

Píšek Gate (Písecká brána)

Mickiewiczova

3

1

Na Baště sv. Jiří

Tychonova

9

Mariánské hradby

Tram 22

Chotkovy sady

Stone Grotto

Pod Bruskou Tram 18, 22, 57

2

20

Chotkova

34

Royal Garden (Královská zahrada)

2

25

Old Castle Steps (Staré Zámecké schody)

Klárov Nábřeží

Tram 12

3

U Prašného mostu

Powder Bridge (Prašný most) Tunnel

Stag Moat (Jelení příkop)

Brusnice

Golden Lane (Zlatá ulička)

Prague Castle (Pražský hrad)

George Street (Jiřská)

See Prague Castle Map (p62)

Palace Gardens Beneath Prague Castle

Valdštejnská

Wallenstein Palace (Valdštejnský palác)

M Malostranská

Letenská

4

Second Courtyard

First Courtyard

Third Courtyard

Garden on the Ramparts (Zahrada na valech)

Castle Steps (Zámecké schody)

Thunovská

Sněmovní

Tomášská

Wallenstein Garden (Valdštejnská zahrada)

Wallenstein Square (Valdštejnské náměstí)

See Staré Město Map (p90)

Vojanovy sady

U lužského semináře

Tram 12, 20, 22, 57

Letenská

Nerudova

Jánský vršek

Malá Strana Square (Malostranské náměstí)

Zámecká

Josefská

St Nicholas Church (kostel sv Mikuláše)

Mostecká

Dražického náměstí

Míšeňská

Cihelná

5

State Police Station

US Embassy

Tržiště

Malá Strana

Saská

Lázeňská

Čertovka

Na Kampě

6

Vrtbov Garden (Vrtbovská zahrada)

Prokopská

Karmelitská Tram 12, 20, 22, 57

Maltese Square (Maltézské náměstí)

Velkopřevorské náměstí

Na Kampě

Charles Bridge (Karlův most)

Kinský Garden (Kinského zahrada)

Harantova

Nebovidská

Pelcozova

Vltava River

Seminářská zahrada

Kampa

HRADČANY

into the halls themselves – it was found that fluctuations in humidity caused by visitors' breath was endangering the frescoes.

The stunning interior of the two-storey-high Philosophy Hall (Filozofický sál; 1780–97) was built to fit around the carved and gilded, floor-to-ceiling walnut shelving that was rescued from another monastery in South Bohemia (access to the upper gallery is via spiral staircases concealed in the corners). The feeling of height here is accentuated by a grandiose ceiling fresco, *Mankind's Quest for True Wisdom* – the figure of Divine Providence is enthroned in the centre amid a burst of golden light, while around the edges are figures ranging from Adam and Eve to the Greek philosophers.

The lobby outside the hall contains an 18th-century Cabinet of Curiosities, displaying the grotesquely shrivelled remains of sharks, skates, turtles and other sea creatures; these flayed and splayed corpses were prepared by sailors, who passed them off to credulous landlubbers as 'sea monsters'. Another case (beside the door to the corridor) contains historical items, including a miniature coffee service made for the Habsburg empress Marie Louise in 1813, which fits into four false books.

The corridor leads to the older but even more beautiful Theology Hall (Teologický sál; 1679). The low, curved ceiling is thickly encrusted in ornate baroque stuccowork, and decorated with painted cartouches depict-

ing the theme of 'True Wisdom', which was acquired, of course, through piety; one of the mottoes that adorns the ceiling is *initio sapientiae timor domini:* 'the beginning of wisdom is the fear of God'.

On a stand outside the hall door is a facsimile of the library's most prized possession, the Strahov Evangeliary, a 9th-century codex in a gem-studded 12th-century binding. A nearby bookcase houses the Xyloteka (1825), a set of booklike boxes, each one bound in the wood and bark of the tree it describes, with samples of leaves, roots, flowers and fruits inside.

In the connecting corridor, look out for the two long, brown, leathery things beside the model ship and narwhal tusk – if you ask, the prudish attendant will tell you they're preserved elephants' trunks, but they're actually whales' penises.

STRAHOV PICTURE GALLERY
Map p70

Strahovská obrazárna; ☎ 220 517 278; www .strahovskyklaster.cz; Strahovské II.nádvoří; adult/ child 60/30Kč; ⏰ 9am-noon & 12.30-5pm; 📷 22
In Strahov Monastery's second courtyard is the Strahov Picture Gallery, with a valuable collection of Gothic, baroque, rococo and romantic art on the 1st floor and temporary exhibits on the ground floor. Some of the medieval works are extraordinary – don't miss the very modern-looking 14th-century Jihlava Crucifix. You can also wander around the monastery's cloister, refectory and chapter house.

PÍSEK GATE

The area northeast of Prague Castle around the Písek Gate (Písecká brána; Map p70) is a quiet, leafy neighbourhood of expensive villas and foreign consulates. It's a bit of a tourist no-man's-land, and few visitors find their way to its one and only sight of note.

BÍLEK VILLA Map p70

Bílkova vila; ☎ 224 322 021; Mickiewiczova 1; adult/child 50/30Kč; ☒ 10am-6pm Tue-Sun; ☒ 18, 22

This striking red-brick villa, designed by sculptor František Bílek in 1912 as his own home, houses a museum of his unconventional stone and wood reliefs, furniture and graphics. It was closed for renovation at the time of research, but should reopen by the end of 2010.

HRADČANY
Walking Tour

1 Písek Gate

As you leave the top of the escalators in Hradčanská metro station, turn right and head for the stairway in the right-hand corner marked 'Pražský hrad'. At street level turn right, and then go right again through the gap in the building. This leads to the street called K Brusce – head for the stone portal of the Písek Gate (Písecká brána) that you'll see straight ahead. The baroque gateway, decorated with carved military emblems, was built by Giovanni Battisti for Charles VI in 1721 as part of Prague's new fortifications; the streets on either side still follow the outlines of the bastions of sv Jiří (St George) to the right and sv Ludmila to the left. A century later, in 1821, the gate became the terminus of Prague's first horse-drawn railway.

2 Cubist houses

Bear right past the gate, then turn right on U Písecké Brány, and then left at the end onto Tychonova. Here you will pass two attractive Cubist houses designed by Josef Gočár.

3 Summer Palace

When you reach Mariánské Hradby (the street with the tram lines), cross it and enter the Royal Garden (p63) beside the beautiful, Renaissance Summer Palace (p64). (The gardens are open from April to October only; at other times of the

year you'll have to go right along Mariánské Hradby and enter Prague Castle via U Prašného mostu.)

4 Ball-Game House

Turn right beyond the Letohrádek, continuing past the equally stunning Ball-Game House (p63), and follow the upper rim of the Stag Moat (Jelení příkop) to the western end of the gardens.

5 Powder Bridge

Go through the gate and turn left to enter the Second Courtyard of Prague Castle (p61) via the Powder Bridge (Prašná most; p63); that's powder as in gunpowder, not a reference to poor-quality construction. Visit the castle if you wish, but for the moment we'll leave the courtyard via the first gate on the right, which leads past a window giving a glimpse into the ruins of a Romanesque chapel, and into Hradčany Square.

6 Hradčany Square

Now watched over by a statue of Tomáš Garrigue Masaryk, the first president of Czechoslovakia, Hradčany Square (p68) was once the social heart of the aristocratic quarter of Hradčany. On the southern side of the square is the extravagant Renaissance status symbol of the Schwarzenberg Palace (p68). On the northern side you can see the rococo Archbishop's Palace (p68) and the sgrafitto-covered Martinic Palace (Martinický palác), which served as Hradčany's town hall. More recently the palace was used as Mozart's house in the film Amadeus.

7 Church of St John Nepomuk

At the far end of the square, bear right on the narrow cobbled street of Kanovnická, and pass the pretty little Church of St John Nepomuk (kostel sv Jan Nepomucký), built in 1729 by the king of Prague baroque, Kilian Dientzenhofer. Take the first lane on the left downhill from the church.

> ## WALK FACTS
> Start Hradčanská metro station
> End Petřín hill (tram 12, 20, 22 or funicular)
> Distance 2.5km
> Time One hour
> Exertion Easy
> Fuel stop U zlaté hrušky

HRADČANY WALKING TOUR

8 Nový Svět

The lane is called Nový Svět (New World) and is a picturesque cluster of little cottages once inhabited by court artisans and tradesmen, a far cry from the fancy palaces at the top of the hill. No 1 Nový Svět was the humble home of court astronomer Tycho Brahe and, after 1600, his successor Johannes Kepler; the atmospheric restaurant U zlaté hrušky (p163) is just

next door. Continue downhill to where Nový Svět ends in a leafy hollow occupied by the Romantik Hotel U Raka (p217).

9 Loreta

Turn left and climb slowly up Černínská to the pretty square in front of the extravagantly baroque Loreta (p69), a shrine to the Virgin Mary and a hugely popular place of pilgrimage for

Roman Catholics. Opposite is the imposing 150m-long facade of the Černín Palace (p68), dating from 1692.

10 Strahov Monastery

At the southern end of the square turn right into Pohořelec and continue to the far western side. A little alley at No 9 leads into the courtyard of Strahov Monastery (p69), where you can visit the library before going through the gate at the eastern end of the courtyard into the gardens above Malá Strana.

11 Petřín Lookout Tower

Turn right on the footpath here (signposted 'Rozhledna & Bludiště') and finish the walk with a nice stroll along to the Petřín Lookout Tower (p86).

MALÁ STRANA

Drinking p183; Eating p164; Shopping p151; Sleeping p218

Almost too picturesque for its own good, the baroque district of Malá Strana (Little Quarter) tumbles down the hillside between Prague Castle and the river. The focal point of the neighbourhood is Malostranské náměstí, a square dominated by the soaring green dome of St Nicholas Church. To its north is a maze of palaces and gardens, home to government offices and foreign embassies; to the south are parks and gardens straggling along the banks of the Vltava before merging into the more commercialised streets of Smíchov (p142).

Once you get away from the crowded pavements of Mostecká and Nerudova – the main tourist route between Charles Bridge and the castle – there are cobbled backstreets to explore, with historic hidden gardens (see the Walking Tour, p86), quaint and colourful house signs perched above doorways, and countless little bars and cafes where you can while away an afternoon.

Malá Strana started life as a market settlement in the 8th or 9th century; Přemysl Otakar II granted it town status in 1257. The district was almost destroyed on two separate occasions: during battles between the Hussites and the Prague Castle garrison in 1419, and then in the Great Fire of 1541. Following this massive devastation Renaissance buildings and palaces sprang up, followed by the many baroque churches and palaces that lend Malá Strana much of its charm.

PRAGUE CASTLE TO CHARLES BRIDGE

Following the tourist crowds downhill from the castle via Ke Hradu, you soon arrive at Nerudova, architecturally the most important street in Malá Strana; most of its old Renaissance facades were 'baroquefied' in the 18th century. It's named after the Czech poet Jan Neruda (famous for his short stories, *Tales of Malá Strana*), who lived at the House of the Two Suns (dům U dvou sluncŭ; Nerudova 47) from 1845 to 1857.

The House of the Golden Horseshoe (dům U zlaté podkovy; Nerudova 34) is named after the relief of St Wenceslas above the doorway – his horse was said to be shod with gold. From 1765 Josef of Bretfeld made his Bretfeld Palace (Nerudova 33) a social hot spot, entertaining Mozart and Casanova. The baroque Church of Our Lady of Unceasing Succour (kostel Panny Marie ustavičné pomoci; Nerudova 24) was a theatre from 1834 to 1837, and staged Czech plays during the Czech National Revival.

Most of the buildings bear house signs. Built in 1566, St John of Nepomuk House (Nerudova 18) is adorned with the image of one of Bohemia's patron saints, while the House at the Three Fiddles (dům U tří houslíček; Nerudova 12), a Gothic building rebuilt in Renaissance style during the 17th century, once belonged to a family of violin makers.

Malostranské náměstí (Map p78), Malá Strana's main square, is divided into an upper and lower part by St Nicholas Church, the district's most distinctive landmark. The square

has been the hub of Malá Strana since the 10th century, though it lost some of its character when Karmelitská street was widened early in the 20th century, and a little more when Prague's first Starbucks opened here in 2008. Today, it's a mixture of official buildings and touristy restaurants, with a tram line through the middle of the lower square.

The nightclub and bar at No 21, Malostranská beseda (see p202), was once the old town hall. Here in 1575 non-Catholic nobles wrote the so-called České Konfese (Czech Confession), a pioneering demand for religious tolerance addressed to the Habsburg emperor and eventually passed into Czech law by Rudolf II in 1609. On 22 May 1618 Czech nobles gathered at the Smiřický Palace (Malostranské náměstí 18) to plot a rebellion against the Habsburg rulers – the next day they flung two Habsburg councillors out of a window in Prague Castle.

CHARLES BRIDGE Map p78 & p90
Karlův most

Strolling across Charles Bridge is everybody's favourite Prague activity. However, by 9am it's a 500m-long fairground, with an army of tourists squeezing through a gauntlet of hawkers and buskers beneath the impassive gaze of the baroque statues that line the parapets (see the boxed text, p82). If you want to experience the bridge at its most atmospheric try to visit it at dawn.

In 1357 Charles IV commissioned Peter Parler (the architect of St Vitus Cathedral) to replace the 12th-century Judith Bridge, which had been washed away by floods in 1342. (You can see the only surviving arch of the Judith Bridge by taking a boat trip with Prague Venice; see p259.)

The new bridge was completed around 1400, and took Charles' name only in the 19th century – before that it was known simply as Kamenný most (Stone Bridge). Despite occasional flood damage, it withstood wheeled traffic for 600 years – thanks, legend says, to eggs mixed into the mortar (though recent investigations have disproved this myth) – until it was made pedestrian-only after WWII.

At the Staré Město end of the bridge, look over the downstream parapet at the retaining wall on the right and you'll see a carved stone head known as Bradáč (Bearded Man). When the river level rose above this medieval marker, Praguers knew it was time to head for the hills. A blue line on the modern flood gauge nearby shows the level of the 2002 flood, no less than 2m above Bradáč!

In the crush, don't forget to look at the bridge itself (the bridge towers have great views) and the grand vistas up and down the river. Pickpocket gangs work the bridge day and night, so keep your purse or wallet safe.

MUSEUM MONTANELLI Map p78
☎ 257 531 220; www.muzeummontanelli.com; Nerudova 13; admission free; ☾ noon-6pm Tue-Sat, noon-4pm Sun; 🚋 12, 20, 22
Tourists, drawn in by an attractive cafe, rub shoulders with connoisseurs of the Czech art world in this private gallery, opened in 2009. Having rapidly become a focus for contemporary art in Prague, it provides a showcase for up-and-coming artists from Central and Eastern Europe, as well as staging exhibitions by more established international names.

MALÁ STRANA BRIDGE TOWER Map p78
Malostranská mostecká věž; ☎ 257 530 487; Charles Bridge; adult/child 70/50Kč; ☾ 10am-10pm Apr-Sep, to 9pm Mar & Oct, to 6pm Nov-Feb; 🚋 12, 20, 22
There are actually two towers at the Malá Strana end of Charles Bridge. The lower one was originally part of the long-gone 12th-century Judith Bridge, while the taller one was built in the mid-15th century in imitation of the Staré Město tower (see Old Town Bridge Tower, p101). The taller tower

TRANSPORT: MALÁ STRANA
Metro Malostranská metro station is in northern Malá Strana, about five minutes' walk from Malostranské náměstí.
Tram Lines 12, 20 and 22 run along Újezd and through Malostranské náměstí.

is open to the public and houses an exhibit on the history of the Judith and Charles Bridges, though like its Staré Město counterpart, the main attraction is the view from the top.

ST NICHOLAS CHURCH Map p78
Kostel sv Mikuláše; ☎ 257 534 215; www.psalterium.cz; Malostranská náměstí 38; adult/child under 10yr 70Kč/free; ☾ 9am-5pm Mar-Oct, to 4pm Nov-Feb; Ⓜ Malostranská or 🚋 12, 20, 22
Malá Strana is dominated by the huge green cupola of St Nicholas Church, one of Central Europe's finest baroque buildings. (Don't confuse it with the other Church of St Nicholas, on Old Town Square, see p94.) It was begun by famed German baroque architect Kristof Dientzenhofer (see p48); his son Kilian continued the work and Anselmo Lurago finished the job in 1755.

On the ceiling, Johann Kracker's 1770 Apotheosis of St Nicholas is Europe's largest fresco (clever trompe l'oeil technique has made the painting merge almost seamlessly with the architecture). In the first chapel on the left is a mural by Karel Škréta, which includes the church official who kept track of the artist as he worked; he is looking out through a window in the upper corner.

Mozart himself tickled the ivories on the 2500-pipe organ in 1787, and was honoured with a requiem Mass here (14 December 1791). Take the stairs up to the gallery to see Škréta's gloomy 17th-century Passion Cycle paintings and the scratchings of bored 1820s tourists and wannabe Franz Kafkas on the balustrade.

You can climb the church's bell tower (adult/child 70/50Kč; ☾ 10am-10pm Apr-Sep, to 8pm Mar & Oct, to 6pm Nov-Feb) via a separate entrance on the corner of Malostranské náměstí and Mostecká. During the communist era, the tower was used to spy on the nearby American embassy – on the way up you can still see a small, white cast-iron urinal that was installed for the use of the watchers.

MALÁ STRANA

See Prague Castle Map (p62)

See Hradčany Map (p70)

Vltava River

Marksmen's Island (Střelecký ostrov)

Children's Island (Dětský ostrov)

Vltava River

Legion Bridge (Legii most)

73

29

Kampa

Janáčkovo nábřeží

Zborovská

náměstí Kinských

Petřínská

Maltézká

Vodní

Nábřežní

69

19

Vítězná

Říční

Besední

Všehrdová

56

72

54

82

Plaská

Melnická

Elišky Peškové

Presslova

Nám. Pě...

60

U lanové dráhy

Štefánikova

Preslova

32

Újezd

Petřínské sady

See Smíchov Map (p143)

tram 6, 9, 12, 20, 58, 59

Kroftova

Zubatého

Holečkova

Drtinova

Funicular Railway (Lanová dráha)

Petřín Funicular Railway (Lower Station)

36

83

Nebozízek Station

15

Kinský Garden (Kinského zahrada)

74

Petřín Funicular Railway (Upper Station)

21

34

Hunger Wall (Hladová zeď)

40

33

20

Olympijská

Jezdecka

Seminářská

64

Chaloupeckého

Strahovský Tunnel

MALÁ STRANA

NORTHERN MALÁ STRANA

From the northern side of Malostranské náměstí, Thunovská and the Castle Steps (Zámecké schody) lead up to the castle. At the eastern end of Thunovská, on Sněmovní, is the Czech Parliament House (Sněmovna), seat of the lower house of parliament, once home to the national assembly that deposed the Habsburgs from the Czech throne on 14 November 1918.

FRANZ KAFKA MUSEUM Map p78

Muzeum Franzy Kafky; ☎ 257 535 507; www .kafkamuseum.cz; Hergetova Cíhelná, Cihelná 2b; adult/child 160/80Kč; ⏰ 10am-6pm; 🚊 12, 20, 22
This much-hyped exhibition on the life and work of Prague's most famous literary son opened here in 2005, after six years in Barcelona and New York. Entitled 'City of K', it explores the intimate relationship between the writer and the city that shaped him, through the use of original letters, photo-

graphs, quotations, period newspapers and publications, and video and sound installations. Does it vividly portray the claustrophobic bureaucracy and atmosphere of brooding menace that characterised Kafka's world? Or is it a load of pretentious bollocks? You decide.

Outside the museum stands one of David Černý's amusing and controversial sculptures, Proudy (Streams; see p142).

PALACE GARDENS BENEATH PRAGUE CASTLE Map p78
Palácové zahrady pod Pražským hradem; ☎ 257 010 401; Valdštejnské náměstí 3, Valdštejnská 12-14; adult/child 79/49Kč; ☯ 9am-9pm Jun & Jul, to 8pm Aug, to 7pm May & Sep, to 6pm Apr & Oct; ⊠ 12, 20, 22

These beautiful, terraced gardens on the steep southern slopes of the castle hill date from the 17th and 18th centuries, when they were created for the owners of the adjoining palaces. They were restored in the 1990s and contain a Renaissance loggia with frescoes of Pompeii and a baroque portal with sundial that cleverly catches the sunlight reflected off the water in a triton fountain.

There are two entrances on Valdštejnská street: one opposite the Wallenstein Palace, and one next to the Palffy Palace Restaurant. There's also one at the top of the hill in the Garden on the Ramparts at Prague Castle.

WALLENSTEIN GARDEN Map p78
Valdštejnská zahrada; Letenská 10; admission free; ☯ 10am-6pm Apr-Oct; Ⓜ Malostranská

This huge, walled garden lurks behind the Wallenstein Palace, an oasis of peace amid the bustle of Malá Strana streets. Its finest feature is the huge loggia decorated with scenes from the Trojan Wars, flanked to one side by an aviary with a pair of Eagle Owls, and an enormous fake stalactite grotto – see how many hidden animals and grotesque faces you can spot. The bronze statues of Greek gods lining the avenue opposite the loggia are copies – the originals were carted away by marauding Swedes in 1648 and now stand outside the royal palace of Drottningholm near Stockholm.

At the eastern end of the garden is an ornamental pond, home to some seriously large carp, and the Wallenstein Riding School (Valdštejnská jízdárna; ☎ 257 073 136; Valdštejnská 3;

adult/child 150/80Kč; ☯ 10am-6pm Tue-Sun), which hosts changing exhibitions of modern art. Enter the garden on Letenská (beside Malostranská metro station) or via the Wallenstein Palace (see the Walking Tour, p86).

WALLENSTEIN PALACE Map p78
Valdštejnský palác; ☎ 257 071 111; Valdštejnské náměstí 4; admission free; ☯ 10am-5pm Sat & Sun Apr-Oct, to 4pm Sat & Sun Nov-Mar; ⊠ 12, 20, 22

The small Wallenstein Square (Valdštejnské náměstí), northeast of Malá Strana Square, is dominated by the monumental 1630 palace of Albrecht of Wallenstein, general of the Habsburg armies, who financed the construction with the confiscated properties of Protestant nobles he defeated at the Battle of Bílá Hora (see White Mountain, p147) in 1620. It now houses the Senate of the Czech Republic, but you can visit some rooms on weekends. The ceiling fresco in the Baroque Hall shows Wallenstein as a warrior at the reins of a chariot, while the unusual oval Audience Hall has a fresco of Vulcan at work in his forge.

SOUTHERN MALÁ STRANA
The southern part of Malá Strana centres on pretty Maltese Square (Maltézské náměstí; Map p78), which takes its name from the Knights of Malta who, in 1169, established a monastery beside the austere, early-Gothic towers of the Church of Our Lady below the Chain (kostel Panny Marie pod řetězem). The knights were charged with protecting the bridge across the river – the chain refers to the barrier they used.

To the east of the square is Kampa (Map p78), an 'island' created by the Čertovka (Devil's Stream) – the most peaceful and picturesque part of Malá Strana. In the 13th century Prague's first mill, the Sovovský mlýn (now Kampa Museum), was built here, and other mills followed. Kampa was once farmland (the name Kampa comes from campus, Latin for 'field'), but the island was settled in the 16th century after being raised above flood level. In 1939 the river was so low that it was again joined to the mainland, and coins and jewellery were found in the dry channel.

The area where the Čertovka passes under Charles Bridge is sometimes called Prague's Venice – the channel is often crowded with dinky tour boats. Cafes beckon from Na Kampě, the small square south of the bridge,

CHARLES BRIDGE STATUES

The first monument erected on the bridge was the crucifix near the eastern end, in 1657. The first statue – the Jesuits' 1683 tribute to St John of Nepomuk – inspired other Catholic orders, and over the next 30 years a score more went up, like ecclesiastical billboards. New ones were added in the mid-19th century, and one (plus replacements for some lost to floods) in the 20th. As most of the statues were carved from soft sandstone, several weathered originals have been replaced with copies. Some originals are housed in the Casemates (p119) at Vyšehrad; others are in the Lapidárium (p135) in Holešovice.

Starting from the western (Malá Strana) end, with odd numbers on your left and even ones on your right, the statues that line the bridge are as follows:

1 Sts Cosmas & Damian (1709) Charitable 3rd-century physician brothers.

2 St Wenceslas (sv Václav; 1858) Patron saint of Bohemia.

3 St Vitus (sv Víta; 1714) Patron saint of Prague (and of dogs, dancers, actors and comedians).

4 Sts John of Matha & Félix de Valois (1714) 12th-century French founders of the Trinitarian order, whose mission was the ransom of enslaved Christians (represented by a Tatar standing guard over a group of them), with St Ivo (No 30).

5 St Philip Benizi (sv Benicius; 1714) Miracle worker and healer.

6 St Adalbert (sv Vojtěch; 1709) Prague's first Czech bishop, canonised in the 10th century. Replica.

7 St Cajetan (1709) Italian founder of the Theatine order in the 15th century.

8 The Vision of St Luitgard (1710) Agreed by many to be the finest piece on the bridge, in which Christ appears to the blind saint and allows her to kiss his wounds.

9 St Augustine (1708) Reformed hedonist, famous for his *Confessions*, theological fountainhead of the Reformation. Also, patron saint of brewers. Replica.

10 St Nicholas of Tolentino (1706) Patron of Holy Souls. Replica.

11 St Jude Thaddaeus (1708) Apostle and patron saint of hopeless causes. Further on the right, beyond the railing, is a column with a statue of the eponymous hero of the 11th-century epic poem *Song of Roland* (Bruncvík).

12 St Vincent Ferrer (1712) A 14th-century Spanish priest, shown with St Procopius, Hussite warrior-priest.

13 St Anthony of Padua (1707) The 13th-century Portuguese disciple of St Francis of Assisi.

14 St Francis Seraphinus (1855) Patron of the poor and abandoned.

though the summer sun is fierce here. Kampa's southern end, beyond the square, is a pleasant wooded park with views across to Staré Město.

Near the southern end of Kampa on the mainland lies one of Malá Strana's oldest Gothic buildings, the Church of St John at the Laundry (kostel sv Jana na prádle; Map p78), built in 1142 as a local parish church. Inside are the remains of 14th-century frescoes.

Marksmen's Island (Střelecký ostrov; Map p78), which is just south of Kampa, is crossed by the Legion Bridge (Legií most). The island's name originates in its use in the 16th century as a cannon and rifle target for the Prague garrison.

During summer it has an open-air bar and cinema (see the boxed text, p185), and there's a little beach at the northern end. To get to the island you take the steps that go down from Legion Bridge.

CHILDREN'S ISLAND Map p78
Dětský ostrov; access from Nábřežní; admission free; 24hr; M Anděl

Prague's smallest island offers a leafy respite from the hustle and bustle of the city, with a selection of swings, slides, climbing frames and sandpits to keep the kids busy, as well as a rope swing, skateboard ramp, mini football pitch, netball court, and lots of open space for older siblings to run wild. There are plenty of benches to take the strain off weary parental legs, and a decent bar and restaurant at the southern end.

JOHN LENNON WALL Map p78
Velkopřevorské náměstí; 12, 20, 22

After his murder on 8 December 1980 John Lennon became a pacifist hero for many young Czechs. An image of Lennon was painted on a wall in a secluded square opposite the French Embassy (there is a niche

15 St John of Nepomuk (1683) Bronze. Patron saint of Czechs. According to the legend on the base of the statue, Wenceslas IV had him trussed up in armour and thrown off the bridge in 1393 for refusing to divulge the queen's confessions (he was her priest), though the real reason had to do with the bitter conflict between church and state; the stars in his halo allegedly followed his corpse down the river. Tradition says that if you rub the bronze plaque, you will one day return to Prague. A bronze cross set in the parapet between statues 17 and 19 marks where he was thrown off.

16 St Wenceslas as a boy (c 1730) With his grandmother and guardian St Ludmilla, patroness of Bohemia.

17 St Wenceslas (1853) With St Sigismund, son of Charles IV, and St Norbert, 12th-century German founder of the Premonstratensian order.

18 St Francis Borgia (1710) A 16th-century Spanish priest.

19 St John the Baptist (1857) By Josef Max.

20 St Christopher (1857) Patron saint of travellers.

21 Sts Cyril & Methodius (1938) The newest statue. These two introduced Christianity and a written script (Cyrillic) to the Slavs in the 9th century.

22 St Francis Xavier (1711) A 16th-century Spanish missionary celebrated for his work in the Orient. Replica.

23 St Anne with Madonna & Child (1707) St Anne is the mother of the Virgin Mary.

24 St Joseph (1854) Husband of the Virgin Mary.

25 Crucifix (1657) Gilded bronze. With an invocation in Hebrew saying 'holy, holy, holy Lord' (funded by the fine of a Jew who had mocked it in 1696); the stone figures date from 1861.

26 Pietá (1859) Mary holding the body of Christ following the crucifixion.

27 Madonna with St Dominic (1709) Spanish founder of the Dominicans, with St Thomas Aquinas. Replica.

28 Sts Barbara, Margaret & Elizabeth (1707) St Barbara, 2nd-century patron saint of miners; St Margaret, 3rd- or 4th-century patron saint of expectant mothers; and St Elizabeth, a 13th-century Slovak princess who renounced the good life to serve the poor.

29 Madonna with St Bernard (1709) Founder of the Cistercian order in the 12th century. Replica.

30 St Ivo of Kermartin (1711) A 13th-century Breton, patron saint of lawyers and orphans. Replica.

on the wall that looks like a tombstone), along with political graffiti and Beatles lyrics. Despite repeated coats of whitewash, the secret police never managed to keep it clean for long, and the Lennon Wall became a political focus for Prague youth (most Western pop music was banned by the communists, and some Czech musicians were even jailed for playing it).

Post-1989 weathering and lightweight graffiti ate away at the political messages and images, until little remained of Lennon but his eyes, but visiting tourists began making their own contributions. The wall is the property of the Knights of Malta, and they have repainted it several times, but it soon gets covered with more Lennon images, peace messages and inconsequential tourist graffiti. In recent years the Knights have bowed to the inevitable and now don't bother to whitewash it any more.

KAMPA MUSEUM Map p78

Muzeum Kampa; ☎ 257 286 147; www.museum kampa.cz; U Sovových Mlýnů 2; adult/concession 150/75Kč; ☼ 10am-6pm; ☒ 12, 20, 22

Housed in a renovated mill building, this gallery is devoted to 20th-century and contemporary art from Central Europe. The highlights of the permanent exhibition are extensive collections of bronzes by Cubist sculptor Otto Gutfreund and paintings by František Kupka, a pioneer of abstract art. The most impressive canvas is Kupka's *Cathedral,* a pleated mass of blue and red diagonals suggesting a curtain with a glimpse of darkness beyond. Outside the museum you can get a close-up look at one of David Černý's famous crawling babies (the ones that swarm over the TV Tower (p133) in Žižkov. Free admission on the first Wednesday of each month.

KAFKA'S PRAGUE

Although he wrote his works in German, Franz Kafka (1883–1924) was very much a son of the Czech capital. He lived in Prague all his life, haunting the city and being haunted by it, both hating it and needing it. His novel *The Trial* can be seen as a metaphysical geography of Staré Město, whose maze of alleys and passageways break down the usual boundaries between outer streets and inner courtyards, between public and private, new and old, real and imaginary.

For most of his life Kafka lived close to Old Town Square, growing up and going to school, working and meeting friends; his own words were: 'this narrow circle encompasses my entire life'. Many guidebooks and walking tours claim to show you 'Kafka's Prague', but any familiarity with his work soon shows that such a place existed only in Kafka's mind. So rather than describe some arbitrary walking trail, we have listed the various places associated with the writer's life in chronological order, so you can wander between them by whichever route you like, as Kafka would have done himself.

- U Radnice 5 (Map p90; 1883–88) is where Kafka was born on 3 July 1883 in an apartment beside the St Nicholas Church; all that remains of the original building is the stone portal. It now houses a Kafka Exhibition, in reality a thinly disguised souvenir shop.
- Celetná 2 (Map p90; 1888–89), 'The Sixt House', was Kafka's childhood home for a brief period.
- House at the Minute (dům U minuty; Map p90; 1889–96) is where Kafka lived as a schoolboy, in the Renaissance corner building that's now part of the Old Town Hall. In a letter he recalled attending primary school in Masná street, and being dragged reluctantly across the square each day by the family cook, whose duty it was to deposit him in class.
- Goltz-Kinský Palace (Map p90) is where Kafka attended high school, at the Old Town State Gymnasium, on the 2nd floor of the palace, between 1893 and 1901. For a time his father ran a clothing shop on the ground floor there, in premises now occupied by the Kafka Bookshop. See also p94.
- Celetná 3 (Map p90; 1896–1907), known as House at the Three Kings, is where Kafka first had a room to himself, and where he wrote his first story. His bedroom window looked out onto the Church of Our Lady before Týn.

CZECH MUSEUM OF MUSIC Map p78

České muzeum hudby; ☎ 257 257 777; www.nm.cz; Karmelitská 2/4; adult/concession 100/60Kč; ☼ 1-6pm Mon, 10am-8pm Wed, 9am-6pm Fri, 10am-6pm Thu, Sat & Sun, closed Tue; ☒ 12, 20, 22
A 17th-century baroque monastery building with an impressive central atrium makes a beautiful setting for Prague's Museum of Music. The museum's permanent exhibition, entitled 'Man-Instrument-Music', explores the relationship between human beings and musical instruments through the ages, and showcases an incredible collection of violins, guitars, lutes, trumpets, flutes and harmonicas – all set to music, of course.

MUSEUM OF THE INFANT JESUS OF PRAGUE Map p78

Muzeum Pražského Jezulátka; ☎ 257 533 646; www.pragjesu.info; Karmelitská 9; admission free; ☼ church 8.30am-7pm Mon-Sat & 8.30am-8pm Sun, museum 9.30am-5.30pm Mon-Sat & 1-6pm Sun, closed 1 Jan, 25 & 26 Dec & Easter Mon; ☒ 12, 20, 22
The Church of Our Lady Victorious (kostel Panny Marie Vítězné), built in 1613, has on its central altar a 47cm-tall waxwork figure of the baby Jesus, brought from Spain in 1628. Known as the Infant Jesus of Prague (Pražské Jezulátko), it is said to have protected Prague from the plague and from the destruction of the Thirty Years' War. An 18th-century German prior, ES Stephano, wrote about the miracles, kicking off what eventually became a worldwide cult; today the statue is visited by a steady stream of pilgrims, especially from Italy, Spain and Latin America. It was traditional to dress the figure in beautiful robes, and over the years various benefactors donated richly embroidered dresses. Today the Infant's wardrobe consists of more than 70 costumes donated from all over the world; these are changed regularly in accordance with a religious calendar.

At the back of the church is the museum, displaying a selection of the frocks used to dress the Infant; shops in the street nearby sell copies of the wax figure. Looking at all this, you can't help thinking about the Second Commandment ('Thou shalt not make unto thee any graven image…') and the objectives of the Reformation. Jan Hus must be spinning in his grave.

- **Assicurazioni Generali** (Map p110; 1907–8) was the Italian insurance firm, located at No 19 Wenceslas Square, where Kafka took his first job, as an insurance clerk, after earning a law degree from Charles University in 1906. Long hours, poor pay and bureaucratic boredom took its toll, and he quit after only nine months.
- **Workers' Accident Insurance Co** (Map p108), an office at Na Poříčí 7 in Nové Město, is where Kafka toiled on the 5th floor for 14 years, from 1908 until his retirement (due to ill health) in 1922.
- **U Jednorožce** (At the Unicorn; Map p90), a house on the southern side of Old Town Square at No 17, was owned by Otto Fanta and his wife Berta, who hosted a regular literary salon popular with fashionable European thinkers of the time, including Kafka and fellow writers Max Brod (Kafka's friend and biographer), Franz Werfel and Egon Erwin Kisch.
- **Pařížská 36** (Map p90; 1907–13), in an apartment overlooking the river beside the Čech Bridge (Čechův most), was where Kafka wrote *The Judgement* and began work on *Metamorphosis*. (The building no longer exists.)
- **Pařížská 1** (Map p90; 1913–14), a luxurious top-floor apartment in the Oppelt House, across from the Church of St Nicholas, was the last place Kafka lived with his parents – and the setting for his horrific parable *Metamorphosis*.
- **Bílkova 22** (Map p90; 1914–15) was where, at the age of 31, Kafka lived in a flat after moving out of his parental home for the first time, and where he began work on *The Trial*.
- **Dlouhá 16** (Map p90; 1915–17) was where Kafka rented a place of his own, at the narrow corner with Masná. He moved around a lot in the next few years, visiting Berlin and Vienna, and visiting with his parents at the Oppelt House when he returned to Prague.
- **Zlatá ulička 22** (Map p62) was Kafka's sister's rented cottage in the castle grounds. During the winter of 1916–17 Kafka stayed here to escape the noise and distraction of his Old Town flat, and produced more than a dozen stories.
- **Tržiště 15** (Map p78; 1917), the Schönborn Palace in Malá Strana (now the US Embassy), was where Kafka took a flat for a few months. He was happy here for a while until he suffered a lung haemorrhage, a symptom of the tuberculosis that would eventually kill him. He spent the rest of his life either seeking medical treatments or staying with his parents, and died in Vienna on 3 June 1924. He was buried in the Jewish Cemetery (see p129) in Žižkov.

VRTBOV GARDEN Map p78

Vrtbovská zahrada; ☎ 257 531 480; www .vrtbovska.cz; Karmelitská 25; adult/concession 55/35Kč; ☽ 10am-6pm Apr-Oct; 🚊 12, 20, 22
This 'secret garden', hidden along an alley at the corner of Tržiště and Karmelitská, was built in 1720 for the Earl of Vrtba, the senior chancellor of Prague Castle. It's a formal baroque garden, climbing steeply up the hillside to a terrace graced with baroque statues of Roman mythological figures by Matthias Braun – see if you can spot Vulcan, Diana and Mars. Below the terrace (on the right, looking down) is a tiny studio once used by Czech painter Mikuláš Aleš, and above is a little lookout with good views of Prague Castle and Malá Strana.

PETŘÍN

This 318m-high hill is one of Prague's largest green spaces. It's great for quiet, tree-shaded walks and fine views over the 'City of a Hundred Spires'. There were once vineyards here, and a quarry that provided the stone for most of Prague's Romanesque and Gothic buildings.

Petřín is easily accessible on foot from Strahov Monastery (p69), or you can ride the funicular railway (lanová draha) from Újezd up to the top. You can also get off two-thirds of the way up at Nebozízek.

In the peaceful Kinský Garden (Kinského zahrada), on the southern side of Petřín, is the 18th-century wooden Church of St Michael (kostel sv Michala), transferred here, log by log, from the village of Medveďov in Ukraine. Such structures are rare in Bohemia, though still common in Ukraine and northeastern Slovakia.

MEMORIAL TO THE VICTIMS OF COMMUNISM Map p78

Památník obětem komunismu; cnr Újezd & Vítězná; 🚊 6, 9, 12, 20, 22
This striking sculptural group consists of several ragged human figures (controversially, all are male) in progressive stages of disintegration, descending a staggered slope. A bronze strip inlaid into the ground in front of them records the terrible human toll of the communist era – 205,486 arrested; 170,938 driven into exile; 248 executed; 4500 who died in prison; and 327 shot while trying to escape across the border.

MIRROR MAZE Map p78

Zrcadlové bludiště; adult/child 70/50Kč; ☺ 10am-10pm Apr-Sep, 10am-8pm Mar & Oct, 10am-6pm Nov-Feb; ⓕ funicular railway

Below the lookout tower is the Mirror Maze, also built for the 1891 Prague Exposition. As well as the maze, which is good for a laugh, there's a diorama of the 1648 battle between Praguers and Swedes on Charles Bridge. Opposite is the Church of St Lawrence (kostel sv Vavřince) which contains a ceiling fresco depicting the founding of the church in 991 at a pagan site with a sacred flame.

MUSAION Map p78

☎ 257 325 766; Kinského zahrada 98; adult/child 70/40Kč; ☺ 10am-6pm Tue-Sun May-Sep, 9am-5pm Tue-Sun Oct-Apr; ⓕ 6, 9, 12, 20

This renovated summer palace houses the National Museum's ethnographic collection, with exhibits covering traditional Czech folk culture and art, including music, costume, farming methods and handicrafts. There are regular folk concerts and workshops demonstrating traditional crafts such as blacksmithing and woodcarving; in the summer months there's a garden cafe.

PETŘÍN FUNICULAR RAILWAY Map p78

Lanová draha na Petřín; ☎ 800 19 18 17; www.dpp.cz; adult/child 26/13Kč; ☺ 9am-11.30pm Apr-Oct, 9am-11.20pm Nov-Mar; ⓕ 12, 20, 22

First opened in 1891, Prague's little funicular railway now uses modern coaches that trundle back and forth on 510m of track, saving visitors a climb up Petřín hill. It runs every 10 minutes (every 15 minutes November to March) from Újezd to the Petřín Lookout Tower, with a stop at Nebozízek. Ordinary 26Kč transfer tickets, valid on tram and metro, are valid on the funicular, too.

PETŘÍN LOOKOUT TOWER Map p78

Petřínská rozhledna; ☎ 257 320 112; adult/child 100/50Kč; ☺ 10am-10pm Apr-Sep, 10am-8pm Mar & Oct, 10am-6pm Nov-Feb; ⓕ funicular railway

The summit of Petřín is topped off with a 62m-tall Eiffel Tower lookalike built in 1891 for the Prague Exposition. You can climb its 299 steps for some of the best views in Prague – on clear days you can see the forests of Central Bohemia to the southwest. (There's also a lift.) On the way to the tower you cross the Hunger Wall (Hladová zeď), running from Újezd to Strahov. These fortifica-tions were built in 1362 under Charles IV, and are so named because they were built by the poor of the city in return for food – an early job-creation scheme.

ŠTEFÁNIK OBSERVATORY Map p78

Štefánikova hvězdárna; ☎ 257 320 540; www.observatory.cz; adult/child 65/45Kč; ☺ hours vary, see website; ⓕ funicular railway

Just south of the funicular's top station is this 'people's observatory', opened in 1928 to further public awareness of astronomy and other sciences. There are exhibitions on astronomy, but the main attraction is the double Zeiss astrograph telescope, which also dates from 1928 and allows observation of the sun and sunspots. On clear nights you can observe the moon, stars and planets.

MALÁ STRANA GARDENS
Walking Tour

1 Prague Castle Lookout

Begin at the lookout just outside the eastern entrance to Prague Castle, which offers a fine view over the rooftops of Malá Strana. On the steep slope directly below are the gardens belonging to the 18th-century aristocratic palaces ranged along Valdštejnská street, now restored and open to the public.

2 Palace Gardens beneath Prague Castle

Go through the gate into the Garden on the Ramparts (Zahrada na valech; p67) and find the entrance to the Palace Gardens Beneath Prague Castle (p81). Note that there is an admission fee, and the gardens are open only from April to October; in winter, begin this walking tour from Malostranská metro station and walk southwest along Valdštejnská to the Wallenstein Palace.

3 Wallenstein Garden

After you have explored the palace gardens, exit via the main gate on Valdštejnská and turn right. When you reach Wallenstein Square (Valdštejnské náměstí), turn left into the main entrance to the Wallenstein Palace (p81) and go through the courtyard into the peace of the Wallenstein Garden (p81). Head for the northeastern corner, to the right of the big fish pond, and leave through the gate beside Malostranská metro station (if the gate

0   400 m
0   0.2 miles

lonelyplanet.com

NEIGHBOURHOODS MALÁ STRANA

is closed, go back along the southern wall and exit through the gate on Letenská).

4 Vojan Gardens

Turn right on Klárov, go straight across the junction with the tram line, and continue along U Lužického Semináře. Just past the Černý Orel restaurant, a gate on the right gives access to the Vojan Gardens (Vojanovy sady), the poor relation of Malá Strana's many parks. Less manicured but more peaceful than the others, it's a public park where local folk take a breather with the kids or sit in the sun on the benches. If you're feeling hungry, the riverside terrace of Hergetova Cihelna (p164) is a great place for lunch.

5 Na Kampě

Continue along U Lužického Semináře, and when the street narrows bear left across the little bridge over the Čertovka (Devil's Stream) onto the island called Kampa (p81). Pass under Charles Bridge and emerge into the picturesque little square of Na Kampě. To your left, at about waist height on the wall to the left of the little gallery under the stairs, is a small memorial plaque that reads *Výska vody 4.žáří 1890*

WALK FACTS

Start Prague Castle (tram 22 or metro Malostranská)

End Petřín hill (tram 12, 20, 22 or funicular)

Distance 4km

Time Two hours

Exertion Moderate

Fuel stops Hergetova Cihelna, Cukrkávalimonáda

(height of waters, 4 September 1890), marking the level reached by the floodwaters of 1890. Directly above it – above head height – is another marking the height of the 2002 floods. (There are several similar plaques around Kampa.) By the way, fans of the Tom Cruise film *Mission: Impossible* might recognise this little square – many of the night scenes in the movie were shot here.

6 Kampa Museum

Head on through the square and into the leafy riverside park known simply as Kampa (from the Latin campus, meaning 'field'); one of the city's favourite chill-out zones, it's usually littered with lounging bodies in summer. If the mood strikes, go for a wander through the modern art collections of the Kampa Museum (p83), housed in a restored mill complex on the edge of the river.

7 John Lennon Wall

Double back north and, as soon as you reach the cobblestones before Na Kampě, bear left along Hroznová, a backstreet that leads to a little bridge over the Čertovka beside Prague's most photographed water wheel. The bridge has become Prague's equivalent of Rome's Ponte Milvio, covered in padlocks placed there by young couples as a sign of their enduring love (a fad inspired by Italian novelist Federico Moccia).

The bridge leads onto a tiny cobbled square with the John Lennon Wall (p82) on one side and the baroque palace that houses the French embassy on the other. The far end of the square curves right, past the severe Gothic towers of the Church of Our Lady below the Chain (p81). Just beyond the church, on the right, is the embassy of the Knights of Malta, which featured in the movie *Amadeus* as the house of Salieri. Turn left opposite the church and bear right along Prokopská; if you fancy a drink – and you may well do by now – Cukrkávalimonáda (p166) is on the right. At the end of Prokopská, cross busy Karmelitská and turn right.

8 Vrtbov Garden

Just past the bar called U malého Glena is an alley on your left that leads to the Vrtbov Garden (p85), one of Malá Strana's least visited but most beautiful gardens. After visiting the garden, turn left along Tržiště and its continuation Vlašská, passing in turn the Irish, US and German embassies.

9 Quo Vadis

A few hundred metres beyond the German embassy there's a little park and playground on the left; leave the street and turn left along the dirt track beyond the wall at the far end of the playground, and you'll be able to peek into the back garden of the German embassy to see David Černý's famous sculpture *Quo Vadis* – a Trabant car perched on four human legs. It's a memorial to the East German asylum seekers who sought refuge here in 1989 during the final death throes of the communist era (for more on David Černý, see the boxed texts, p38 and p142).

10 Petřín Lookout Tower

Follow Vlašská to its end and climb the steps that lead up to the top of Petřín hill and finish your walk at the Petřín Lookout Tower (p86). From here you can take the Petřín Funicular Railway (p86) back down to Újezd or slowly wander down one of the many footpaths.

STARÉ MĚSTO

Drinking p184; Eating p166; Shopping p151; Sleeping p220

Staré Město – meaning 'Old Town' – is the historic heart of medieval Prague, centred on one of Europe's most spectacular town squares. Its origins date back to the 10th century, when a marketplace and settlement grew up on the east bank of the river. In the 12th century this was linked to the castle district by Judith Bridge, the forerunner of Charles Bridge, and in 1231 Wenceslas I honoured it with a town charter and the beginnings of a fortification.

The town walls are long gone, but their line can still be traced along the streets Národní třída, Na Příkopě (which means 'on the moat') and Revoluční, and the Old Town's main gate – the Powder Gate – still survives.

Staré Město shared in the boom when Charles IV gave Prague a Gothic face befitting its new status as capital of the Holy Roman Empire. He founded Charles University in 1348 and commissioned Charles Bridge in 1357. When Emperor Joseph II united Prague's towns into a single city in 1784 the Old Town Hall (Staroměstská radnice) became its seat of government.

In an attempt to escape the frequent floods caused by the Vltava River, the level of the town was gradually raised. Beginning in the 13th century, new houses were simply built on top of older ones (many of Staré Město's Gothic buildings have Romanesque basements). A huge fire in 1689 created space for an orgy of rebuilding during the Catholic Counter-Reformation of the 17th and 18th centuries, giving this originally Gothic district a baroque makeover.

The only intrusions into Staré Město's medieval maze of a street plan have been the appropriation of a huge block in the west for the Jesuits' massive college, the Klementinum, in the 16th and 17th centuries, and the slum clearance of Josefov, the Jewish quarter, at the end of the 19th century.

At the centre of everything is Old Town Square (Staroměstské náměstí). If the labyrinth of narrow streets around the square can be said to have a 'main drag' it's the so-called Royal Way, the ancient coronation route to Prague Castle, running from the Powder Gate along Celetná to Old Town Square and Little Square (Malé náměstí), then along Karlova and across Charles Bridge.

OLD TOWN SQUARE

One of Europe's biggest and most beautiful urban spaces, the Old Town Square (Staroměstské náměstí, or Staromák for short; Map p90) has been Prague's principal public square since the 10th century, and was its main marketplace until the beginning of the 20th century.

Despite the swarms of tourists, crowded pavement cafes and over-the-top commercialism, it's impossible not to enjoy the spectacle: tour leaders thrusting through crowds, umbrellas borne aloft like battle standards, with clients straggling behind like a gaggle of ducklings; students dressed as frogs and chickens handing out flyers for a drama production; middle-aged couples in matching, too-short shorts and sensible shoes, frowning at pink-haired, leather-clad punks with too many piercings; gangs of red-faced lads in football shirts slopping beer and ice cream on the cobblestones; and a bored-looking guy with a placard advertising a museum of torture instruments.

There are busking jazz bands and alfresco concerts, political meetings and fashion shows, plus Christmas and Easter markets, all watched over by Ladislav Šaloun's brooding art nouveau statue of Jan Hus (see the boxed text, p22). It was unveiled on 6 July 1915, which was the 500th anniversary of Hus' death at the stake.

The brass strip on the ground nearby is the so-called Prague Meridian. Until 1915 the square's main feature was a 17th century plague column (see the boxed text, p120), whose shadow used to cross the meridian at high noon.

TRANSPORT: STARÉ MĚSTO

Metro Staroměstská station is a few minutes' walk northwest of Old Town Square, and Můstek station is five minutes' walk to the south.

Tram No trams run close to Old Town Square. Trams 17 and 18 run along the western edge of Staré Město near the river, while lines 5, 8 and 14 stop at Republic Square (náměstí Republiky), across the street from the Municipal House (Obecní dům). Trams 6, 9, 18, 21 and 22 run along Národní třída on the southern edge of Staré Město.

STARÉ MĚSTO

See Holešovice,
Bubeneč
& Dejvice Map (p136)

See Nové Město &
Vyšehrad
Map (p108)

Vltava River

Josefov

Old Jewish
Cemetery
(Starý židovský hřbitov)

See Nové Město Map (p110)

Staré Město

Former Fruit Market (Ovocný trh)

Old Town Square (Staroměstské náměstí)

Little Square (Malé náměstí)

New City Hall (Novoradnice)

Mariánské náměstí

City Library (Knihovna)

Open-Air Market

Bethlehem Square (Betlémské náměstí)

Charles Bridge (Karlův most)

Wenceslas Square (Václavské náměstí)

Jungmannovo náměstí

Adria Palace

Národní třída

Ahenské náměstí

Karoliny Světlé

Legion Bridge (Legii most)

STARÉ MĚSTO

INFORMATION

CHURCH OF OUR LADY BEFORE TÝN
Map p90

Kostel Panny Marie před Týnem; Staroměstské náměstí; admission free; ⊙ 3-5pm Tue-Fri; Ⓜ **Staroměstská**

The distinctive, spiky-topped Týn Church is early Gothic, though it takes some imagination to visualise the original in its entirety because it's partly hidden behind the four-storey Týn School (not a Habsburg plot to obscure this 15th-century Hussite stronghold, but almost contemporaneous with it). The church's name originates from the Týn Courtyard (p96) behind the church.

Though Gothic on the outside, the church's interior is smothered in heavy ba-

roque. Two of the most interesting features are the huge rococo altar on the northern wall and the tomb of Tycho Brahe, the Danish astronomer who was one of Rudolf II's most illustrious 'consultants' (he died in 1601 of a burst bladder following a royal piss-up – he was too polite to leave the table to relieve himself). On the inside of the southern wall of the church are two small windows – they are now blocked off, but once opened into the church from rooms in the neighbouring house at Celetná 3, where the teenage Franz Kafka once lived (from 1896 to 1907; see the boxed text, p84).

As for the exterior of the church, the north portal overlooking Týnská ulička is

STARÉ MĚSTO

topped by a remarkable 14th-century tympanum that shows the Crucifixion and was carved by the workshop of Charles IV's favourite architect, Peter Parler. Note that this is a copy; the original is in the Lapidárium (p135).

The entrance to the church is along a passage from the square, through the third (from the left) of the Týn School's four arches. The Týn Church is an occasional concert venue and has a very grand-sounding pipe organ.

CHURCH OF ST JAMES Map p90

Kostel sv Jakuba; Malá Štupartská 6; admission free; 9.30am-noon & 2-4pm; M Staroměstská

The great Gothic mass of the Church of St James, located to the east of Týn Courtyard, began in the 14th century as a Minorite monastery church, and was later given a beautiful baroque facelift in the early 18th century. Pride of place inside goes to the over-the-top tomb of Count Jan Vratislav of Mitrovice, an 18th-century lord chancellor of Bohemia, found in the northern aisle.

In the midst of the gilt and stucco is a grisly memento: on the inside of the western wall (look up to the right as you enter) hangs a shrivelled human arm. Legend claims that when a thief tried to steal the jewels from the statue of the Virgin around

THE MISSING MONUMENTS

Prague witnessed several profound changes of political regime during the 20th century: from Habsburg empire to independent Czechoslovak Republic in 1918; to Nazi Protectorate from 1938 to 1945; to communist state in 1948; and back to democratic republic in 1989.

Each change was accompanied by widespread renaming of city streets and squares to reflect the heroes of the new regime. The square in front of the Rudolfinum in Staré Město, for example, has been known variously as Smetanovo náměstí (Smetana Square; 1918–39); Mozartplatz (Mozart Square; 1939–45); náměstí Krasnoarmějců (Red Army Square; 1948–89); and náměstí Jana Palacha (Jan Palach Square; 1989–present).

This renaming was often followed by the removal of monuments erected by the previous regime. Here are four of Prague's most prominent 'missing monuments'.

The Missing Virgin

If you look at the ground in Old Town Square (Staroměstské náměstí; Map p90) about 50m south of the Jan Hus monument, you'll see a circular stone slab set among the cobblestones at the far end of the brass strip marking the Prague Meridian (p89). This was the site of a Marian column (a pillar bearing a statue of the Virgin Mary), erected in 1650 in celebration of the Habsburg victory over the Swedes in 1648. It was surrounded by figures of angels crushing and beating down demons – a rather unsubtle symbol of a resurgent Catholic Church defeating the Protestant Reformation.

The column was toppled by a mob – who saw it as a symbol of Habsburg repression – on 3 November 1918, five days after the declaration of Czechoslovak independence. Its remains can be seen in the Lapidárium (p135).

The Missing General

A prominent victim of the change of regime in 1918 was the statue of Field Marshal Václav Radecký (1766–1858) – or Count Josef Radetzky, to give him his Austrian name – that once stood in the lower part of Malá Strana Square (Malostranské náměstí; Map p78); it is now in the Lapidárium (p135). Although Radecký was a Czech, his fame derived from leading the Habsburg armies to victory against Napoleon and crushing the Italians at the battles of Custoza and Novara. (Composer Johann Strauss the Elder wrote the *Radetzky March* in his honour.) The Starbucks coffee shop here was once called the Radetzky Café.

the year 1400, the Virgin grabbed his wrist in such an iron grip that his arm had to be lopped off. (The truth may not be far behind: the church was a favourite of the guild of butchers, who may have administered their own justice.)

It's well worth a visit to enjoy St James' splendid pipe organ and famous acoustics. Recitals – free ones at 10.30am or 11am after Sunday Mass – and occasional concerts are not always advertised by ticket agencies, so check the noticeboard outside.

CHURCH OF ST NICHOLAS Map p90

Kostel sv Mikuláše; Staroměstské náměstí; admission free; ⏰ noon-4pm Mon, 10am-4pm Tue-Sat, noon-3pm Sun; Ⓜ Staroměstská

The baroque wedding cake in the northwestern corner of Old Town Square is the Church of St Nicholas, built in the 1730s by Kilian Dientzenhofer (not to be confused with at least two other St Nicholas churches in Prague, including the Dientzenhofers' masterwork in Malá Strana; see p77). Considerable grandeur has been worked into a very tight space; originally

the church was wedged behind the Old Town Hall's northern wing (destroyed in 1945). Chamber concerts are often held beneath its stucco decorations, a visually splendid (though acoustically mediocre) setting.

GOLTZ-KINSKÝ PALACE Map p90

Palác Kinských; ☎ 224 810 758; Staroměstské náměstí 12; adult/child 100/50Kč; ⏰ 10am-6pm Tue-Sun; Ⓜ Staroměstská

Fronting the late-baroque Goltz-Kinský Palace is probably Prague's finest rococo facade, finished in 1765 by the redoubtable Kilian Dientzenhofer (see also p48). Alfred Nobel, the Swedish inventor of dynamite, once stayed here; his crush on pacifist Bertha Kinský may have influenced him to establish the Nobel Peace Prize. Many older Praguers have a darker memory of the place, for it was from its balcony in February 1948 that Klement Gottwald proclaimed communist rule in Czechoslovakia.

There are Kafka connections here, too – young Franz once attended a school around the back of the building, and his

The Missing Dictator

If you stand on Old Town Square (Map p90) and look north along the arrow-straight avenue of Pařížská you will see, on a huge terrace at the far side of Čechův most, a giant metronome (see also Letná Terása, p137). If the monumental setting seems out of scale that's because the terrace was designed to accommodate the world's biggest statue of Stalin. Unveiled in 1955 – two years after Stalin's death – the 30m-high, 14,000-tonne colossus showed Uncle Joe at the head of two lines of communist heroes, Czech on one side, Soviet on the other. Cynical Praguers accustomed to constant food shortages quickly nicknamed it *fronta na maso* (the meat queue).

The monument was dynamited in 1962, in deference to Khrushchev's attempt to airbrush Stalin out of history. The demolition crew was instructed, 'it must go quickly, there mustn't be much of a bang, and it should be seen by as few people as possible'. The Museum of Communism (p113) has a superb photo of the monument – and of its destruction.

The Missing Tank

Náměstí Kinských (Map p78), at the southern edge of Malá Strana, was until 1989 known as náměstí Sovětských tankistů (Soviet Tank Crews Square), named in memory of the Soviet soldiers who 'liberated' Prague on 9 May 1945. For many years a Soviet T-34 tank – allegedly the first to enter the city – squatted menacingly atop a pedestal here (in fact it was a later Soviet 'gift').

In 1991 artist David Černý (see the boxed text, p38) decided that the tank was an inappropriate monument to the Soviet soldiers and painted it bright pink. The authorities had it painted green again, and charged Černý with a crime against the state. This infuriated many parliamentarians, 12 of whom repainted the tank pink. Their parliamentary immunity saved them from arrest and secured Černý's release.

After complaints from the Soviet Union the tank was removed. Its former setting is now occupied by a circular fountain surrounded by park benches; the vast granite slab in the centre is split by a jagged fracture, perhaps symbolic of a break with the past. The tank still exists, and is still pink – it's at the Military Museum in Lešany, near Týnec nad Sázavou, 30km south of Prague.

father ran a shop in the premises now occupied by the Kafka Bookshop (see the boxed text, p84).

Today, the palace is home to a branch of the National Gallery, housing a collection of 17th- to 20th-century Czech landscape art and temporary art exhibitions. It was closed for refurbishment at the time of research, but was due to reopen soon with the addition of the National Gallery's collection of oriental art.

HOUSE AT THE GOLDEN RING Map p90

Dům U zlatého prstenu; ☎ 224 827 022; Týnská 6; adult/child 120/60Kč; ☽ 10am-6pm Tue-Sun; Ⓜ Staroměstská

The restored Renaissance House at the Golden Ring, located at the corner of Týnská just outside the western entrance to Týn courtyard, contains another branch of the Prague City Gallery; the original painted ceiling beams can still be seen in some of the rooms. It was closed for reconstruction work at the time of research, but was due to reopen soon with a collection of Central European art from the second half of the 20th century.

HOUSE AT THE STONE BELL Map p90

Dům U kamenného zvonu; ☎ 224 827 526; Staroměstské náměstí 13; adult/child 120/60Kč; ☽ 10am-6pm Tue-Sun; Ⓜ Staroměstská

Next door to the Goltz-Kinský Palace is this elegant medieval building, its 14th-century Gothic dignity rescued from a second-rate baroque renovation. During restoration in the 1980s the stucco facade was stripped away to reveal the original stonework, the eponymous stone bell is on the building's corner. Inside, two restored Gothic chapels now serve as branches of the Prague City Gallery (with changing exhibits of modern art) and as chamber-concert venues.

OLD TOWN HALL Map p90

Staroměstská radnice; ☎ 12444; Staroměstské náměstí 1; separate tickets for guided tour adult/child 100/50Kč & admission to tower 100/50Kč; ☽ 11am-6pm Mon, 9am-6pm Tue-Sun Apr-Oct, 9am-5pm Tue-Sat, 11am-5pm Sun Nov-Mar; Ⓜ Staroměstská

Prague's Old Town Hall, founded in 1338, is a hotchpotch of medieval buildings acquired piecemeal over the centuries, presided over by a tall Gothic tower with a splendid Astronomical Clock (see the boxed

THE ASTRONOMICAL CLOCK

The Old Town Hall tower was given a clock in 1410 by the master clockmaker Mikuláš of Kadaně; this was improved in 1490 by one Master Hanuš, producing the mechanical marvel you see today. Legend has it that Hanuš was afterwards blinded so he could not duplicate the work elsewhere, and in revenge crawled up into the clock and disabled it. (Documents from the time suggest that he carried on as clock-master for years – unblinded – although the clock apparently didn't work properly until it was repaired in about 1570.)

Four figures beside the clock represent the deepest civic anxieties of 15th-century Praguers: Vanity (with a mirror), Greed (with his money bag; originally a Jewish moneylender, but cosmetically altered after WWII), Death and Pagan Invasion (represented by a Turk). The four figures below these are the Chronicler, Angel, Astronomer and Philosopher.

On the hour, Death rings a bell and inverts his hourglass, and the 12 Apostles parade past the windows above the clock, nodding to the crowd. On the left side are Paul (with a sword and a book), Thomas (lance), Jude (book), Simon (saw), Bartholomew (book) and Barnabas (parchment); on the right side are Peter (with a key), Matthew (axe), John (snake), Andrew (cross), Philip (cross) and James (mallet). At the end, a cock crows and the hour is rung.

On the upper face, the dark disk in the middle of the fixed part depicts the world known at the time – with Prague at the centre, of course. The gold sun traces a circle through the blue zone of day, the brown zone of dusk (*Crepusculum* in Latin) in the west *(Occasus)*, the black disc of night, and dawn *(Aurora)* in the east *(Ortus)*. From this the hours of sunrise and sunset can be read. The curved lines with black Arabic numerals are part of an astrological 'star clock'.

The sun arm points to the hour (without any daylight-saving time adjustment) on the Roman-numeral ring; the top XII is noon and the bottom XII is midnight. The outer ring, with Gothic numerals, reads traditional 24-hour Bohemian time, counted from sunset; the number 24 is always opposite the sunset hour on the fixed (inner) face.

The moon, with its phases shown, also traces a path through the zones of day and night, riding on the offset moving ring. On the ring you can also read which houses of the zodiac the sun and moon are in. The hand with a little star at the end of it indicates sidereal (stellar) time.

The calendar wheel beneath all this astronomical wizardry, with 12 seasonal scenes celebrating rural Bohemian life, is a duplicate of one painted in 1866 by the Czech Revivalist Josef Mánes. You can have a close look at the beautiful original in the Prague City Museum (p108). Most of the dates around the calendar wheel are marked with the names of their associated saints; 6 July honours Jan Hus.

text, above). The main entrance is to the left of the clock; beyond that is the House at the Minute (dům U minuty), an arcaded building covered with Renaissance *sgraffito* – Franz Kafka lived here (1889–96) as a child just before the building was bought by the town council.

As well as housing the Old Town's main tourist information office, the town hall has several historic attractions, and hosts art exhibitions (adult/concession 40/20Kč) on the ground floor and the 2nd floor. The guided tour takes you through the council chamber and assembly room, with beautiful mosaics dating from the 1930s, before visiting the Gothic chapel and taking a look at the inner workings of the 12 apostles who parade above the Astronomical Clock every hour. The tour is rounded off with a trip through the Romanesque and Gothic cellars beneath the building. However, the town hall's best feature is the view from the 60m-tall tower, which is well worth the climb (there's also a lift).

The area outside the town hall is one of the most crowded corners of Old Town Square, especially during the hourly show

put on by the Astronomical Clock. Around the corner to the right, a plaque on the building's eastern face lists the 27 Protestant nobles who were beheaded here in 1621 after the Battle of Bílá Hora; white crosses on the ground mark where the deed was done. Another plaque commemorates a critical WWII victory by Red Army and Czechoslovak units at Dukla Pass in Slovakia, and yet another the Czech partisans who died during the Prague Rising on 8 May 1945. If you look at the neo-Gothic eastern gable, you can see that its right-hand edge is ragged – the wing that once extended north from here was blown up by the Nazis in 1945, on the day before the Soviet army marched into the city.

TÝN COURTYARD Map p90

Týnský dvůr; entrances on Malá Štupartská & Týnská ulička; admission free; 🕑 24hr; Ⓜ Staroměstská
This picturesque courtyard tucked behind the Church of Our Lady before Týn was originally a sort of medieval caravanserai – a fortified hotel, trading centre and customs office for visiting foreign merchants. First established as long ago as the 11th

century, it's still often called by its German name, Ungelt (meaning 'customs duty'), and was busiest and most prosperous during the reign of Charles IV. Now attractively renovated, the courtyard houses shops, restaurants and hotels.

In the northwest corner is the 16th-century Granovsky Palace, with an elegant Renaissance loggia, and *sgraffito* and painted decoration depicting biblical and mythological scenes. Across the yard, to the right of the V Ungeltu shop, is dům U černého medvěda (House at the Black Bear), whose baroque facade is adorned with a statue of St John of Nepomuk above the door and a bear in chains on the corner, a reminder of the kind of 'entertainment' that once took place here.

JOSEFOV

Half-a-dozen historic synagogues, a town hall and the Old Jewish Cemetery are all that survive of the once-thriving Jewish quarter of Josefov – the slice of Staré Město bounded by Kaprova, Dlouhá and Kozí. Most of the district's buildings were demolished around the turn of the 20th century, when massive redevelopment saw the old slums replaced with expensive new apartments.

When the ghetto was cleared at the turn of the 20th century, the broad boulevard of Pařížská třída (Paris Ave) was driven in a straight line through the heart of the old slums. This was a time of widespread infatuation with the French art nouveau style, and the avenue and its side streets were lined with elegant apartment buildings adorned with stained glass and sculptural flourishes. In the last decade Pařížská has become a glitzy shopping strand, studded with expensive brand names such as Dior, Louis Vuitton and Fabergé.

Jan Palach Square (náměstí Jana Palacha; Map p90) is named after the young Charles University student who in January 1969 set himself alight in Wenceslas Square in protest against the Soviet invasion (see the boxed text, p29). On the eastern side of the square, beside the entrance to the philosophy faculty building where Palach was a student, is a bronze memorial plaque with a ghostly death mask.

Presiding over the square is the Rudolfinum, home to the Czech Philharmonic Orchestra. This and the National Theatre, both designed by architects Josef Schulz and Josef Zítek, are considered Prague's finest neo-Renaissance buildings. Completed in 1884, the Rudolfinum served between the wars as the seat of the Czechoslovak parliament, and during WWII as the administrative offices of the occupying Nazis (see the boxed text, p100).

CONVENT OF ST AGNES Map p90

Klášter sv Anežky; ☎ 224 810 628; www.ng prague.cz; U Milosrdných 17; adult/child 150/80Kč; ⏰ 10am-6pm Tue-Sun; ⎇ 5, 8, 14; ♿

In the northeastern corner of Staré Město is the former Convent of St Agnes, Prague's oldest surviving Gothic building. The 1st-floor rooms hold the National Gallery's permanent collection of medieval art (1200–1550) from Bohemia and Central Europe.

In 1234 the Franciscan Order of the Poor Clares was founded by Přemysl king Wenceslas I, who made his sister Anežka (Agnes) its first abbess. Agnes was beatified in the 19th century and, with hardly accidental timing, Pope John Paul II canonised her as St Agnes of Bohemia just weeks before the revolutionary events of November 1989.

In the 16th century the buildings were handed over to the Dominicans, and after Joseph II dissolved the monasteries, they became a squatters' paradise. It is only since the 1980s that the convent complex has been restored and renovated. In addition to the 13th-century cloister, you can visit the French Gothic Church of the Holy Saviour, which contains the tombs of St Agnes and of Wenceslas I's Queen Cunegund. Alongside this is the smaller Church of St Francis, where Wenceslas I is buried; part of its ruined nave now serves as a chilly concert hall.

The gallery is fully wheelchair-accessible, and the ground-floor cloister has a tactile presentation of 12 casts of medieval sculptures with explanatory text in Braille.

MUSEUM OF DECORATIVE ARTS
Map p90

Umělecko-průmyslové muzeum; ☎ 251 093 111; www.upm.cz; 17.listopadu 2; permanent collection adult/child 80/40Kč, temporary exhibitions 80/40Kč, combined 120/70Kč; ⏰ 10am-7pm Tue, to 6pm Wed-Sun; Ⓜ Staroměstská

This museum opened in 1900 as part of a European movement to encourage a return to the aesthetic values sacrificed to the Industrial Revolution. Its four halls are a feast for the eyes, full of 16th- to

19th-century artefacts such as furniture, tapestries, porcelain and a fabulous collection of glasswork.

The neo-Renaissance building is itself a work of art, the facade decorated with reliefs representing the various decorative arts and the Bohemian towns famous for them. The staircase leading up from the entrance hall to the main exhibition on the 2nd floor is beautifully decorated with colourful ceramics, stained-glass windows and frescoes representing graphic arts, metalworking, ceramics, glassmaking and goldsmithing. It leads to the ornate Votive Hall, which houses the Karlštejn Treasure, a hoard of 14th-century silver found hidden in the walls of Karlštejn Castle (see p234) in the 19th century.

To the right is a textiles exhibit and a fascinating collection of clocks, watches, sundials and astronomical devices, but the good stuff is to the left in the glass and ceramics hall – exquisite baroque glassware, a fine collection of Meissen porcelain and a range of Czech glass, ceramics and furniture in cubist, art nouveau and art deco styles, the best pieces being by Josef Gočár and Pavel Janák. The graphic arts section has some fine art nouveau posters, and the gold and jewellery exhibit contains some real curiosities – amid the Bohemian garnet brooches, 14th-century chalices, diamond-studded monstrances and art nouveau silverware you will find a Chinese rhino-horn vase in a silver mount, a delicate nautilus shell engraved with battle scenes, and a silver watchcase in the shape of a skull.

Labels are in Czech, but detailed English and French texts are available in each room. What you see is only a fraction of the collection; other bits appear now and then in single-theme exhibitions. Admission is free from 5pm to 7pm on Tuesdays.

PRAGUE JEWISH MUSEUM

Židovské muzeum Praha; ☎ 222 317 191; www .jewishmuseum.cz; Reservation Centre, U Starého Hřbitova 3a; ordinary ticket adult/child 300/200Kč, combined ticket 480/320Kč; ☯ 9am-6pm Sun-Fri Apr-Oct, to 4.30pm Sun-Fri Nov-Mar, closed on Jewish hols; Ⓜ Staroměstská

In one of the most grotesquely ironic acts of WWII, the Nazis took over the management of the Prague Jewish Museum – first established in 1906 to preserve artefacts from synagogues that were demolished during the slum clearances in Josefov

around the turn of the 20th century – with the intention of creating a 'museum of an extinct race'. They shipped in materials and objects from destroyed Jewish communities throughout Bohemia and Moravia, helping to amass what is probably the world's biggest collection of sacred Jewish artefacts and a moving memorial to seven centuries of oppression.

The museum consists of six Jewish monuments clustered together in Josefov: the Maisel Synagogue; the Pinkas Synagogue; the Spanish Synagogue; the Klaus Synagogue; the Ceremonial Hall; and the Old Jewish Cemetery. There is also the Old-New Synagogue, which is still used for religious services, and requires a separate ticket or additional fee. If you are pressed for time, the highlights are the Old-New Synagogue and the Old Jewish Cemetery.

An ordinary ticket gives admission to all six main monuments; a combined ticket includes the Old-New Synagogue as well. Admission to the Old-New Synagogue alone costs 200/140Kč. You can buy tickets at the Reservation Centre (see address preceding), the Pinkas Synagogue, the Spanish Synagogue and the shop opposite the entrance to the Old-New Synagogue. Queues tend to be shortest at the Spanish Synagogue.

Completed around 1270, the Old-New Synagogue (Staronová synagóga; Map p90; Červená 2) is Europe's oldest working synagogue and one of Prague's earliest Gothic buildings. You step down into it because it pre-dates the raising of Staré Město's street level in medieval times to guard against floods. Men must cover their heads (a hat or bandanna will do; paper yarmulkes are handed out at the entrance). Around the central chamber are an entry hall, a winter prayer hall and the room from which women watch the men-only services. The interior, with a pulpit surrounded by a 15th-century wrought-iron grill, looks much as it would have 500 years ago. The 17th-century scriptures on the walls were recovered from beneath a later 'restoration'. On the eastern wall is the Holy Ark that holds the Torah scrolls. In a glass case at the rear, little light bulbs beside the names of the prominent deceased are lit on their death days.

With its steep roof and Gothic gables, this looks like a place with secrets, and at least one version of the Golem legend ends here. Left alone on the Sabbath, the creature runs amok; Rabbi Loew rushes out in the middle of a service, removes its magic talisman and carries the lifeless body into the synagogue's attic, where some insist it still lies.

Across the narrow street is the elegant 16th-century High Synagogue (Vysoká synagóga; Map p90), so-called because its prayer hall (closed to the public) is upstairs. Around the corner is the Jewish Town Hall (Židovská radnice; Map p90), also closed to the public, built by Mordechai Maisel in 1586 and given its rococo facade in the 18th century. It has a clock tower with one Hebrew face where the hands, like the Hebrew script, run 'backwards'.

The handsome Pinkas Synagogue (Pinkasova synagóga; Map p90; Široká 3) was built in 1535 and used for worship until 1941. After WWII it was converted into a memorial, with wall after wall inscribed with the names, birth dates, and dates of disappearance of the 77,297 Czech victims of the Nazis. It also has a collection of paintings and drawings by children held in the Terezín concentration camp (see p239) during WWII.

The Pinkas Synagogue contains the entrance to the Old Jewish Cemetery (Starý židovský hřbitov; Map p90; entrance on Široká), Europe's oldest surviving Jewish graveyard. Founded in the early 15th century, it has a palpable atmosphere of mourning even after two centuries of disuse (it was closed in 1787); however, remember that this is one of Prague's most popular sights, so if you're hoping to have a moment of quiet contemplation you'll probably be disappointed. Around 12,000 crumbling stones (some brought from other, long-gone cemeteries) are heaped together, but beneath them are perhaps 100,000 graves, piled in layers because of the lack of space.

The most prominent graves, marked by pairs of marble tablets with a 'roof' between them, are near the main gate; they include those of Mordechai Maisel and Rabbi Loew. The oldest stone (now replaced by a replica) is that of Avigdor Karo, a chief rabbi and court poet to Wenceslas IV, who died in 1439. Most stones bear the name of the deceased and his or her father, the date of death (and sometimes of burial), and poetic texts. Elaborate markers from the 17th and 18th centuries are carved with bas-reliefs, some of them

indicating the deceased's occupation – look out for a pair of hands marking the grave of a pianist.

Since the cemetery was closed, Jewish burials have taken place in the Jewish Cemetery (p129) in Žižkov. There are remnants of another old Jewish burial ground at the foot of the TV Tower (p133) in Žižkov.

You exit the cemetery through a gate between the Klaus Synagogue (Klausová Synagóga; Map p90) and the Ceremonial Hall (Obřadní síň; Map p90), both of which house exhibitions on Jewish forms of worship, family ceremonies and traditions such as birth, circumcision, bar mitzvah and marriage.

A block to the southeast lies the neo-Gothic Maisel Synagogue (Maiselova synagóga; Map p90; Maiselova 10), which replaced a Renaissance original built by Mordechai Maisel, mayor of the Jewish community, in 1592. It houses an exhibit on the history of the Jews in Bohemia and Moravia from the 10th to the 18th centuries, with displays of ceremonial silver, textiles, prints and books.

Finally, about two blocks east of the Maisel is the Spanish Synagogue (Španělská synagóga; Map p90; Vězeňská 1). Named after its striking Moorish interior and dating from 1868, its exhibit continues the story of the Jews in the Czech Republic from emancipation to the present day.

RUDOLFINUM Map p90
☎ 227 059 270; www.rudolfinum.cz; Alšovo nábřeží 12; 🚊 17, 18

This complex of concert halls and offices built in neo-Renaissance style in the late 19th century is the home turf of the Czech Philharmonic Orchestra – the impressive Dvořák Hall, its stage dominated by a vast organ, is one of the main concert venues for the Prague Spring festival (see the boxed text, p206). The building served as the seat of the Czechoslovak parliament from 1918 to 1938.

The northern part of the complex (entrance facing the river) houses the Galerie Rudolfinum (☎ 227 059 205; www.galerierudolfinum .cz; adult/child 120/60Kč, combined admission with Museum of Decorative Arts 180/100Kč; 🕙 10am-6pm Tue-Sun, to 8pm Thu), a gallery that specialises in changing exhibitions of contemporary art. There's also a sumptuous cafe with tables ranged amid the Corinthian splendour of the Column Hall.

MENDELSSOHN IS ON THE ROOF

The roof of the Rudolfinum (p99) is decorated with statues of famous composers. It housed the German administration during WWII, when the Nazi authorities ordered that the statue of Felix Mendelssohn – who was Jewish – should be removed.

In *Mendelssohn is on the Roof*, a darkly comic novella about life in wartime Prague, the Jewish writer Jiří Weil weaves a wryly amusing story around this true-life event. The two Czech labourers given the task of removing the statue can't tell which of the two dozen or so figures is Mendelssohn – they all look the same, as far as they can tell. Their Czech boss, remembering his lectures in 'racial science', tells them that Jews have big noses. 'Whichever one has the biggest conk, that's the Jew.'

So the workmen single out the statue with the biggest nose – 'Look! That one over there with the beret. None of the others has a nose like his' – then sling a noose around its neck and start to haul it over. As their boss walks across to check on their progress, he gapes in horror as they start to topple the figure of the only composer on the roof that he does recognise – Richard Wagner.

ALONG THE ROYAL WAY

The Royal Way (Královská cesta) was the ancient processional route followed by Czech kings on their way to St Vitus Cathedral for coronation. The route leads from the Powder Gate (Prašná brána; p102) along Celetná, through Old Town Square and Little Square (Malé náměstí), along Karlova and across Charles Bridge to Malá Strana Square (Malostranské náměstí), before climbing up Nerudova to the castle. The only procession that makes its way along these streets today is the daily crush of tourists shouldering their way through a gauntlet of gaudy souvenir shops and bored-looking leaflet touts. For a less crowded alternative route, see the Walking Tour (p105).

Celetná, leading from the Powder Gate to Old Town Square, is an open-air museum of pastel-painted baroque facades covering Gothic frames resting on Romanesque foundations, deliberately buried to raise Staré Město above the floods of the Vltava River. But the most interesting building – Josef Gočár's delightful House of the Black Madonna (dům U černé Matky Boží), now the Museum of Czech Cubism (p102) – dates only from 1912.

Little Square (Malé náměstí; Map p90), the southwestern extension of Old Town Square, has a Renaissance fountain with a 16th-century wrought-iron grill. Here several fine baroque and neo-Renaissance exteriors adorn some of Staré Město's oldest structures. The most colourful is the VJ Rott Building (1890), decorated with wall paintings by Mikuláš Aleš, which now houses the Prague incarnation of the Hard Rock Café.

A dog-leg from the southwestern corner of the square leads to narrow, cobbled Karlova (Charles St; Map p90), which continues as far as Charles Bridge – this section is often choked with tourist crowds. On the corner of Liliová is the house called At the Golden Snake (U zlatého hada), the site of Prague's first coffee house, opened in 1708 by an Armenian named Deomatus Damajan.

Karlova sidles along the massive southern wall of the Klementinum (opposite) before emerging at the riverside on Křižovnické náměstí. On the north side of the square is the 17th-century Church of St Francis Seraphinus (kostel sv Františka Serafinského), its dome decorated with a fresco of the Last Judgment. It belongs to the Order of Knights of the Cross, the only Bohemian order of Crusaders still in existence.

Just south of Charles Bridge, at the site of the former Old Town mill, is Novotného lávka (Map p90), a riverside terrace full of sunny, overpriced *vinárny* (wine bars) with great views of the bridge and castle, its far end dominated by a statue of composer Bedřich Smetana.

CHARLES BRIDGE MUSEUM Map p90

Muzeum Karlova mostu; ☎ 776 776 779; www .charlesbridgemuseum.com; Křižovnické náměstí 3; adult/concession 150/70Kč; ☽ 10am-8pm May-Sep, to 6pm Oct-Apr; Ⓜ Staroměstská
Founded in the 13th century, the Order of the Knights of the Cross with the Red Star were the guardians of Judith Bridge (and its successor Charles Bridge), with their 'mother house' at the Church of St Francis Seraphinus on Křižovnické náměstí. This museum, housed in the order's headquarters, covers the history of Prague's most famous landmark, with displays on ancient bridge-building techniques, masonry and carpentry, and models of both Judith and Charles Bridges. In Room 16 you can

descend into the foundations of the building to see some of the original stonework of Judith Bridge (dating from 1172), but perhaps the most impressive exhibits are the old photographs of flood damage to Charles Bridge in 1890, when three arches collapsed and were swept away.

OLD TOWN BRIDGE TOWER Map p90
Staroměstská mostecká věž; Charles Bridge; adult/child 70/50Kč; ⏰ 10am-11pm Apr-Sep, to 10pm Mar & Oct, to 8pm Nov-Feb; Ⓜ Staroměstská

Perched at the eastern end of Charles Bridge, this elegant late-14th-century tower was built not only as a fortification but also as a triumphal arch marking the entrance to the Old Town. Like the bridge itself, it was designed by Peter Parler and incorporates many symbolic elements. Here, at the end of the Thirty Years' War, an invading Swedish army was finally repulsed by a band of students and Jewish ghetto residents.

On the 1st floor there's a small exhibition and a video explaining the astronomical and astrological symbolism of Charles Bridge and the bridge tower, while the 2nd floor has a rather dull exhibit about Charles IV. The main justification for paying the admission fee, however, is the amazing view from the top of the tower.

CZECH MUSEUM OF FINE ARTS Map p90
České muzeum výtvarných umění; ☎ 222 220 218; www.cmvu.cz; Husova 19-21; adult/child 50/20Kč; ⏰ 10am-6pm Tue-Sun; Ⓜ Staroměstská

Housed in three beautifully restored Romanesque and Gothic buildings, this often-overlooked little gallery stages temporary exhibitions of 20th-century and contemporary art, though it's worth the admission fee just for a look at the architecture.

KLEMENTINUM Map p90
☎ 222 220 879; www.klementinum.cz; entrances to courtyards on Křížovnická, Karlova & Mariánské náměstí; Ⓜ Staroměstská

When the Habsburg emperor Ferdinand I invited the Jesuits to Prague in 1556 to boost the power of the Roman Catholic Church in Bohemia, they selected one of the city's choicest pieces of real estate and in 1587 set to work on the Church of the Holy Saviour (kostel Nejsvětějšího Spasitele), Prague's flagship of the Counter-Reformation. The western facade faces Charles Bridge, its sooty stone saints glaring down

at the traffic jam of trams and tourists on Křížovnické náměstí.

After gradually buying up most of the adjacent neighbourhood, the Jesuits started building their college, the Klementinum, in 1653. By the time of its completion a century later it was the largest building in the city after Prague Castle. When the Jesuits fell out with the pope in 1773, it became part of Charles University.

The Klementinum today is a vast complex of beautiful baroque and rococo halls, now occupied by the Czech National Library. Most of the buildings are closed to the public, but you can take a 50-minute guided tour of the baroque Library Hall & Astronomical Tower and the Chapel of Mirrors (adult/child 220/140Kč; ⏰ 10am-7pm daily, hourly Mon-Thu, every 30min Fri-Sun). The chapel dates from the 1720s and is an ornate confection of gilded stucco, marbled columns, fancy frescoes and ceiling mirrors – think baroque on steroids. Concerts of classical music are held here daily (tickets are available at most ticket agencies). The library hall, chapel and tower were closed for renovation at the time of research, and may not reopen till 2011.

There are two other interesting churches in the Klementinum. The Church of St Clement (kostel sv Klimenta; ⏰ services 8.30am & 10am Sun), lavishly redecorated in the baroque style from 1711 to 1715 to plans by Kilian Dientzenhofer, is now a Greek Catholic chapel. Conservatively dressed visitors are welcome to attend the services. And then there's the elliptical, Italian Chapel of the Assumption of the Virgin Mary (Vlašská kaple Nanebevzetí Panny Marie), built in 1600 for the Italian artisans who worked on the Klementinum (it's still technically the property of the Italian government).

MARIONETTE MUSEUM Map p90
Muzeum loutek; ☎ 222 228 511; www.puppetart.com; Karlova 12; adult/child 100/50Kč; ⏰ noon-8pm; ☐ 17, 18

Rooms peopled with a multitude of authentic, colourful marionettes illustrate the evolution of this wonderful Czech tradition from the late 17th to early 19th centuries. The star attractions are the Czech children's favourites, Spejbl and Hurvínek – kids and adults alike can enjoy the Czech equivalent of Punch and Judy at the Spejbl & Hurvínek Theatre (p207).

MUNICIPAL HOUSE Map p90

Obecní dům; ☎ 222 002 101; www.obecni-dum
.cz; náměstí Republiky 5; guided tours adult/child
270/220Kč; ☺ public areas 7.30am-11pm, information centre 10am-7pm; Ⓜ Náměstí Republiky

Prague's most exuberant and sensual
building stands on the site of the Royal
Court, seat of Bohemia's kings from 1383
to 1483 (when Vladislav II moved to Prague
Castle), which was demolished at the end
of the 19th century. Between 1906 and
1912 the Municipal House was built in its
place – a lavish joint effort by around 30
leading artists of the day, creating a cultural
centre that was the architectural climax of
the Czech National Revival. Restored in the
1990s after decades of neglect during the
communist era, the entire building was a
labour of love, every detail of design and
decoration carefully considered, every painting and sculpture loaded with symbolism.

The mosaic above the entrance, *Homage to Prague,* is set between sculptures
representing the oppression and rebirth of
the Czech people; other sculptures ranged
along the top of the facade represent history, literature, painting, music and architecture. You pass beneath a wrought-iron
and stained-glass canopy into an interior
that is art nouveau down to the doorknobs
(you can look around the lobby and the
downstairs bar for free). The restaurant
and the *kavárna* (cafe; see Kavárna Obecní
dům in the boxed text, p188) flanking the
entrance are like walk-in museums of art
nouveau design.

Upstairs are half a dozen sumptuously
decorated halls and assembly rooms that
you can visit by guided tour (90 minutes,
three or four per day), which can be
booked at the building's information centre
(through the main entrance, and around to
the left of the stairs).

First stop on the tour is Smetana Hall
(p205), Prague's biggest concert hall, with
seating for 1200 ranged beneath an art
nouveau glass dome. The stage is framed
by sculptures representing the Vyšehrad
legend (to the right) and Slavonic dances
(to the left).

Several impressive official apartments
follow, but the highlight of the tour is
the octagonal Lord Mayor's Hall (Primatorský
sál), whose windows overlook the main
entrance. Every aspect of its decoration
was designed by Alfons Mucha, who also
painted the superbly moody murals that
adorn the walls and ceiling. Above you is
an allegory of *Slavic Concord,* with intertwined figures representing the various
Slavic peoples watched over by the Czech
eagle. Figures from Czech history and my-
thology, representing the civic virtues, oc-
cupy the spaces between the eight arches,
including Jan Hus as *Spravedlnost* (justice),
Jan Žižka as *Bojovnost* (military prowess)
and the Chodové (medieval Bohemian
border guards) as beady-eyed *Ostražitost*
(vigilance).

On 28 October 1918 an independent
Czechoslovak Republic was declared in
Smetana Hall, and in November 1989 meetings took place here between the Civic
Forum and the Jakeš regime. The Prague
Spring (Pražské jaro) music festival (see the
boxed text, p206) always opens on 12 May,
the anniversary of Smetana's death, with a
procession from Vyšehrad to the Municipal
House followed by a gala performance of
his symphonic cycle *Má Vlast* (My Country)
in Smetana Hall.

MUSEUM OF CZECH CUBISM Map p90

Muzeum Českého kubismu; ☎ 224 211 746; Ovocný
trh 19; adult/child 100/50Kč, 50/30Kč after 4pm;
☺ 10am-6pm Tue-Sun; Ⓜ Náměstí Republiky

Though dating from 1912, Josef Gočár's
House of the Black Madonna (dům U černé Matky
Boží) – Prague's first and finest example
of cubist architecture – still looks modern
and dynamic. It now houses three floors of
remarkable cubist paintings and sculpture,
as well as furniture, ceramics and glassware
in Ccubist designs.

POWDER GATE Map p90

Prašná brána; ☎ 724 063 723; Na Příkopě; adult/
child 70/50Kč; ☺ 10am-10pm Apr-Sep, to 8pm Oct
& Mar, to 6pm Nov-Feb; Ⓜ Náměstí Republiky

The 65m-tall Powder Gate was begun in
1475 on the site of one of Staré Město's
original 13 gates. Built during the reign of
King Vladislav II Jagiello as a ceremonial
entrance to the city, it was left unfinished
after the king moved from the neighbouring Royal Court to Prague Castle in 1483.
The name comes from its use as a gunpowder magazine in the 18th century. Josef
Mocker rebuilt and decorated it and put up
a steeple between 1875 and 1886, giving it
its neo-Gothic icing.

The tower houses exhibitions on the
Hussites (dull) and the history of the Royal
Court (see Municipal House, above) and the

towers that once punctuated Prague's town walls (more interesting), but the main attraction is the view from the top.

SMETANA MUSEUM Map p90

Muzeum Bedřicha Smetany; ☎ 222 220 082; Novotného lávka 1; adult/child 50/25Kč; ☒ 10am-noon & 12.30-5pm Wed-Mon; Ⓜ Staroměstská
This small museum is devoted to Bedřich Smetana, Bohemia's favourite composer. It isn't that interesting unless you're a Smetana fan, and has only limited labelling in English, but there's a good exhibit on popular culture's feverish response to Smetana's opera *The Bartered Bride* – it seems Smetana was the Andrew Lloyd Webber of his day.

HAVELSKÉ MĚSTO

In about 1230 a market district named Havelské Město (St Gall's Town), named after the 7th-century Irish monk who helped introduce Christianity to Europe, was laid out for the pleasure of the German merchants invited to Prague by Wenceslas I.

Modern-day Rytířská and Havelská streets were at that time a single plaza surrounded by arcaded merchants' houses. Specialist markets included those for coal (Uhelný trh) at the western end of the plaza and for fruit (Ovocný trh) at the eastern end. In the 15th century an island of stalls was built down the middle.

All that remains of St Gall's market today is the touristy open-air market on Havelská and the clothes hawkers in adjacent V Kotcích. Though no match for the original, it's still Prague's most central open-air market.

At the eastern end of Havelská is the Church of St Gall (kostel sv Havla; Map p90), as old as St Gall's Town itself, where Jan Hus and his predecessors preached religious reform. The Carmelites took possession of it in 1627, and in 1723 added its shapely baroque facade. The Czech baroque painter Karel Škréta (1610–74) is buried in the church.

Near the former Uhelný trh (coal market) is the plain, 12th-century Church of St Martin in the Wall (kostel sv Martin ve zdi; Map p90), a parish church enlarged and Gothicised in the 14th century. The name comes from its having had the Old Town wall built right around it. In 1414 the church was the site of the first-ever Hussite communion service *sub utraque specie* (with both bread and wine), from which the name 'Utraquist' derives.

ESTATES THEATRE
Map p90

Stavovské divadlo; ☎ 224 902 231; www.narod ni-divadlo.cz; Ovocný trh 1; Ⓜ Náměstí Republiky
Beside the Karolinum is Prague's oldest theatre and finest neoclassical building, the Estates Theatre, where the premiere of Mozart's *Don Giovanni* was performed on 29 October 1787, with the maestro himself conducting. Opened in 1783 as the Nostitz Theatre (after its founder, Count Anton von Nostitz-Rieneck), it was patronised by upper-class German citizens and thus came to be called the Estates Theatre – the Estates being the traditional nobility.

After WWII it was renamed the Tylovo divadlo (Tyl Theatre) in honour of the 19th-century Czech playwright Josef Kajetán Tyl. One of his claims to fame is the Czech national anthem, *Kde domov můj?* (Where Is My Home?), which came from one of his plays. In the early 1990s the theatre's name reverted to Estates Theatre. Around the corner is the 17th-century Kolowrat Theatre (Divadlo Kolowrat; Ovocný trh 6), now also a National Theatre venue. See also p204 for more information on classical-music venues.

KAROLINUM
Map p90

Univerzita Karlova; ☎ 224 491 250; www.cuni.cz/ ukeng-4.html; Ovocný trh 3; Ⓜ Můstek
Central Europe's oldest university, founded by Charles IV in 1348, was originally housed in the so-called Rotlev House. With Protestantism and Czech nationalism on the rise, the reforming preacher Jan Hus became Charles University's rector in 1402 and soon persuaded Wenceslas IV to slash the voting rights of the university's German students – thousands of them left Bohemia when this was announced.

The facilities of the ever-expanding university were concentrated here in 1611, and by the 18th century the old burgher's house had grown into a sizeable complex known as the Karolinum. After the Battle of Bílá Hora (1620) it was handed over to the Jesuits, who gave it a baroque makeover; when they were booted out in 1773 the university took it back. Charles University now has faculties all over Prague, and the Karolinum today houses only some faculty offices, the University Club and a ceremonial hall. It is open to the public only on 'open doors' days (details from tourist information offices).

Among pre-university Gothic survivals is the Chapel of Sts Cosmas & Damian (kaple sv Kosmas a Damian), with its extraordinary oriel window protruding from the southern wall. Built around 1370, it was renovated in 1881 by Josef Mocker.

SOUTHWESTERN STARÉ MĚSTO

The meandering lanes and passageways between Karlova and Národní třída are Prague's best territory for aimless wandering. When the crowds thin out late in the day, this area can cast such a spell that it's quite a surprise to emerge from its peaceful backstreets into the bustle of the 21st century.

The charm goes a bit cold along Bartolomějská, however, and not just because it is lined with police offices. Before November 1989 this block was occupied by the StB (Státní bezpečnost, or State Security), the hated secret police. Older Czechs are still understandably twitchy about police of any kind and it's a common suspicion that a few former StB officers are still around, just wearing new uniforms.

Backing onto Bartolomějská is an old convent and the once-lovely 18th-century Church of St Bartholomew (kostel sv Bartoloměje; Map p90), for a time part of the StB complex but now returned to the Franciscans. The area boasts a couple more historic churches in the shape of the Bethlehem Chapel and the Rotunda of the Holy Cross.

BETHLEHEM CHAPEL
Map p90

Betlémská kaple; ☎ 224 248 595; Betlémské náměstí 3; adult/child 50/30Kč; ❤ 10am-6.30pm Tue-Sun Apr-Oct, to 5.30pm Tue-Sun Nov-Mar; 🚊 6, 9, 18, 21, 22
The Bethlehem Chapel is one of Prague's most important churches, being the true birthplace of the Hussite cause. In 1391, Reformist Praguers won permission to build a church where services could be held in Czech instead of Latin, and proceeded to construct the biggest chapel Bohemia had ever seen, able to hold 3000 worshippers. Architecturally it was a radical departure, with a simple square hall focused on the pulpit rather than the altar. Jan Hus preached here from 1402 to 1412, marking

the emergence of the Reform movement from the sanctuary of the Karolinum (where he was rector).

In the 18th century the chapel was torn down. Remnants were discovered around 1920, and from 1948 to 1954 – because Hussitism had official blessing as an ancient form of communism – the whole thing was painstakingly reconstructed in its original form, based on old drawings, descriptions, and traces of the original work. It's now a national cultural monument.

Only the southern wall of the chapel is brand new. You can still see some original parts in the eastern wall: the pulpit door, several windows and the door to the preacher's quarters. These quarters, including the rooms used by Hus and others, are also original; they are now used for exhibits. The wall paintings are modern, and are based on old Hussite tracts. The indoor well pre-dates the chapel.

The chapel has an English text available at the door. Every year on the night of 5 July, the eve of Hus' burning at the stake in 1415, a commemorative celebration is held here, with speeches and bell-ringing.

CHURCH OF ST GILES
Map p90

Kostel sv Jiljí; cnr Zlatá & Husova; 🚊 6, 9, 18, 21, 22
With stocky Romanesque columns, tall Gothic windows, and an exuberant baroque interior, the Church of St Giles – founded in 1371 – is a good place to ponder the architectural development of Prague's religious buildings. The proto-Hussite reformer Jan Milíč of Kroměříž preached here before the Bethlehem Chapel was built. The Dominicans gained possession during the Counter-Reformation, built a cloister next door and 'baroquefied' it in the 1730s. Václav Reiner, the Czech painter who created the ceiling frescoes, is buried here.

NÁPRSTEK MUSEUM Map p110

Náprstkovo muzeum; ☎ 224 497 500; www .nm.cz; Betlémské náměstí 1; adult/child 80/50Kč; ❤ 10am-6pm Tue-Sun; 🚊 6, 9, 18, 21, 22
The small Náprstek Museum houses an ethnographical collection of Asian, African and American cultures, founded by Vojta Náprstek, a 19th-century industrialist with a passion for both anthropology and modern technology (his technology exhibits are now part of the National Technical Museum (p137) in Holešovice).

ROTUNDA OF THE HOLY CROSS
Map p110
Kaple sv kříže; Konviktská; 🕒 **services 5pm Sun & Tue, in English 5.30pm 1st Mon of each month;** 🚋 **6, 9, 18, 21, 22**

This tiny Romanesque rotunda is one of Prague's oldest buildings, starting as a parish church around 1100. Saved from demolition and restored in the 1860s by a collective of Czech artists, it still has the remnants of some 600-year-old wall frescoes, though you will have to attend Mass to see them.

NOT QUITE THE ROYAL WAY
Walking Tour
1 Republic Square
At Republic Square (náměstí Republiky), three ages of Prague architecture face each other across the intersection of Na Příkopě and Celetná – the sooty Gothic tracery of the Powder Gate (p102), the elegant art nouveau convolutions of the Municipal House (p102), and the stern functionalist facades of the Czech National Bank (Česká národní banka) and the Commercial Bank (Komerční banka). As you look west along Celetná you'll see the tower of the Old Town Hall framed at the end of the street like a target in a gun-sight; set off towards it.

2 House of the Black Madonna
In addition to the many souvenir shops, Celetná is lined with many interesting buildings. As you reach the open space of Ovocný trh you'll see an unusual, origami-like facade on the left. It belongs to the House of the Black

Madonna (dům U černé Matky Boží), one of Prague's finest examples of cubist architecture, and home of the Museum of Czech Cubism (p102). If you fancy coffee and cake or a cold beer, head for the Grand Café Orient (p188) on the first floor.

3 Celetná Theatre
A little further along Celetná, turn right into the passage at No 17, which leads to a peaceful little courtyard beside the Celetná Theatre (p206).

4 Church of St James
The passage on the far side of the courtyard leads out onto Štupartská; go straight ahead along Malá Štupartská for a look at the baroque sculptures adorning the facade of the Church of St James (p93). If it's open, go inside for a peek at its gloomy, gilded splendour and the grisly exhibit hanging next to the door.

5 Týn Courtyard
Retrace your steps for a few metres and turn right through the cobbled passage just beyond Big Ben Bookshop to enter the Týn Courtyard (p96). This lovely square is lined with posh shops, good restaurants and a Renaissance loggia, and

WALK FACTS
Start Republic Square (metro Náměstí Republiky)
End Charles Bridge (tram 17, 18)
Distance 1.5km
Time 45 minutes
Exertion Easy
Fuel stop Grand Café Orient

NOT QUITE THE ROYAL WAY WALKING TOUR

has a fine view of the twin steeples of the Church of Our Lady before Týn (p92). Exit at the far end of the courtyard and go along the narrow alley to the right of the church, stopping to look up at the semicircular tympanum above the northern door, decorated with a superb Gothic relief of the Last Judgment.

6 Old Town Square

You emerge from the alley into the melee of Old Town Square (p89), dominated by the brooding statue of Jan Hus and the Gothic tower of the Old Town Hall (p95). If you've timed it right, you'll be able to join the crowd at the foot of the tower to watch a performance by the Astronomical Clock (see the boxed text, p96) set into the tower wall.

7 Little Square

Continue past the clock and the *sgraffito*-clad House at the Minute (dům U minuty) to reach Little Square (Malé náměstí). To your left you'll see the beautiful baroque shop called U zlaté koruny (At the Golden Crown); it was once a pharmacy (you can still see the original fittings) but now houses a jewellery shop. Ahead is the neo-Renaissance facade of the VJ Rott Building, decorated with colourful murals by Mikuláš Ales (now home to the Hard Rock Café). You'll see the main tourist throng bearing left into Karlova, but bear right towards the opposite end of the square and then turn left into Linhartská.

8 Mariánské náměstí

This leads to the quieter space of Mariánské náměstí (Virgin Mary Square), dominated by New City Hall (Nova radnice), seat of Prague's city council. The facade is framed by brooding art nouveau statues by Ladislav Šaloun, the same chap who created the Jan Hus Monument in Old Town Square, and decorated with red and yellow flags, Prague's municipal colours.

9 Klementinum

Facing City Hall across the square is the main gate of the Klementinum (p101). Go through the gate into the courtyard and turn left; on your right is the entrance to the Chapel of Mirrors (Zrcadlová kaple;), where classical concerts are held daily. Continue past the chapel and through the triple arch, then turn right and continue through the quiet courtyards (look up to your right to spot a modern sculpture of a child with a paper plane perched on a ledge).

10 Old Town Bridge Tower

At the far end of the Klementinum courtyards you emerge again into the bustling traffic and tourist crowds of Křížovnické náměstí. End your walk by climbing up the Old Town Bridge Tower (p101) for a view over Prague's most famous bridge, before visiting the nearby Charles Bridge Museum (p100).

Drinking p186; Eating p169; Shopping p154; Sleeping p222

Nové Město means 'New Town', although this crescent-shaped district to the east and south of Staré Město was new only when it was founded by Charles IV in 1348. It extends eastwards from Revoluční and Na Příkopě to Wilsonova and the main railway line, and south from Národní třída to Vyšehrad.

Most of Nové Město's outer fortifications were demolished in 1875 – a section of wall still survives in the south, facing Vyšehrad – but the original street plan of the area has been essentially preserved, with three large market squares that once provided the district's commercial focus: Senovážné náměstí (Hay Market Square), Wenceslas Square (Václavské náměstí; originally called Koňský trh, or Horse Market) and Charles Square (Karlovo náměstí; originally called Dobytčí trh, or Cattle Market).

Though originally a medieval neighbourhood, most of the surviving buildings in this area are from the 19th and early 20th centuries, many of them among the city's finest examples of art nouveau, neo-Renaissance, Czech National Revival and functionalist architecture. Many blocks are honeycombed with pedestrian-only arcades – Prague's famous *pasáž̌y* (passages) – lined with shops, cafes, cinemas and theatres.

In the south, overlooking the river, is the ancient citadel of Vyšehrad. Since the 1920s the old fortress has been a quiet park, with splendid panoramas of the Vltava Valley. It retains a fond place in Czech hearts and is a popular destination for weekend family outings – take along a picnic and find a quiet spot among the trees, or on the battlements with a view over the river.

NORTHERN NOVÉ MĚSTO

The northern part of Nové Město stretches from the Vltava River down to Wenceslas Square. The area is mostly rather nondescript, but there are a few gems hidden away among the bland facades.

JINDŘIŠSKÁ TOWER
Map p110

Jindřišská věž; ☎ 224 232 429; www.jindrisskavez .cz; Jindřišská 1; adult/child 80/35Kč; ☒ 10am-6pm; ▣ 3, 9, 14, 24

This bell tower, dating from the 15th century but rebuilt in the Gothic style in the 1870s, dominates the end of Jindřišská, a busy street running northeast from Wenceslas Square. Having stood idle for decades, the tower was renovated and reopened in 2002 as a tourist attraction, complete with exhibition space, shop, cafe and restaurant, and a lookout gallery on the 10th floor.

JUBILEE SYNAGOGUE
Map p110

Jubilejní synagóga; ☎ 222 319 002; Jeruzalémská 7; adult/child 80/50Kč; ☒ 11am-5pm Sun-Fri Apr-Oct, closed on Jewish hols; Ⓜ Hlavní Nádraží

The colourful Moorish facade of the Jubilee Synagogue, also called the Velká synagóga (Great Synagogue), dates from 1906. Note the names of the donors on the stained-glass windows, and the grand organ above the entrance.

MUCHA MUSEUM
Map p110

Muchovo muzeum; ☎ 221 451 333; www.mucha .cz; Panská 7; adult/child 160/80Kč; ☒ 10am-6pm; Ⓜ Můstek

This fascinating (and busy) museum features the sensuous art nouveau posters, paintings and decorative panels of Alfons Mucha (1860–1939), as well as many sketches, photographs and other memorabilia. The exhibits include countless artworks showing Mucha's trademark Slavic maidens with flowing hair and piercing blue eyes, bearing symbolic garlands and linden boughs; photos of the artist's Paris studio,

TRANSPORT: NOVÉ MĚSTO

Metro The city's three metro lines all intersect in Nové Město, at Muzeum and Můstek stations at the eastern and western ends (respectively) of Wenceslas Square, and at Florenc station in northern Nové Město, while Karlovo náměstí station on line B serves southern Nové Město.

Tram Cutting across the middle of Wenceslas Square, trams 3, 9, 14 and 24 run along Vodičkova and Jindřišská. Lines 17 and 21 run along the river embankment in the west.

NOVÉ MĚSTO & VYŠEHRAD

NOVÉ MĚSTO & VYŠEHRAD

one of which shows a trouserless Gaugin playing the harmonium; a powerful canvas entitled *Old Woman in Winter;* and the original of the 1894 poster of actress Sarah Bernhardt as Giselda, which shot him to international fame. The fascinating 30-minute video documentary about Mucha's life is well worth watching, and helps to put his achievements in perspective. For more information on Mucha see the boxed text, p39.

POSTAL MUSEUM
Map p108

Poštovní muzeum; ☎ 222 312 006; Nové Mlýny 2; adult/child 50/10Kč; ♥ 9am-noon & 1-5pm Tue-Sun; ◉ 5, 8, 14

Philatelists will love this tiny museum with its letterboxes, mail coach and drawers of old postage stamps, including a rare Penny Black. Look for the beautiful stamps created in the early 20th century by Czech artists Josef Navrátil and Alfons Mucha.

Across the street is the Petrská Waterworks Tower (Petrská vodárenská věž), which was built about 1660 on the site of earlier wooden ones. From here, wooden pipes once carried river water to buildings in Nové Město.

PRAGUE CITY MUSEUM Map p108

Muzeum hlavního města Prahy; ☎ 224 816 773; www.muzeumprahy.cz; Na Poříčí 52; adult/child 100/40Kč, 1st Thu of each month 1Kč; ♥ 9am-6pm Tue-Sun, to 8pm 1st Thu of each month; ◉ Florenc

This excellent museum, opened in 1898, is devoted to the history of Prague from prehistoric times to the 20th century. Among the many intriguing exhibits are the brown silk funeral cap and slippers worn by astronomer Tycho Brahe when he was interred in the Týn Church in 1601 (they were removed from his corpse in 1901) and the Astronomical Clock's original 1866 calendar wheel with Josef Mánes' beautiful painted panels representing the months – that's January at the top, toasting his toes by the fire, and August near the bottom, sickle in hand, harvesting the corn.

But what everybody comes to see is Antonín Langweil's astonishing 1:480 scale model of Prague as it looked between 1826 and 1834. The display is most rewarding after you get to know Prague a bit, as you can spot the changes – look at St Vitus Cathedral, for example, still only half-finished.

Most labels are in English as well as Czech, but you'll need the English text (available at the ticket desk) for Room I (prehistory to medieval).

PRAGUE MAIN TRAIN STATION
Map p110

Praha hlavní nádraží; Wilsonova; ♥ closed 12.40-3.15am; Ⓜ Hlavní Nádraží

What? The Prague Main Train Station is actually a tourist attraction? Perhaps not

NOVÉ MĚSTO & VYŠEHRAD

NEIGHBOURHOODS

lonelyplanet.com

A   B   C   D

Charles Bridge
(Karlův
most)

Little Square
(Malé náměstí)

1

Novotného
lávka

Anenská

Rétězová

Staré
Město

Open-Air
Market

Anenské
náměstí

Liliová

Karlovy Světlé

Náprstkova

Boršov

Betlémská

See Staré Město
Map (p90)

Bethlehem Square
(Betlémské
náměstí)

Zlatá

Michalská

Skořepka

Uhelný
trh

Můstek

2

Konviktská

Na Perštýně

Martinská

28 října

7

Bartolomějská

Národní třída

Jungmannovo
náměstí

Divadelní

Tram 6, 9, 18, 22, 23, 51, 54, 57

80

Vladislavova

Národní
třída

Adria
Palace

4

3

Legion Bridge
(Legií most)

P

11

51

1

Voršilská

Mikulandská

Purkyňova

55

Palackého

3

87

Divadelní

Ostrovní

V Jirchářích

68

Masarykovo nábřeží

45

43

Nádražní

Petrská

V Jirchářích

71

Opatovická

Nové
Město

M. Rettigové

Vladislavova

62

84

44

20

Černá

Spálená

Lazarská

4

49

Slav Island
(Slovanský
ostrov)

69

64

86

Kremencová

Opatrniků

76

Navrátilova

38

Řeznická

Pštrossova

81

63

22

Na zbořenci

Myslíkova

Odborů

Pinská

92

Vltava River

39

Tram 21

Vojtěšská

Resslova

Na Zderaze

Charles Square
(Karlovo
náměstí)

Malá Štěpánská

5

46

Záhořanského

Jirásek Square
(Jiráskovo
náměstí)

Karlovo
Náměstí

Tram 4, 6, 10, 22

Jiráskův most

Resslova

35   16

Karlovo
Náměstí

85

6

19

67

Gorazdova

Dittrichova

15

Vyšehradská

Tram 3, 4, 10, 14, 16, 18, 24

41

96

Trojanova

110

0 _____ 0.2 km
0 _____ 0.1 miles

Former Fruit Market
(Ovocný trh)

Myslbek pasáž

94

95
73

Na Příkopě

Havířská

Senovážná

78
65
49

Na Poříčí

Nekázanka

57

60

34

26

Panská

Václav

33

28

Jindřišská

Jeruzalémská

Senovážné
náměstí

Tram 5, 9, 26, 55, 58

56

Opletalova

Vrchlického
sady

Wilsonova

24

Tram 3, 9, 14, 24, 51, 52, 54, 55, 56, 58

Jungmannova

25

Opletalova

Politických vězňů

5

Růžová

Hlavní
Nádraží

16

Wilsonova

Mùstek

21

48

88

Prague Main
Tram Station
(Praha hlavní
nádraží)

Franciscan Garden
(Františkánská
zahrada)

74

52

51

75
29

27
53
59

58

Wenceslas Square
(Václavské náměstí)

2

Opletalova

40

93

U zlvodla

79

Radio Free
Europe/Radio
Liberty Building

37
72

Vodičkova

Štěpánská

26

Novák Arcade
(Pasáž U
Nováků)

Vltava

89

82

91

Na Smečkách

32

47

Muzeum

Washingtonova

Wilsonova

Škretova

Polská

Mánesova

Information-Advisory
Centre of Charles
University (IPC)

1

23

36

Krakovská

Mezibranská

Lazarská

Legerova

Rímská

Vinohradská

Tram 11

Vinohrady

50

Žitná

Štěpánská

Svetová

Londýnská

Balbínova

5

Škotská

42

Na Rybníčku II

14

Na Rybníčku

Tram 4, 6, 10, 16, 22, 51, 56, 57

Ječná

IP Pavlova

Ječná

Tram 6, 11

Anglická

See Vinohrady &
Vršovice
Map (p125)

6

Lípová

90

Myslíkova

Kateřinská

IP Pavlova

Na
Boišti

Sokolská

Legerova

Lublaňská

Bělehradská

Tram 6, 11

NOVÉ MĚSTO

all of it, but it is certainly worth going to the top floor for a look at the grimy, soot-blackened splendour of the original art nouveau building that was designed by Josef Fanta and built between 1901 and 1909.

The domed interior is adorned with a mosaic of two nubile ladies, the words *Praga: mater urbium* (Prague, Mother of Cities) and the date '28.října r:1918' (28 October 1918, which is Czechoslovakia's Independence Day).

WENCESLAS SQUARE & AROUND

Originally a medieval horse market, and more a broad, sloping boulevard than a typical city square, Wenceslas Square (Václavské náměstí, also called Václavák) got its present name during the nationalist revival of the mid-19th century. Since then it has witnessed a great deal of Czech history – a giant Mass was held here during the revolutionary upheavals of 1848; in 1918 the creation of the new Czechoslovak Republic was celebrated here; and in 1989 the fall of communism was announced here.

Following the police attack on a student demonstration on 17 November 1989 (see the boxed text, p29), angry citizens gathered in Wenceslas Square by the thousands night after night. A week later, in a stunning mirror image of Klement Gottwald's 1948 proclamation of communist rule in Old Town Square, Alexander Dubček and Václav Havel stepped onto the balcony of the Melantrich Building to a thunderous and tearful ovation, and proclaimed the end of communism in Czechoslovakia.

At the southern end of the square is Josef Myslbek's muscular equestrian statue of St Wenceslas (sv Václav; Map p110), the 10th-century pacifist Duke of Bohemia and the 'Good King Wenceslas' of Christmas carol fame (he was never a king, only a prince, but was widely regarded as being a good man). Flanked by other patron saints of Bohemia – Prokop, Adalbert, Agnes and Ludmila – he has been plastered with posters and bunting at every one of the square's historical moments. Near the statue, a small memorial to the victims of communism bears photographs and handwritten epitaphs to Jan Palach and other anticommunist rebels.

In contrast to the solemnity of this shrine, the square around it has become a monument to capitalism, a gaudy gallery of cafes, fast-food outlets, expensive shops, greedy cabbies and pricey hotels, haunted at night by drunken British stag parties, prostitutes and strip-club touts.

CHURCH OF OUR LADY OF THE SNOWS Map p110

Kostel Panny Marie sněžné; Jungmannovo náměstí 18; M Můstek
The most sublime attraction in the neighbourhood is this Gothic church at the northern end of Wenceslas Square. It was begun in the 14th century by Charles IV but only the chancel was ever completed, which accounts for its proportions – seemingly taller than it is long. Charles had intended it to be the grandest church in Prague; the nave is higher than that of St Vitus Cathedral, and the altar is the city's tallest. It was a Hussite stronghold, ringing with the sermons of Jan Želivský, who led the 1419 defenestration that touched off the Hussite Wars.

The church is approached through an arch in the Austrian Cultural Institute on Jungmannovo náměstí, but you can get a good view of the exterior from the neighbouring Franciscan Garden (see p123). Beside the church is the Chapel of the Pasov Virgin, now a venue for temporary art exhibitions.

LUCERNA PALACE Map p110

Palác Lucerna; Vodičkova 36; ☒ 3, 9, 14, 24
The most elegant of Nové Město's many shopping arcades runs beneath the art nouveau Lucerna Palace (1920), between Štěpánská and Vodičkova streets. The complex was designed by Václav Havel (grandfather of the ex-president), and is still partially owned by the family. It includes theatres, a cinema, shops, a rock club and several cafes and restaurants. In the marbled atrium hangs artist David Černý's sculpture Kun (Horse; see also the boxed text, p142), a wryly amusing counterpart to the equestrian statue of St Wenceslas in Wenceslas Square. Here St Wenceslas sits astride a horse that is decidedly dead; Černý never comments on the meaning of his works, but it's safe to assume that this Wenceslas (Václav in Czech) is a reference to Václav Klaus, former prime minister and now president of the Czech Republic.

The neighbouring Novák Arcade, connected to the Lucerna and riddled by a maze of passages, has one of Prague's finest art nouveau facades (overlooking Vodičkova), complete with mosaics of country life.

MUSEUM OF COMMUNISM Map p110

Muzeum komunismu; ☎ 224 212 966; www .muzeumkomunismu.cz; Na Příkopě 10; adult/concession/child under 10yr 180/140Kč/free; ✆ 9am-9pm; M Můstek
It's difficult to think of a more ironic site for a museum of communism – it occupies part of an 18th-century aristocrat's palace, stuck between a casino on one side and a McDonald's burger restaurant on the other. Put together by an American expat and his

Czech partner, the museum tells the story of Czechoslovakia's years behind the Iron Curtain in photos, words and a fascinating and varied collection of…well, stuff. The empty shops, corruption, fear and double-speak of life in socialist Czechoslovakia are well conveyed, and there are rare photos of the Stalin monument that once stood on Letná terrace – and its spectacular destruction. Be sure to watch the video about protests leading up to the Velvet Revolution: you'll never think of it as a pushover again.

NA PŘÍKOPĚ Map p110

Na Příkopě (On the Moat), along with Revoluční (Revolution), 28.října (28 October 1918; Czechoslovak Independence Day) and Národní třída (National Ave), follows the line of the moat that once ran along the foot of Staré Město's city walls (the moat was filled in at the end of the 18th century).

Na Příkopě meets Wenceslas Square at Na Můstku (On the Little Bridge; Map p110). A small stone bridge once crossed the moat here – you can still see a remaining arch in the underground entrance to Můstek metro station, on the left just past the ticket machines.

In the 19th century this fashionable street was the haunt of Prague's German cafe society. Today it is (along with Wenceslas Square and Pařížská) the city's main upmarket shopping precinct, lined with banks, shopping malls and tourist cafes.

NÁRODNÍ TŘÍDA Map p110

Národní třída (National Ave) is central Prague's 'high street', a stately row of mid-range shops and grand public buildings, notably the National Theatre at the Vltava River end.

Fronting Jungmannovo náměstí, at the eastern end, is an imitation Venetian palace known as the Adria Palace. Its distinctive, chunky architectural style, dating from the 1920s, is known as 'rondocubism'. Note how the alternating angular and rounded window pediments echo similar features in neoclassical baroque buildings such as the Černín Palace (p68).

Beneath it is the Adria Theatre, birthplace of Laterna Magika and meeting place of Civic Forum in the heady days of the Velvet Revolution. From here, Dubček and Havel walked to the Lucerna Palace and their 24 November 1989 appearance on the balcony of the Melantrich Building. Wander through

the arcade for a look at the lovely marble, glass and brass decoration; the main atrium has a 24-hour clock from the 1920s, flanked by sculptures depicting the signs of the zodiac. It was once the entrance to the offices of the Adriatica insurance company (hence the building's name).

Along the street, inside the arcade near No 16, is a bronze plaque on the wall with a cluster of hands making the peace sign and the date '17.11.89', in memory of students beaten up by police on that date (see the boxed text, p29).

West of Voršilská, the lemon-yellow walls of the Convent of St Ursula (klášter sv Voršila) frame a pink church, which has a lush baroque interior that includes a battalion of Apostle statues. Out front is the figure of St John of Nepomuk, and in the facade's lower-right niche is a statue of St Agatha holding her severed breasts – one of the more gruesome images in Catholic hagiography.

Across the road at No 7 is the art nouveau facade (by Osvald Polívka) of the Viola Building (Map p90), former home of the Prague Insurance Co, with the huge letters 'PRAHA' entwined around five circular windows, and mosaics spelling out *život, kapitál, důchod, věno* and *pojišťuje* (life, capital, income, dowry and insurance). The building next door, a former publishing house, is also a Polívka design.

On the southern side at No 4, looking like it has been built out of old TV screens, is the Nová Scéna (1983), the 'New National Theatre' building, now home of Laterna Magika (see p206).

Finally, facing the Vltava near Smetanovo nábřeží is the National Theatre (Národní divadlo), neo-Renaissance flagship of the Czech National Revival and one of Prague's most impressive buildings. Funded entirely by private donations and decorated inside and out by a roll-call of prominent Czech artists, architect Josef Zítek's masterpiece burned down within weeks of its 1881 opening but, incredibly, was funded again and restored under Josef Schulz in less than two years. It's now used mainly for ballet and opera performances (see p205).

Across from the theatre is the Kavárna Slavia (see the boxed text, p188), known for its art deco interior and river views, once *the* place to be seen or to grab an after-theatre meal. Now renovated, it's once again the place to be seen – though mainly by other tourists.

NATIONAL MUSEUM Map p110

Národní muzeum; ☎ 224 497 111; www.nm.cz; Václavské náměstí 68; adult/child 150/100Kč, admission free 1st Mon of each month; ⊙ 10am-6pm, to 8pm 1st Wed of the month, closed 1st Tue of the month; Ⓜ Muzeum

Looming above Wenceslas Square is the neo-Renaissance bulk of the National Museum, designed in the 1880s by Josef Schulz as an architectural symbol of the Czech National Revival.

The main displays of rocks, fossils and stuffed animals have a rather old-fashioned feel – serried ranks of glass display cabinets arranged on creaking parquet floors – but even if trilobites and taxidermy are not your thing it's still worth a visit just to enjoy the marbled splendour of the interior and the views down Wenceslas Square. The opulent main staircase is an extravaganza of polished limestone and serpentine, lined with paintings of Bohemian castles and medallions of kings and emperors. The domed pantheon, with four huge lunette paintings of (strangely womanless) Czech legend and history by František Ženíšek and Václav Brožík, houses bronze busts and statues of the great and the good of Czech art and science.

The light-coloured areas on the facade of the museum are patched-up bullet holes. In 1968 Warsaw Pact troops apparently mistook the museum for the former National Assembly or the radio station, and raked it with gunfire. It's also here where you'll find a cross-shaped memorial set into the pavement, to the left of the fountain in front of the museum, that marks the spot where Jan Palach fell (see the boxed text, p29).

The main museum building is badly in need of a facelift, and in 2011 it will close for four years to allow for major renovation. Meanwhile, the museum has expanded into the old Radio Free Europe/Radio Liberty building next door. The so-called New Building (adult/child 100/70Kč, combined admission with main bldg 200/150Kč) houses an exhibition on Czechoslovakia under communist rule, which provides some grimly fascinating insights into this dark period of recent history. Between 1948 and 1989 at least 280 civilians died trying to cross the border to the west, but during the same period 584 of the 19,000-strong border guard died, including 185 suicides, 39 shot, and 243 through injury and accident; only 11 were killed by escapees. The New

top picks

ARCHITECTURE

Despite the parade of garish ads and globalised brand names, Wenceslas Square still manages some architectural dignity, having retained some of the city's finest early-20th-century buildings. Here are the edited highlights, starting at the southern (uphill) end and working down, with even numbers on the western (left) side:

- No 25 Grand Hotel Evropa (1906) is perhaps the most beautiful building on the square, art nouveau inside and out; have a peep at the French restaurant at the rear of the ground floor, and at the 2nd-floor atrium.
- No 36 Melantrich Building (1914), now a Marks & Spencer; the balcony overlooking the Tramvaj Café is where Havel and Dubček appeared to announce the end of communist rule in November 1989.
- No 34 Wiehl House (Wiehlův dům; 1896) has a gorgeous facade decorated with neo-Renaissance murals by top Czech artist Mikuláš Aleš and others; it's named after its designer, Antonín Wiehl.
- No 6 Baťa shoe store (1929) is a functionalist masterpiece, designed by Ludvík Kysela for Tomáš Baťa, art patron, progressive industrialist and founder of the worldwide shoe empire.
- No 4 Lindt Building (1927) was also designed by Ludvík Kysela, and is one of the republic's earliest functionalist buildings.
- No 1 Koruna Palace (Palác Koruna; 1914), with an art nouveau design by Antonín Pfeiffer, has a tower topped with a crown of pearls; note its tiny but charming facade around the corner on Na Příkopě.

Building has the same opening hours as the National Museum (see above).

PEČEK PALACE Map p110

Pečkův palác; Politických Vězňů 20; ⊙ closed to the public; Ⓜ Muzeum

This gloomy neo-Renaissance palace served as the wartime headquarters of the Gestapo. A memorial on the corner of the building honours the many Czechs who were tortured and executed in the basement detention cells; it reads 'In the time of the Nazi occupation this building housed the torture chambers of the Gestapo. Fighters for the freedom of our country fought, suffered and died here. We will never forget their memory, and will be loyal to their legacy. PEOPLE, BE AWARE.' Today, it is home to the Ministry of Trade & Industry.

top picks

FOR CHILDREN

- Boat trips (p259)
- Children's Island (p82)
- Mirror Maze (p86)
- National Technical Museum (p137)
- Prague Zoo (p145)

ALONG THE RIVER

The Nové Město riverfront, stretching south from the National Theatre to Vyšehrad, is lined with some of Prague's grandest 19th- and early-20th-century architecture – it's a great place for an evening stroll, when the setting sun gilds the facades with a beautiful golden light.

Masarykovo nábřeží (Masaryk Embankment; Map p110) sports a series of stunning art nouveau buildings. At No 32 is the duck-egg green Goethe Institute, once the East German embassy, while No 26 is a beautiful apartment building with owls perched in the decorative foliage that twines around the door, dogs peeking from the balconies on the 5th floor, and birds perched atop the balustrade.

No 16 is the House of the Hlahol Choir, built in 1906 by Josef Fanta for a patriotic choral society associated with the Czech National Revival. It's decorated with elaborate musical motifs topped by a giant mosaic depicting *Music* – the motto beneath translates as 'Let the song reach the heart; let the heart reach the homeland'.

At the next bridge is Jirásek Square (Jiráskovo náměstí), dedicated to writer Alois Jirásek (1851–1930), author of *Old Czech Legends* (studied by all Czech schoolchildren) and an influential figure in the drive towards Czechoslovak independence. His statue is overlooked by the famous Dancing Building.

A little further along the riverbank is Rašínovo nábřeží 78, an apartment building designed by the grandfather of ex-president Václav Havel – this was where Havel first chose to live (in preference to Prague Castle) after being elected as president in December 1989, surely the world's least pompous presidential residence.

Two blocks south, sitting on Palackého náměstí, is Stanislav Suchárda's extraordinary art nouveau František Palacký Memorial (Map

p108); a swarm of haunted bronze figures (allegories of the writer's imagination) swirling around a stodgy statue of the 19th-century historian and giant of the Czech National Revival.

DANCING BUILDING Map p110
Tančící dům; Rašínovo nábřeží 80; 🚊 17, 21
The junction where Resslova meets the river at Rašínovo nábřeží is dominated by the Dancing Building, built in 1996 by architects Vlado Milunić and Frank Gehry. The curved lines of the narrow-waisted glass tower clutched against its more upright and formal partner led to it being christened the 'Fred & Ginger' building, after legendary dancing duo Fred Astaire and Ginger Rogers. It's surprising how well it fits in with its ageing neighbours.

MÁNES GALLERY Map p110
Galerie Mánes; ☎ 224 932 938; www.galerie manes.cz; Masarykovo nábřeží 1; adult/child 60/30Kč; 🕙 10am-6pm Tue-Sun; 🚊 17, 21
Spanning a branch of the river beneath a 15th-century water tower is the Mánes Building (1927–30), which houses an art gallery founded in the 1920s by a group of artists, headed by painter Josef Mánes, as an alternative to the Czech Academy of Arts. It is still one of Prague's best venues for viewing contemporary art, with a lively program of changing exhibitions. The building itself, designed by Otakar Novotný, is considered a masterpiece of functionalist architecture.

SLAV ISLAND Map p110
Slovanský ostrov; Masarykovo nábřeží; 🚊 17, 21
This island is a sleepy, dog-eared sandbank with pleasant gardens, river views and several jetties where you can hire rowing boats. Its banks were reinforced with stone in 1784, and a spa and a dye works were built in the early part of the following century. Bohemia's first train had a demonstration run here in 1841, roaring down the island at a rattling 11km/h. In 1925 the island was named after the Slav conventions that had taken place here since 1848.

In the middle stands Žofín, a 19th-century cultural centre that has been restored and opened as a restaurant and social venue. At the southern end is Šítovská věž, a 15th-century water tower (once part of a mill) with an 18th-century onion-dome roof.

CHARLES SQUARE & AROUND

With an area of more than seven hectares, Charles Square (Karlovo náměstí; Map p110) is the city's biggest square; it's more like a small park, really. Presiding over it is the Church of St Ignatius (kostel sv Ignáce; Map p110), a 1660s baroque tour de force designed for the Jesuits by Carlo Lurago.

The baroque palace found at the southern end of the square belongs to Charles University. It's known as Faust House (Faustův dům; Map p108) because, according to a popular story, this house was where Mephisto took Dr Faust away to hell through a hole in the ceiling, and because of associations with Rudolf II's English court alchemist, Edward Kelley, who toiled here in the 16th century trying to convert lead into gold.

Resslova runs west from Karlovo náměstí to the river. Halfway along is the baroque Church of Sts Cyril & Methodius (Kostel sv Cyril a Metoděj; Map p110), a 1730s work by Kilian Dientzenhofer and Paul Bayer. The crypt now houses the moving National Memorial to the Victims of Post-Heydrich Terror (Národní památník obětí Heydrichiády; Map p110).

On the other side of Resslova you'll find the 14th-century Gothic Church of St Wenceslas in Zderaz (Kostel sv Václava na Zderaza; Map p110), the former parish church of Zderaz, a village that pre-dates Nové Město. On its western side are parts of a wall and windows from its 12th-century Romanesque predecessor.

The area to the east of Karlovo náměstí is occupied by Charles University's medical faculty, and is full of hospitals and clinics. Halfway between Žitná and Ječná on Štěpánská is the 14th-century Church of St Stephen (kostel sv Štěpána; Map p110). Behind it on Na Rybníčku II is one of Prague's three surviving Romanesque rotundas, the Rotunda of St Longinus (rotunda sv Longina), built in the early 12th century.

CHARLES UNIVERSITY BOTANICAL GARDEN Map p108

Botanická zahrada Univerzity Karlovy; ☎ 221 951 879; www.bz-uk.cz; Viničná 7; admission to garden free, to glasshouses adult/child 50/25Kč; ◷ 10am-7.30pm Apr-Aug, to 6pm Aug & Sep, to 5pm Feb & Mar, to 4pm Nov-Jan; ⓰ 18, 24

Just south of Karlovo náměstí (main entrance on Na Slupi) is Charles University's botanical garden. Founded in 1775 and moved from Smíchov to its present site in 1898, it's the country's oldest botanical

garden. The steep, hillside garden concentrates on Central European flora and is especially pretty in spring.

CHURCH OF THE ASSUMPTION OF THE VIRGIN MARY & CHARLEMAGNE Map p120

Kostel Nanebevzetí Panny Marie a Karla Velikého; Ke Karlovu; ◷ 10am-5pm Mon-Sat; ⓰ 6, 11 to Bělehradská or Ⓜ IP Pavlova

At the southern end of Ke Karlovu is a little church with a big name, founded by Charles IV in 1350 and modelled on Charlemagne's burial chapel in Aachen. In the 16th century it acquired its fabulous ribbed vault, the revolutionary unsupported span of which was attributed by some to witchcraft.

From the terrace beyond the church you can see some of Nové Město's original fortifications, and look out towards ancient Vyšehrad and the modern Nusle Bridge (Nuselský most), which vaults across the valley of the Botič creek, with six lanes of traffic on top and the metro inside.

DVOŘÁK MUSEUM Map p108

Muzeum Antonína Dvořáka; ☎ 224 923 363; www.nm.cz; Ke Karlovu 20; adult/child 50/25Kč; ◷ 10am-1.30pm & 2-5pm Tue, Wed & Fri-Sun, 11am-3.30pm & 4-7pm Thu Apr-Sep, 9.30am-1.30pm & 2-5pm Tue-Sun Oct-Mar; Ⓜ IP Pavlova

The most striking building in the drab neighbourhood south of Ječná is the energetically baroque Vila Amerika, a 1720s, French-style summer house designed by (you guessed it) Kilian Dientzenhofer. It's one of the city's finest baroque buildings, and now houses a museum dedicated to the composer Antonín Dvořák. Special concerts of Dvořák's music are staged here from May to October.

EMMAUS MONASTERY Map p108

Klášter Emauzy; Vyšehradská 49; ◷ 8am-6pm Mon-Fri, services noon Mon-Fri, 10am Sun; ⓰ 18, 24

Founded for a Slavonic Benedictine order at the request of Charles IV, and originally called Na Slovanech, the Emmaus Monastery dates from 1372. During WWII the monastery was seized by the Gestapo and the monks were sent to Dachau concentration camp, then in February 1945 it was almost destroyed by a stray Allied fire-bomb. Some monks returned after the war, but the reprieve was short-lived: in 1950 the communists closed down the monastery, and

THE HEYDRICH ASSASSINATION

In 1941, in response to a series of crippling strikes and sabotage operations by the Czech resistance movement, the German government appointed SS general Reinhard Heydrich, an antisubversion specialist, as Reichsprotektor of Bohemia and Moravia. Heydrich immediately cracked down on resistance activities with a vengeance.

In a move designed to support the resistance and boost Czech morale, Britain secretly trained a team of Czechoslovak paratroopers to assassinate Heydrich. It was code-named Operation Anthropoid and, astonishingly, it succeeded. On 27 May 1942, two paratroopers, Jan Kubiš and Jozef Gabčík, attacked Heydrich as he rode in his official car through the city's Libeň district (see V Holešovičkách, p147) – he died from the wounds. The assassins and five co-conspirators fled but were betrayed in their hiding place in the Church of Sts Cyril & Methodius; all seven died in the ensuing siege.

The Nazis reacted with a frenzied wave of terror, which included the annihilation of two entire Czech villages, Ležáky and Lidice (see p239 for more on the grim fate of Lidice) and the shattering of the underground movement.

tortured the prior to death. It was finally restored to the Benedictine order in 1990, and reconstruction has been going on ever since.

The monastery's Gothic Church of Our Lady (kostel Panny Marie), badly damaged by the 1945 bombing, reopened in 2003, though the swooping, twin spires were added back in the 1960s. The atmospheric Gothic cloisters have some fine, but faded, original frescoes dating from the 14th century, salted with bits of pagan symbolism.

Across Vyšehradská is the baroque Church of St John of Nepomuk on the Rock (kostel sv Jana Nepomuckého na Skalce), built in 1739 and one of the city's most beautiful Dientzenhofer churches.

NATIONAL MEMORIAL TO THE HEROES OF THE HEYDRICH TERROR
Map p110

Národní památník hrdinů Heydrichiády; ☎ 224 916 100; Resslova 9; adult/concession 75/35Kč; ☉ 9am-5pm Tue-Sun Mar-Oct, 9am-5pm Tue-Sat Nov-Feb; Ⓜ Karlovo Náměstí

In 1942 seven Czech paratroopers who were involved in the assassination of Reichsprotektor Reinhard Heydrich (see the boxed text, above) hid in the crypt of the Church of Sts Cyril & Methodius for three weeks after the killing, until their hiding place was betrayed by the Czech traitor Karel Čurda. The Germans besieged the church, first attempting to smoke the paratroopers out and then flooding the church with fire hoses. Three paratroopers were killed in the ensuing fight; the other four took their own lives rather than surrender to the Germans.

The crypt now houses a moving memorial to the men, with an exhibit and video about Nazi persecution of the Czechs. In the crypt itself you can still see the bullet marks and shrapnel scars on the walls,

and signs of the paratroopers' last desperate efforts to dig an escape tunnel to the sewer under the street. On the Resslova side of the church, the narrow gap in the wall of the crypt where the Germans inserted their fire hoses is still pitted with bullet marks.

NEW TOWN HALL Map p110

Novoměstská radnice; ☎ 224 948 229; www.novomestskaradnice.cz; Karlovo náměstí 23; adult/child 50/30Kč; ☉ 10am-6pm Tue-Sun May-Sep; Ⓜ Karlovo Náměstí

The historical focus of Charles Square is the New Town Hall, built in the late 14th century when the New Town was still new. From the window of the main hall (the tower was not built until 1456), two of Wenceslas IV's Catholic councillors were flung to their deaths in 1419 by followers of the Hussite preacher Jan Želivský, giving 'defenestration' (throwing out of a window) a lasting political meaning and sparking off the Hussite Wars. (This tactic was repeated at Prague Castle in 1618.) You can visit the Gothic Hall of Justice, which was the site of the defenestration, and climb the 221 steps to the top of the tower.

U KALICHA Map p108

☎ 224 912 557; www.ukalicha.cz; Na Bojišti 12; ☉ 11am-11pm; Ⓜ IP Pavlova

A few blocks east of Karlovo náměstí is the pub U kalicha (At the Chalice). This is where the eponymous antihero was arrested at the beginning of Jaroslav Hašek's comic novel of WWI, The Good Soldier Švejk (which Hašek cranked out in instalments from his own local pub). The pub is milking the connection for all it's worth – it's an essential port of call for Švejk fans, but the rest of us can find cheaper beer and dumplings elsewhere.

VYŠEHRAD

Legend has it that Vyšehrad (High Castle) is the place where Prague was born. According to myth the wise chieftain Krok built a castle here in the 7th century, and Libuše, the cleverest of his three daughters, prophesied that a great city would rise here. Taking as her king a ploughman named Přemysl, she founded both the city of Prague and the Přemysl dynasty.

Archaeologists have discovered that various early Slavonic tribes set up camp at Vyšehrad, a crag above the Vltava River south of the Nusle Valley. The site may have been permanently settled as early as the 9th century, and Boleslav II (r 972–99) may have lived here for a time. By the mid-11th century there was a fortified settlement, and Vratislav II (r 1061–92) moved his court here from Hradčany, beefing up the walls and adding a castle, the Basilica of St Lawrence, the original Church of Sts Peter & Paul and the Rotunda of St Martin. His successors stayed until 1140, when Vladislav II returned to Hradčany.

Vyšehrad then faded into the background until Charles IV, aware of its symbolic importance, repaired the walls and joined them to those of his new town, Nové Město. He built a small palace and decreed that the coronations of Bohemian kings should begin with a procession from here to Hradčany.

Nearly everything there was wiped out during the Hussite Wars. The fortress remained a ruin – except for a ramshackle township of artisans and traders – until after the Thirty Years' War, when Leopold I refortified it.

The Czech National Revival generated new interest in Vyšehrad as a symbol of Czech history. Painters painted it, poets sang about the old days, and Smetana set his patriotic opera *Libuše* here. In 1866 many of the old fortifications were dismantled, various buildings were restored, and the parish graveyard was converted into a national memorial cemetery. Today it is a peaceful green park with great views across the river, the haunt of old ladies walking their dogs, mothers playing with their children on the lawns, and young lovers canoodling on park benches.

BRICK GATE & CASEMATES Map p120

Vratislavova; ☾ **9.30am-6pm Apr-Oct, to 5pm Nov-Mar;** Ⓜ **Vyšehrad**

At the 19th-century Brick Gate (Cihelná brána; admission 20Kč) on the northern side of the

fortress you can see an exhibit explaining the history of Vyšehrad and Prague's other fortifications.

Here you will also find the entrance to the Casemates (adult/child 50/30Kč), a system of vaulted brick tunnels beneath the ramparts. The largest of these is the barrel-vaulted Gorlice Hall, which served as an air-raid shelter and potato store during WWII. It now houses six of the original baroque statues from Charles Bridge, including *St Ludmila with the Young St Wenceslas* by Matthias Braun (the other originals are in the Lapidárium; see p135), as well as temporary art exhibitions in summer. The Casemates ticket also gives admission to the Gothic Cellar (below).

CHURCH OF STS PETER & PAUL
Map p120

Kostel sv Petra a Pavla; ☎ **249 113 353; K Rotundé 10; adult/child 10/5Kč;** ☾ **9am-noon & 1-5pm Wed-Mon;** Ⓜ **Vyšehrad**

Vratislav II's Church of Sts Peter & Paul has been built and rebuilt over the centuries, culminating in a neo-Gothic work over by Josef Mocker in the 1880s. The twin steeples, a distinctive feature of the Vyšehrad skyline, were added in 1903. The interior is a swirling acid trip of colourful art nouveau frescoes, painted in the 1920s by various Czech artists.

GOTHIC CELLAR
Map p120

Gotický sklep; Vyšehradský sady; adult/child 50/30Kč; ☾ **9.30am-6pm Apr-Oct, to 5pm Nov-Mar;** Ⓜ **Vyšehrad**

The restored Gothic cellars that once lay beneath Charles IV's palace (now gone) house an exhibition dedicated to the history and legend of Vyšehrad. It is packed with archaeological finds and religious relics associated with life in the fortress from 3800 BC until the present day.

TRANSPORT: VYŠEHRAD

Metro Vyšehrad metro station (on line C) is five minutes' walk east of the citadel, past the Congress Centre (Kongresové centrum).

Tram Lines 17 and 21 run along the riverbank below the citadel; trams 7, 18 and 24 run along the Nusle Valley to its east. From the tram stop on either line, it's a steep climb up to the citadel.

ROTUNDA OF ST MARTIN
Map p120

Rotunda sv Martina; V Pevnosti; ☺ closed to the public; Ⓜ Vyšehrad

Vratislav II's little chapel, the 11th-century Rotunda of St Martin, is Prague's oldest surviving building. In the 18th century it was used as a powder magazine. The door and frescoes date from a renovation made about 1880.

Nearby are a 1714 plague column and the baroque St Mary Chapel in the Ramparts (kaple Panny Marie v hradbách), dating from about 1750, and behind them the remains of the 14th-century Church of the Beheading of St John the Baptist (kostelíkStětí sv Jana Křtitele).

VYŠEHRAD CEMETERY
Map p120

Vyšehradský hřbitov; ☎ 249 198 815; K Rotundé 10; admission free; ☺ 8am-7pm May-Sep, to 6pm Mar, Apr & Oct, to 5pm Nov-Feb; Ⓜ Vyšehrad

For Czechs, the Vyšehrad Cemetery is the hill's main attraction. In the late 19th century the parish graveyard was made into a memorial cemetery for famous figures of Czech culture, with a graceful,

neo-Renaissance arcade running along the northern and western sides. For the real heroes, an elaborate pantheon called the Slavín (loosely, 'Hall of Fame'), designed by Antonín Wiehl, was added at the eastern end in 1894; its 50-odd occupants include painter Alfons Mucha, sculptor Josef Myslbek and architect Josef Gočár. The motto reads *Ač Zemeřeli Ještě Mluví* (Though dead, they still speak).

The 600 or so graves in the rest of the cemetery include those of composers Smetana and Dvořák and writers Karel Čapek, Jan Neruda and Božena Němcová; there's a directory of famous names at the entrance. One word that you will see all over the place is *rodina* – it means 'family'.

Many of the tombs and headstones are themselves works of art – Dvořák's is a sculpture by Ladislav Šaloun, the art nouveau sculptor who created the Jan Hus monument in Old Town Square. To find it from the gate beside the church, head straight across to the colonnade on the far side, and turn left; it's the fifth tomb on your right. To find Smetana's grave, go to the Slavín and stand facing the monument; it's the pale-grey obelisk to your right.

VYŠEHRAD

The annual Prague Spring music festival (see the boxed text, p206) kicks off on 12 May, the anniversary of Smetana's death, with a procession from his grave at Vyšehrad to the Municipal House (p102).

VYŠEHRAD CITADEL Map p120

☎ 241 410 348; www.praha-vysehrad.cz; V Pevnosti 5; admission free; ☽ grounds 24hr, information centre 9.30am-6pm Apr-Oct, to 5pm Nov-Mar; Ⓜ Vyšehrad

The main entrance to the citadel is through Tábor Gate (Táborská brána) at the southeastern end. On the other side of the brick ramparts and ditch are the remnants of the Gothic Peak Gate (Špička brána), a fragment of arch that is now part of the information office – all that remains of Charles IV's 14th-century fortifications. Beyond that lies the grand 17th-century Leopold Gate (Leopoldova brána), the most elegant fortress gate here.

You can walk around most of the battlements, with grand views over the river and city. Beside the southwestern bastion are the foundations of a royal palace built by Charles IV but dismantled in 1655. Perched on the bastion itself is the Vyšehrad Gallery (galérie Vyšehrad; admission 20Kč), which holds temporary exhibitions and opens the same hours as the information centre, except for January and February, when it closes. Below the bastion are some ruined guard towers named Libuše's Bath. You can also examine the foundations of the 11th-century Romanesque Basilica of St Lawrence (bazilika sv Vavřince; admission 10Kč; ☽ 11am-5pm Mon-Fri, 11.30am-4pm Sat & Sun). Ask for the key at the snack bar next door.

South of the Church of Sts Peter & Paul lie the Vyšehrad Gardens (Vyšehradské sady), with four imposing statues by Josef Myslbek based on Czech legends. Prague's founders Libuše and Přemysl are in the northwestern corner; in the southeast are Šárka and Ctirad (see p134). On Sundays in May, June and September, open-air concerts are held here at 2.30pm, with anything from jazz to oompah bands to chamber music.

In the northwestern corner is the former New Provost's House (Nové proboštství), built in 1874. In the adjacent park, Štulcovy sady, there is an open-air Summer Theatre (Letní scéna) where you can catch a concert or cultural show at 6pm on most Thursdays or the odd children's performance on Tuesday afternoon (usually around 2pm).

The information centre sells a map and guide to Vyšehrad's buildings in English, German, French and Italian.

AROUND WENCESLAS SQUARE
Walking Tour
1 National Museum

Begin at the steps in front of the neo-Renaissance National Museum (Národní muzeum; p115), which dominates the upper end of Wenceslas Square (Václavské náměstí). From the steps you have a grand view down the square, a focal point of Czech history since the 19th century. At the foot of the steps is a pavement memorial to student Jan Palach (see the boxed text, p29).

AROUND WENCESLAS SQUARE WALKING TOUR

WALK FACTS

Start National Museum (metro Muzeum)

End Na Můstku (metro Můstek)

Distance 1.5km

Time 45 minutes

Exertion Easy

Fuel stops Various cafes around Nové Město

2 Statue of St Wenceslas

Cross the busy traffic artery of Mezibranská to Prague's famous landmark, the equestrian statue of St Wenceslas (sv Václav), the 10th-century 'Good King Wenceslas' of Christmas-carol fame.

3 Memorial to the Victims of Communism

A flower bed a short distance downhill from the statue contains a modest memorial to those who died for their resistance to communism (see also p85). Around the anniversary of Jan Palach's death (19 January) the memorial is surrounded by votive candles, flowers and photographs.

4 Grand Hotel Evropa

Wander down the middle of the square, admiring the grand buildings on either side. The finest is the 1906 art nouveau Grand Hotel Evropa (see the boxed text, p115) at No 25, about halfway down on the right.

5 Melantrich Building

Across the street at No 36 is the Melantrich Building, from whose balcony the death of Czech communism was pronounced by Alexander Dubček and Václav Havel on 24 November 1989 (it now houses a Marks & Spencer store).

6 Lucerna Palace

Turn left into Pasáž Rokoko, a glittering, mirror-lined art deco shopping arcade directly across the street from the Grand Hotel Evropa. It leads to the central atrium of the Lucerna Palace (palác Lucerna; p113), dominated by David Černý's Kun (Horse), an ironic twist on the St Wenceslas statue in the square outside (it helps to know that the first prime minister of the Czech Republic was also a Václav). For more on David Černý, see the boxed texts, p38 and p142. Turn right beneath the dead horse (you'll see when you get there), and follow the passage to Vodičkova. Bear right across the street and enter the Světozor arcade. Up ahead you'll see a beautiful stained-glass window dating from the late 1940s – it's actually an advertisement for Tesla Radio, an old Czech electronics company.

7 Franciscan Garden

At the far end of the Světozor arcade, turn left into the Franciscan Garden (Františkánská zahrada), a hidden oasis of peace and greenery that is dominated by the soaring nave of the Church of Our Lady of the Snows. Make your way to the far northern corner of the garden, which is diagonally opposite from where you came in, and you will find an exit to Jungmann Square (Jungmannovo náměstí).

8 Church of Our Lady of the Snows

Go past the arch leading to the Church of Our Lady of the Snows (p113), an old Gothic church and former Hussite stronghold, and turn right.

9 Cubist lamppost

Keep to the right of the Lancôme shop, and you will come to what must be the only cubist lamppost in the entire world, dating from 1915. Turn left here and then duck right through the short Lindt arcade and you will emerge at the foot of Wenceslas Square.

10 Koruna Palác

Across the street, on the corner with Na Příkopě, is the art nouveau Koruna Palác (Crown Palace) – look up and you will see the corner tower with the crown of pearls that gives the building its name. From here you can head right along Na Příkopě to the Municipal House and the beginning of the Not Quite the Royal Way Walking Tour (p105), or retire to one of the many nearby bars and cafes.

VINOHRADY & VRŠOVICE

Drinking p186; Eating p171; Shopping p156; Sleeping p223

Upmarket Vinohrady is one of the few parts of Prague that has a consistent personality throughout. In Vinohrady's case, that would be bourgeois. An address in an early 20th-century town house on one of Vinohrady's leafy streets marks one as upwardly mobile, enjoying the good life, and perhaps eyeing a move someday to a villa in Střešovice or the nether reaches of Dejvice (in Prague terms, the sign that one's *really* arrived).

The name Vinohrady means 'vineyards' and refers to the vines that were cultivated here in centuries past; as recently as 200 years ago there was little urbanisation. There is still some wine cultivation in the area and even a lovely, restored wooden gazebo where you can sample some of the local product (see Viniční Altán, p189).

Vinohrady's physical and commercial heart is Peace Square (náměstí Míru), dominated by the neo-Gothic Church of St Ludmilla (kostel sv Ludmily). Right behind it is the neo-Renaissance National House (Národní dům), holding exhibitions and concerts. On the north side of the square is the Vinohrady Theatre (divadlo na Vinohradech), built in 1909, a popular drama venue.

For visitors, there are not many traditional sights, but it's a great place to ramble. The streets to the right or left of the main avenue, Vinohradská, are filled with small cafes and restaurants. There are plenty of parks and at least one terrific open-air beer garden (see Riegrovy sady, p124). It's also become the unofficial centre of Prague's gay community, with small bars tucked here and there (p186).

Vršovice is not quite as sophisticated, yet it's hoping a little of Vinohrady's polish might rub off. The area along Francouzská, where it meets Moskevká, including Voroněžská and Krymská, is slowly gentrifying and worth a look.

CHURCH OF THE MOST SACRED HEART OF OUR LORD Map p125

Kostel Nejsvětějšího Srdce Páně; náměstí Jiřího z Poděbrad 19, Vinohrady; ☾ services 8am & 6pm Mon-Sat, 7am, 9am, 11am & 6pm Sun; Ⓜ Jiřího z Poděbrad

This church was built in 1932 and is one of Prague's most original and unusual pieces of 20th-century architecture. It's the work of Jože Plečnik, the Slovenian architect who also raised a few eyebrows with his additions to Prague Castle. Inspired by Egyptian temples and early Christian basilicas, the glazed-brick building sports a massive, tombstone-like bell tower pierced by a circular glass clock-window. Unfortunately it's rarely open to the public. The best time to get a look inside is during Mass.

TRANSPORT: VINOHRADY & VRŠOVICE

Metro Line A runs east through Vinohrady starting at Náměstí Míru station.

Tram Line 11 runs east along Vinohradská and south down Bělehradská; lines 10 and 16 run east along Korunní; lines 4 and 22 run east along Francouzská, turning south to meet up with lines 6, 7 and 24, which also run east along Vršovická.

RIEGROVY SADY (RIEGER GARDENS) Map p125

Park entrance on Chopinova, across from Na Švíhance, Vinohrady; Ⓜ Jiřího z Poděbrad

Vinohrady's largest and prettiest park was designed as a classic English garden in the 19th century. These days it's looking a little bit worn from overuse, but it's still worth searching out on a sunny day for a leisurely stroll or a place to put down a blanket and chill out. The bluff towards the back of the park affords photo-op-worthy shots of Prague Castle in the distance and the main train station and Old Town below. On a warm summer eve, the open-air beer garden (p187) is *the* place to be in this part of town.

VINOHRADY & VRŠOVICE
Walking Tour

This walk covers a lot of ground but thankfully has few hills. It meanders along some of Prague's nicest residential streets, allowing you to indulge your inner real estate agent for a moment. In the first years after the 1989 revolution, apartments in Vinohrady were going for a song; now (even with the worldwide economic slowdown) they fetch prices that would not be out of place in Paris or London. You could plan a midmorning start,

VINOHRADY & VRŠOVICE

See Nové Město Map (p110)

See Žižkov & Karlín Map (p130)

See Vyšehrad Map (p120)

Vinohradská
Vinohradská

Tram 10, 16, 19, 26, 58
Tram 5, 10, 11, 16, 51, 58

Olšany Cemetery
(Olšanské hřbitovy)

Jičínská   Tram 5, 58

Tram 10, 16

Piseckâ

Koubmská

Tram 5

Jičínská
Sudoměřská
Baranova
Radhošťská
Žižkovo náměstí
Bořivojova
Fibichova
Ondříčkova
Kubelíkova
Orlická
Velehradská
Jiřiho z Poděbrad
Jiřiho z Poděbrad
Mánesova
Třebízského
Slavíkova
Blodkova

Přemyslovská
Libická
Kolínská
Perunova
Nitranská
U Vodárny
Laubova

Slezská
Slezská

Chvalova
Chopinova
Polská
Manesova
Blanická
Španělská
Italská
Balbínova
Krkonošská
Rumunská
Manesova
Tram 11

Riegrovy sady
Vinohrady
Náměstí Míru
Peace Square
Náměstí Míru

Korunní
Korunní
Ripská
Dykova
Chorvatská
Slovenská
Ruská
Ruská
Budečská

Moravská
Lužická
Chodská
Mánesova
Trojická

Šumavská
Francouzská
Šumavská
Šafaříkova
Londýnská
U Zvonařky
Belgická
Bělehradská

Vršovice
Vršovice

Mexická
Kodaňská
Vršovická
Tram 4, 22, 37, 39
Tram 6, 7, 74

Tram 4, 10, 16, 22
Tram 10, 16, 51

Donská
Kozácká
Kodaňská

Krymská
Ruská
Voroněžská

Vinohradská
Ke Karlovu
Na Smetance
Škrétova
Anglická
Lublaňská
Bělehradská
Sarajevská

Tram 6, 11
Tram 6, 11

Tram 17, 22, 24, 55, 57, 59

See Vyšehrad Map (p120)
P Pavlova
P Pavlova
Legerova
Legerova

0   500 m
0   0.25 miles

125

VINOHRADY & VRŠOVICE

with a light lunch at Viniční Altán or a bigger meal at Mozaika, or an early-afternoon start and wind up with a beer at the Riegrovy sady beer garden.

1 Peace Square (náměstí Míru)

Known affectionately to Czechs as 'Mirák' – a diminutive form of 'Míru' – this leafy square is the lively heart of Vinohrady. The name still has faint echoes of communist times, when everything was labelled 'Peace' this or 'Peace' that. After 1989, there was talk of scrapping the name. In the end, though, Prague residents decided they didn't mind, and the 'Peace' stayed.

2 Americká

Leave the square via Americká, a quiet residential street leading south. It's hard to believe now, but by the time of the Velvet Revolution this street was badly run-down; several apartment houses were even abandoned. Under communism, older buildings such as these were poorly maintained and the vogue was to get a new place in a high-rise housing estate – a *panelák* – on the outskirts of town. Now the trend is exactly the opposite. Follow the street and walk through the small roundabout, marked by a modern fountain built a

couple of years ago chiefly to keep people from parking here. At this point Americká becomes Kopernikova and ends at the park Havlíčkovy sady.

3 Havlíčkovy sady

This rocky hillside park marks the border between Vinohrady and Vršovice and is particularly popular with lovers (since it's relatively secluded) and mothers with strollers (which is arguably a logical consequence of the 'lovers' part). There's no prescribed walk for exploring the park – just choose the most inviting path leading vaguely downhill. Look for signs to the wine garden and gazebo Viniční Altán.

4 Viniční Altán

At this stage you're likely to have one of those moments when everything suddenly seems clear: this is how Vinohrady ('vineyards') got its name. Open-air wine gardens are a rarity in Prague and none are as nice as this one (p189), with its wooden gazebo overlooking a terraced hillside lined with grapevines. The wine list includes bottles from around the world, but go with a local vintage. On the food side, the choices are limited to salads and sausages – mostly to accompany the beverages.

5 U Havlíčkových Sadů
Retrace your steps as best you can through the park, back to the street that lines the park, U Havlíčkových Sadů. Follow this to the right, then make a left at the end of the street onto Rybalkova. Follow Rybalkova, passing the

WALK FACTS

Start Peace Square (metro Náměstí Míru or tram 4, 10, 16, 22)
End Riegrovy sady beer garden (metro Jiřího z Poděbrad or tram 11)
Distance 4km to 5km
Time Two to three hours
Exertion Moderate
Fuel stops Viniční Altán, Mozaika, Riegrovy sady beer garden

street Voroněžská, which leads down into Vršovice, and continue on to Máchova. At Máchova turn right, crossing busy Francouzská onto Šumavská, and then make a right at Lužická.

6 Lužická
This is another classic, tree-lined Vinohrady street, filled with handsome apartment houses and rapidly rising housing valuations – which is just the way the locals like it. Lužická empties out into a small park. Cut straight ahead through the park, and onto the street Hradešínská.

7 Hradešínská
This street and the one that parallels it to the right, Na Šafránce, have some of the most beautiful private villas in this part of the city. The most famous of these is at Hradešínská 6,

VINOHRADY & VRŠOVICE WALKING TOUR

the family home of early modern Czech architect Jan Kotěra, built in 1908. Turn left at Chorvatská and left again onto Dykova, then right onto Řípská, with a dead-on view of Žižkov's TV Tower (p133) in the background. If it's mealtime, walk one more block to the left to Nitranská to Mozaika (p172), one of the most popular restaurants in the city. At lunch you probably won't have to book ahead, but it can get crowded at dinner.

8 Church of the Most Sacred Heart of Our Lord

Řípská takes you eventually to Vinohradská and náměstí Jiřího z Poděbrad, defined by the imposing dark-red brickwork and enormous clock of one of the city's most controversial churches (p124), the work of the modern Slovene master Jože Plečnik. Unless it's Sunday around Mass time, you're unlikely to get a glimpse inside, but walk around to the front entrance just in case the door is open. To continue the walk, find the street Slavíkova that runs past the church's front entrance and follow it to the right, arriving at Polská.

9 Polská

Walk left onto Polská for another row of handsome town houses in various states of disre-pair and renovation. About 200m down the road, you'll see the small street Chopinova, which runs to the right. Take this and walk uphill, passing the streets Krkonošská (with another great view of the Žižkov TV Tower) and then Na Švíhance.

10 Riegrovy sady

You'll see the entrance to Vinohrady's largest park, Riegrovy sady (p124), to the left, just opposite Na Švíhance. Before dipping into the park you might want to meander down Krkonošská or Na Švíhance. Both are lined with beautifully restored town houses, many with art nouveau facades.

11 Riegrovy sady beer garden

The entrance to the beer garden (p187) is about 50m from the park entrance; you'll see it to the left as you follow the walkway in. End the walk here or continue another 100m along the path for an amazing panorama of Prague, with Prague Castle in the distance. To return to the centre, retrace your steps to the Jiřího z Poděbrad metro. Alternatively, follow the path in the park downhill, which takes you to the bottom of Vinohradská, from where you can walk to the centre or take tram 11.

Drinking p189; Eating p174; Sleeping p226

Named after the one-eyed Hussite hero, Jan Žižka, who defeated the Holy Roman Emperor Sigismund here in 1420, Žižkov was one of Prague's earliest industrial suburbs. It has long had a reputation as a rough-and-ready, working-class neighbourhood, and was full of left-wing revolutionary fervour well before the communist takeover of 1948 – in fact, Žižkov was an independent municipality from 1881 till 1922 and was widely known as the 'people's republic of Žižkov'.

Today it is one of Prague's liveliest districts, with more bars per capita than any other part of Prague (or indeed, it is claimed, any other part of Europe). It's still pretty rough around the edges and much of the district is still grimy and run-down, but the streets near the city centre are slowly getting a facelift as gentrification creeps in – the upper part of the district is already being referred to in estate agents' adverts as 'Lower Vinohrady'.

The district is dominated by two prominent hilltop landmarks – the communist-vintage TV Tower and the National Monument. The latter sits atop Žižkov Hill, originally known as Vítkov. The famous Battle of Vítkov Hill took place in July 1420 on the long, narrow ridge that separates the Žižkov and Karlín districts. A colossal statue of Jan Žižka (Map p130), the victorious Hussite general, was erected here in 1950, commanding superb views across Staré Město to Prague Castle.

The mostly residential suburb of Karlín lies to the north of Žižkov, squeezed between Žižkov Hill and the Vltava River. It was devastated by the floods of 2002, and since then has been undergoing massive redevelopment, with new glass-and-steel office complexes rising along the banks of the river. The older part of the district, along Křižíkova, is another up-and-coming area, with lots of lovely old art nouveau buildings – Lyčkovo náměstí is one of the prettiest squares in the city.

ARMY MUSEUM Map p130

Armádní muzeum; ☎ 973 204 924; www.vhu.cz; U Památníku 2, Žižkov; admission free; ☼ 9.30am-6pm Tue-Sun; Ⓜ Florenc

On the way up Žižkov Hill you will find this grim-looking barracks of a museum, with a rusting T34 tank parked outside, and exhibits on the history of the Czechoslovak Army and resistance movement from 1918 to 1945. There is also an exhibition on the experiences of the Czechoslovak Army following the communist coup of 1948.

JEWISH CEMETERY Map p130

Židovské hřbitovy; Izraelská, Žižkov; admission free; ☼ 9am-5pm Sun-Thu & 9am-2pm Fri Apr-Oct, 9am-4pm Sun-Thu & 9am-2pm Fri Nov-Mar, closed on Jewish hols; Ⓜ Želivského

Franz Kafka is buried in this cemetery, which opened around 1890 when the older Jewish cemetery – now at the foot of the TV Tower (p133) – was closed. To find Kafka's grave, follow the main avenue east (signposted), turn right at row 21, then left at the wall; it's at the end of the 'block'. Fans make a pilgrimage on 3 June, the anniversary of his death.

The entrance is beside Želivského metro station; men should cover their heads (yarmulkes are available at the gate). Last admission is 30 minutes before closing.

KARLÍN STUDIOS Map p130

☎ 251 511 804; www.karlinstudios.cz; Křižíkova 34, Karlín; admission free; ☼ noon-6pm Tue-Sun; Ⓜ Křižíkova

Housed in a converted factory building, this complex of artists' studios includes a public art gallery that showcases the best of Czech contemporary art, plus two small commercial galleries. This is the place to come and see what's happening at the cutting edge of art in the city.

TRANSPORT: ŽIŽKOV & KARLÍN

Bus Buses 133 and 175 run from outside Florenc metro station along Husitská at the foot of Žižkov Hill, useful for the Army Museum and National Monument.

Metro There are no metro stations in Žižkov itself – the nearest is Jiřího z Poděbrad on line A, a five-minute walk south from the TV Tower. Line B runs through Karlín.

Tram Lines 5, 9 and 26 run along Seifertova, in the centre of Žižkov, while lines 8 and 24 run along Sokolovská in Karlín.

ŽIŽKOV & KARLÍN

NEIGHBOURHOODS ŽIŽKOV & KARLÍN

0 — 0.5 km
0 — 0.25 miles

SIGHTS	(p129)
Army Museum	1 B4
Chapel of St Roch (Kaple sv Rocha)	2 E5
Former Jewish Cemetery	3 C5
Jan Palach's Grave	4 F6
Jan Žižka Statue	5 C4
Jewish Cemetery (Židovské Hřbitovy)	6 G6
Kafka's Grave	7 H6
Karlín Studios	8 C3
Miminka (Mummy) – David Černy Sculpture	(see 11)
National Monument (Národní památník)	9 C4
Olšany Cemetery (Olšanské Hřbitovy)	10 F6
TV Tower	11 C6

EATING	(p159)
Hanil	12 B6
Kuře v Hodinkách	13 C5
Mailsi	14 C5
Restaurace Akropolis	(see 17)

ENTERTAINMENT	(p197)
Bunkr Parukářka	15 D5
Kino Aero	16 G3
Palác Akropolis	17 B5
Sedm Vlků	18 B5
XT3	19 D4

DRINKING	(p179)
Bukowski's	20 C5
Parukářka	21 D5
Pivovarský Klub	22 A3
U Slovanské Lípy	23 C4
U Vystřeleného Oka	24 C4

SPORTS & ACTIVITIES	(p209)
Cybex Health Club & Spa	25 A2
FK Viktoria Žižkov Stadium	26 B5

SLEEPING	(p215)
Armedia Hotel Theatrino	27 C5
Clown & Bard Hostel	28 B5
Hostel Elf	29 B4
Hotel Alwyn	30 B3

TRANSPORT	(p248)
Florenc Bus Station	31 A3

NATIONAL MONUMENT Map p130

Národní památník; ☎ 222 781 676; www.nm.cz;
U Památníku 1900, Žižkov; exhibition adult/child
60/30Kč, roof terrace 80/40Kč, combined ticket
110/60Kč; ⏱ 10am-6pm Thu, Sat & Sun, to 8pm
Fri, closed Mon-Wed; Ⓜ Florenc

Although not, strictly speaking, a legacy
of the communist era – it was completed
in the 1930s – the huge monument atop
Žižkov Hill is, in the minds of most Praguers
over a certain age, inextricably linked with
the Communist Party of Czechoslovakia,
and in particular with Klement Gottwald,
the country's first 'worker-president'.

Designed in the 1920s as a memorial to
the 15th-century Hussite commander Jan
Žižka, and to the soldiers who had fought
for Czechoslovak independence, it was still
under construction in 1939 when the occupation of Czechoslovakia by Nazi Germany
made the 'Monument to National Liberation', as it was called, seem like a sick joke.

After 1948 the Communist Party appro-
priated the story of Jan Žižka and the Hussites for propaganda purposes, extolling
them as shining examples of Czech peasant
power. The communists completed the
National Monument with the installation
of the Tomb of the Unknown Soldier and
Bohumil Kafka's gargantuan bronze statue
of Žižka. But they didn't stop there.

In 1953 the monument's mausoleum –
originally intended to hold the remains of
Tomáš Garrigue Masaryk, Czechoslovakia's
founding father – received the embalmed
body of the recently deceased Klement
Gottwald, displayed to the public in a
refrigerated glass chamber, just like his
more illustrious comrade Lenin in Moscow's

Red Square. It soon became a compulsory
outing for school groups and busloads of
visiting tourists from around the Soviet
bloc. Gottwald's morticians, however, were
not as adept as the Russians – by 1962 the
body had decayed so badly that it had to
be cremated.

After 1989, the remains of Gottwald and
other communist dignitaries were removed,
and the building lay closed for 20 years.
However, after a two-year renovation
project it reopened to the public recently
as a museum of 20th-century Czechoslovak
history. Although the massive functionalist
structure has all the elegance of a nuclear
power station, the interior is a spectacular
extravaganza of polished art deco marble,
gilt and mosaics.

The central hall – once home to a dozen
marble sarcophagi bearing the remains of
communist luminaries – houses a moving
war memorial with sculptures by Jan Sturša,
and exhibits recording the founding of the
Czechoslovak Republic in 1918, WWII, the
1948 coup, and the Soviet invasion of 1968
and its aftermath. Steps lead down to the
columbarium, where the ashes of prominent Czechs were once stored.

But the most grimly fascinating part is
the Frankenstein laboratory beneath the
Liberation Hall, where scientists once bat-
tled to prevent Klement Gottwald's corpse
from decomposing. On display in a glass-
walled sarcophagus by day, his body was
lowered into this white-tiled crypt every
night for another frantic round of main-
tenance and repair (it still smells faintly of
embalming fluid). In the corner is the refrigerated chamber where Gottwald spent
his nights (now occupied by the shattered
remains of his sarcophagus), and in the adjoining room is a phalanx of 1950s control
panels, switches and instruments that once
monitored the great leader's temperature
and humidity.

The monument's roof terrace offers a
superb view over the city, and there's an
appealing cafe on the first floor with an
outdoor terrace.

OLŠANY CEMETERY Map p130

Olšanské hřbitovy; Vinohradská 153, Žižkov; admission free; ⏱ 8am-7pm May-Sep, to 6pm Mar, Apr &
Oct, to 5pm Nov-Feb; Ⓜ Flora

Huge and atmospheric, Prague's main
burial ground was founded in 1680 to handle the increased deaths during a plague

NEIGHBOURHOODS   ŽIŽKOV & KARLÍN

JAROSLAV SEIFERT

Born into a working-class family in Žižkov, the poet
and journalist Jaroslav Seifert (1901–86) is the only
Czech (so far) to be awarded the Nobel Prize for Literature. Although he was originally a member of the
Communist Party, he was later expelled after pro-
testing against its increasingly 'Bolshevik tendencies'
and, along with Václav Havel, was a signatory of the
1977 human rights charter, Charter 77. Hailed as a
spokesman for the people of Czechoslovakia, and a
standard-bearer for freedom of expression during the
years of communist suppression, he was a vocal critic
of the communist government; one of his best-known
sayings was, 'If a writer is silent, he is lying.'

epidemic; the oldest stones can be found in the northwestern corner, near the 17th-century Chapel of St Roch (kaple sv Rocha). There are several entrances to the cemetery running along Vinohradská, east of Flora metro station, and also beside the chapel on Olšanská.

Jan Palach, the student who set himself on fire on the steps of the National Museum in January 1969 to protest the Soviet invasion (see the boxed text, p29), is buried here. To find his grave, enter the main gate (flanked by flower shops) on Vinohradská and turn right – it's about 50m along on the left of the path.

TV TOWER Map p130

Televizní vysílač; ☎ 242 418 784; www.tower
.cz; Mahlerovy sady 1, Žižkov; adult/child under 6yr/
child 6-14yr/student 150/free/60/120Kč; ☯ 10am-
11.30pm; Ⓜ Jiřího z Poděbrad

Prague's tallest landmark – and, depending on your tastes, either its ugliest or its most futuristic feature – is the 216m-tall TV Tower, erected between 1985 and 1992. It dominates the skyline from most parts of the city, and is floodlit at night in the national colours of red, white and blue.

The viewing platforms, reached by high-speed lifts, have comprehensive information boards in English and French explaining what you can see; there's also a restaurant at 66m up (closed for renovation at the time of research, but due to reopen by 2011). But the most bizarre thing about it is the 10 giant crawling babies with coin-slots for faces that appear to be exploring the outside of the tower – an installation called *Miminka* (Mummy) by artist David Černý (see the boxed texts, p38 and p142).

The tower is built on the site of a former Jewish cemetery (admission 20Kč; ☯ 9am-1pm Tue & Thu). The cemetery was opened after the Old Jewish Cemetery (p99) in Josefov was closed, and remained in use until 1890, when the much larger Jewish Cemetery (p129) off Vinohradská was opened.

Drinking p190; Eating p175; Shopping p157; Sleeping p227

Holešovice, Bubeneč and Dejvice are contiguous neighbourhoods, running east to west, north of the Old Town across the Vltava River. Holešovice, the furthest east, nestles inside the big bend of the Vltava. It's unfortunately bisected by a major rail line and highway into distinct eastern and western halves. Bubeneč, in the middle and largely residential, occupies the land directly north of the Old Town on the other side of Letná park. Its defining features are two major parks, Letná Gardens (Letenské sady; p136) and Stromovka (p138). Dejvice, a sprawling, mostly green residential area to the west, is situated north of Malá Strana and Hradčany.

For decades, Holešovice was badly neglected. It was long considered the 'German' area of the city and became run-down in the decades after WWII when many of the residents left or were forcibly expelled. It didn't help that the district was chopped in two by insensitive rail and road construction. The far eastern half, built around the container ports on the Vltava, for decades was the closest thing Prague had to a true slum.

All of that changed in 2002, when the Vltava flood inundated the low-level areas around the river, including much of Holešovice. The flood's aftermath saw a massive injection of development funds into the neighbourhood. The district's former brewery is now being converted into luxury apartments and office complexes. High-priced condos and office towers now line the western bank of the Vltava, and clubs, restaurants, galleries and hotels are slowly moving in. The future looks bright.

Holešovice is home to the vast exhibition grounds known as the Výstaviště (Map p136). Many of the buildings were built to house the 1891 Jubilee Exhibition and are still impressive in a faded-glory kind of way. These include the Prague Pavilion and the grand art nouveau Industrial Palace. Sadly, though, the Výstaviště grounds have been allowed to fall into disrepair and look a little shabby these days. To add insult to injury, a fire in November 2008 destroyed part of the Industrial Palace (though it's being faithfully rebuilt). There are a couple of attractions here, including an amusement park, a 'singing' fountain, and Tesla Aréna, one of the leading concert and ice-hockey venues in town, but you're not likely to want to linger long.

Bubeneč, up the hill from the western side of Holešovice, has always been a comfortable middle-class neighbourhood, and it's no different now. Anchored by two of Prague's nicest parks, the late 19th-century town houses on both sides of the central avenue, Milady Horákové, and to the north around Stromovka park are in high demand. Many embassies and villas, including the spectacular residence of the US ambassador, are here.

Dejvice, further to the west, is a mix of university campuses and residential areas in the western part that merges into the leafy backstreets of Prague's embassy district in the eastern section. There's not too much to see out here, but there are some good restaurants and accommodation options.

Just north of Dejvice is the unusual 1930s villa suburb of Baba, a functionalist project designed by a team of artists and designers that aimed to provide cheap, attractive, single-family houses. The Hanspaulka suburb to its southwest was a similar project, built between 1925 and 1930. Both are now highly desirable addresses.

DIVOKÁ ŠÁRKA Map p58
Evropská, Dejvice; 🚊 **20, 26**

The valley of the Šárecký potok (Šárka Creek) is one of Prague's best-known and most popular nature parks. It's named after the mythical warrior Šárka, who is said to have thrown herself off a cliff here after the death of her enemy, the handsome Ctirad – whom she either seduced and murdered (committing suicide afterwards to avoid capture), or fell in love with and failed to protect (killing herself out of grief and guilt), depending on which version of the legend you prefer.

The most attractive area is nearby, among the rugged cliffs near the Džbán Reservoir. People sunbathe on the rocks, and you can swim in the Džbán Reservoir.

From there it's a 7km walk northeast down the valley on a red-marked trail to the suburb of Podbaba, where the creek empties into the Vltava River. There's a bus stop by the Vltava at Podbaba, for the trip back to the centre, or you can walk south about 1.5km on Podbabská to the northern terminus of tram 8, opposite the Hotel Crowne Plaza (p135) in Dejvice.

DOX CENTRE FOR CONTEMPORARY ART Map p136

☎ 774 145 434; www.doxprague.org; Osadní 34, Holešovice; adult/family 180/300Kč; ☻ 10am-6pm Wed-Mon; ⛔ 5, 12, Ⓜ Ortenovo náměstí

This edgy, noncommercial art gallery and exhibition space forms the nucleus of Holešovice's expanding rep as one of the city's hippest districts. The exhibitions highlight a wide range of media, including video, sculpture, photography and painting. The shows are hit-and-miss, but recent exhibitions like Andy Warhol's *Chelsea Hotel* and Robert Mapplethorpe's photography have definitely pushed the envelope for what remains a relatively conservative art public. You'll find a cafe and an excellent bookstore heavy on art and architecture on the upper level. In 2009 and 2010, DOX hosted David Černý's controversial, EU-mocking installation *Entropa* (see p38), though it wasn't clear if this would remain the work's permanent home.

ECOTECHNICAL MUSEUM Map p136

Ekotechnické muzeum; ☎ 777 170 636; www.ekotechnickemuseum.cz; Papírenská 6, Bubeneč; adult/family 120/250Kč; ☻ 10.30am-4pm Tue-Sun May-Oct; ⛔ 131 from Ⓜ Hradčanská

Prague's former wastewater treatment plant was built between 1895 and 1906 following a design by English architect WH Lindley. Surprisingly, as the plant was designed to service a city of 500,000 people, it remained in operation until 1967, by which time Prague had a population of over a million. Several steam-powered engines are on display and more are being repaired; there are also guided tours (included with admission) of the labyrinth of sewers beneath the building.

HOTEL CROWNE PLAZA Map p136

☎ 296 537 111; www.austria-hotels.at; Koulova 15, Dejvice; ⛔ 8 (stop: Podbaba)

The silhouette of this huge Stalin-era building in northern Dejvice will be familiar to anyone who has visited the Russian capital. Originally called the Hotel International, it was built in the 1950s to a design inspired by the tower of Moscow University, right down to the Soviet-style star on top of the spire (though this one is gold, not red).

Nip into the gleamingly restored, marble-clad lobby bar (to the right), and take a look at the large tapestry hanging on the wall in the far left-hand corner. Entitled *Praga Regina Musicae* (Prague, Queen of Music) and created by Cyril Bouda around 1956, it shows an exaggerated aerial view of central Prague. Bang in the centre is the former Stalin Monument on Letná terása, and at the bottom edge you can spot the now-departed Soviet tank memorial (see the boxed text, p95). For a review of the hotel see p229.

KŘIŽÍK'S FOUNTAIN Map p136

Křižíkova fontána; ☎ 723 665 694; www.krizikova fontana.cz; U Výstaviště 1, Holešovice; admission to shows around 200Kč; ☻ performances hourly 7-11pm Mar-Oct; ⛔ 5, 12, 14, 15, 17

Each evening from spring to autumn the musical Křižík's Fountain performs its computer-controlled light and water dance. Performances range from classical music such as Dvořák's *New World Symphony* to rousing works performed by Andrea Bocelli, Vangelis and Queen, and theme music from popular films. Call ahead or check the website for details of what's on. The light show is best after sunset – from May to July go for the later shows.

LAPIDÁRIUM Map p136

☎ 233 375 636; U Výstaviště 1, Holešovice; adult/child 40/20Kč; ☻ noon-6pm Tue-Fri, 10am-6pm Sat & Sun; ⛔ 5, 12, 14, 15, 17

An outlying branch of the National Museum and an often-overlooked gem, the Lapidárium is a repository for some 400

TRANSPORT: HOLEŠOVICE & BUBENEČ

Metro The Vltavská and Nádraží Holešovice metro stations on line C serve the southern and northern parts of Holešovice respectively.

Tram Lines 5, 12, 14, 15 and 17 run along Dukelských Hrdinů, the main north–south street in Holešovice, while trams 1, 8, 15, 25 and 26 run east–west on Milady Horákové, serving both Holešovice and Bubeneč.

TRANSPORT: DEJVICE

Metro Dejvická station is the northwestern terminus of line A; Hradčanská, the last stop but one, serves the southern part of the district.

Tram Lines 2, 8, 20 and 26 all pass through Vítézné náměstí in the centre of Dejvice.

NEIGHBOURHOODS HOLEŠOVICE, BUBENEČ & DEJVICE

sculptures from the 11th to the 19th centuries. The exhibits include the Lions of Kouřim (Bohemia's oldest surviving stone sculpture), parts of the Renaissance Krocín Fountain that once stood in Old Town Square, 10 of Charles Bridge's original statues, and many other superb sculptures. Note that the Lapidárium was closed in January 2010 for technical reasons and it wasn't clear when it would reopen.

LETNÁ Map p136

Letná is a vast open space between Milady Horákové and the river, with a parade ground to the north and a peaceful park, the Letná Gardens (Letenské sady), in the south, offering picture-postcard views over the city and its bridges. In summer you'll find an open-air beer garden (see Letenský zámeček, p191). In 1261 Přemysl Otakar II held his coronation celebrations here, and during communist times, Letná was the site of Moscow-style May Day military parades. In 1989 around 750,000 people gathered here in support of the Velvet Revolution. In 2008 work began in the northwestern corner of the park on the enormous Blanka Tunnel, part of Prague's future ring-road system. When the work is finished the tunnel will lead under both Letná and Stromovka parks.

In the southwestern corner is the charming, neobaroque Hanavský Pavilón (p175), built by Otto Prieser for the 1891 Jubilee Exposition.

For a walking tour through the park, see p139.

LETNÁ TERÁSA Map p136

The monumental, stepped terrace overlooking the river on the southern edge of Letná Gardens dates from the mid-1950s, when a huge statue of Stalin – the world's largest – was erected here by the Communist Party of Czechoslovakia, only to be blown up in 1962 by the same sycophants when Stalin was no longer flavour of the decade (see the boxed text, p95). A giant metronome – a symbolic reminder of the passing of time – has stood in its place since 1991.

MOŘSKÝ SVĚT Map p136

☎ 220 103 275; U Výstaviště 1, Holešovice; adult/child 240/145Kč; ☺ 10am-7pm; ☒ 5, 12, 14, 15, 17
The Czech 'Sea World' has the largest water tank in the country, with a capac-ity of around 100,000L. Some 4500 living species of fish and sea creatures are on display, with a good and suitably scary set of sharks. The cramped interior will be disappointing if you're used to larger 'Sea World'-type amusement parks around the world. Nevertheless, it's a fun day out for little kids.

NATIONAL TECHNICAL MUSEUM Map p136

Národní technické muzeum; ☎ 220 399 111; www.ntm.cz; Kostelní 42, Holešovice; adult/child 100/50Kč; ☺ 9am-5pm Tue-Fri, 10am-6pm Sat & Sun; ☒ 1, 8, 15, 25
The museum was closed in 2008 for long-term renovations and was expected to reopen late in 2010. We recommend checking the museum website to make sure the

HOLEŠOVICE, BUBENEČ & DEJVICE

museum is open. Before it was closed, the museum had a huge main hall chock-full of vintage trains, planes and automobiles, including 1920s and '30s Škoda and Tatra cars and even a couple of Bugattis, plus an active program of other temporary technical exhibits aimed at machine-loving geeks and gearheads.

PRAGUE PLANETARIUM
Map p136

Planetárium Praha; ☎ 220 999 001; www
.planetarium.cz; Královská Obora 233, Holešovice;
exhibition adult/child 25/15Kč; shows in Czech/
English 80/160Kč; ⏰ 8.30am-noon & 1-8pm Mon-
Thu, 9.30am-noon & 1-8pm Sat & Sun; ⓐ 5, 12,
14, 15, 17

The planetarium in Stromovka park, just west of Výstaviště, presents various slide and video presentations in addition to the star shows. Most shows are in Czech only, but one or two of the more popular ones provide a text summary in English (check the website for details). There's also an astronomical exhibition in the main hall.

STROMOVKA
Map p136

ⓐ 5, 12, 14, 15, 17

Stromovka, west of Výstaviště, is Prague's largest park. In the Middle Ages it was a royal hunting preserve, which is why it's sometimes called the Královská obora (Royal Deer Park). Rudolf II had rare trees planted here and several lakes created (fed from the Vltava River via a still-functioning canal). It's now the preserve of strollers, joggers, cyclists and in-line skaters. For a walking tour through the park, see p139.

VELETRŽNÍ PALACE

Map p136

Veletržní palác; ☎ 224 301 122; www.ngprague
.cz; Dukelských Hrdinů 47, Holešovice; adult/child
200/100Kč, after 4pm 100/50Kč, free entry after
3pm 1st Wednesday of the month; ⊗ 10am-6pm
Tue-Sun; 🚋 12, 14, 17

The huge, functionalist Veletržní palác
(Trade Fair Palace), which was built in 1928
to house trade exhibitions, is now the
home of the National Gallery's superb collection of 20th- and 21st-century Czech and
European artwork.

You could easily spend an entire day
wandering through here – the collection
is spread over three floors of this vast,
ocean-liner-like building – but if you
have only got an hour to spare, head for
the 3rd floor (Czech Art 1900–30, and
19th- and 20th-century French Art), where
you can see the paintings of František
Kupka, pioneer of abstract art, and the
art, furniture and ceramics of the Czech
cubists. The French section includes some
sculpture by Rodin, a few Impressionist
artworks, Gaugin's *Flight* and Van Gogh's
Green Wheat.

The 1st floor (20th-century Foreign
Art) includes works by Klimt, Schiele and
Picasso, while the 2nd floor (Czech Art
1930 to present day) has early examples of
kinetic art, some socialist realist stuff from
the communist era and various amusing
works by contemporary artists.

LETNÁ & STROMOVKA
Walking Tour

1 Stone grotto

Begin at the Summer Palace (Letohrádek) at
the eastern end of the Royal Garden (p63), north
of Prague Castle. A path at the southern end
of the Summer Palace leads east into the
neighbouring park of Chotkovy sady; in the
centre of the park you will find a little stone
grotto that is dedicated to the historical novelist
Josef Zeyer and, nearby, a park bench with a
superb view over the river and Staré Město.
Doing this part of the route is possible only
from April to October, as the Royal Garden
is closed in winter. An alternative start involves taking tram 18 to the Chotkova stop
and following Gogolova east into Letná Gardens (Letenské sady). You can visit Chotkovy
sady by doubling back across the bridge at the
eastern end of the gardens.

2 Hanavský Pavilón

A footbridge at the eastern end of the gardens
leads across Chotkova and into the huge Letná
Gardens, crossing a broad grassy ditch lined
with red-brick walls that once formed part of
Prague's fortifications. Follow the main path,
which bears right from the park entrance, but
then detour further right to visit the Hanavský
Pavilón (p175), where you can enjoy a superb
panorama and, perhaps, a little lunch.

3 Metronome

The path continues along the top of a bluff
directly above the Vltava, with great views
over the river and the eastern and southern
parts of the city, before arriving at a monumental stepped terrace topped by a giant,
creaking metronome that sits on a spot once
occupied by a giant statue of Stalin (see the
boxed text, p95).

4 Letná beer garden

Continue east along the path at metronome
level and you will eventually arrive at Letná's
popular beer garden, Letenský zámeček (p191),
where it's almost compulsory to stop for a
cold one.

5 Expo 58 Restaurant

Beyond the beer garden, the path slopes down
through pretty flower gardens and along an
avenue of plane trees, past the futuristic Expo 58
Restaurant. Built for the Brussels World Exposition of 1958, and later re-erected here, it is no
longer a restaurant but has been beautifully
renovated and now houses some fortunate
office workers.

If the Hanavský Pavilón didn't tempt you
into a lunch stop, perhaps cosy La Crêperie (p177)
on nearby Janovského will.

6 Veletržní Palace

Leave the park and continue downhill on Ska-
lecká, then turn left along busy Dukelských
Hrdinů. Follow this street north for 400m –
stopping to visit the Veletržní Palace (above),
Prague's premier collection of modern art, if
you wish – to the entrance of the Výstaviště
exhibition grounds; if you don't fancy walking this section, hop on a tram for a couple
of stops (lines 5, 12 or 17 will do).

7 Lapidárium

If the Veletržní Palace has whetted your appetite for cultural attractions (or maybe it's
just started raining), you might like to detour

NEIGHBOURHOODS HOLEŠOVICE, BUBENEČ &DEJVICE

139

LETNÁ & STROMOVKA WALKING TOUR

WALK FACTS

Start Summer Palace (tram 22 to Letohrádek stop)
End Troja (bus 112 to metro Nádraží Holešovice)
Distance 6km
Time Three hours
Exertion Moderate
Fuel stops Hanavský Pavilón, Letná beer garden, La Crêperie

into the Lapidárium (p135) for a wander among some of the city's finest sculptures. The entire Výstaviště grounds are normally open to the public. In addition to the Lapidárium, you'll find a relatively run-down amusement park, a 'singing' fountain and lots of sausage stands and *pivo* (beer) joints.

8 Prague Planetarium

If you're in the mood for something more educational, bear left at the entrance to Výstaviště and follow the path just to the right of the terminal loop of tram 5, passing the dome of the Prague Planetarium (p138) on your right as you enter the former royal hunting ground, Stromovka (p138).

9 Old restaurant

Follow your nose as the path curves to the left, past people playing boules on the gravel verge, then bear right towards the pond. Turn left when you reach a broad main path (signposted 'Dejvice & Bubeneč'), which leads between a series of artificial lakes on the right and a once-grand but now ruined old restaurant and bandstand on the left.

10 Mistodržitelský Summer Palace

Beyond this you'll see the Renaissance Mistodržitelský Summer Palace perched on a hill to the left, where Bohemian royals used to hang out on their hunting trips to Stromovka. It was remodelled in neo-Gothic style in the early 19th century.

11 Emperor's Island

At the T-junction below the palace, turn right and continue along an avenue of trees, following the path as it curves around to the right. Take the first path on the left (following the signs to 'Troja' and 'Zoo'), continue through the short tunnel under the railway line, and go up the steps ahead in the distance. Cross the bridge and go left, then right (signposted 'Zoo'; if you're planning on taking the boat back into town, this is where it leaves from). You are now on Emperor's Island (Císařský ostrov); the road leads to a sweeping pedestrian bridge over the main branch of the Vltava, with a canoe slalom course visible upstream. At the far end of the pedestrian bridge go left along the riverbank path, and in about 300m you'll reach a parking area; turn right, and the road will lead you to the 112 bus terminus. On one side of the bus terminus is Troja Chateau (p145), with a museum of winemaking in the cellar; on the other is the entrance to Prague Zoo (p145). Take your pick.

SMÍCHOV

Drinking p194; Eating p177; Shopping p157; Sleeping p230

Smíchov arguably deserves a reputation as Prague's most economically varied – even schizo-phrenic – district. For years it languished as a depressed industrial backwater that was (by some accounts) home to Prague's largest Roma community. At the same time, the hills southwest of the Anděl metro station, not far from the Barrandov film studios, had some of the city's swanki-est villas. These days, those jarring contrasts are seen in the area around Anděl, which is filled with gleaming office towers, the vast Nový Smíchov shopping centre (p157), the Staropramen brewery (see the boxed text, p190), and some of the city's hottest boutique hotels. Just down the road, near the Smíchovské Nádraží train station, the poverty and neglect set in again.

As with the city's other riverside districts, Smíchov both suffered and benefited from the 2002 flood. Low-lying areas were submerged, but the aftermath saw a big infusion of develop-ment capital. Like Holešovice and Karlín, Smíchov is hoping to play off its industrial chic a bit. That effort got a huge boost in 2007 when artist David Černý (see the boxed texts, p38 and below) decided to relocate his 'Meet Factory' performance art space amid the tenements and abandoned factories south of Smíchovské Nádraží.

FUTURA GALLERY Map p143

☎ 251 511 804; www.futuraprojekt.cz; Holečkova 49; admission free; �'t 11am-6pm Wed-Sun; ☒ 4, 7, 9, 10

The Futura Gallery focuses on all aspects of contemporary art, ranging from painting, photography and sculpture to video, instal-lations and performance art. The gallery spaces, which include two floors of 'white cube' halls, a more intimate brick-vaulted cellar and a garden, host changing exhi-bitions by both Czech and international artists. The most notorious exhibit is in the garden, a permanent installation by David Černý (see the boxed texts, p38 and below). It consists of two huge, naked human figures, bent over at the waist with their heads buried in a blank wall. Ladders allow you to climb up and place your head – there's really no polite way to say this – up each figure's arse, where you can watch a video of Czech president Václav Klaus and the director of Prague's National Gallery spoon-ing mush into each other's mouths. Richly metaphorical, to say the least.

MEET FACTORY Map p143

☎ 251 551 796; http://meetfactory.cz; Ke Sklárně 15; admission free; �'t vary by event; ☒ 12, 14, 20 stop to Lihovar

Don't come here looking for a polished art experience. For the time being, David Černý's 'Meet Factory' remains very much a work in progress. The idea is to invite artists

WEIRD ART

David Černý's sculpture is often controversial, occasionally outrageous and always amusing. Here are six of his best-known works that are permanently on view in Prague. See also the boxed text, p38.

- *Quo Vadis* (Where Are You Going; 1991) – in the garden of the German Embassy in Malá Strana (Map p78). A Trabant (an East German car) on four human legs serves as a monument to the thousands of East Germans who fled the communist regime in 1989 prior to the fall of the Berlin Wall, and camped out in the embassy garden seeking political asylum. See the Malá Strana Gardens Walking Tour, p86.
- *Viselec* (Hanging Out; 1997) – above Husova street in Staré Město (Map p90). A bearded, bespectacled chap with a passing resemblance to Sigmund Freud, casually dangling by one hand from a pole way above the street.
- *Kun* (Horse; 1999) – in the Lucerna Palace shopping arcade, Nové Město (Map p110). Amusing alternative version of the famous St Wenceslas Statue in Wenceslas Square, only this time the horse is dead.
- *Miminka* (Mummy; 2000) – on the TV Tower (p133), Žižkov. Creepy, giant, slot-faced babies crawling all over a TV transmitter tower – something to do with consumerism and the media. We think.
- *Brownnosers* (2003) – in the Futura Gallery, Smíchov (Map p142). Stick your head up a statue's backside and watch a video of the Czech president and the director of the National Gallery feeding each other baby food.
- *Proudy* (Streams; 2004) – in the courtyard of Hergetova Cíhelná, Malá Strana (Map p78). Two guys pissing in a puddle (whose irregular outline, you'll notice, is actually the map outline of the Czech Republic) and spelling out famous quotations from Czech literature with their pee. (Yes, the sculpture moves! It's computer controlled.)

SMÍCHOV

lonelyplanet.com

0 — 250 m
0 — 0.1 miles

INFORMATION
Austrian Embassy 1 C2
White Circle of Safety (Bílý
  Kruh Bezpečí) 2 A3

SIGHTS (p142)
Brownnosers – David Černy
  Sculpture ....(see 3)
Futura Gallery..................................3 A2
Meet Factory....................................4 C6
Mozart Museum (Vila
  Bertramka).....................................5 A3

SHOPPING (p149)
Mapis ....(see 16)
Nový Smíchov 6 C2

EATING (p159)
Anděl...7 C3
Artisan..8 C1
Corte di Angelo...............................9 C3
Na Verandách.............................(see 22)
Pizzeria Corleone.........................10 C3
U Mikuláše Dačického.................11 C2
Zlatý Klas.......................................12 B3

ENTERTAINMENT (p197)
Bunkr Klub.....................................13 C4
Futurum..14 C2
Jazzdock...15 D1
Švandovo Divadlo na
  Smíchově......................................16 C1

DRINKING (p179)
Back Doors.....................................17 C3
Dog's Bollocks..............................18 C4
Hells Bells......................................19 C3
Káva Káva Káva.............................20 C3
Lokal Blok......................................21 C2
Na Verandách................................22 C3
Staropramen Brewery.............(see 22)
Wash Café......................................23 C4

SPORTS & ACTIVITIES (p209)
Holmes Place.................................24 D5

SLEEPING (p215)
Admirál Botel................................25 D3
Anděl's Hotel Prague...................26 C3
Angelo Hotel.................................27 B3
Arpacay Hostel.............................28 C5
Hotel Arbes-Mepro......................29 C2
Hotel Julian...................................30 C1
Ibis Praha Malá Strana................31 B3

TRANSPORT (p248)
Lihovar Tram Stop.......................32 D6

TRANSPORT: SMÍCHOV

Metro Line B has stations at Anděl, in the heart of Smíchov, and at Smíchovské Nádražíin the south.
Tram Lines 4, 7, 10 and 14 rumble across Palackého most from Charles Square (Karlovo náměstí) to Smíchov; from Malá Strana take trams 12 or 20 south from Malostranské náměstí or Újezd.

from around the world to live and create in this cavernous, abandoned factory south of Smíchovské Nádraží. The Meet Factory also holds visual and performance art happenings, film screenings and concerts. The problem is that the group that runs it, headed by prominent local artists, is still scraping together the cash to patch the walls. Be sure to check the website before venturing this far out.

There's no easy way to get here. The best bet is to take tram 12, 14 or 20 from Smíchovské Nádraží two stops to Lihovar, find the narrow gate on the right side of the road, cross five or six sets of railway tracks (be sure to look both ways!), and there it is – a crumbling greenish factory with two red fibreglass cars hanging from hooks outside, courtesy of David Černý himself.

MOZART MUSEUM Map p143
Vila Bertramka; ☎ 257 318 461; www.bertramka .com; Mozartova 169; museum admission adult/ child 110/30Kč, concerts around 500Kč; ☽ closed; ☒ 4, 7, 9, 10

For years, this 17th-century villa was a major tourist attraction for those on the hunt for Mozart memorabilia. Mozart stayed here in 1787 and 1791 as the guest of composer František Dušek – and it was here that he finished his opera *Don Giovanni*. Unfortunately, the museum was forced to close in November 2009 following a squabble between art bureaucrats and the Mozart Society, which owns the villa. At the time of research the museum's future was unclear, though there were plans afoot to continue holding occasional concerts. Check the website to get the latest information before venturing out here.

OUTER NEIGHBOURHOODS

Clustered around the city's historic core are the largely 20th-century suburbs of Troja, Kobylisy, Kbely, Barrandov, Střešovice and Břevnov. Except to visit the Prague Zoo and Troja Chateau, few tourists venture into these outer regions and you will often have the attractions here to yourself.

PRAGUE ZOO Map p58

Zoo Praha; ☎ 296 112 111; www.zoopraha.cz;
U Trojského Zámku 120, Troja; adult/child/family
150/100/450Kč; ⏱ 9am-7pm Jun-Aug, to 6pm
Apr, May, Sep & Oct, to 5pm Mar, to 4pm Nov-Feb;
🚌 112 from Ⓜ Nádraží Holešovice

Prague's attractive zoo is set in 60 hectares of wooded grounds on the banks of the Vltava River. Pride of place, at the top of the hill, goes to a herd of Przewalski's horses – the zoo's breeding program played an important part in saving them from extinction (the zoo's logo is a Przewalski's horse) – and the Komodo dragons, which bred in captivity for the first time in 2006. Other attractions include a miniature cable car and an extensive kids' play area with adventure playground and paddling pool.

TROJA CHATEAU Map p58

Trojský zámek; ☎ 283 851 614; U Trojského Zámku
1,Troja; adult/child 120/60Kč; ⏱ 10am-6pm
Tue-Sun Apr-Oct, closed Nov-Mar; 🚌 112 from
Ⓜ Nádraží Holešovice

Troja Chateau is a 17th-century baroque palace built for the Šternberk family, inspired by the Roman country villas seen by the architect on a visit to Italy. The sumptuously decorated palace now houses the Prague City Gallery's collection of 19th-century Czech art, a gallery of paintings of dogs and horses owned by the Bohemian aristocracy, and exhibits explaining the sculptures and frescoes that adorn the palace itself. There's free admission to the palace grounds, where you can wander in the beautiful French gardens, watched over by a gang of baroque stone giants on the balustrade outside the southern door.

KOBYLISY ANTI-FASCIST RESISTANCE MEMORIAL off Map p58

Památník protifašistického odboje v Kobylisích;
Žernosecká; admission free; ⏱ 24hr; 🚋 10, 17, 24

This grassy quadrangle of earthen embankments, ringed by trees and overlooked by apartment blocks, was once the Kobylisy

Rifle Range. More than a hundred Czechs were executed here by firing squads during WWII. Today it's the site of a national memorial: a huge bronze plaque lists all the names of the dead and – such is the legacy of Nazi bureaucracy – the dates and times of their executions. Take tram 10, 17 or 24 to the terminal at Ďáblická, then walk west for 800m (about 10 minutes) along Žernosecká.

KBELY AIRCRAFT MUSEUM off Map p58

Letecké muzeum Kbely; ☎ 973 207 500; Mladoboleslavská; admission free; ⏱ 10am-6pm Tue-Sun
May-Oct; 🚌 185 or 259 from Ⓜ Českomoravská

The Kbely airfield in northeastern Prague is home to this aircraft museum, where you can have a close look at Russian MiG fighter planes and a host of exhibits on aeronautics and space flight. The impressive collection amounts to no fewer than 275 aircraft, including several British and American machines such as a 1931 De Havilland Tiger Moth, a Gloster Meteor jet-fighter (1950) and a McDonnell Douglas F4 Phantom (1954).

BARRANDOV Map p58

🚌 246, 247, 248 from Ⓜ Smíchovské Nádraží

The southern suburb of Barrandov, on the western bank of the Vltava River, was developed in the 1930s by Václav Havel, the father of ex-president Havel. It is famous for the Barrandov Studios, the film studios founded by Miloš Havel (the ex-president's uncle) in 1931 and increasingly popular

---

TRANSPORT: TROJA

Boat Take a boat trip (see p259) from the city centre to the Troja landing.

Bus Take bus 112 from Nádraží Holešovice metro station to the end of the line. From April to September a free shuttle bus (Linka Zoo) runs on this route at weekends.

On foot Walk from Výstaviště to Troja through Stromovka (3km).

with Hollywood producers in recent years: *Mission: Impossible* (1996), *The League of Extraordinary Gentlemen* (2003), *Casino Royale* (2006) and the first two 'Chronicles of Narnia' movies (2005 and 2008) all made use of the facilities here.

The district was deliberately developed as an homage to 1920s Hollywood, with the jazz age architect Max Urban commissioned to create the Barrandov Terraces, an upmarket complex of art deco mansions, villas and apartments ranged along a bluff overlooking the Vltava River, in conscious imitation of the Hollywood Hills. Sadly, the district was 'nationalised' and neglected during the communist era and fell into disrepair; the best views of its crumbling splendour are from the opposite side of the river.

The suburb was named after the 19th-century French geologist Joachim Barrande, who studied the fossils in the contorted limestone of the Barrandov Cliffs (Barrandovské skály; Map p58) – hundreds of them are on display in the National Museum.

PUBLIC TRANSPORT MUSEUM
Map p70

Muzeum MHD; ☎ 296 124 900; www.dpp.cz; Patočkova 4, Střešovice; adult/child 35/20Kč; ☺ 9am-5pm Sat, Sun & hols Apr-Oct; ⊠ 1, 2, 15, 18, 25

The museum at the Střešovice tram depot has a large collection of trams and buses, from an 1886 horse-drawn tram to present-day vehicles. It's a great place for kids as they can climb into some of the vehicles, and you can board a vintage tram (see p260) for a sightseeing tour of the city.

VILLA MÜLLER
Map p58

Müllerova vila; ☎ 224 312 012; www.muller ovavila.cz; Nad Hradním Vodojemem 14, Střešovice; guided tours in Czech adult/concession 300/200Kč, in English or German 400/300Kč; ☺ 9am-6pm Tue, Thu, Sat & Sun Apr-Oct, 10am-5pm Tue, Thu, Sat & Sun Nov-Mar; ⊠ 1, 2, 18 to Ořechovka

Fans of functionalist architecture will enjoy this masterpiece of domestic design. It was built in 1930 for construction entrepreneur František Müller, and designed by the Viennese architect Adolf Loos, whose clean-cut, ultramodernist exterior contrasts with the polished wood, leather and oriental rugs of the classically decorated interior. The villa can be visited only by guided tour, which must be booked in advance; tours begin every two hours from 9am April to October, from 10am November to March.

BŘEVNOV MONASTERY
Map p58

Břevnovský klášter; ☎ 220 406 111; Patočková 72, Břevnov; gardens admission free, guided tour of church, crypt & monastery 50Kč; ☺ gardens 5.30-8am & 5-8.30pm Mon-Fri, 5.30am-8.30pm Sat & Sun, tours 10am & 2pm Sat & Sun, plus 4pm May-Sep; ⊠ 15, 22, 25

Břevnov Monastery is the Czech Republic's oldest Benedictine monastery, founded in 993 by Boleslav II and Bishop Vojtěch Slavníkovec (later to be canonised as St Adalbert). The two men, from powerful and opposing families intent on dominating Bohemia, met at Vojtěška spring, each having had a dream that this was the place where they should found a monastery. Its name comes from *břevno* (beam), after the beam laid across the spring where they met.

The present baroque monastery building and the nearby Basilica of St Margaret (Bazilika sv Markéty) were completed in 1720 by Kristof Dientzenhofer. During the communist era the monastery housed a secret-police archive; Jan Patočka (1907–77), a leading figure of the Charter 77 movement, who died after interrogation by the secret police, is buried in the cemetery behind the monastery. In 1993 (the 1000th anniversary of the monastery's founding) the restored 1st floor, with its fine ceiling frescoes, and the Romanesque crypt, with the original foundations and a few skeletons, were opened to the public for the first time.

The church, crypt and monastery can be visited only by guided tour (minimum 10 people for a tour in Czech, 20 people in English or German), but at weekends you can wander the gardens at your leisure. There is also a good restaurant, Klášterní Šenk (☎ 220 406 294; mains 125-350Kč; ☺ 11.30am-11pm), serving rustic Czech cuisine.

TRANSPORT: STŘEŠOVICE

Tram Lines 1, 2 and 18 run along Střešovická, the main street.

STAR SUMMER PALACE
off Map p58

Letohrádek hvězda; ☎ 235 357 938; Obora hvězda, entrances on Libocká & Bělohorská, Liboc; adult/child 30/15Kč; ⏲ 10am-6pm Tue-Sun May-Sep, to 5pm Tue-Sun Apr & Oct, closed Nov-Mar; 🚊 15, 22, 25

The Letohrádek hvězda is a Renaissance summer palace in the shape of a six-pointed star, built in 1556 for Archduke Ferdinand of Tyrol. It sits at the end of a long avenue through the lovely wooded park of Obora hvězda, a hunting reserve established by Ferdinand I in 1530. The palace houses a small museum about its history and an exhibit on the Battle of Bílá Hora (see White Mountain, below).

From the Vypich tram stop, bear right across open parkland to the white archway in the wall; the avenue on the far side leads to the palace (a 1.5km walk from the tram).

WHITE MOUNTAIN
off Map p58

Bílá Hora; access from Karlovarská; 🚊 22, 25
The 381m-high White Mountain – more of a gentle hillock, actually – on the western outskirts of Prague was the site of the 1620 collapse of Protestant military forces that ended Czech independence for almost 300 years. The only reminder of the battle is a small memorial cairn located on a mound in the middle of a field, with the roof of the Star Summer Palace poking above the forest to the northeast.

Take the tram to the end of the line, then continue west past the Church of Our Lady Victorious (kostel Panny Marla Vítězná), an early 18th-century celebration of the Habsburg

TRANSPORT: BŘEVNOV
Tram Lines 15, 22 and 25 run along Patočkova and Bělohorská, the main drag. Tram 15 terminates at the Vypich stop; 22 and 25 continue to Bílá Hora.

victory at White Mountain, and turn right; the field is visible up ahead.

V HOLEŠOVIČKÁCH
Map p58

🚊 10, 24, 25
The spot in the suburb of Libeň where Reichsprotektor SS Obergruppenführer Reinhard Heydrich was assassinated (see the boxed text, p118) has changed considerably since 1942 – the tram tracks have gone and a modern road intersection has been built. It's near where the slip road exits north from V Holešovičkách to Zenklova. A tall steel monument – topped by three human figures with upraised arms – was finally built here in 2009, 67 years after the event. Because the Czech paratroopers who carried out the assassination were trained in Britain, the communist regime had preferred not to remember them.

To get to the site, take tram 10, 24 or 25 to the Vychovatelna stop (Map p58). From the downhill end of the tram stop, look across to the prominent yellow building with a green spire on the skyline – you can see the monument directly below, a short walk away across a grassy park, where information boards (Czech only) explain what happened here. The neighbouring streets, Gabčíkova and Kubišova, are named after the parachutists who carried out the attack.

top picks

SHOPPING

In the last decade or so Prague's shopping scene has changed beyond recognition. A massive influx of global brand names and a wave of glitzy new malls crammed with designer outlets, smart cafes and big Western brand names has left the city's main shopping streets looking very much like those of any other European capital.

Imported goods often carry Western European prices, but Czech products remain affordable for Czechs and cheap for Westerners. While tourist gift shops outside Prague – see Karlštejn (p234) or Mělník (p238) – have smaller selections, prices are significantly lower. If you're hunting for bargains, the word 'sleva' means 'discount'.

SHOPPING AREAS

The city centre's single biggest – and most exhausting – retail zone is around Wenceslas Square (Václavské náměstí), its pavements jammed with browsing visitors and locals making beelines for their favourite stores. You can find pretty much everything here, from high fashion and music megastores to run-of-the-mill department stores and gigantic book emporia. Many of the more interesting shops are hidden away in arcades and passages, such as the Lucerna Palace (Map p110).

The other main shopping drag intersects with the lower end of Wenceslas Square, comprising Na Příkopě, 28.října and Národní třída (Map p90 and Map p110). Most of the big stores and malls are concentrated on Na Příkopě, with the biggest of them all – the Palladium Praha Shopping Centre (Map p108; náměstí Republiky, Nové Město; M Náměstí Republiky) – at its northeast end, opposite the Municipal House.

In Staré Město, the elegant avenue of Pařížská (Map p90) is lined with international designer houses including Dior, Boss, Armani and Louis Vuitton, while the backstreets to its east are home to boutiques operated by Czech fashion designers. In contrast, the winding lanes between the Old Town Square and Charles Bridge are thronged with tacky souvenir shops flaunting puppets, Russian dolls and 'Czech This Out' T-shirts. However, other parts of Staré Město – notably Dlouhá, Dušní and Karoliny Světlé – are becoming known for a concentration of designer fashion boutiques, art galleries and quirky independent shops.

As Prague's ritziest residential district, it is not very surprising that Vinohrady is also home to the greatest number of furniture and home decor shops in the city. If you are a fan of design or decoration, you should definitely hike the miracle mile along Vinohradská from the Muzeum metro stop to Jiřího z Poděbrad to see the latest in couches, kitchens and carpets. Worth peeking in are Haestens and KA International (both at Vinohradská 33) for high-end bedding and fabrics, and Huelsta (Vinohradská 30) for furniture.

OPENING HOURS

Prague shops usually open anywhere between 8am and 10am, and close between 5pm and 7pm on Monday to Friday and 8.30am to noon or 1pm on Saturday; major shops, departments stores and tourist businesses also open on weekends, but local shops may be closed on Saturday afternoon and Sunday.

CONSUMER TAXES

Value-added tax (VAT, or DPH in Czech) is applied at 10% on food (including restaurant meals), books and periodicals, and 20% on the sale of most goods and services This tax is included in the marked price and not added at the cash register.

It is possible to claim VAT refunds of up to 14% of the purchase price for purchases totalling more than 2000Kč that are made in shops displaying the 'Tax Free Shopping' sticker. They will give you a Tax Free Shopping voucher, which you then need to present to customs for validation when you leave the country (which must be within three months of the date of purchase). You can then claim your refund either at a duty-free shop in the airport (after passing through passport control) or from a cash-refund office back home (within six weeks of the purchase date). For more information, see www.globalrefund.com.

HRADČANY

ANTIQUE MUSIC INSTRUMENTS
Map p70   Antiques

☎ 220 514 287; www.antiques.cz; Pohořelec 9;
🕒 9am-6pm; 🚊 22

It may not get the prize for most inventive shop name, but this place is a real treasure-trove of vintage stringed instruments. You'll find an interesting stock of antique violins, violas and cellos dating from the 18th century to the mid-20th century, as well as bows, cases and other musical accessories. In the same premises you'll find the Icons Gallery, a luminous collection of Russian and Eastern European religious icons, as well as lots of other decorative objets d'art, watches, porcelain and art nouveau glassware.

HOUPACÍ KŮŇ
Map p70   Toys

☎ 603 515 745; Loretánské náměstí 3; 🕒 9.30am-6.30pm; 🚊 22

The 'Rocking Horse' toyshop houses a collection of carved wooden folk dolls, old 1950s wind-up tractors, toy cars and – surprise – even a couple of rocking horses. There are quality toys and art supplies you won't find anywhere else in Prague, but for a typically Czech souvenir look out for the famous and ubiquitous Little Mole character, available here in several guises.

MALÁ STRANA

VETEŠNICTVI
Map p78   Antiques

☎ 257 530 624; Vítezná 16; 🕒 10am-5pm Mon-Fri, to noon Sat; 🚊 6, 9, 12, 20, 22

This is an Aladdin's cave of secondhand goods, bric-a-brac and junk with, in all likelihood, some genuine antiques for those who know what they're looking for. There's affordable stuff for all, from communist-era lapel pins, medals, postcards, old beer mugs and toys to crystal, shot glasses, porcelain, china, pipes and spa cups, all presided over by a bust of Lenin.

SHAKESPEARE & SONS Map p78   Books

☎ 257 531 894; www.shakes.cz; U Lužického Seminaře 10; 🕒 11am-7pm; 🚊 12, 20, 22

This is a newer and smaller branch of the famous English-language bookshop of the same name in Vinohrady (see p156).

PAVLA & OLGA Map p78   Fashion

☎ 728 939 872; Vlašská 13; 🕒 2-6pm Mon-Fri; 🚊 12, 20, 22

Sisters Pavla and Olga Michalková originally worked in the film and TV industry before setting up their own fashion label, creating a unique collection of quirky and cute hats, clothes and accessories. Past customers have included Czech supermodel Tereza Maxová, Britpop band Blur and photographer Helmut Newton.

STARÉ MĚSTO

ART DECO GALERIE Map p90   Antiques

☎ 224 223 076; www.artdecogalerie-mili.com; Michalská 21; 🕒 2-7pm Mon-Fri; Ⓜ Můstek

Specialising in early-20th-century items, this shop has a wide range of 1920s and '30s stuff including clothes, handbags, jewellery, glassware and ceramics, along with knick-knacks such as the kind of cigarette case you might imagine Dorothy Parker pulling from her purse.

CLOTHING SIZES

Women's clothing

Aus/UK	8	10	12	14	16	18
Europe	36	38	40	42	44	46
Japan	5	7	9	11	13	15
USA	6	8	10	12	14	16

Women's shoes

Aus/USA	5	6	7	8	9	10
Europe	35	36	37	38	39	40
France only	35	36	38	39	40	42
Japan	22	23	24	25	26	27
UK	3½	4½	5½	6½	7½	8½

Men's clothing

Aus	92	96	100	104	108	112
Europe	46	48	50	52	54	56
Japan	S		M	M		L
UK/USA	35	36	37	38	39	40

Men's shirts (collar sizes)

Aus/Japan	38	39	40	41	42	43
Europe	38	39	40	41	42	43
UK/USA	15	15½	16	16½	17	17½

Men's shoes

Aus/UK	7	8	9	10	11	12
Europe	41	42	43	44½	46	47
Japan	26	27	27½	28	29	30
USA	7½	8½	9½	10½	11½	12½

Measurements approximate only; try before you buy

BRIC A BRAC
Map p90   Antiques

☎ 224 815 763; Týnská 7; ⏱ 10am-6pm; Ⓜ Náměstí Republiky

Hidden up a narrow lane behind the Týn Church, this is a wonderfully cluttered cave of old household items and glassware and toys and apothecary jars and 1940s leather jackets and cigar boxes and typewriters and stringed instruments and… Despite the junky look of the place, the knick-knacks are surprisingly expensive; there are two 'showrooms', a small one on Týnská, and a larger one in a nearby courtyard (follow the signs), and the affable Serbian owner can give you a guided tour around every piece in his extensive collection.

ART DÉCORATIF
Map p90   Arts & Crafts

☎ 222 002 350; U Obecního Domu 2; ⏱ 10am-8pm; Ⓜ Náměstí Republiky

This is a beautiful shop dealing in Czech-made reproductions of fine art nouveau and art deco glassware, jewellery and fabrics, including some stunning vases and bowls. It's also an outlet for the gorgeously delicate creations of Jarmila Plockova, granddaughter of Alfons Mucha, who uses elements of his paintings in her work.

KERAMIKA V UNGELTU
Map p90   Arts & Crafts

Týn 7; ⏱ 10am-8pm; Ⓜ Náměstí Republiky

This little shop in a corner of the Týn Courtyard is a good place to look for both traditional Bohemian pottery and modern blue-and-white wares, as well as wooden toys and marionettes, at prices up to 25% lower than at many other outlets in Staré Město.

KUBISTA
Map p90   Arts & Crafts

☎ 224 236 378; www.kubista.cz; Ovocný trh 19; ⏱ 10am-6pm Tue-Sun; Ⓜ Náměstí Republiky

Appropriately located in the Museum of Czech Cubism (p102) in Prague's finest cubist building, this shop specialises in limited-edition reproductions of distinctive cubist furniture and ceramics, and designs by masters of the form such as Josef Gočár and Pavel Janák. It also has a few original pieces for serious collectors with serious cash to spend.

QUBUS
Map p90   Arts & Crafts

☎ 222 313 151; www.qubus.cz; Rámová 3; ⏱ 10am-6pm Mon-Fri; Ⓜ Staroměstská

This small design studio looks more impressive online than in the flesh, but Qubus – run by leading Czech designers Maxim Velčoský and Jakon Berdych – is worth a visit if you're interested in cutting-edge household accessories ranging from 'liquid lights' (lamps in the form of teardrops) to crystal wine glasses in the shape of disposable plastic cups. Whatever floats your avant-garde boat…

ANAGRAM
Map p90   Books

☎ 224 895 737; www.anagram.cz; Týn 4; ⏱ 10am-8pm Mon-Sat, to 7pm Sun; Ⓜ Náměstí Republiky

An excellent English-language bookshop, Anagram offers a vast range of fiction and nonfiction, with an especially good selection on European history, philosophy, religion, art and travel, as well as Czech works in translation and children's books. Seek out the remainders section for some bargain new books as well as secondhand offerings on various topics.

BIG BEN
Map p90   Books

☎ 224 826 565; www.bigbenbookshop.com; Malá Štupartská 5; ⏱ 9am-7pm Mon-Fri, 10am-6pm Sat, noon-5pm Sun; Ⓜ Náměstí Republiky

Big Ben is a small but well-stocked English-language bookshop, with shelves devoted to Czech and European history, books on Prague, travel (including Lonely Planet guides), science fiction, children's books, poetry and all the latest fiction best sellers. There are also English-language newspapers and magazines at the counter.

BOTANICUS
Map p90   Cosmetics

☎ 234 767 446; www.botanicus.cz; Týn 3; ⏱ 10am-8pm; Ⓜ Náměstí Republiky

Prepare for olfactory overload in this always-busy outlet for natural health and beauty products. The scented soaps, herbal bath oils and shampoos, fruit cordials and handmade paper products are made using herbs and plants grown on an organic farm at Ostrá, east of Prague.

BOHÈME
Map p90   Fashion

☎ 224 813 840; www.boheme.cz; Dušní 8; ⏱ 11am-7pm Mon-Fri, to 5pm Sat; Ⓜ Staroměstská

This trendy fashion store showcases the designs of Hana Stocklassa and her associates, with collections of knitwear, leather and suede clothes for women. Sweaters, turtlenecks, suede skirts, linen blouses, knit dresses and stretch denim suits seem to be the stock in trade, and there's a range of jewellery to choose from as well.

KLARA NADEMLÝNSKÁ Map p90   Fashion

☎ 224 818 769; www.klaranademlynska.cz; Dlouhá 3; 🕑 10am-7pm Mon-Fri, to 6pm Sat; Ⓜ Staroměstská

Klara Nademlýnská is one of the Czech Republic's top fashion designers, having trained in Prague and worked for almost a decade in Paris. Her clothes are characterised by clean lines, simple styling and quality materials, making for a very wearable range that covers the spectrum from swimwear to evening-wear via jeans, halter tops, colourful blouses and sharply styled suits.

TEG Map p90   Fashion

☎ 222 327 358; www.timoure.cz; V Kolkovně 6; 🕑 10am-7pm Mon-Fri, 11am-5pm Sat; Ⓜ Staroměstská

TEG (Timoure et Group) is the design team created by Alexandra Pavalová and Ivana Šafránková, two of Prague's most respected fashion designers. This boutique showcases their quarterly collections, which feature a sharp, imaginative look that adds zest and sophistication to everyday, wearable clothes.

MODERNISTA Map p90   Furniture

☎ 224 241 300; www.modernista.cz; Celetná 12; 🕑 11am-7pm; Ⓜ Náměstí Republiky

Modernista is an elegant gallery specialising in reproduction 20th-century furniture in classic styles ranging from art deco and cubist to functionalist and Bauhaus. Its collection includes those sensuously curved chairs by Jindřich Halabala that are a feature of the Icon Hotel (p222) and an unusual chaise longue by Adolf Loos, a copy of the one you can see in the drawing room of the Villa Müller (p146). The shop is inside the arcade at Celetná 12 (not visible from the street).

ARZENAL Map p90   Glassware

☎ 224 814 099; Valentinská 11; 🕑 10am-6pm Mon-Fri, 11am-5pm Sun; Ⓜ Staroměstská

Arzenal is a design salon and showroom for the striking and colourful glassware of

top picks

DESIGNER BOUTIQUES

- Bohème (opposite)
- Helena Fejková Gallery (p154)
- Pavla & Olga (p151)
- Klara Nademlýnská (left)
- TEG (left)

Bořek Šípek (www.boreksipek.cz), one of the Czech Republic's leading architects and designers. His work may not be to everyone's taste, but it's certainly eye-catching.

LE PATIO LIFESTYLE Map p90   Homewares

☎ 222 310 310; www.lepatio.cz; Dušní 8; 🕑 10am-7pm Mon-Sat, 11am-7pm Sun; Ⓜ Staroměstská

There are lots of high-quality household accessories here, from wrought-iron chairs and lamps forged by Bohemian blacksmiths to scented wooden chests made by Indian carpenters. Plus you'll find funky earthenware plant pots, chunky crystal wine glasses in contemporary designs, and many more tempting items that you just *know* will fit into your already crammed suitcase…

FREY WILLE Map p90   Jewellery

☎ 272 142 228; www.frey-wille.com; Havířská 3; 🕑 10am-7pm Mon-Sat, noon-6pm Sun; Ⓜ Můstek

An Austrian jewellery maker famed for its enamel work, Frey Wille produces a distinctive range of highly decorative pieces. Its traditional paisley and Egyptian designs are complemented by a range of art nouveau designs based on the works of Alfons Mucha.

GRANÁT TURNOV Map p90   Jewellery

☎ 222 315 612; www.granat.eu; Dlouhá 28-30; 🕑 10am-6pm Mon-Fri, to 1pm Sat; Ⓜ Náměstí Republiky

Part of the country's biggest jewellery chain, specialising in Bohemian garnet, with a huge range of gold and silver rings, brooches, cufflinks and necklaces featuring the small, dark blood-red stones. There's also pearl and diamond jewellery, and less expensive pieces set with the dark green semi-precious stone known in Czech as *vltavín* (moldavite).

SHOPPING STARÉ MĚSTO

MAXIMUM UNDERGROUND

Map p90   Music

☎ 724 307 198; www.maximum.cz; Jílská 22;
🕓 11am-7pm Mon-Sat; Ⓜ Můstek

On the 1st floor in an arcade just off Jílská,
this place is stocked with CDs and LPs of
indie, punk, hip hop, techno and other
genres. It also has a selection of new and
secondhand street and club wear for those
seeking that Central European grunge look.

TALACKO Map p90   Music

☎ 224 813 039; www.talacko.cz; Rybná 29;
🕓 10am-6pm Mon-Fri, to 4pm Sat; Ⓜ Náměstí
Republiky

Pick up the score for Mozart's *Don Giovanni*
or Dvořák's *New World Symphony* at this
eclectic sheet-music shop. Or you might
enjoy some popular music favourites – how
about *101 Beatles Songs for Buskers*?

NOVÉ MĚSTO

GALERIE ČESKÉ PLASTIKY

Map p108   Arts & Crafts

Czech Sculpture Gallery; ☎ 222 310 684; www
.art-pro.cz; Revoluční 20; 🕓 10am-6pm Mon-Sat;
🚊 5, 8, 14

This commercial gallery is a treasure house
of 20th-century and contemporary Czech
sculpture, paintings, prints and photography. There are regular themed exhibitions,
and all items are for sale, at prices ranging
from 2000Kč to 2 million Kč.

GLOBE BOOKSTORE & CAFÉ

Map p110   Books

☎ 224 934 203; www.globebookstore.cz;
Pštrossova 6; 🕓 9.30am-midnight Sun-Wed,
9.30am-1am Thu-Sat; Ⓜ Karlovo Náměstí

A popular hang out for book-loving expats, the Globe is a cosy English-language
bookshop with an excellent cafe-bar (see
the boxed text, p165) in which to peruse
your purchases. There's a good range of
new fiction and nonfiction, a big selection
of secondhand books, and newspapers
and magazines in English, French, Spanish,
Italian, German and Russian. Plus art exhibitions and film screenings.

PALÁC KNIH NEO LUXOR

Map p110   Books

☎ 296 110 372; www.neoluxor.cz; Václavské
náměstí 41; 🕓 8am-8pm Mon-Fri, 9am-7pm Sat,
10am-7pm Sun; Ⓜ Muzeum

Palác Knih Neo Luxor is Prague's biggest
bookshop – head for the basement to find
a wide selection of fiction and nonfiction
in English, German, French and Russian, including Czech authors in translation. You'll
also find internet access (1Kč per minute),
a cafe and (just inside the main entrance) a
good selection of international newspapers
and magazines.

KANZELSBERGER

Map p110   Books & Maps

☎ 224 219 214; www.dumknihy.cz; Václavské
náměstí 4; 🕓 9am-8pm; Ⓜ Můstek

Housed in the tall, glass-fronted Lindt
building at the foot of Wenceslas Square,
Kanzelsberger has five floors of bookshelves, with a cafe on the 1st floor overlooking the square. You'll probably want
the top floor, where there's a selection of
books in English, German and French, plus
hiking and city maps covering the whole of
the Czech Republic.

KIWI Map p110   Books & Maps

☎ 224 948 455; www.kiwick.cz; Jungmannova 23;
🕓 9am-6.30pm Mon-Fri, to 2pm Sat; Ⓜ Národní
Třída

This small specialist travel bookshop stocks
a huge range of maps covering not only
the Czech Republic but also many other
countries. It also an extensive selection of
Lonely Planet guidebooks.

HELENA FEJKOVÁ GALLERY

Map p110   Fashion

☎ 724 125 262; www.helenafejkova.cz; Lucerna
Pasáž, Štěpánská 61; 🕓 10am-7pm Mon-Fri, to
3pm Sat; Ⓜ Muzeum

Kit yourself out in the latest Czech fash-
ions at this *très chic* boutique and showroom. Contemporary men's and women's
fashion and accessories by Prague designer Helena Fejková and others are on
display, and private fashion shows can be
arranged.

MANUFACTURA ABRAM KELLY

Map p110   Gifts

☎ 224 233 282; www.manufactura.cz; Senovážné
náměstí 16; 🕓 9am-6pm Mon-Fri; 🚊 3, 9, 14, 24

This little workshop and studio produces
handmade paper using traditional techniques, and sells it in the form of greeting
cards, business cards, stationery, calligra-
phy, antique map prints and photographic
prints.

MOSER Map p110   Glassware
☎ 224 211 293; www.moser-glass.com; Na Příkopě 12; ⏰ 10am-8pm; Ⓜ Můstek
One of the most exclusive and highly respected of Bohemian glassmakers, Moser was founded in Karlovy Vary in 1857 and is famous for its rich and flamboyant designs. The shop on Na Příkopě is worth a browse as much for the decor as for the goods – it's in a magnificently decorated, originally Gothic building called the House of the Black Rose (dům U černé růže).

BELDA JEWELLERY Map p110   Jewellery
☎ 224 931 052; www.belda.cz; Mikulandská 10; ⏰ 10am-6pm Mon-Thu, to 5pm Fri; Ⓜ Národní Třída
Belda & Co is a long-established Czech firm dating from 1922. Nationalised in 1948, it was revived by the founder's son and grandson, and continues to create gold and silver jewellery of a very high standard. Its range includes its own angular, contemporary designs, as well as reproductions based on art nouveau designs by Alfons Mucha.

BAZAR Map p110   Music
☎ 602 313 730; www.cdkrakovska.cz; Krakovská 4; ⏰ 9am-7pm Mon-Fri, 10am-3pm Sat; Ⓜ Muzeum
There's a vast selection of secondhand CDs, LPs and videos to browse through here at Bazar, representing a wide range of genres. Czech and Western pop jostle with jazz, blues, heavy metal, country and world music, though with most LPs costing around 300Kč to 450Kč this place is not exactly what you'd call a bargain basement.

BONTONLAND Map p110   Music
☎ 224 473 080; www.bontonland.cz; Václavské náměstí 1-3; ⏰ 9am-8pm Mon-Sat, 10am-7pm Sun; Ⓜ Můstek
Supposedly the biggest music megastore in the Czech Republic, with pretty much everything including Western chart music, classical, jazz, dance and heavy metal, as well as an extensive collection of Czech pop. It also sells videos and DVDs, iPods and accessories, and has a large PlayStation arena and internet cafe.

FOTO ŠKODA Map p110   Photography
☎ 222 929 029; www.fotoskoda.cz; Vodičkova 37; ⏰ 9am-8pm Mon-Fri, 10am-6pm Sat; Ⓜ Můstek

top picks

BOOKSHOPS

- Anagram (p152)
- Big Ben (p152)
- Globe Bookstore & Café (opposite)
- Palác Knih Neo Luxor (opposite)
- Shakespeare & Sons (p156)

One of Prague's biggest camera shops, Foto Škoda stocks a wide range of digital and film cameras, camcorders, binoculars, film (professional as well as amateur) and photographic accessories. It also sells used cameras, and offers a camera repair service.

JAN PAZDERA Map p110   Photography
☎ 224 216 197; Vodičkova 28; ⏰ 10am-6pm Mon-Fri, to 1pm Sat; 🚊 3, 9, 14, 24
The friendly and knowledgeable staff members at this long-standing shop are happy to show you around their impressive stock of secondhand cameras, darkroom gear, lenses, binoculars and telescopes. Models range from the basic but unbreakable Russian-made Zenit to expensive Leicas.

BAŤA Map p110   Shoes
☎ 221 088 478; www.bata.cz; Václavské náměstí 6; ⏰ 9am-9pm Mon-Fri, 9am-8pm Sat, 10am-8pm Sun; Ⓜ Můstek
Established by Tomáš Baťa in 1894, the Baťa footwear empire is still in family hands and is one of the Czech Republic's most successful companies. The flagship store on Wenceslas Square, built in the 1920s, is considered a masterpiece of modern architecture, and houses six floors of shoes (including international brands such as Nike, Salomon and Cat, as well as Baťa's own), handbags, luggage and leather goods.

ZERBA Map p110   Toys
☎ 221 014 616; www.zerba.cz; 1st fl, Černa Růže Shopping Centre, Na Příkopě 12; ⏰ 10am-7pm Mon-Fri, to 6pm Sat, to 5pm Sun; Ⓜ Můstek
This place is a paradise for model-railway enthusiasts of all ages, with a huge range of track and rolling stock in N- and OO-gauge, as well as a good selection of Scalextric racing sets and Matchbox model cars.

VINOHRADY & VRŠOVICE

OBCHOD S UMĚNÍM Map p125   Art
☎ 224 252 779; Korunní 34, Vinohrady; ☙ 11am-5pm Mon-Fri; Ⓜ Náměstí Míru, 🚊 10, 16
Prague is filled with antique shops and secondhand-book stores that specialise in selling paintings and prints from the early modern period. Trouble is it's hard to separate the wheat from the chaff. The 'Shop with Art' is the real deal, specialising in original paintings, prints and sculpture from 1900 to 1940, when Czech artists were at the forefront in movements such as constructivism, surrealism and cubism. Naturally, these art works fetch astronomical prices these days, but it's still fun to drop by and browse.

SHAKESPEARE & SONS
Map p125   Books
☎ 271 740 839; www.shakes.cz; Krymská 12, Vršovice; ☙ 4pm-midnight; 🚊 4, 22
Though its shelves groan with a formidable range of literature in English, both new and secondhand, Shakes is more than a bookshop – it's a congenial literary hang out, with a cosy cafe that regularly hosts poetry readings, author events and live jazz. Here you can buy magazines, such as the *New York Review of Books, Harper's* and *Atlantic Monthly,* and settle down for a read over coffee and cakes. Occasionally the bookshop opens earlier on weekends for brunch; best to check the website.

ORIENTÁLNÍ KOBERCE PALÁCKA
Map p125   Carpets
☎ 222 518 354; www.orientalni-koberce.cz; Vinohradská 42, Vinohrady; ☙ 10am-7pm Mon-Fri, to 2pm Sat; Ⓜ Náměstí Míru
The 'Oriental Carpet Palace' is a sumptuous showroom stocked with handmade carpets, rugs and wall hangings from Iran and other Central Asian states. The colourful pieces come in all sizes and prices and in intricate traditional designs, and the knowledgeable staff will be happy to help you make an informed purchase.

DŮM PORCELÁNU Map p125   Glass & Crystal
☎ 221 505 320; www.dumporcelanu.cz; Jugoslávská 16, Vinohrady; ☙ 9am-7pm Mon-Fri, 9am-5pm Sat, 2-5pm Sun; Ⓜ IP Pavlova

The House of Porcelain is a kind of factory outlet for the best Czech porcelain makers, including Haas & Czjzek and Thun, both based in western Bohemia. The flatware, china, blue onion pattern porcelain and other items are priced to draw in local buyers – not tourists. Prices here are a fraction what they are downtown for similar items.

KAREL VÁVRA Map p125   Musical Instruments
☎ 222 518 114; Lublaňská 65, Vinohrady; ☙ 9am-5pm Mon-Fri; Ⓜ IP Pavlova
Handmade fiddles decorate the interior of this old-fashioned violin workshop where Karel and his assistants beaver away making and repairing these instruments in time-honoured fashion. Even if you are not in search of a custom-made violin, it's worth a look just for the time-warp atmosphere.

PALÁC FLÓRA Map p130   Shopping Centre
☎ 255 741 712; www.palacflora.cz; Vinohradská 151, Vinohrady; ☙ 9am-9pm Mon-Sat, 10am-9pm Sun; Ⓜ Flóra
You could be anywhere in the capitalist world in this shiny, glittering shrine to consumerism. Slick cafes share floor space with girly emporia of tiny T-shirts, sparkly make-up and globalised brand names (Hilfiger, Sergio Tacchini, Nokia, Puma, Lacoste, Guess, Diesel, Apple), a full food court upstairs, an eight-screen multiplex and an IMAX cinema that keep the crowds coming in the evenings. Convenient entry direct from the Flóra metro stop.

VINOHRADSKÝ PAVILON
Map p125   Shopping Centre
☎ 222 097 100; www.pavilon.cz; Vinohradská 50, Vinohrady; ☙ 9.30am-9pm Mon-Sat, noon-8pm Sun; Ⓜ Jiřího z Poděbrad
Vinohrady's main shopping arcade is worth a look in if only for a glimpse into the interior of this lovingly restored 1902 market pavilion. Try as they might, the arcade's management has never really succeeded in luring enough real shoppers here to make this work as a commercial venture; though there are a few upmarket boutiques scattered around and the cafe on the ground floor (run by the Ambiente local restaurant group) has excellent coffee and small meals. There's also a large Albert supermarket in the basement, in case you're staying in the area and need to stock up on picnic or train provisions.

HOLEŠOVICE, BUBENEČ & DEJVICE

ANTIKVITA Map p136   Antiques

☎ 233 336 601; www.antikvita.cz; Na Hutích 9, Bubeneč; ☾ 10am-5pm Mon-Fri; Ⓜ Dejvická

This antique shop is a collector's delight, crammed with cases and cabinets overflowing with vintage toys, model trains, dolls, coins, medals, jewellery, clocks, watches, militaria, postcards, porcelain figures, glassware and much, much more. If you have something to sell, Antikvita holds buying sessions on Wednesday and Thursday (from 10am to noon and 2pm to 5pm).

PIVNÍ GALERIE Map p136   Food & Drink

☎ 220 870 613; www.pivnigalerie.cz; U Průhonu 9, Holešovice; ☾ noon-7pm Tue-Fri; 🚊 1, 3, 5, 25

If you think that Czech beer begins and ends with Pilsner Urquell, a visit to the tasting room at Pivní Galerie (the Beer Gallery) will soon lift the scales from your eyes. Here you can sample and purchase a huge range of Bohemian and Moravian beers – nearly 150 varieties from 30 different breweries – with expert advice from the owners.

PRAŽSKÁ TRŽNICE Map p136   Market

Prague Market Hall; ☎ 220 800 945; Bubenské nábřeží 306, Holešovice; ☾ 7am-6pm Mon-Fri, to 2pm Sat; 🚊 1, 3, 5, 25

Almost a suburb in itself, Prague's sprawling, slightly depressing city market includes a large open-air area selling fresh fruit, vegetables and flowers, large covered halls housing supermarkets, electrical goods and car accessories, and dozens of stalls selling everything from cheap clothes to garden gnomes. In the eastern part of the market are several antiques warehouses, some of which look like they have emptied a baroque palace or two. The market is also, ironically, home to SaZaZu (p176), Prague's reigning super club and highbrow Asian restaurant.

SMÍCHOV

MAPIS Map p143   Maps

☎ 257 315 459; Štefánikova 63; ☾ 9am-6.30pm Mon-Fri; 🚊 6, 9, 12, 20

Mapis is a specialist map shop with a wide selection of local, national and international maps, including hiking maps and city plans covering not just the city but also the whole of the Czech Republic.

NOVÝ SMÍCHOV Map p143   Shopping Centre

☎ 251 511 151; www.novysmichov.eu; Plzeňská 8; ☾ 9am-9pm; Ⓜ Anděl

Nový Smíchov is a vast shopping centre that occupies an area the size of several city blocks. It's an airy, well-designed space with plenty of fashion boutiques and niche-market stores – for example, you could check out Profimed, which has all the dental-care products you never knew you needed. Besides all the big brand names, there's a large computer store, a food court, a virtual games hall, a bowling alley, a 12-screen multiplex cinema and a huge, well-stocked Tesco hypermarket.

EATING

top picks

Traditional Czech cuisine is a cardiologist's nightmare, a cholesterol-laden menu of meat, fat, salt and more meat, accompanied by high-calorie dumplings and washed down with copious quantities of beer. When it comes to food, the ultimate Czech put-down is to describe it as *neslaný* or *nemaslý* ('not salty' or 'not fatty').

But if you put aside your notions of healthy eating for a few days (you're on holiday, after all – live a little!), you'll find traditional Czech food to be very tasty. The country can boast some top-notch produce, from game to fish to smoked meats to wild mushrooms, and Prague's top chefs are beginning to reinvent Czech cuisine with a lighter, more inventive touch.

Since the Czech Republic joined the EU in 2004, the steady increase in the number, quality and variety of Prague's restaurants has, if anything, accelerated. You can now enjoy a wide range of international cuisine, from Afghan to Argentinean, Korean to Cantonese, and even – miracle of miracles – expect service with a smile in many eating places.

However, don't let this kaleidoscope of cuisines blind you to the pleasures of good old-fashioned Czech grub. The city's many pubs dish up tasty pork and dumplings, often at very low prices, and a lot of the more upmarket restaurants offer gourmet versions of classic Bohemian dishes such as pork knuckle or roast duck.

CELEBRATING WITH FOOD

Christmas is the most important celebration on the Czech domestic calendar, and food and drink play an important part. Christmas Eve (*Štědrý den*, or 'generous day') is a day of abstinence from meat, with people saving their appetite for the evening meal, which is traditionally *smažený kapr* (crispy, fried carp) served with *bramborový salát* (potato salad). The carp are farmed in medieval *rybníky* (fish ponds) in the countryside, mostly in South Bohemia, and in December they are brought to city markets where they are sold, live, from water-filled barrels. In many homes, the Christmas carp then gets to swim around in the bathtub until it's time for the frying pan.

There is no national tradition as to what is served on Christmas Day (*vánoce*), but meat is definitely back on the menu; *pečená kachna* (roast duck), served with gravy and dumplings, is a widespread favourite. There are also Christmas cookies (*vánoční cukrovi*), baked according to traditional family recipes, and *vánočka*, Bohemia's answer to Christmas cake,

though it's actually made with bread dough, sweetened with sugar, flavoured with lemon, nutmeg, raisins and almonds, and plaited; it is usually served after the Christmas Eve dinner.

New Year's Eve *(Silvestr)* is also a big celebration. These days few people still prepare the traditional New Year's Eve dinner of *vepřový ovar* (boiled pig's head) served with grated horseradish and apple, but the day is still a big party day, with plates of *chlebíčky* (small, open sandwiches), *brambůrky* (potato pancakes) and other snacks, and bottles of *šampaňské* or other sparkling wine on hand to toast the bells at midnight.

ETIQUETTE

Although the vast majority of Prague's tourist-oriented restaurants have long since adopted international manners, a dinner in a Czech home or a traditional eatery still demands traditional Czech etiquette.

To the Czech way of thinking, only barbarians would begin a meal without first saying *dobrou chuť* (the Czech equivalent of *bon appetit* – the correct response is to repeat the phrase); even the waiters in tourist restaurants will murmur *dobrou chuť* as they place the plates on your table. And the first drink of the evening is always accompanied by a toast – usually *na zdraví* (nahz-drah-vee; literally, 'to health') – as you clink first the tops and then the bottoms of your glasses, and finally touch the glass to the table before drinking.

THE SMOKING BAN

In 2010, pubs and restaurants in the Czech Republic had to choose one of the following three labels to be displayed at the entrance to the premises: smoking allowed, smoking prohibited, or mixed. The latter is reserved for establishments that have separate (ie physically isolated) spaces for smokers and nonsmokers.

SPANISH BIRDS & MORAVIAN SPARROWS

Many Czech dishes have names that don't offer a clue as to what's in them, but certain words will give you a hint: *šavle* (sabre; something on a skewer); *tajemství* (secret; cheese inside rolled meat); *překvapení* (surprise; meat, capsicum and tomato paste rolled into a potato pancake); *kapsa* (pocket; a filling inside rolled meat); and *bašta* (bastion; meat in spicy sauce with a potato pancake).

Two strangely named dishes that are familiar to all Czechs are *Španělský ptáčky* (Spanish birds; sausage and gherkin wrapped in a slice of veal, served with rice and sauce) and *Moravský vrabec* (Moravian sparrow; a fist-sized piece of roast pork). But even Czechs may have to ask about *Meč krále Jiřího* (the sword of King George; beef and pork roasted on a skewer), *Tajemství Petra Voka* (Peter Voka's mystery; carp with sauce), *Šíp Malínských lovců* (the Malín hunter's arrow; beef, sausage, fish and vegetables on a skewer) and *Dech kopáče Ondřeje* (the breath of grave-digger Andrew; fillet of pork filled with extremely smelly Olomouc cheese).

It's considered bad manners to talk while eating, and especially to distract a guest while they are enjoying their food, so conversation is usually kept to a minimum while food is being consumed; the time for talk is between courses and after the meal.

SPECIALITIES

The first course of a meal is usually a hearty *polévka* (soup) – often *bramboračka* (potato soup), *houbová polévka* (mushroom soup) or *hovězí vývar* (beef broth). Ones worth looking out for are *cibulačka* (onion soup), a delicious, creamy concoction of caramelised onions and herbs, and *česnečka* (garlic soup), a powerfully pungent broth that is curiously addictive.

Other common appetisers include *Pražská šunka* (Prague ham), for which the capital is famous. It is cured in brine and smoked; the best stuff is *šunka od kosti* (ham off the bone).

What roast beef and Yorkshire pudding is to the English, so *vepřová pečeně s knedlíky a kyselé zelí* (roast pork with dumplings and sauerkraut) is to the Czechs; it's a dish so ubiquitous that it is often abbreviated to *vepřo-knedlo-zelo*. The pork is rubbed with salt and caraway seeds, and roasted long and slow – good roast pork should fall apart, meltingly tender, at the first touch of fork or finger.

The dumplings should be light and fluffy – *houskové knedlíky* (bread dumplings) are made from flour, yeast, egg yolk and milk, and are left to rise like bread before being cooked in boiling water and then sliced. The best *knedlíky* are homemade, but the ones you'll find in most pubs and restaurants will be factory-produced. Alternatively, you may be served *bramborové knedlíky* (potato dumplings); if you thought bread dumplings were filling, just wait until you try these stodge-bombs.

Other staples of Czech restaurant menus include *svíčková na smetaně* (slices of mari-nated roast beef served with a sour-cream sauce garnished with lemon and cranberries); *guláš* (a casserole of beef or pork in a tomato, onion and paprika gravy); and *vepřový řízek* (Wiener schnitzel, a thin fillet of pork coated in breadcrumbs and fried, served with potato salad or *hranolky* – French fries).

Poultry is another popular main course, either roasted or served as *kuře na paprice* (chicken in spicy paprika-cream sauce). *Kachna* (duck), *husa* (goose) and *krůta* (turkey) usually come roasted, with gravy, dumplings and sauerkraut. A few restaurants specialise in game; the most common are *jelení* (venison), *bažant* (pheasant), *zajíc* (hare) and *kanec* (boar) – fried or roasted and served in a mushroom sauce or as *guláš*.

Seafood is found only in a handful of expensive restaurants, but freshwater fish – usually *kapr* (carp) or *pstruh* (trout) – are plentiful. *Štika* (pike) and *úhoř* (eel) are found on more specialised menus. Note that the price of fish on the menu is sometimes not for the whole fish but per 100g. Ask how much the trout weighs before you order it!

The classic Czech dessert is *ovocné knedlíky* (fruit dumplings), but once again the best are to be found at domestic dinner tables rather than in restaurants. Large, round dumplings made with sweetened, flour-based dough are stuffed with berries, plums or apricots, and served drizzled with melted butter and a sprinkle of sugar.

Desserts on offer in traditional restaurants and pubs consist of *kompot* (canned/pre-served fruit), either on its own or *pohár* – in a cup with *zmrzlina* (ice cream) and whipped cream. *Palačinky* or *lívance* (pancakes) are also very common. Other desserts include *jablkový závin* (apple strudel), *makový koláč* (poppy-seed cake) and *ovocné koláče* (fruit slices). For cakes and pastries it is better to go to a *kavárna* (cafe) or *cukrárna* (cake shop).

A typical Czech breakfast *(snídaně)* is a light affair consisting of *chléb* (bread) or *rohlík* (bread roll) with butter, cheese, jam or yoghurt, washed down with tea or coffee. A hotel breakfast buffet will normally also include cereals, eggs, ham or sausage. Some Czechs eat breakfast at self-service *bufety*, which are open between 6am and 8am – these serve up soup or hot dogs, which are washed down with coffee or even beer. Some eateries serving Western-style breakfasts are noted in the boxed text, p165.

You can also go to a *pekárna* or *pekařství* (bakery), or to one of the French or Viennese bakeries, for *loupáčky* (like croissants but smaller and heavier). Czech bread, especially rye, is excellent and varied.

Oběd (lunch) is traditionally the main meal of the day and, except for on Sundays, it's often a hurried affair. Czechs are usually early risers, and so they may sit down to lunch as early as 11.30am, though latecomers can still find leftovers for lunch in many restaurants as late as 3pm.

Having stuffed themselves at lunchtime, for many Czechs *večeře* (dinner) is a light meal, perhaps only a platter of cold meats, cheese and pickles with bread.

PRACTICALITIES

Opening Hours

In general, lunch is served from noon to 3pm, and dinner from 6pm to 9pm. Most Prague restaurants, however, are open all day, from 10am or noon to 10pm or 11pm, allowing a laid-back approach to meal times. Cafes are usually open from 8am; see the boxed text, p165, for breakfast recommendations.

How Much?

On average, you can expect to pay around 300Kč to 600Kč per person for a meal in a midrange restaurant, not including drinks. In the more upmarket places you can double that, and in the very best restaurants the

bill will be in the area of 1500Kč per person before drinks.

On the other hand, it's possible to eat well for very little. You can fill up in a pub or cafe for less than 200Kč per person – and that includes a glass of beer.

Unless otherwise indicated, price ranges quoted in this chapter's restaurant reviews are for main courses at dinner; prices for main courses at lunch are often cheaper.

Booking Tables

It's always a good idea to reserve a table at upmarket restaurants, especially during the high season; almost without fail the phone will be answered by someone who speaks English. That said, we have spent months researching in Prague and mostly did just fine without making any reservations at all.

Tipping

Traditionally, Prague restaurants have not included a service charge on the bill (check, though; more and more places seem to be tacking a 10% service charge to the tab). In most tourist-area places the helpful message 'Tips Not Included', in English (hint, hint), is printed (or even handwritten, as an extra reminder) on the bill. The normal rate for tipping is 10% of the total.

Normal practice in pubs, cafes and midrange restaurants is to round up the bill to the next 10Kč (or the next 20Kč if it's over 200Kč). The usual protocol is for the staff to hand you the bill and for you, as you hand over the money, to tell them the total amount you want to pay with the tip included.

Change is usually counted out starting with the big notes, on down to the smallest coins. If you say *děkuji* (thank you) during this process the staff will stop and assume the rest is a tip.

Self-Catering

There is a wide variety of self-catering options available with *potraviny* (grocery or food shops) and supermarkets everywhere, the best-stocked and priciest being in flashy department stores near the centre. Note that some perishable supermarket food items bear a date of manufacture *(datum výroby)* plus a 'consume-within…' *(spotřebujte do…)* period, whereas others (such as long-life milk) have a stated minimum shelflife *(minimální trvanlivost)* date, after which the freshness of the product is not guaranteed.

PRICE GUIDE

The price guide indicates the average cost of a dinner mains dish:

€€€	more than 600Kč (more than €24)
€€	250Kč to 599Kč (€10 to €24)
€	less than 250Kč (less than €10)

FUNNY, I DON'T REMEMBER ORDERING THAT!

Keep in mind that nothing comes for free in Prague restaurants – if the waiter offers you fries with that, and you accept, you'll be charged for them. Bread, mayonnaise, mustard, vegetables… almost everything has a price tag. Many restaurants also have a *couvert* (cover charge), which every diner must pay regardless of what they eat and even if they eat nothing. It's not a scam; it's just the way things are done. If the menu has no prices, ask for them. Don't be intimidated by the language barrier; know exactly what you're ordering. If something's not available and the waiter suggests an alternative, ask for the price. Immediately return anything you didn't order and don't want, such as bread, butter or side dishes; don't just leave it to one side or chances are they'll appear on your bill. Most importantly, though, don't let paranoia ruin your meal. The majority of overcharging happens at tourist-oriented restaurants in the city centre. If you're not eating in Old Town Square or Wenceslas Square, or if you're at a new place run by young Czechs, you're unlikely to have any problems.

For supermarket supplies, head over to the Albert Supermarket (Map p108; náměstí Republiky, Staré Město; ☺ 9am-9pm Sun-Wed, 9am-10pm Thu-Sat; Ⓜ Náměstí Republiky), which is beneath the Palladium shopping mall, or to Tesco (Map p110; Národní třída 26, Nové Město; ☺ 8am-9pm Mon-Sat, 9am-8pm Sun; Ⓜ Národní Třída), which is in the basement of the MY Národní Mall.

In Malá Strana you will find the handy Vacek Bio-Market (Map p78; Mostecká 3, Malá Strana; ☺ 7am-10pm Mon-Sat, 10am-10pm Sun), a well-stocked mini-supermarket.

The city has several open-air produce markets. The biggest one in the city centre is the tourist-oriented open-air market (Map p90; Havelská, Staré Město; ☺ 8am-6pm) south of the Old Town Square. More authentic neighbourhood markets – mainly open in the mornings only and closed on Sundays – include the open-air market (off Map p136) on Dejvická, near Hradčanská metro station in Dejvice.

In Staré Město, Bakeshop Praha (Map p90; Kozí 1, Staré Město; ☺ 7am-7pm) is a fantastic bakery that sells some of the best bread in the city, along with pastries, cakes and takeaway sandwiches, salads and quiche.

Delicatessens that are good for stocking up on picnic supplies include Centrum Delikates (Map p108; Palladium Praha Shopping Centre, náměstí Republiky, Nové Město; ☺ 9am-9pm Sun-Wed, 9am-10m Thu-Sat; Ⓜ Náměstí Republiky), which sells smoked meats, cheese, pastries and more. There's also Culinaria (Map p90; Skořepká 9, Staré Město; ☺ 8.30am-8pm Mon-Fri, 10am-7pm Sat, noon-5pm Sun; Ⓜ Národní třída), which sells handmade bread, pastries, French and Italian specialities, and freshly made sandwiches.

Cellarius (Map p110; Lucerna pasáž, Václavské náměstí 36, Nové Město; ☺ 9.30am-9pm Mon-Sat, 3-9pm Sun; Ⓜ Můstek) is the place to head if you're looking for Czech and imported wines.

PRAGUE CASTLE & HRADČANY

Most of the restaurants in the castle district are aimed squarely at the tourist crowds, and the whole area becomes pretty quiet in the evenings after the castle closes. The following places, which are a cut above the usual tourist eateries regarding character and cuisine, are worth seeking out – Vikárka and U zlaté hrušky for Czech food with some atmosphere, Malý Buddha for authentic Asian cooking, and Villa Richter for the view.

U ZLATÉ HRUŠKY
Map p70   Czech €€
☎ 220 514 778; Nový Svět 3, Hradčany; mains 400-700Kč; ☺ 11.30am-3pm & 6.30pm-midnight; 🚊 22

'At the Golden Pear' is a cosy, wood-panelled gourmets' corner, serving beautifully prepared Bohemian fish, fowl and game dishes (tripe fricasee is a speciality) and frequented as much by locals and visiting dignitaries as by tourists (the Czech foreign ministry is just up the road, and Margaret Thatcher once dined here). In summer get a table in its leafy *zahradní restaurace* (garden restaurant) across the street.

VIKÁRKA
Map p62   International €€
☎ 233 311 962; Vikářská 39, Prague Castle; mains 200-400Kč; ☺ 11am-8pm; 🚊 22

The best of the restaurants within the Prague Castle grounds, Vikárka inhabits a warren of beautifully restored medieval rooms, the simple Romanesque and Gothic shapes tastefully set off with splashes of bold colour and period decoration. The menu runs from Czech classics to steak and chicken – the goulash, roast goose and roast pork knuckle are all recommended – and there's a separate kids' menu offering fish fingers, spaghetti or chicken and chips.

VILLA RICHTER Map p70   Czech, French €€

☎ 257 219 079; Staré zamecké schody 6, Hradčany; mains 150-300Kč; ⊙ 10am-11pm; Ⓜ Malostranská
Housed in a restored 18th-century villa in the middle of a replanted medieval vineyard, this place is aimed squarely at the hordes of tourists thronging up and down the Old Castle Steps. But the setting is indeed something special – outdoor tables set on terraces with one of the finest views in the city – and the menu of classic Czech dishes doesn't disappoint. If you want something fancier, the Piano Nobile restaurant within the villa itself offers a French fine-dining menu (three-course dinner 990Kč).

MALÝ BUDDHA Map p70   Asian €

☎ 220 513 894; Úvoz 46, Hradčany; mains 100-250Kč; ⊙ noon-10.30pm Tue-Sun; Ⓡ 22; Ⓥ
Candlelight, incense and a Buddhist shrine characterise this intimate, vaulted restaurant that tries to capture the atmosphere of an oriental tearoom. The menu is a mix of Asian influences, with authentic Thai, Chinese and Vietnamese dishes, many of them vegetarian, and a drinks list that includes ginseng wine, Chinese rose liqueur and all kinds of tea. Credit cards are not accepted.

MALÁ STRANA

You'll be spoilt for choice looking for somewhere to eat in Malá Strana. The tourist crowds are swelled by hungry office workers from the district's many embassies and government offices, and this well-heeled clientele ensures that there are lots of quality restaurants offering a wide range of cuisines. Many of the best restaurants take advantage of a riverside location, or are perched on a hillside with a view over the city.

TERASA U ZLATÉ STUDNĚ
Map p78   International €€€

☎ 257 533 322; U Zlaté Studně 4; mains 720-1150Kč; ⊙ noon-11pm; Ⓜ Malostranská
Perched atop a Renaissance mansion within a champagne cork's pop of the castle, 'At the Golden Well' enjoys one of the finest settings in Prague. Weather will dictate

whether you sit in the plush red-and-gold dining room, or head upstairs to the outdoor terrace – both command a stunning panorama across the red-tiled rooftops of Malá Strana. The kitchen, which has French, Mediterranean and Asian influences, conjures up dishes such as carpaccio of kohlrabi and cucumber, traditional French bouillabaisse, and Argentinian beef steak with foie gras and truffles.

KAMPA PARK Map p78   International €€€

☎ 296 826 112; Na Kampě 8b; mains 500-900Kč; ⊙ 11.30am-1am; Ⓡ 12, 20, 22
Opened way back in 1994, Kampa Park was a pioneer of Prague's fine-dining scene and has attracted countless celebrity visitors including Mick Jagger, Johnny Depp, Lauren Bacall, Robbie Williams, and Bill and Hillary Clinton. The cuisine is as famous as the clientele, from the seared scallops with raisins and capers *beurre blanc,* to the saddle of venison with sweet potato purée and cardamom sauce. Some think that the place has been resting on its laurels in recent years, but it's still hard to beat for a romantic dinner – book a candlelit table on the cobblestoned terrace, draped in fairy lights, right beside the river, with the lights of Charles Bridge glittering on the water.

HERGETOVA CIHELNA
Map p78   International €€

☎ 296 826 103; Cihelná 2b; mains 150-600Kč; ⊙ 11.30am-1am; Ⓜ Malostranská
Housed in a converted 18th-century *cihelná* (brickworks), this place enjoys one of Prague's hottest locations, with a riverside terrace offering sweeping views of Charles Bridge and the Old Town waterfront. The menu is as sweeping as the view, ranging from Czech specialities to burgers and pasta dishes, plus an organic menu that includes crab salad with caviar and dill, and pike-perch with lentil ragout and potato gnocchi. Note that there are two wine lists, one reasonably priced, the other eye-poppingly expensive.

U MALTÉZSKÝCH RYTÍŘŮ
Map p78   Czech, International €€

☎ 257 530 075; Prokopská 10; mains 180-400Kč; ⊙ 1-11pm; Ⓡ 12, 20, 22
'At the Maltese Knights' is a cosy and romantic olde-worlde restaurant, with candlelit tables tucked into niches in the stone-and-brick Gothic vaults downstairs

(the ground-floor tables are much less atmospheric). Classic Bohemian offerings include roast wild boar with rosehip sauce, and organic carp stuffed with tomatoes, mushrooms and capers, but there are also international dishes such as steak Chateaubriand, and a couple of vegetarian dishes such as stuffed aubergine, and fettuccine with spinach, goat's cheese and roast walnuts.

U MALÉ VELRYBY Map p78   International €€
☎ 257 214 703; Valdštejnská 14; mains 280-380Kč; ☽ noon-3pm & 6-11pm; Ⓜ Malostranská
Restaurants come and go quickly in Prague's rapidly evolving dining scene, so it's good to see that this one has survived those crucial first few years. It's a tiny place – only eight tables – run by a chef-proprietor from Cork, Ireland, who gets fresh seafood flown in daily from French markets. The seared calamari with chilli, lime and ginger is meltingly tender, the seafood pie (fish and mussels topped with crispy potatoes) is tasty and filling, and the crab pasta with lemon and black pepper is deliciously delicate. There is occasional live music from a local guitarist.

CANTINA Map p78   Mexican €€
☎ 257 317 173; Újezd 38; mains 230-340Kč; ☽ 11.30am-midnight Mon-Sat; 🚋 6, 9, 12, 20, 22
This homely hacienda, decked out in bleached pine and Brazilian coffee sacks, serves up the most authentic margaritas in Prague – perhaps a little light on the tequila, but nicely iced and with a good zing of fresh lime. The menu is as good as Tex-Mex gets in the city centre, with big portions of burrito, chimichanga, quesadilla and fajitas with both meat and vegetarian fillings; if the salsa isn't hot enough for you, there are bottles of chilli sauce on the table to add a bit of bite. This place is insanely popular, so get here early, book a table, or be prepared to wait.

NOI Map p78   Asian €€
☎ 257 311 411; Újezd 19; mains 200-300Kč; ☽ 11am-1am; 🚋 12, 20, 22
A restaurant that feels a bit like a club, Noi is super-stylish but with a chilled-out, Far Eastern atmosphere. The decor is based around Buddha statues, lotus blossoms, lanterns and soft lighting, with curtains made from mother-of-pearl disks. The menu follows the Asian theme, with com-

top picks

BEST BREAKFASTS

- **Red Hot & Blues** (Map p90; ☎ 222 314 639; Jakubská 12, Staré Město; mains 200-400Kč; ☽ 9am-11pm; Ⓜ Náměstí Republiky) Serves a range of breakfasts, including pancakes and maple syrup, and a full British fry-up; the 'Home Run Special' will soak up the heaviest hangover, and lay a firm foundation for further debauchery. Breakfast is served to 11.30am weekdays and to 4pm on weekends.

- **Kavárna Pavilón** (Map p125; ☎ 222 097 201; Vinohrady Pavilón, Vinohradská 50, Vinohrady; mains 115-200Kč; ☽ 8am-9pm Mon-Fri, 9am-9pm Sat & Sun; Ⓜ Náměstí Míru; 🛜 Ⓥ) Bright, airy cafe in upmarket shopping centre; offers excellent coffee, eggs several ways, and the best almond croissants in town.

- **Globe Bookstore & Café** (Map p110; ☎ 224 934 203; Pštrossova 6, Nové Město; mains 110-210Kč; ☽ 9.30am-midnight; Ⓜ Karlovo Náměstí; 🛜) Excellent brunch served 9.30am to 3pm Saturday and Sunday, including bacon, egg and hash browns, blueberry pancakes, and freshly squeezed juices. Lighter breakfasts served 9.30am to 11.30am weekdays.

- **Káva Káva Káva** (Map p90; ☎ 224 228 862; Platýz pasáž, Národní třída 37, Staré Město; snacks 30-70Kč; ☽ 7am-10pm Mon-Fri, 9am-10pm Sat & Sun; Ⓜ Národní Třída; 🛜) Has some of the best coffee in town, accompanied by toasted bagels, croissants, cakes and pastries. Breakfast served all day.

- **Fraktal** (Map p136; ☎ 777 794 094; Šmeralova 1, Holešovice; mains 100-300Kč; ☽ 1am-midnight; 🚋 6, 9, 22; 🛜) This expat bar (see p190) offers a brunch menu from 11am to 3.30pm Saturday and Sunday, with dishes ranging from omelette with salmon, garlic and dill, to steak and eggs, to huevos rancheros (eggs Mexican style).

petent Thai dishes such as chicken in red curry sauce, and pad thai noodles, which – unusually for a Prague restaurant – actually have a hefty chilli kick.

CAFÉ DE PARIS Map p78   French €€
☎ 603 160 718; Maltézské náměstí 4; mains 190-290Kč; ☽ noon-midnight; 🚋 6, 9, 12, 20, 22
A little corner of France tucked away on a quiet square, the Café de Paris is small, straightforward and unpretentious. So is

top picks

VEGETARIAN RESTAURANTS

- Beas Vegetarian Dhaba (p168)
- Café FX (p173)
- Country Life (p168)
- Lehká Hlava (p168)
- Maitrea (p168)

the menu – just a couple of choices, onion soup or foie gras terrine to start, followed by entrecôte steak with chips, salad and a choice of sauces (they're very proud of the Café de Paris sauce, made to a 75-year-old recipe with 35 ingredients, and very nice it is too). There are also one or two daily specials, including a vegetarian alternative. The wine list offers a decent range of French wines, including a Muscadet that's good value at 399Kč a bottle.

CAFÉ SAVOY Map p78   International €

☎ 257 311 562; Vítězná 5, Malá Strana; mains 120-250Kč; � 8am-10.30pm Mon-Fri, 9am-10.30pm Sat & Sun; 🚊 6, 9, 22; 🛜

The Savoy is a beautifully restored belle époque cafe, with haughty black-and-white suited waiting staff and a Viennese-style menu of hearty soups, salads and roast meats. There's also a good breakfast menu with plenty of healthy choices, but a 'Full English' that includes German frankfurters and slices of fresh apple along with the bacon and egg? Surely some mistake!

CUKRKÁVALIMONÁDA

Map p78   International €

☎ 257 530 628; Lázeňská 7; mains 100-200Kč; � 9am-7pm; 🚊 12, 20, 22; Ⓥ

A cute little cafe-cum-restaurant that combines minimalist modern styling with Renaissance-era painted timber roof-beams, CKL offers fresh, homemade pastas, frittatas, ciabattas, salads and pancakes (sweet and savoury) by day and a slightly more sophisticated bistro menu in the early evening. The coffee is excellent, the hot chocolate is to die for, and the house special elderflower drink (flavoured with mint and lemon) is crisp and refreshing. Since you ask, the name means 'sugar, coffee, lemonade' – the phrase is the Czech equivalent of 'eeny-meeny-miny-moe'.

STARÉ MĚSTO

The Old Town is littered with tourist traps, especially around Old Town Square, but there are also plenty of excellent restaurants to discover. The maze of streets leading away from Old Town Square contains many hidden gems, while the swanky strip of Pařížská boasts a more obvious string of stylish, up-market eateries. The classic Staré Město dining room is in a brick-lined cellar – you'll soon become a connoisseur of subterranean decor.

ALLEGRO Map p90   Italian €€€

☎ 221 427 000; Veleslavínova 2a; 4/5-course dinner 2550/2950Kč; � 11.30am-10.30pm; Ⓜ Staroměstská

The Czech Republic's first (and so far only) Michelin-starred restaurant, part of the Four Seasons Hotel, oozes understated elegance with lots of polished wood panelling and art deco–style glass, and boasts a terrace with stunning night-time views of the floodlit castle. It's a superb setting for superb food – the Italian chef turns out inspired dishes that range from roulade of marinated sea bream scented with jasmine, to grilled red snapper with ginger-marinated octopus and smoked carrot sauce.

CASA ARGENTINA

Map p90   South American €€€

☎ 222 311 512; Dlouhá 35; mains 250-1600Kč; � 9am-2am; Ⓜ Náměstí Republiky

Prague now boasts around half a dozen South American steakhouses specialising in charcoal-grilled Argentine or Brazilian beef, but the consensus among expat diners is that the kitchen at Casa Argentina serves up the best rare steak in town. Service can be laid-back, verging on lackadaisical, and the atmosphere is idiosyncratic, to say the least, with kitschy Latin American trappings, a caged lizard, a live toucan on a perch, and a couple of professional dancers who tango among the tables. Whatever; you're only here for the beef.

V ZÁTIŠÍ

Map p90   International, Modern Czech €€€

☎ 222 221 155; Liliová 1; 2-/3-course meal 890/990Kč; � noon-3pm & 5.30-11pm; 🚊 17, 18

'Still Life' is one of Prague's top restaurants, famed for the quality of its cuisine. The decor is bold and modern, with quirky glassware, boldly patterned wallpapers and cappuccino-coloured crushed-velvet chairs.

Of the 10 or so main courses on offer, four are seafood and the rest are meat – nothing vegetarian. There are also gourmet versions of traditional Czech dishes – the crispy roast duckling with red cabbage and herb dumplings is superb. If the three-course dinner is not enough, you can lash out on the five-course *dégustation* menu (1170Kč; plus 770Kč extra for wines to match the dishes).

LA PROVENCE
Map p90   French €€
☎ 296 826 155; Štupartská 9; mains 300-700Kč; ☷ 11am-11pm; Ⓜ Náměstí Republiky
With its dark-wood beams, cushion-strewn benches, dim yellow lighting and shelves crammed with cooking implements, the basement restaurant at La Provence makes a good fist of passing itself off as a French country kitchen. The menu matches the decor, ranging from escargots with parsley and garlic butter to rabbit Provençal in a creamy tarragon sauce. In the evening, when candlelight and soft piano music add to the atmosphere, it's an ideal spot for a romantic tête-à-tête.

KHAJURAHO Map p90   Indian €€
☎ 224 242 860; Richtrův dům, Michalská 25; mains 400-650Kč; ☷ 11am-11pm; Ⓜ Můstek; Ⓥ
The Khajuraho sprawls through a series of vaulted medieval rooms given an oriental atmosphere with Persian rugs scattered on the floor, Indian statues tucked into niches, and sequinned textiles glowing colourfully beneath glass tabletops. Service is friendly and attentive, and the food is bursting with authentic flavours – cumin, coriander, ginger, garlic and chilli – ranging from Kashmiri dishes to *handi* (curry cooked in a deep metal pot) and South Indian specialities, with plenty of choices that will appeal to vegetarians. There's a range of good-value thalis (Indian platters) and set menus costing from 300Kč per person.

LES MOULES Map p90   Belgian €€
☎ 222 315 022; Pařížská 19; mains 300-600Kč; ☷ 11am-midnight; ☷ 17
This impressive, wood-panelled, Belgian-style brasserie serves up steaming pans of mussels (295Kč for a kilo) in a range of sauces, from traditional *marinière* (white wine, cream and garlic) to Thai style (lemongrass, lime and coconut milk), as

well as steaks, pork ribs, boeuf bourgignon and lobster fresh from the *vivier* (live tank; be prepared to shell out 990Kč). The bar offers a selection of Belgian beers, including Stella Artois, Leffe and Hoegaarden on tap, and Chimay, Achel and La Trappe in bottles.

AMBIENTE PASTA FRESCA
Map p90   Italian €€
☎ 224 230 244; Celetná 11; mains 175-430Kč; ☷ 11am-midnight; Ⓜ Náměstí Republiky; Ⓥ
Slick styling and service with a smile complement an extensive menu at this busy Italian restaurant. Choose from dishes such as melt-in-the-mouth carpaccio of beef, piquant spaghetti *aglio-olio* with chilli and crisp pancetta, and rich creamy risotto with *porcini*, along with a wide range of Italian and Czech wines. There's a long, narrow cafe at street level, but you'll find a more formal, intimate cellar restaurant located down below.

KOLKOVNA
Map p90   Czech €€
☎ 224 819 701; V Kolkovně 8; mains 155-400Kč; ☷ 11am-midnight; Ⓜ Staroměstská
Owned and operated by the Pilsner Urquell brewery, Kolkovna is a stylish, modern take on the traditional Prague beer hall, with decor by top Czech designers, and posh (but hearty) versions of classic Czech dishes such as goulash, roast duck and Moravian sparrow (see the boxed text, p161), including the Czech favourite, pork and dumplings (the dish of the day is only 95Kč). All washed down with exquisite Urquell beer, of course.

AMBIENTE PIZZA NUOVA
Map p90   Italian €€
☎ 221 803 308; Revoluční 1; mains 165-370Kč; ☷ 11.30am-11.30pm; Ⓜ Náměstí Republiky
Another good idea from the Ambiente team is this cool 1st-floor space next door to the Kotva shopping centre, filled with big tables and banquettes with picture windows overlooking náměstí Republiky. For a fixed price (298Kč per person before 6pm, 398Kč after) you get an all-you-can-eat deal – either help yourself from the salad and antipasti buffet, or choose from the hot pasta dishes and pizzas offered by a band of wandering waiters (buffet and pizza-pasta combined costs 475/528Kč). Wine by the glass is around 75Kč.

EATING STARÉ MĚSTO

KABUL Map p90 Afghan €

☎ 224 235 452; Karolíny Světlé 14; mains 145-270Kč; ✸ noon-11pm; ⓡ 6, 9, 18, 22; Ⓥ

Cosy rather than cramped, the Kabul has a welcoming, old-world atmosphere with worn wooden furniture and oriental rugs draped on the walls. It serves a range of unusual Afghani dishes, including *ashak* (a sort of ravioli stuffed with chopped leeks and mint, served with a rich sauce of minced beef and tomato), various lamb and chicken kebabs, and tasty vegetarian specialities (roast aubergine, okra with tomato, garlic and spices), served with warm, tasty flatbread on the side. For those who don't fancy the Afghan offerings, the flatbread oven is also used for pizza.

LOKÁL Map p90 Czech €

☎ 222 316 265; Dlouhá 33; mains 120-220Kč; ✸ 11am-1am Mon-Fri, noon-1am Sat, noon-10pm Sun; ⓡ 5, 8, 14

Who'd've thought it possible? A classic Czech beer hall (albeit with slick modern decor), excellent *tankové pivo* (tanked Pilsner Urquell), a daily-changing menu of traditional Bohemian dishes, and – can this be true? – smiling, efficient, friendly service! Top Prague restaurant chain Ambiente has finally turned its hand to Czech cuisine, and the result has been so successful the place is always busy, mostly with locals. The menus are all in Czech, but the staff seem happy to translate for tourists. This beer hall has entrances on both Dlouhá and Rybna.

LEHKÁ HLAVA Map p90 Vegetarian €

☎ 222 220 665; Boršov 2; mains 120-210Kč; ✸ 11.30am-11.30pm Mon-Fri, noon-11.30pm Sat & Sun; ⓡ 17, 18; Ⓥ

Tucked away down a narrow cul-de-sac, Lehká Hlava (the name means 'clear head') exists in a little world of its own. A peaceful atrium leads to two unusually decorated dining rooms, both with a vaguely psychedelic vibe – one with a rocket-shaped light fitting that projects coloured images onto the walls, the other topped by a dark blue vault pierced by twinkling stars. Both have tables lit from within, either studded with glowing glass spheres or with a radiant wood-grain effect. In the kitchen the emphasis is on healthy, freshly prepared vegetarian and vegan dishes, ranging from hummus and roast veggies to tofu Thai red

curry to a spicy oriental stir-fry that could easily feed two at lunch.

MAITREA Map p90 Vegetarian €

☎ 221 711 631; Týnská ulička 6; mains 120-160Kč; ✸ 11.30am-11.30pm Mon-Fri, noon-11.30pm Sat & Sun; Ⓜ Staroměstská; Ⓥ

The new sister restaurant to Lehká Hlava, Maitrea (a Buddhist term meaning 'the future Buddha') is a beautifully designed space full of flowing curves and organic shapes, from the sensuous polished-oak furniture and fittings to the blossom-like lampshades, set off by Buddha statues and Tibetan mantras. The menu is inventive and wholly vegetarian, with dishes such as red bean chilli tortillas, beetroot cakes with sauerkraut and polenta, and pasta with smoked tofu, spinach, cream and parmesan. The weekday lunchtime special offers soup, main course and glass of mineral water for 108Kč, and the Bernard *švestkové pivo* (nonacoholic plum-flavoured beer) makes a great accompaniment.

COUNTRY LIFE Map p90 Vegetarian €

☎ 224 213 366; Melantrichova 15; mains 90-180Kč; ✸ 10.30am-8pm Mon-Thu, 10.30am-3pm Fri, noon-6pm Sun, closed Sat; Ⓜ Můstek; Ⓥ

Prague's first-ever health-food shop opened in 1991, and is an all-vegan cafeteria and sandwich bar offering inexpensive salads, sandwiches, pizzas, vegetarian goulash, sunflower-seed burgers and soy drinks (food is sold by weight, around 30Kč per 100g). There is plenty of seating in the rear courtyard but it can still get crowded at lunchtime, so go early or buy sandwiches to go.

BEAS VEGETARIAN DHABA

Map p90 Vegetarian, Indian €

☎ 608 035 727; Týnská 19; mains 90-130Kč; ✸ 11am-8pm Mon-Sat, 11am-6pm Sun; Ⓜ Náměstí Republiky; Ⓥ

Tucked away in a courtyard off Týnská, this friendly, informal little restaurant offers vegetarian curries (cooked by chefs from North India), served with rice, salad, chutneys and raita; the samosas are excellent, especially with a dab of fig chutney on the side. Unusually for Prague, there's some genuine chilli heat in the food, which is tasty and good value (food sold by weight, around 16Kč per 100g). This is also a great place to meet Czechs of an alternative bent.

NOVÉ MĚSTO & VYŠEHRAD

The New Town has an eclectic collection of eating places, with cafes and traditional Czech pubs as well as a range of international restaurants. The main eating streets are Wenceslas Square and Na Příkopě, lined with restaurants offering cuisines that cross the world from Italy to India and Argentina to Japan; there are also lots of less obvious and more appealing eateries hidden in the backstreets between Wenceslas Square and the river.

CÉLESTE Map p110   French €€€

☎ 221 984 160; Rašínovo nábřeží 80, Nové Město; mains 550-700Kč; ⏰ noon-2.30pm & 6.30-10.30pm Mon-Sat; Ⓜ Karlovo Náměstí

Located on the 7th floor of the spectacular **Dancing Building** (p116), Céleste's dining room and outdoor terrace offer stunning views across the river to Malá Strana and Prague Castle. The cuisine is French, with the accent on seafood and meat dishes – only one vegetarian main course on the menu here – and the atmosphere is crisply formal. The Breton chef turns out imaginative dishes such as salad of purple artichoke, seared squid and fava beans, and pan-fried skate with cockles, Provençal herbs and rosé wine sauce. The two- or three-course lunch menu (450/550Kč) is good value.

ZAHRADA V OPEŘE

Map p110   Italian, International €€

☎ 224 239 685; Legerová 75, Vinohrady; mains 280-500Kč; ⏰ 11.30am-1am; Ⓜ Muzeum or ⓡ 11

This may be the best food for the money in the city, with excellently prepared Czech dishes such as *svíčková* as well as Italian-inflected recipes of steaks and seafood. The sophisticated contemporary decor manages to be both unstuffy and elegant at the same time. For years, the restaurant was trapped in the security cordon of US-funded Radio Free Europe/Radio Liberty next door, making it a real effort to find the front door, but the radio station moved to a more remote location in 2009, leaving the entryway relatively unobstructed. The location, right next to the Prague State Opera, makes it a natural for a pre- or post-concert repast. The kitchen is open until midnight.

KOGO Map p110   Italian €€

☎ 221 451 259; Slovanský dům, Na Příkopě 22, Nové Město; pizzas 200-300Kč, mains 250-680Kč; ⏰ 11am-11pm; Ⓜ Náměstí Republiky; 🛜

Chic and businesslike, but also relaxed and child-friendly (highchairs provided), Kogo is a stylish restaurant serving top-notch pizza, pasta, steak and seafood – the rich, tomatoey *zuppa di pesce* (fish soup) is delicious, as is the *risotto alla pescatora* (made with squid, mussels, shrimp and octopus). There's also a good range of wines available by the glass. On summer evenings, tables filled with conversation and candlelight spill over into the leafy courtyard.

RIO'S VYŠEHRAD

Map p120   Mediterranean €€

☎ 224 922 156; Štulcova 2, Vyšehrad; mains 250-600Kč; ⏰ 10am-midnight; Ⓜ Vyšehrad

Located opposite the Church of Sts Peter & Paul in the Vyšehrad fortress, this is an attractive modern restaurant set in an ancient building. There's an elegant indoor dining room and an informal terrace, but the main attraction is the garden, a lovely spot for an outdoor meal in summer. The international gourmet menu includes dishes such as salad of grilled octopus, veal saltimbocca, and chargrilled Argentian beef, plus Czech classics such as roast duck and spicy goulash.

OLIVA Map p120   Mediterranean €€

☎ 222 520 288; Plavecká 4, Vyšehrad; mains 400-485Kč; ⏰ 11.30am-3pm & 6pm-midnight Mon-Fri, 6pm-midnight Sat; ⓡ 3, 7, 16, 17, 21

A small, friendly, family-run restaurant focusing on fresh Mediterranean cuisine, Oliva has become a victim of its own popularity. A menu of carefully prepared dishes that include rocket salad with avocado, gorgonzola, Parma ham and sesame dressing; mussel, prawn and fennel chowder; and veal with beetroot gratin and buttered Brussels sprouts, has pulled in so many customers that on weekend evenings the waiters can be overwhelmed. But the food is so good that it's well worth enduring the occasional spell of slow service.

SUTERÉN Map p110   International €€

☎ 224 933 657; Masarykovo nábřeží 26, Nové Město; mains 275-400Kč; ⏰ 11.30am-midnight Mon-Sat; ⓡ 17, 21

'The Basement' is a beautiful cellar space, where modern detailing complements the

TALKING FOOD WITH CZECH PLEASE'S 'BREWSTA'

Restaurant blogs in the Czech Republic are still fairly rare, even less common in English. Czech Please (http://czechoutchannel.blogspot.com), which debuted in February 2007, was the first on the Prague scene. Written by an enigmatic American expat known only as 'Brewsta', Czech Please covers everything from lowly burgers and pizzas to the best high-end Italian, Thai and, naturally, Czech cooking. The blog's accessibility and photos have gained it a wide following. Brewsta's reviews are now published regularly on the leading local expat website (www.expats.cz) and the blog itself racks up some 8000 unique page views each month, with the majority of visitors being from the UK, US and Czech Republic. We contacted Brewsta with the hope he might share a few tips on dining out in Prague, including, naturally, where he himself likes to eat.

During the course of living in Prague and writing your blog the past couple of years, what are some of the main trends you've seen in local restaurants? Are things getting better or worse? The quality and diversity of Prague's restaurant scene is dramatically better than it was 10 years ago. There are many more high-end spots these days, including one, Allegro (p166), with a Michelin star. But the city still doesn't come close to the depth or diversity of major European capitals such as London or Paris.

Are there any special tricks that visitors should watch out for? What are some classic scams that waiters use to pad the bill? One common method is the addition of a 'service charge' without informing the customer. Other tricks include charging for unordered bread or pretzels placed on the table, pouring a very expensive wine by the glass, or just throwing an extra charge on the bill, hoping it won't be read too carefully.

The centre of Prague is filled with tourists and very specious-looking restaurants that in reality are thinly veiled tourist traps. Are there any decent places near the centre where you can find an affordably priced authentic Czech meal? In the centre of Prague, I'd recommend Lokál (p168) or any of the Pilsner Urquell Original Restaurant franchises, such as Kolkovna (p167).

Can you let us in on a couple Brewsta favourites? If you only had a couple of meals to spend in Prague, where would you eat? A great-looking room with a quality kitchen that's good for breakfast, lunch or dinner is the Café Savoy (p166). Personal favourites include Aromi (p172), Céleste (p169), Perpetuum (p176), Osteria Da Clara (p172), Noi (p165), Bohemia Bagel (p176), and the Potrefená husa restaurants. *An interview with Czech Please blogger 'Brewsta' by Mark Baker.*

old red-brick and wooden beams perfectly. Cream linen chairs, set at gleaming black tables with a single, deep-pink rose in the middle of each one, surround a circular glass bar with a colourful aquarium along one wall. The menu leans towards seafood, beef and game, with intriguing dishes such as grilled salmon fillet in a saffron cream sauce with pea-and-mint pancakes; and more traditional fare such as roast lamb shank with rosemary gravy and mashed potato.

U MATĚJE KOTRBY Map p110 Czech €€

☎ 224 930 768; Křemencova 17, Nové Město; mains 130-390Kč; ⊗ noon-11pm; ⓑ 6, 9, 18, 21, 22
It's only 50m away from the tourist trap that is U Fleků, but this place is the real deal – an atmospheric Czech pub strewn with more bric-a-brac, musical instruments and old photos than the average antique shop and, more importantly, sporting a menu of classic Czech grub from goulash made with Pilsner Urquell to pork knuckle braised in dark beer, mustard and horseradish. There's also a range of traditional 'beer snacks' including *utopenci* (sausage pickled in vinegar), Czech cheeses with walnuts and olives, and *libová tlačenka* (pork brawn, or potted head), amusingly translated on the menu as 'homemade headcheese'.

NA RYBÁRNĚ Map p110 Seafood €€

☎ 224 918 885; Gorazdova 17, Nové Město; mains 100-300Kč; ⊗ 10am-11pm Mon-Fri, 11am-11pm Sat & Sun; ⓑ 17, 21
This unassuming little fish restaurant has been around for almost a century and has seen more than a few celebrity diners, ranging from writer Karel Čapek to ex-president Václav Havel, Rolling Stone Mick Jagger and former US secretary of state Madeleine Albright. The menu here offers everything from salmon and tuna to cuttlefish and tiger prawns, but the best dishes are the simplest

and most traditional – trout with herb butter, and daily specials such as baked carp or grilled eel with lemon butter.

MODRÝ ZUB Map p110 *Asian €*
☎ 222 212 622; Jindrvíšská 5, Nové Město; mains 165-275Kč; ⏲ 11am-10.30pm Mon-Fri, noon-10pm Sat & Sun; ▣ 3, 9, 14, 24; Ⓥ

This slick, stylish and deservedly popular noodle bar is ideal for a quick hit of chilli and ginger, just a few paces away from the busy and overpriced eateries of Wenceslas Square. Sit on the high bench along the back wall, or grab a small, square table near the window, and peruse a menu that includes dim sum, warm Thai salads, red, green and yellow Thai curries, stir-fries with fresh Asian flavours, and noodles served all ways, including a yummy pad thai with chicken or prawns.

U NEKLANA Map p120 *Czech €*
☎ 224 916 051; Neklanova 30, Vyšehrad; mains 140-290Kč; ⏲ 11am-midnight; ▣ 7, 18, 24

U Neklana is a welcoming local pub nestled in the corner of one of Prague's coolest apartment buildings, a cubist classic dating from 1915. Decked out in the cheerful red colours of the Budvar brewery, it dishes up hearty Czech fare such as potato and mushroom soup served in a scooped-out loaf of rye bread (the menu is in English and German as well as Czech), and there's a hits-of-the-'80s jukebox providing a suitably retro soundtrack.

KARAVANSERÁJ Map p110 *Lebanese €*
☎ 224 930 390; Masarykovo nábřeží 22, Nové Město; mains 90-260Kč; ⏲ 11am-11pm Mon-Thu, 11am-midnight Fri, noon-midnight Sat, noon-10pm Sun; ▣ 17, 21; 🛜 Ⓥ

Serving as the home base of a travellers' club, this restaurant and tearoom cultivates a ramshackle, relaxed and welcoming atmosphere, with its batik tablecloths, wicker chairs, oriental knick-knacks and library of travel guidebooks. The menu is mostly Lebanese – baba ganoush, falafel, hummus and lamb kebabs – with a couple of Indian dishes thrown in, and there's a huge range of speciality teas to choose from. It's child-friendly too, with highchairs, kids' portions and a collection of toys to play with.

SIAM ORCHID Map p108 *Thai €€*
☎ 222 319 410; Na Poříčí 21, Nové Město; mains 150-210Kč; ⏲ 10am-10pm; ▣ 3, 8, 24, 26

The setting – a scatter of plastic tables and chairs on a 1st-floor balcony hidden up a passage beside a department store – looks none too promising, but this tiny restaurant, tucked away beside a Thai massage studio, offers some of the city's most authentic Thai cuisine. From the crisp, grease-free *po-pia thot* (spring rolls with pork and black mushrooms) and succulent *kai sa-te* (chicken satay) to the fiery *kaeng khiao wan kai* (chicken in green curry with basil), pretty much everything on the menu is a delight.

COUNTRY LIFE Map p110 *Vegetarian €*
☎ 224 247 280; Jungmannova 1, Nové Město; mains 60-180Kč; ⏲ 8.30am-6pm Mon-Fri; ▣ 3, 9, 14, 24; Ⓥ

Country Life is a cafeteria-style health-food restaurant with all-vegan food and buffet service – load up your plate, and pay by weight (that's right! You weigh in at the till). There are only four tables at this branch, which caters mainly to the takeaway trade – if you want a better chance of a seat, head for the branch in Staré Město (p168).

PIZZERIA KMOTRA Map p110 *Pizza €*
☎ 224 934 100; V Jirchářích 12, Nové Město; pizza 100-160Kč; ⏲ 11am-midnight; Ⓜ Národní Třída; v

One of Prague's oldest and best pizzerias, 'the Godmother' can rustle up more than two dozen varieties of pizza, from margherita to marinara, cooked in a genuine wood-fired pizza oven. Sit beside the bar upstairs, or head down to the basement where you can watch the chef slinging pizza dough in the open kitchen – both areas are nonsmoking. It gets busy here after 8pm, so try to snag a table before then.

VINOHRADY & VRŠOVICE

Outside the centre, Vinohrady has Prague's largest concentration of good restaurants, and the choice is only getting better as the area moves steadily upmarket. Most are clustered around náměstí Míru and the long residential street, Mánesova, that parallels Vinohradská from the Muzeum to the Jiřího z Poděbrad metro stops. Vršovice, a mostly working-class district, starts at the southeast corner of Vinohrady. It's not as fruitful, but has a couple of pleasant surprises, including one of the city's best Tuscan-style hideaways.

AROMI Map p125   Italian €€€

☎ 222 713 222; Mánesova 78, Vinohrady; mains 450-600Kč; ☽ noon-11pm Mon-Sat, to 10pm Sun; Ⓜ Jiřího z Poděbrad or Ⓔ 11

Red brick, polished wood, country-style furniture and sprigs of rosemary and thyme on each table create a rustic atmosphere in this gourmet Italian restaurant. Brisk and businesslike at lunchtime, romantic in the evening, Aromi has a reputation for authentic Italian cuisine, from the *zuppa di cannellini* (cannellini bean soup) to the *branzino al guazzetto* (sea bass baked in a sea-salt crust; seafood is a speciality). The service can get a little over the top, with one waiter giving you the specials list, while another pours water and a third brings the bread basket, but just relax and let yourself be pampered.

AMBIENTE Map p125   International €€

☎ 222 727 851; Mánesova 59, Vinohrady; mains 200-450Kč; ☽ 11am-midnight Mon-Fri, noon-midnight Sat & Sun; Ⓜ Jiřího z Poděbrad or Ⓔ 11

'Ambiente' means atmosphere, and the warm yellow walls, banquettes, bamboo-and-basketwork chairs and rich mahogany woodwork help create a relaxing one at this flagship of the well-run Ambiente chain. The American-themed menu offers a huge range of salads (including Caesar, goat's cheese, roast veggies, avocado), tasty pasta dishes, barbecue ribs, fajitas, steaks and chicken wings, and there are excellent house wines for around 90Kč a glass.

MOZAIKA Map p125   International €€

☎ 224 253 011; Nitranská 13, Vinohrady; mains 220-400Kč; ☽ 11.30am-11pm; Ⓜ Jiřího z Poděbrad

Not quite the undiscovered gem it was a couple of years ago, nevertheless this is one of the most dependably good restaurants in the neighbourhood. The theme is an updated French bistro, with beef *tournedos* and boeuf bourguignon sharing the spotlight with international entrees like stir-fries, BBQ pork ribs and our personal favourite: salmon wrapped in seaweed and served with wasabi mashed potatoes. The service is usually spot-on and, rare for Prague, it has a good selection of wines by the glass. Reserve on the tiny sidewalk terrace in warm weather.

AMIGOS Map p125   Mexican €€

☎ 222 250 594; Anny Letenské 16 (cnr Mánesova), Vinohrady; mains 200-400Kč; ☽ 11.30am-midnight; Ⓜ Muzeum or Ⓔ 11

Amigos offers decent Mexican and South American cooking, just a short walk up Mánesova from the Muzeum metro station. There are tasty burritos, tacos, enchiladas and quesadillas, as well as steaks, hamburgers, stir-fries and big dinner salads. The atmosphere often feels more like a pub than a restaurant, and the mood can get rowdy on occasion. Fun.

OSTERIA DA CLARA Map p125   Italian €€

☎ 271 726 548; Mexická 7, Vršovice; mains 200-400Kč; ☽ 11am-3pm & 6-11pm Mon-Fri, noon-3.30pm & 6-11pm Sat; Ⓜ Náměstí Míru & Ⓔ 4, 22

This minuscule Tuscan-style trattoria offers some of the most authentic and best-value Italian cooking in the city, though it will take a good map or a taxi to find the place. The menu varies from month to month, but expect a handful of creative pasta dishes and main courses built around duck, beef, pork and seafood. The chef prides himself on choosing the best ingredients he can find, including fresh seafood from Italy every Wednesday and Friday. Best to reserve in advance – there are only eight tables.

PASTIČKA Map p125   Czech €€

☎ 222 253 228; Blanická 25 (cnr Mánesova), Vinohrady; mains 200-400Kč; ☽ 11am-10pm Mon-Fri, 5-11pm Sat & Sun; Ⓜ Jiřího z Poděbrad or Ⓔ 11

A warm, inviting ground-floor pub with a little garden out the back, Pastička is great for a beer or a meal. The decor is part 1920s Prague and part Irish pub. In the evenings, the rows of tables stretching past the bar are normally filled with students. Most come for the beer, but the mix of international and traditional Czech dishes is very good. The garden is popular with a local office crowd at lunchtime.

U BILÉ KRÁVY Map p125   French, Steakhouse €€

☎ 224 239 570; Rubešova 10, Vinohrady; mains 150-300Kč; ☽ 11.30am-11pm Mon-Fri; 5-11pm Sat; Ⓜ Náměstí Míru or Muzeum

Steak lovers have a special treat in store. This French-run, Lyonnais-styled bistro has some of the best steaks, at the best prices, in town. The name 'White Cow' refers to the Charollais breed of white cows from Burgundy used to make the restaurant's signature steaks. The chef insists the meat is never frozen and that the beef is allowed to age 21 days to maximise tenderness and flavour. Added to that is the authentic bistro feel, the solicitous service and the excellent wine selection, both by the bottle and the glass. It's is a little hard to find, on a forgotten side street just behind the National Museum, within easy walking distance of the Muzeum metro stop.

CHEERS Map p125 — International €

☎ 222 513 108; cnr náměstí Míru & Belgická, Vinohrady; mains 150-340Kč; ⏲ 11am-1am; Ⓜ Náměstí Míru

Cheers is a modern take on the traditional Czech pub, with bright and breezy colours, lots of stainless steel and a splash of contemporary art. The menu plays in pretty close to the Czech vest, with staples like goulash, roast chicken and pork and our choice: smaz/vený sýr (fried cheese). Lunchtimes can get packed as this is a favourite haunt of the local office crowd. Lunch specials easily bring this restaurant into the budget range.

CHUDOBA Map p125 — Czech €

☎ 222 250 624; Vinohradská 67, Vinohrady; mains 130-260Kč; ⏲ 11am-1am Mon-Sat, 11am-midnight Sun; 🚋 11

This upmarket Czech tavern-restaurant occupies a choice corner on a leafy section of Vinohradská. The patrons are mostly young professionals and couples out for an after-work beer or a very good and reasonably priced Czech meal. The decor plays with the 'Ye Olde Vinohrady' theme, with sepia-tone photos on the wall, and polished wooden floors. The food is a mix of Czech and Continental, with standards like roast duck and goulash sharing the menu with pork ribs and a very hearty meat fondue. There's a sidewalk terrace in nice weather.

MASALA Map p125 — Indian €

☎ 222 251 601; Mánesova 13, Vinohrady; mains 150-250Kč; ⏲ noon-11pm Mon-Fri, 5-11pm Sat & Sun; Ⓜ Muzeum or 🚋 11; Ⓥ

Just what Prague needed: an excellent, unpretentious Indian restaurant, with all of the good food and none of the stultifying atmosphere and stiff service you normally find at Indian places here. The Indian couple who run Masala aim for what they call home-style service, meaning relaxed presentation and good home cooking. One minor quibble is that the food could use more spice. On a recent visit the lamb rogan josh had a hint of ketchup, but the meat was tender and the accompanying naan bread was just right: crispy on the edges and soft in the centre.

U DĚDKA Map p125 — International €

☎ 222 522 784; Na Kozačce 12, Vinohrady; mains 150-250Kč; ⏲ 10am-11pm Mon-Fri, 2pm-1am Sat; Ⓜ Náměstí Míru, 🚋 4, 22

This pleasantly upmarket pub-restaurant, situated near the top of Voroněžská on the border between Vinohrady and Vršovice, has a quiet, tree-covered terrace out the front. The modern decor pulls in a mix of Czech professionals, students and the occasional tourist from a nearby pension, while the menu is a blend of Czech specialities plus well-done bar food, such as chicken quesadillas and cheeseburgers. The latter are easily the best in this part of town.

CAFÉ FX Map p125 — Vegetarian €

☎ 224 254 776; Bělehradská 120, Vinohrady; mains 120-240Kč; ⏲ 11am-midnight; Ⓜ IP Pavlova; Ⓥ

For nearly two decades Café FX has been a vegetarian beacon in the gritty neighbourhood surrounding the IP Pavlova metro stop. The food – mostly salads, stir-fries and veggie burgers – is reliably good, though the menu has changed little since opening day and it's hard not to get the feeling the place is coasting. Diners seem not to mind and most days finds the cafe bustling with students, clubbers and even the odd businessperson or two. The cafe is part of the nightclub Radost FX (p200), lending a kind of glittery sheen to the place (which sadly doesn't extend to the lavatories, which make the public toilets in the metro look good).

LAS ADELITAS Map p125 — Mexican €

☎ 222 542 031; Americká 8, Vinohrady; mains 150-200Kč; ⏲ 11am-11pm Mon-Fri, 2-11pm Sat & Sun; Ⓜ Náměstí Míru

This small and informal Mexican restaurant run by a group of friends from Mexico offers the closest thing to authentic Tex-Mex you're likely to find from here to Warsaw. Delicious tacos, burritos and enchiladas are crafted with love from handmade tortillas. The ambience is a little sterile, but no one is here for a candlelight dinner – just very good and good-value nosh.

PIZZERIA GROSSETO

Map p125 — Italian, Pizza €

☎ 224 252 778; Francouzská 2, Vinohrady; mains 120-180Kč; ⏲ 11.30am-11pm; Ⓜ Náměstí Míru; Ⓥ

This bustling Vinohrady pizzeria, just off Náměstí Míru, serves very good pizzas, with inventive toppings such as asparagus and ricotta cheese, as well as homemade pastas and original desserts. Too often in Prague, pizzas come only with standard toppings like ham or mushrooms – but not here. The garden terrace at the back is a secluded gem and something of a local secret. To find it, walk left past the front entrance of the pizzeria in the direction of Francouzská and through a small passageway to the right.

HA NOI Map p125   Vietnamese €
☎ 222 514 448; Slezská 57, Vinohrady; mains 80-100Kč; ☺ 10am-10pm Mon-Fri, 2-11pm Sat; Ⓜ Jiřího z Poděbrad or Flora

Though Prague is home to thousands of Vietnamese immigrants, outside of being invited into a family's home it's nearly impossible to find decent Vietnamese cooking. Ha Noi remains by far the best of a handful of mostly mediocre options. Decent spring rolls, both fresh and fried, and two types of seasoned *pho* (broth with noodles), with either beef or chicken as a base, are on offer. The unfussy decor – just a few wooden tables and the typical oriental kitsch – make it better suited to a hearty lunch than that special night out.

ŽIŽKOV & KARLÍN

Žižkov is more famous for its pubs than its restaurants, but there are new places springing up every year to add to the old stalwarts that have been around for ages. We haven't been able to recommend any restaurants in Karlín yet, but if you're in the area check out Pivovarský Klub (p189), a drinking venue that serves good traditional pub grub.

HANIL Map p130   Japanese, Korean €€
☎ 222 715 867; Slavíkova 24, Žižkov; mains 350-500Kč; ☺ 11am-2.30pm & 5.30-11pm Mon-Sat, 5.30-11pm Sun; Ⓜ Jiří z Poděbrad

White walls, blond-wood lattice screens, paper lanterns and polished granite tables create a relaxed and informal setting where a mixed crowd of businesspeople, locals and expats enjoys authentic Japanese and Korean cuisine without the fuss and formality of more expensive restaurants. Tuck into a hot bowl of tasty *bibimbap* (rice topped with meat and pickled vegetables and spiced with hot pepper paste), or order a sashimi platter – the sushi here is probably the best value in town (70Kč to 150Kč per piece).

MAILSI Map p130   Pakistani €€
☎ 222 717 783; Lipanská 1, Žižkov; mains 200-400Kč; ☺ noon-3pm & 6-11.30pm; ⓖ 5, 9, 26; Ⓥ

Mailsi was Prague's first Pakistani restaurant, and is still one of the city's best for authentic, home-style curry cuisine. The outside is inconspicuous, and it's only the qawwali music that guides you into the attractively decorated green and burgundy dining room with its tropical fishtank. Service is courteous and the food delicious, though prices have edged up in recent years. The *bhaji* is rather plain – just onion and potato thinly sliced, dipped in spiced flour and fried, but very light and crisp – while the *murgh dal* consists of tender chicken in a cumin-spiced lentil sauce.

KUŘE V HODINKÁCH
Map p130   Czech, International €
☎ 222 734 212; Seifertova 26, Žižkov; mains 85-220Kč; ☺ 11am-1am Mon-Fri, noon-1am Fri, 6pm-1am Sun; ⓖ 5, 9, 26

This rock music–themed pub is named after a 1972 album by Czech jazz-rock band Flamengo, which was banned by the communist authorities (it means 'Chicken in the Watch' – hey, it was the '70s, psychedelic drugs and all that…). Decked out in rock memorabilia, and with a choice of buzzing street-level bar or more intimate brick-vaulted basement, it's more upmarket than most Žižkov pubs and has a classy kitchen to match – the menu includes mushroom ragout with potato gnocchi and sour cream, Caesar salad, barbecued chicken drumsticks in ginger, honey and chilli, and a rich, dark and tasty goulash with bacon dumplings.

RESTAURACE AKROPOLIS
Map p130   International €
☎ 296 330 913; Kubelíkova 27, Žižkov; mains 80-230Kč; ☺ 11am-12.30am Mon-Thu, 11am-1.30am Fri, 3pm-12.30am Sat & Sun; ⓖ 5, 9, 26; Ⓥ

The cafe in the famous Palác Akropolis (p202) club is a Žižkov institution, with its eccentric combination of marble panels, quirky metal-work light fittings and weird fishtank installations designed by local artist František Skála. The menu has a good selection of vegetarian dishes, from nachos to gnocchi, plus great garlic soup, searingly hot buffalo wings and steak tartare. Kids are welcome (though it can get a bit smoky) – you'll find toys and colouring books. Dogs are welcome too, and can choose from their own menu of biscuits and chew toys.

HOLEŠOVICE, BUBENEČ & DEJVICE

The outlying neighbourhoods north and west of the city centre are finally coming into their own in terms of quality restaurants. Most of the better places are clustered along the residential streets around the Dejvická metro station. You'll find another grouping within walking distance of Strossmaycrovo náměstí. The far eastern section of Holešovice has seen a boom in property development but is still lacking in decent eateries, yet even here are there are a few new names.

DA EMANUEL
Map p136   Italian €€€

☎ 224 312 934; Charlese De Gaulla 4, Dejvice; mains 500-700Kč; ☽ noon-11pm; Ⓜ Dejvická or Ⓡ 8

This small, elegant Italian-owned place, on a quiet residential street, is one of Dejvice's true destination restaurants. The main dining room, perched romantically below an arched brick ceiling, holds around a dozen tables, each with a vase of fresh flowers and covered in white linens. Try the *tagliata con rucola* (tender slices of filet mignon sprinkled with rocket) or the mussels, served in a salty tomato sauce. Since it's small, you'll have to book in advance.

HANAVSKÝ PAVILÓN
Map p136   Czech, International €€€

☎ 233 323 641; Letenské sady 173, Bubeneč; mains 345-490Kč; ☽ 11am-1am, terrace to 11pm; Ⓡ 18

Perched on a terrace high above the river, this ornate, neobaroque pavilion dating from 1891 houses a smart restaurant with a postcard-perfect view of the Vltava bridges – from April to September you can dine on the outdoor terrace. There's also a three-course set menu (from 375Kč) of Czech classics.

MIRELLIE Map p136   Italian €€

☎ 222 959 999; VP Čkalova 14, Dejvice; mains 180-410Kč; ☽ 11am-11pm; Ⓜ Dejvická or Hradčanská

Given Da Emanuel's wallet-shredding prices, Dejvice was crying out for a more affordable Italian option that doesn't cut too many corners. Mirellie delivers. Like many 'Italian' places around town, Mirellie is run by ex-Yugoslavs, who decamped en masse to Prague in the 1990s. But don't let that dissuade you from trying the delicious

beef carpaccio (served with hot 'pizza' bread), followed by a homemade pasta topped with an inventive sauce like spiced lamb ragout. The seafood is fresh, and the pizzas are also very good, relatively cheap and filling.

KAVALA Map p136   Greek €€

☎ 224 325 181; Charlese De Gaulla 5, Dejvice; mains 290-350Kč; ☽ 11.30am-11.30pm; Ⓜ Dejvická or Ⓡ 8

If you can't get in at De Emanuel (left), try this Greek taverna across the street. There are the usual classics such as souvlaki and moussaka, plus a delicious seafood mezze (320Kč) that could easily be a meal in itself. The indoor dining room, with sponged walls and light woods, is a little too cute – a better bet is the front garden. The Greek Society runs a small grocery next door, which is great for stocking up on fresh olives, Greek wines, authentic Greek yoghurt and fresh feta.

ČÍNSKÁ ZAHRADA
Map p136   Chinese €€

☎ 233 379 656; Šmeralová 11, Bubeneč; mains 150-300Kč; ☽ 11am-11pm; Ⓡ 1, 8, 15, 25, 26

Čínská Zahrada (Chinese Garden) is a neighbourhood joint that's just authentic enough to draw people from around the city. In fact, it's not uncommon to see lines of Asian tourists streaming down the sidewalks, all headed here, at mealtimes. The very hot 'dry fried chicken' (pieces of chicken cooked on the bone in red pepper flakes) is one of the local favourites; ask the waiter to advise. Dine on the terrace in nice weather.

IL GATTOPARDO
Map p136   Italian €€

☎ 774 999 027; Šmeralová 15, Bubeneč; mains 140-300Kč; ☽ 11am-11pm; Ⓡ 1, 8, 15, 25, 26

This is a small, family-run Italian restaurant and food store near Letenské náměstí that's not easy to find (located on the ground floor and basement of a residential town house), but it's worth the effort. Nearly everything on the menu is imported from Sicily, lending an authenticity that many so-called Italian restaurants in Prague can't match, with excellent pastas and salads and a list of daily specials for under 200Kč. The wine selection (mostly from Sicily) is enormous and reasonably priced. The owner/ chef, Salvatore, apparently makes the gelato by hand.

SASAZU Map p136   Asian €€

☎ 284 097 455; Bubenské nábřeží 306 (inside the Holešovice market), Holešovice; mains 240-480Kč; ⏲ noon-midnight Sun-Thu, noon-1am Fri & Sat; Ⓜ Vltavská & 🚊 1, 3, 5, 25

This upmarket Asian restaurant connected to the club of the same name (p200) was arguably Prague's hottest opening of 2009, certainly the biggest thing working-class Holešovice had ever seen. Head chef Shahaf Shabtay has imported five cooking techniques from Southeast Asia, mixing cuisines from India, Malaysia, Indonesia, Thailand and Singapore. While prices for individual entrees are not outrageous for what's on offer (Vietnamese Ga curry, for example, is 180Kč), portions are on the small side and 100Kč bottles of water and 50Kč beers (for small ones) inflate the tab in a hurry. On the other hand, if you're looking for world-class Asian, this is the first address in town. Be sure to book in advance for Thursday, Friday and Saturday night, when snagging a walk-in table is well-nigh impossible.

PERPETUUM Map p136   Czech €€

☎ 233 323 429; Na hutích 9, Dejvice; mains 230-380Kč; ⏲ 11.30am-11pm Mon-Sat; Ⓜ Dejvická

Having a meal of expertly prepared duck is one of the culinary highlights of a visit to the Czech Republic, where it's a national favourite. Here, duck is the only thing on the menu and the guys in the kitchen clearly know what they are doing. Choose the Czech standard of a roast bird, served with bread dumplings and red cabbage or dabble in gamier wild duck or the sweetish Barbarie duck. It's all delicious. The secluded dining room is romantic enough for a meal to remember, and nonsmoking during mealtimes.

SAKURA Map p136   Japanese €€

☎ 774 785 077; Náměstí Svobody 1, Dejvice; mains 180-320Kč; ⏲ 11am-10pm; Ⓜ Dejvická

Crown for crown, this may be one of the best sushi places in Prague. It occupies a smart 1930s functionalist building, and the open interior is a soothing blend of contemporary Japanese and Czech high modern. There's even a small play area for children. The sushi is excellent, but the rolls really stand out. The 'volcano' roll features spicy tuna; the 'crunch' roll comes lightly fried, with gently cooked salmon tucked inside.

MOLO 22 Map p136   International €€

☎ 220 563 348; U Průhonu 22, Holešovice; mains 160-280Kč; ⏲ 8am-midnight Mon-Fri, 9am-midnight Sat & Sun; Ⓜ Vltavská & 🚊 5, 12, 15

This slick restaurant – done out in dark panelled walls and lime green accents – just across the street from the dance club Mecca (p199) – is a beacon of optimism on an otherwise drab street in the eastern section of Holešovice. The menu is ambitious and eclectic, with Italian risottos and Thai curries listed alongside traditional Czech favourites such as Svíčková na smetaně and roast duck, though the chef could use a little less salt. Good cheesecake desserts.

BOHEMIA BAGEL Map p136   International €

☎ 220 806 541; Dukelských Hrdinů 48, Holešovice; mains 120-240Kč; ⏲ 9am-11pm; 🚊 5, 14, 15, 17

When this outlet of the local Bohemia Bagel empire opened in 2007, it was widely heralded as a sign of Holešovice's imminent rebirth. It hasn't exactly worked out that way. Nevertheless, this remains the best all-round sandwich and light meal joint in the neighbourhood, with the usual range of bagels, breakfasts and burgers, plus seared tuna and filet mignon entrees for bigger appetites. Bohemia Bagel is only two tram stops from Nádraží Holešovice (take tram 15), making this a feasible meal option if you're waiting for a train.

STAROČESKÁ KRČMA Map p136   Czech €

☎ 224 321 505; V.P. Čkalova 15, Dejvice; mains 150-230Kč; ⏲ 11am-midnight; Ⓜ Hradčanská or Dejvická

A very good traditional Czech tavern, Staročeská Krčma specialises in huge portions of grilled meats, such as steaks, pork and chicken. The setting is meant to evoke an old-fashioned koliba (inn or country cottage), with big wooden tables, an open fireplace and stacks of wood sitting around. The pork dishes excel, while the steaks are only good. Reserve in advance, especially on weekends.

CAPUA Map p136   Pizza €

☎ 233 382 659; Milady Horákové 9, Holešovice; mains 100-150Kč; ⏲ 11am-1am, terrace to 11pm; 🚊 1, 8, 15, 25, 26

This corner restaurant just above Strossmayerovo náměstí is widely considered the best pizza place in the neighbourhood, and even the *Prague Post* in recent years has listed it among the city's top picks. But in truth it's only good, not great. The inviting interior is divided into two rooms, with nonsmokers getting the larger and nicer one to the right. The pizzas are thin-crust and follow the usual formula of Italian combinations. 'Capriccioso' is a filling mix of ham and fresh mushrooms. There's a shaded terrace out the front in nice weather.

NAD KRÁLOVSKOU OBOROU
Map p136   Czech €

☎ 220 912 319; Nad Královskou oborou 31, Bubeneč; mains 140-250Kč; ☻ 11.30am-11pm; 🚃 1, 8, 15, 25, 26

The sad fact is many pub renovations destroy any semblance of what was nice about the pub in the first place. The good news here is that they've taken a great old neighbourhood pub and made it even better. Sure, they had to clear out some colourful locals and scrape the nicotine off the walls, but they've spruced the place up while keeping the relaxed vibe and improved the Czech cooking immensely by adding some hard-to-find-venison dishes (try the venison goulash). The park-side location makes it an ideal lunch or beer spot after a stroll through Stromovka.

NA URALE
Map p136   Czech €

☎ 224 326 820; Uralská 9, Dejvice; mains 100-200Kč; ☻ 11am-1am; Ⓜ Dejvická or 🚃 8

A formerly grotty Czech pub that's greatly cleaned up its act in recent years, adding some beautiful crimson walls and solid stone-tile floors. The kitchen has also had an upgrade, but the prices for well-done Czech dishes such as *guláš* and roast pork are barely higher than at a typical workers' pub. Na Urale anchors an increasingly interesting set of shops on lovely Puškinovo náměstí (Pushkin Square), which now includes both an Italian and Russian grocery store.

PIZZERIA GROSSETO
Map p136   Italian, Pizza €

☎ 233 342 694; Jugoslávských Partyzánů 8, Dejvice; mains 120-180Kč; ☻ 11.30am-11pm; Ⓜ Dejvická or 🚃 8; Ⓥ

This is a lively, friendly pizzeria with a genuine, wood-fired pizza oven that pulls in crowds of students from the nearby university campus. As well as a huge choice

of tasty pizza varieties, the menu also offers salads, pastas, risotto, roast chicken, steak and grilled salmon. The main dining room, where you can watch the pizza chefs twirling their dough, is complemented by an attractive timber-decked conservatory out the back. Reservations are absolutely essential, and the staff takes an unseemly pleasure in telling walk-ins there's not a free table to be had.

LUCKY LUCIANO
Map p136   Pizza €

☎ 220 875 900; Dělnická 28, Holešovice; mains 100-150Kč; ☻ 11.30am-11pm; Ⓜ Vltavská & 🚃 1, 5, 12, 14, 15, 25; Ⓥ

You're in luck if you're staying at Sir Toby's Hostel (p229) – this little pizzeria next door serves very good pizza, as well as traditional Italian appetisers such as beef carpaccio and *insalata caprese*. The service is friendly, and the best part of all is the big tree-covered terrace in the front – a nice, cool spot to chill out on a hot summer day.

LA CRÊPERIE
Map p136   French €

☎ 220 878 040; Janovského 4, Holešovice; mains 60-140Kč; ☻ 9am-11pm Mon-Sat, to 10pm Sun; Ⓜ Vltavská or 🚃 1, 5, 8, 12, 14, 15, 17, 25, 26

Odd place to put an authentic French crêperie, in a forgotten corner of Holešovice next to the district's massive administrative office complex. Still, if you happen to be in the area, it's worth a stop for excellent sweet and savoury open-faced crêpes called *galettes*. Everything is made to order, so you may have to wait. That's fine, since the space – fitted out like a rustic inn in Bretagne – is warm and there's usually some rousing, vintage French music piping from the speakers. The *galette complet* (ham and cheese with an egg on top) makes an excellent and filling breakfast.

SMÍCHOV

With the arrival in recent years of the Nový Smíchov shopping centre and surrounding office complexes, the area around the Anděl metro station has exploded with restaurants. Most of these, like TGI Friday's and Potrefená husa, are actually upmarket chains that cater to the lunchtime business crowd. Authentic and really decent places are harder to find, though there are a few of those too. If you don't see something you like, the food court on the top floor of the shopping centre has at least a dozen more dining options.

ARTISAN Map p143   International €€
☎ 257 218 277; Rošickýh 4; mains 240-400Kč;
🕐 11am-midnight Mon-Thu, to 1am Fri & Sat, to
11pm Sun; 🚊 6, 9, 12, 20 (to Švandovo divadlo)
The owners of this upmarket restaurant,
hidden around a back corner near náměstí
Kinských and on the edge of Smíchov and
Malá Strana, have taken a real gamble:
that residents in this workaday part of
Prague are willing to shell out for genuinely high-class cooking. So far, the jury
is still out. On some nights, the tastefully
contemporary dining room is only half
full. That's a shame, since Artisan is simply
the best meal to be had in Smíchov, bar
none. Try the homemade ravioli stuffed
with spicy duck ragout or the pumpkin
risotto or one of the excellent aged steaks.
The dining area is nonsmoking; eat on the
back terrace in nice weather.

NA VERANDÁCH Map p143   International €€
☎ 257 191 200; Nádražní 84; mains 150-300Kč;
🕐 11am-midnight Mon-Thu, to 1am Fri & Sat, to
11pm Sun; Ⓜ Anděl
Na Verandách, the combination pub-
restaurant located in the Staropramen
Brewery (see the boxed text, p190), is no
longer privately run but managed by the
Staropramen-owned Potrefená husa restaurant chain. Nevertheless, it's still wildly
popular with *Czuppies,* the local version of
yuppies, at lunch and dinnertime. There's
no shortage of quality beers (eight varieties
on tap) to wash down the very good rendi-
tions of ribs, burgers, and chicken and pork
dishes. In nice weather, try to snag a table
on the verandah in the back.

PIZZERIA CORLEONE Map p143   Pizza €€
☎ 251 511 244; Na Bělidle 42; mains 120-340Kč;
🕐 11am-11.30pm; Ⓜ Anděl; Ⓥ
This lively neighbourhood restaurant is
arguably the best pizza option in Smíchov.
The wood-fired pizza oven turns out all the
classics, from margherita to *moscardina,*
and also allows you to choose your own
toppings. The dining room shows a taste
for the art of Jack Vettriano, whose paintings are reproduced in large murals. There's
a nonsmoking area in the basement.

U MÍKULÁŠE DAČÍCKÉHO
Map p143   Czech €€
☎ 257 322 334; ul Victora Huga; mains 200-300Kč;
🕐 11am-midnight; Ⓜ Anděl

An honest-to-goodness, old-fashioned
vinárna (wine bar). These slightly more
upmarket wine-oriented equivalents of the
beer-focused *hospody* (pubs) – complete with
traditional atmosphere and excellent Czech
cooking – have been dying out in recent
years. The owners here have gone for the 'Ye
Olde Middle Ages' look, with dark woods, red
tablecloths, and pictures showing the lords
enjoying their wine. Reserve in advance.

ANDĚL Map p143   Czech €
☎ 257 323 234; Nádražní 114; mains 90-220Kč;
🕐 11am-11pm; Ⓜ Anděl
If you happen to be staying at one of the
gleaming new boutique hotels in the
neighbourhood, you need walk only a few
metres to stumble into one of the better
Pilsner Urquell pubs in town. Though Anděl
is relatively new, it has the look and feel of a
well-worn Czech pub, complete with crusty
regulars, very good traditional Czech entrees such as *svičková na smetaně* and *guláš,*
and offers super-fresh, direct-from-the-
brewery 'tank beer' *(tankové pivo).* Reservations recommended for lunch and dinner.

ZLATÝ KLAS Map p143   Czech €
☎ 251 562 539; Plzeňská 9; mains 120-200Kč;
🕐 11am-11pm Sun-Thu, 11am-1am Fri & Sat;
Ⓜ Anděl
This is the best and most tourist-friendly of
the traditional pubs in the area. Zlatý klas
also offers super-fresh *tankové pivo* from
Plzeň, a local badge of honour meaning the
beer is served from large tanks and is free
of the carbon dioxide used to pump the
beer through the taps. The menu is filled
with well-done Czech grub such as roast
pork, goulash and fried breast of chicken in
a kitsch but comfortable space. The service
is fast and friendly, but you'll have to book
in advance in the evenings, since it can get
impossibly crowded.

CORTE DI ANGELO Map p143   Pizza €
☎ 257 326 167; Nádražní 116; mains 120-180Kč;
🕐 11am-11pm; Ⓜ Anděl; Ⓥ
Another decent pizza option in the Anděl
area, this one goes for a 'Wild West' motif.
The main draws here are thin-crust pizza
from a wood-fired oven, decent starters
like beef carpaccio, and a pleasant terrace
situated off the street in a small courtyard. It
also operates the adjacent, street-side cafe,
with excellent Illy espresso and a handy row
of tables for people-watching.

DRINKING

top picks

DRINKING

Bars in Prague go in and out of fashion with alarming speed, and trend spotters are forever flocking to the latest 'in' place only to desert it as soon as it becomes mainstream. The best areas to go looking for good drinking dens include Vinohrady, Žižkov, Smíchov, Holešovice, the area south of Národní třída in Nové Město and the lanes around Old Town Square in Staré Město.

Most pubs serve beer snacks; some of the most popular are *utopenci* (sliced sausage pickled in vinegar with onion), *topinky* (fried toast) and, of course, the famous *Pražská šunka* (Prague ham) with gherkin. Many of the places listed in this chapter also serve more substantial meals.

The wave of stag parties that once afflicted Prague seems to have moved east to pastures new (and cheaper), but if you want to be sure of avoiding any, stay away from Wenceslas Square, Irish and English pubs in the city centre, and the sports bars on and around Ve Smečkách in the New Town.

SPECIALITIES
Beer

The Czech lands have been famous for centuries for producing some of the finest amber nectar in the world. The earliest historical mention of beer-making and hop-growing dates back to 1088 in the founding charter of Opatovice monastery in East Bohemia. Apparently the taste of beer was quite different in those days – by today's standards it would be considered undrinkable. It was not until 1842 that a smart group of Plzeň brewers pooled their experience, installed 'modern' technology and founded a single municipal brewery, with spectacular results. Their golden lager beer, labelled Plzeňský Prazdroj (*prazdroj* is old Czech for 'the original source'), or Pilsner Urquell in German, is now one of the world's best, and most imitated, beers.

Even in these times of encroaching coffee culture, *pivo* (beer) remains the lifeblood of Prague. Czechs drink more beer per capita than anywhere else in the world (around 157L per head per year, easily beating both Germany and Australia), and the local *hospoda* or *pivnice* (pub or small beer hall) remains the social hub of the neighbourhood. Many people drink at least one glass of beer every day – local nicknames for beer include *tekutý chleb* (liquid bread) and *živá voda* (life-giving water) – and it's still possible to see people stopping off for a small glass of beer on their way to work in the morning.

Most Czech beers are bottom-fermented lagers, naturally brewed using Moravian malt and hand-picked hops from Žatec in northwestern Bohemia. The whole brewing and fermentation process uses only natural

---

PUB ETIQUETTE

There's an etiquette to be observed if you want to sample the atmosphere in a traditional *hospoda* (pub) without drawing disapproving stares and grumbles from the regulars. First off, don't barge in and start rearranging chairs and tables – if you want to share a table or take a spare seat, ask *'je tu volno?'* (is this free?) first. It's normal practice in crowded Czech pubs to share tables with strangers. Take a beer mat from the rack and place it in front of you, and wait for the bar staff to come to you; waving for service is guaranteed to get you ignored.

You can order without saying a single thing – it's automatically assumed that you're here for the beer. When the waiter approaches, just raise your thumb for one beer, thumb and index finger for two, etc – providing you want a 0.5L glass of the pub's main draught ale. Even just a nod will do. The waiter will keep track of your order by marking a slip of paper that stays on your table; whatever you do, don't write on it or lose it (you'll have to pay a fine if you do). As soon as the level of beer in your glass falls to within an inch of the bottom, the eagle-eyed waiter will be on his/her way with another. But never, as people often do in Britain, pour the dregs of the old glass into the new – this is considered to be deeply uncivilised behaviour.

If you don't want any more beer brought to your table, place a beer-mat on top of your glass. When you want to pay up and go, get the waiter's attention and say *'zaplatím'* (I'll pay). He or she will tot up the marks on your slip of paper, and you pay there, at the table (try to have some smallish change; handing over a 2000Kč note will prompt a display of amateur dramatics). It's normal to leave a tip (see p182).

ingredients – water, hops, yeast and barley. As in neighbouring Germany, strict regulations prevent the use of chemicals in the beer-making process.

There are two main varieties of beer – *světlé* (light) and *tmavy* or *černé* (dark). The *světlé* is a pale amber or golden lager-style beer with a crisp, refreshing, hoppy flavour. Dark beers are sweeter and more full-bodied, with a rich, malty or fruity flavour.

Draught beers are often labelled either *dvanáctka* (12°) or *desítka* (10°). This indicator of specific gravity is known as the Balling rating, and was invented by Czech scientist Karl Josef Balling in the 19th century. One degree (°) Balling represents 1% by weight of malt-derived sugar in the brewing liquid before fermentation. However, not all the sugar turns to alcohol, so the Balling rating gives an indication of the 'body' as well as the likely alcohol content of the finished beer – 12° is richer in flavour, as well as being stronger in alcohol, than 10°, with a slight malty sweetness that cuts the bitterness of the hops.

In 1997 Czech law adopted a new system to indicate the alcohol-by-volume (ABV) content of beer, which recognises three categories – *výcepni pivo* (less than 4.5% ABV), *ležák* (4.5% to 5.5% ABV) and *special* (more than 5.5% ABV). However, tradition dies hard, and most breweries and pubs still use the *dvanáctka* and *desítka* labels.

Czechs like their beer served at cellar temperature (around 6°C to 10°C) with a tall, creamy head (known as *pěna*, meaning foam). Americans and Australians may find it a bit warm, but this improves the flavour. Most draught beer is sold in *půl-litr* (0.5L) glasses; if you prefer a small beer, ask for a *malé pivo* (0.3L). Some bars confuse the issue by using 0.4L glasses, while others offer a German-style 1L mug known as a *tuplák*.

The world-famous Pilsner Urquell and Budvar (Budweiser) beers are brewed in the provincial towns of Plzeň (West Bohemia) and České Budějovice (South Bohemia) respectively, but Prague has its own native brews. The largest concern is Prague Breweries, which operates the Staropramen and Braník breweries in Prague, and the Ostravar brewery in Ostrava (Northern Moravia). Its brands include the traditional Staropramen lager and the newer Kelt stout and Velvet bitter, and account for just over 15% of the domestic beer market.

Prague Breweries is now owned by the multinational company StarBev, the largest brewery group in the world, and Pilsner Urquell is a subsidiary of SABMiller. In fact, the Budweiser Budvar Brewery in Ceské Budějovice, which is still partly owned by the state, is the only major brewery in the country that is still 100% Czech-owned.

The takeover of the Czech Republic's breweries by multinational companies has been accompanied by a resurgence of interest in traditional beer-making, which has seen a wave of microbreweries (beer halls that brew their own beer on the premises) springing up all over the country. There are several microbreweries in Prague – see the boxed text, p182, for details.

Wine

Czech beer is, of course, world famous, and beer-heads come to Prague from all over the world to worship at the mother lode of all lagers. What is less well known is that Czech wines have improved enormously in recent years, and are well worth getting to know.

Grapes have been grown in the Czech lands since the 14th century, when Charles IV imported vines from Burgundy; their descendants are still thriving on the slopes beneath Mělník Chateau (p238).

The standard of Czech wine has soared since the fall of communism, as small producers have concentrated on the quality end of the market. The total area of land given over to viticulture increased from 120 sq km in 1989 to 193 sq km by 2006. The main wine-growing region in the country is South Moravia, which accounts for 96% of Czech vineyards, with the remaining 4% scattered across northern Bohemia.

Although Czech red wines – such as the South Moravian speciality, Svatovavřinecké (St Lawrence) – are mostly pretty average, Czech whites can be very good indeed. The varieties to look out for are Veltinské zelené (Grüner Veltlin), Rýnský ryzlink (riesling) and Müller-Thurgau. Tanzberg and Sonberk are both excellent winemakers.

Although not as popular as beer, *víno* (wine) is widely available in *vinárny* (wine bars), restaurants and pubs – but not in many beer halls. *Suché víno* is dry wine and *sladké* is sweet; a sign advertising *sudové víno* means that it is served straight from the barrel. If you want to sample a range of Czech wines, head for a wine bar such as Bokovka (p186), Monarch Vinný Sklep (p186) or Viniční Altán (p189), or go shopping at Cellarius (p163).

SMALL IS BEAUTIFUL

While big multinational brewing companies have been busy taking over traditional Czech breweries, a growing number of enthusiasts have been setting up microbreweries that stay true to the origins of Bohemian beer, serving tasty, unpasteurised brews in atmospheric brewery pubs. Here are six in the capital:

Klášterní pivovar Strahov (Strahov Monastery Brewery; Map p70; ☎ 233 353 155; Strahovské nádvoří 301, Hradčany; ☽ 10am-10pm; ⊠ 22) Dominated by two polished copper brewing kettles, this convivial little pub serves up two varieties of its St Norbert beer – *tmavý* (dark), a rich, tarry brew with a creamy head, and *polotmavý* (amber), a full-bodied, hoppy lager, both 59Kč per 0.4L.

Novoměstský pivovar (New Town Brewery; Map p110; ☎ 224 232 448; Vodičkova 20, Nové Město; ☽ 8am-11.30pm Mon-Fri, 11.30am-11.30pm Sat, noon-10pm Sun; ⊠ 3, 9, 14, 24) Like U Fleků, the 'New Town Brewery' has largely been taken over by coach-party invasions, with similar high beer prices (65Kč for 0.5L, available in both light and dark varieties), though the food is not only edible but actually rather good. If you haven't booked, you'll be lucky to get a table.

Pivovar U Bulovky (Bulovka Brewery; Map p58; ☎ 284 840 650; Bulovka 17, Libeň; ☽ 11am-11pm Mon-Thu, to midnight Fri, noon-midnight Sat; ⊠ 10, 15, 24, 25) Opened in 2004, this is a genuine neighbourhood bar out in the suburbs, a homely wood-panelled room with quirky metalwork, much of it home-built by the owner. The delicious house *ležák* (lager; 29Kč for 0.5L) is a yeast beer, cloudy in appearance, and crisp, citrusy and refreshing in flavour. Well worth the tram trip, but don't expect the staff to speak English!

For about three weeks each year from the end of September to mid-October, you will see shops and street stalls selling *burčák*. This is 'young wine', freshly extracted grape juice in the early stages of fermentation. It is sweet and refreshing, more reminiscent of fruit juice than wine, but contains around 3% to 5% alcohol; beware – the stuff sneaks up on you.

Later in the year, as winter sets in and the weather gets colder, you'll notice the *svařák* stalls appearing in the streets. Short for *svařené vino* (mulled wine), *svařák* is what you would expect – red wine heated and flavoured with sugar and spices.

Spirits

Probably the most distinctive of Czech *lihoviny* (spirits) is Becherovka. Produced in the West Bohemian spa town of Karlovy Vary, famous for its 12 sulphurous, thermal springs, the bitter, herbal liqueur is famously known as the '13th spring' – a few shots will leave you feeling sprightlier than a week's worth of spa treatment. It is often served as an apéritif, and is increasingly used as an ingredient in cocktails.

The fiery and potent *slivovice* (plum brandy) is said to have originated in Moravia, where the best brands still come from. The best commercially produced *slivovice* is R Jelínek from Vizovice. Other regional spirits include *meruňkovice* (apricot brandy) and juniper-flavoured *borovička*.

The deadliest locally produced spirit is Hills Liquere absinthe from Jindřichův Hradec. While it's banned in many countries, in part because of its high alcohol content, absinthe is legal in the Czech Republic. Unfortunately, connoisseurs of absinthe consider Hills little better than highly alcoholic mouthwash.

Spirits are traditionally drunk neat and usually chilled. An exception is *grog*, a popular year-round hot drink: half rum, half hot water or tea, with a slice of lemon.

PRACTICALITIES
How Much?

Gone are the days of cheap beer. A combination of generally increasing tourist prices and a strong Czech crown have seen bar prices begin to approach those in Germany, France and even the UK.

The price of a half-litre of draught beer varies enormously, from around 25Kč to 40Kč in pubs catering mainly to local drinkers, to 90Kč and up at outdoor tables in tourist-thronged Old Town Square. Most tourist-oriented bars in the city centre charge 40Kč to 80Kč.

Cocktails in the city centre range from 150Kč to 300Kč, depending on the quality of the ingredients and the fanciness of the surroundings, while good-quality Czech wine in a specialist wine bar will cost from 300Kč to 400Kč a bottle.

Tipping

It's customary to tip the staff in Prague pubs, bars and cafes. Normal practice is to round up the bill to the next 10Kč (or the next 20Kč

Pivovarský dům (Brewery House; Map p110; ☎ 296 216 666; cnr Ječná & Lipová, Nové Město; ☯ 11am-11.30pm; ▣ 4, 6, 10, 16, 22) While the tourists flock to U Fleků, locals gather here to sample the classic Czech lager (in light, dark and mixed varieties; 38Kč per 0.5L) that is produced on the premises, as well as wheat beer and a range of flavoured beers (including coffee, banana and cherry, 38Kč per 0.3L). The pub itself is a pleasant place to linger, decked out with polished copper vats and brewing implements and smelling faintly of malt and hops (no smoking).

U Fleků (Map p110; ☎ 224 934 019; Křemencová 11, Nové Město; ☯ 9am-11pm; Ⓜ Karlovo Náměstí) A festive warren of drinking and dining rooms, U Fleků is a Prague institution, though usually clogged with tour groups high on oompah music and the tavern's home-brewed, 13° black beer (59Kč for 0.4L), known as Flek. Purists grumble but go along anyway because the beer is good, though tourist prices have nudged out many locals. Beware the waiter asking if you want to try a Becherovka (Czech liqueur) – it's not a great accompaniment to beer, and it'll add 80Kč to the bill.

U Medvídků (At the Little Bear; Map p90; ☎ 224 211 916; Na Perštýně 7, Staré Město; ☯ beer hall 11.30am-11pm, museum noon-10pm; Ⓜ Národní Třída) The most micro of Prague's microbreweries, with a capacity of only 250L, U Medvídků started producing its own beer only in 2005, though its beer hall has been around for many years. What it lacks in size, it makes up for in strength – the dark lager produced here, marketed as X-Beer, is the strongest in the country, with an alcohol content of 11.8% (as strong as many wines). Available in bottles only (50Kč for 0.33L), it's a malty, bitter-sweet brew with a powerful punch; handle with caution! There's also Budvar on tap at 35Kč for 0.5L.

if it's over 200Kč). Change is usually counted out starting with the big notes, then on down to the smallest coins. If you say *děkuji* (thank you) during this process, the bartender will stop and assume that the rest is a tip.

PRAGUE CASTLE & HRADČANY

This is a fairly quiet district, with drinking venues limited to laid-back cafes and a couple of traditional pubs.

U ZAVĚŠENÝHO KAFE Map p70   Bar
☎ 605 294 595; Úvoz 6, Hradčany; ☯ 11am-midnight; ▣ 12, 20, 22
This is a superb drinking den barely five minutes' walk from the castle. Head for the cosy, wood-panelled back room, quirkily decorated with weird art and mechanical curiosities by local artist Kuba Krejci (all for sale), and an ancient jukebox with Beatles, Stones and Czech rock. Foaming Pilsner Urquell is 35Kč a half-litre, and the coffee (42Kč for a cappuccino) is damn fine too.

LOBKOWICZ PALACE CAFÉ Map p62   Cafe
☎ 233 312 925; Jiřská 3, Prague Castle; ☯ 10am-6pm; ▣ 22
This cafe housed in the 16th-century Lobkowicz Palace is the best in the castle complex by an imperial mile. Try to grab one of the tables on the balconies at the back – the view over Malá Strana is superb,

as are the cafe's chocolate brownies, served with a splash of mango sauce and fresh strawberries. The coffee is good too (if a tad pricey at 95Kč for a cappuccino), and service is fast and friendly.

PIVNICE U ČERNÉHO VOLA
Map p62   Pub
☎ 220 513 481; Loretánské náměstí 1, Hradčany; ☯ 10am-10pm; ▣ 22
Many religious people make a pilgrimage to the Loreta, but just across the road is a shrine that pulls in pilgrims of a different kind – the 'Black Ox'. This surprisingly authentic and inexpensive beer hall is visited by real-ale aficionados for its authentic atmosphere and lip-smackingly delicious draught beer, Velkopopovický Kozel (29Kč for 0.5L), which is brewed in a small town southeast of Prague.

MALÁ STRANA

Malá Strana is the place to go for pavement table people-watching, with lots of cafes and bars spilling out onto the streets – especially on main square Malostranské náměstí and on Nerudova, which leads up to the castle. Places here range from cute tea houses and cafes to traditional cellar-pubs and funky bars.

KLUB ÚJEZD Map p78   Bar
☎ 257 316 537; Újezd 18; ☯ 2pm-4am; ▣ 6, 9, 12, 20, 22
Klub Újezd is one of Prague's many 'alternative' bars, spread over three floors (DJs

in the cellar, and a cafe upstairs) and filled with a fascinating collection of handmade furniture and fittings, original art and weird wrought-iron sculptures. Clamber onto a two-tonne bar stool in the agreeably grungy street-level bar, and sip on a beer while you watch a thick rope of herbal-scented smoke uncoil across the ceiling beside the scaly, fire-breathing sea-monster that dangles over your head. Trippy.

KAFÍČKO Map p78   Cafe
☎ 724 151 795; Míšenská 10; ☻ 10am-10pm; ▣ 12, 20, 22
This smoke-free, family-friendly little cafe, with its cream walls, bentwood chairs, fresh flowers and arty photographs, is an unexpected setting for some of Prague's finest tea and coffee. Choose from a wide range of quality roasted beans from all over the world, and have them freshly ground and made into espresso, cappuccino or latte (40Kč to 55Kč); the espresso is served, as it should be, with a glass of water.

U ZELENÉHO ČAJE Map p78   Cafe
☎ 257 530 027; Nerudova 19; ☻ 11am-10pm; ▣ 12, 20, 22
'At the Green Tea' is a charming little oldeworlde tea house on the way up to the castle. The menu offers around a hundred different kinds of tea (45Kč to 80Kč a pot) from all over the world, ranging from classic green and black teas from China and India to fruit-flavoured teas and herbal infusions, as well as tempting cakes and tasty sandwiches.

BLUE LIGHT Map p78   Cocktail Bar
☎ 257 533 126; Josefská 1; ☻ 6pm-3am; ▣ 12, 20, 22
The Blue Light is an appropriately dark and atmospheric jazz cavern, as popular with locals as with tourists, where you can sip a caipirinha or cranberry colada as you cast an eye over the vintage jazz posters, records, old photographs and decades-worth of scratched graffiti that adorn the walls. The background jazz is recorded rather than live, but on a quality sound system that never overpowers your conversation. Often heaving on weekend nights.

HOSTINEC U KOCOURA Map p78   Pub
☎ 257 530 107; Nerudova 2; ☻ 11am-11pm; ▣ 12, 20, 22
'The Tomcat' is a long-established traditional pub, still enjoying its reputation as

a former favourite of ex-president Havel, and still managing to pull in a mostly Czech crowd despite being in the heart of touristville (maybe it's the ever-present pall of cigarette smoke). It has relatively inexpensive beer for this part of town – 33Kč for 0.5L of draught Budvar, Pilsner Urquell or Bernard yeast beer.

STARÉ MĚSTO
The Old Town is tourist central, with crowded pubs and prices to match. But all you have to do is explore the maze of narrow backstreets that radiate from Old Town Square to find hidden gems like Čili Bar, Duende and Literární Kavárna Řetězová.

DUENDE Map p90   Bar
☎ 775 186 077; Karoliny Světlé 30; ☻ 1pm-midnight Mon-Fri, 3pm-midnight Sat, 4pm-midnight Sun; Ⓜ Národní Třída
Barely five minutes' walk from Charles Bridge but half a world away in atmosphere, this cute little bar is the opposite of touristy – a bohemian drinking den that pulls in an arty, mixed-age crowd of locals. Here you can enjoy a drink while casting an eye over the fascinating photos and quirky art that cover the wall, or listen to live guitar or violin. As well as wines and cocktails, the bar serves the excellent Bernard beer for 29Kč per 0.5L.

FRIENDS Map p90   Bar
☎ 226 211 920; Bartolomějská 11; ☻ 6pm-4am; Ⓜ Národní Třída
Friends is a welcoming gay music-and-video bar serving excellent coffee, cocktails and wine. It's a good spot to sit back with a drink and check out the crowd, or join in the party spirit on assorted theme nights, which range from Czech pop music and movies to cowboy parties (see www.friendsprague.cz for listings). DJs add their own spin from 9pm Friday and Saturday.

KOZIČKA Map p90   Bar
☎ 224 818 308; Kozí 1; ☻ noon-4am Mon-Fri, 6pm-4am Sat, 7pm-3am Sun; Ⓜ Staroměstská
The 'Little Goat' is a buzzing, red-brick basement bar decorated with cute steel goat sculptures, serving Krušovice on tap at 45Kč for 0.5L (though watch out – the bartenders will occasionally sling you a 1L tuplák if they think you're a tourist). It fills

up later in the evening with a mostly Czech crowd, and is a very civilised setting for a late-night session.

KÁVA KÁVA KÁVA
Map p90   Cafe

☎ 224 228 862; Platýz pasáž, Národní třída 37; ☺ 7am-10pm Mon-Fri, 9am-10pm Sat & Sun; Ⓜ Národní Třída; 🛜

Tucked away in the peaceful Platýz courtyard, this American-owned cafe has some of the best coffee in town – the *grande cappuccino* is big enough to bathe in – and a selection of bagels, croissants, chocolate brownies, carrot cake and other goodies. You can find a second branch in Smíchov (see p195).

KRÁSNÝ ZTRÁTY Map p90   Cafe

☎ 775 755 143; Náprstkova 10; ☺ 9am-1am Mon-Fri, noon-1am Sat & Sun; Ⓜ Národní Třída or 🚋 17, 18; 🛜

This cool cafe – the name translates as something like 'beautiful destruction' – doubles as an art gallery and occasional music venue, and is hugely popular with students from nearby Charles University. There are newspapers and books to leaf through, chilled tunes on the sound system, and a menu of gourmet teas and coffees to choose from.

LITERÁRNÍ KAVÁRNA ŘETĚZOVÁ
Map p90   Cafe

☎ 222 221 244; ☺ noon-11pm Mon-Fri, 5-11pm Sat & Sun; 🚋 17, 21

This is the kind of place where you can imagine yourself tapping out the Great Prague Novel on your laptop with a half-finished coffee on the table beside you. It's a plain, vaulted room with battered wooden furniture, a scatter of rugs on the floor, old black-and-white photos on the wall, and the sort of quiet, relaxed atmosphere where you can read a book without feeling self-conscious. If you fancy something stronger than coffee, try the fruity, full-flavoured Bernard *kvasnicové* (yeast beer).

ČILI BAR Map p90   Cocktail Bar

☎ 777 945 848; Kožná 8; ☺ 5pm-2am; Ⓜ Můstek

Hidden in the crook of a narrow Old Town alley but only a few paces from Old Town Square, this tiny cocktail bar could not be further removed in atmosphere from your typical Old Town drinking place. Cramped and smoky – there are Cuban cigars for sale – with a couple of battered leather armchairs competing for space with a handful of tables and the crowd at the bar, it's friendly, relaxed and lively. Don't miss the speciality of the house – a shot of rum mixed with finely chopped red chillis.

BEER GARDENS

On a hot summer day, what could be finer than sitting outdoors with a chilled glass of Bohemia's finest beer, admiring a view over river or city? Many of Prague's pubs have small beer gardens or courtyards, but the following summer-only spots are truly out in the open air. Opening times are weather-dependent, but are typically noon to midnight April to September; expect to pay around 25Kč to 35Kč for a half-litre of beer.

Letenský zámeček (Map p136; Letenské sady, Bubeneč) A slew of rickety benches and tables spread along a dusty scarp beneath the trees at the eastern end of Letná Gardens enjoys one of the city's most stunning views, looking across the river to the spires of Staré Město, and southwest to Malá Strana. Gambrinus on tap. See p191.

Letní bar (Map p78; Střelecký ostrov, Malá Strana) Basically a shack serving Budvar in plastic cups, this is the place to pick up a beer before hitting the little beach at the northern end of the island.

Občerstvení U okénka (Map p120; Soběslavova, Vyšehrad) Not a proper beer garden as such, but a collection of outdoor tables with a view over Vyšehrad Gardens – a pleasant spot for a beer on a sunny day, with bottled Braník at only 16Kč for 0.5L.

Riegrovy sady (Map p125; Riegrovy sady, Vinohrady) Perched on top of precipitous Riegrovy park, this bustling beer garden has awesome night-time views of the castle, a big screen showing sport, and the opportunity to play table football and table hockey with half of Prague. Pilsner Urquell and Gambrinus. See p187 for a full review.

Parukářka (Map p130; Olšanská, Žižkov) Ramshackle wooden hut in park overlooking Žižkov, with plenty of outdoor tables and lots of sweet-smelling smoke wafting about in the evenings. Gambrinus on tap.

Petřínské terasy (Map p78; Petřín, Malá Strana) Traditional country-style pub with large, outdoor wooden deck and a stunning view over the city. Pilsner Urquell on tap.

U ZLATÉHO TYGRA
Map p90   Pub
☎ 222 221 111; Husova 17; ⏰ 3-11pm;
Ⓜ Staroměstská

The 'Golden Tiger' is one of the few Old Town drinking holes that has hung on to its soul – and its low prices (36Kč per 0.5L of Pilsner Urquell), considering its location. It was novelist Bohumil Hrabal's favourite hostelry – there are photos of him on the walls – and the place that Václav Havel took fellow president Bill Clinton in 1994 to show him a real Czech pub.

MONARCH VINNÝ SKLEP
Map p90   Wine Bar
☎ 224 239 602; Na Perštýně 15; ⏰ 3pm-midnight Mon-Sat; Ⓜ Národní Třída

The Monarch wine cellar is one of the best places in town to get to know Czech wines. Despite its knowledgeable staff and vast selection of vintages, it manages to avoid any air of pretentiousness, and has a tempting menu of nibbles – cheeses, olives, prosciutto, salami and smoked duck – to accompany your wine, which is not as expensive as you might expect. A range of Moravian wines are available by the glass from only 39Kč.

NOVÉ MĚSTO

Nové Město, particularly the area around Wenceslas Square, is still a bit of a magnet for stag parties and groups of young lads on the piss – best avoided if you're looking for a quiet drink. But there are plenty of good drinking holes, too. Check out the streets south of Národní třída near the river, where you'll find plenty of studenty cafes and quirky wine bars.

JÁMA
Map p110   Bar
☎ 224 222 383; V Jámě 7; ⏰ 11am-1am; Ⓜ Muzeum

Jáma ('the Hollow'), southeast off Vodičkova, is a popular American expat bar with vaulted ceilings plastered with old rock gig posters ranging from Led Zep and REM to Kiss and Shania Twain. There's a leafy little beer garden out the back shaded by lime and walnut trees, smiling staff serving up rotating selection of high-quality regional beers and microbrews on draught, and a menu that includes good burgers, steaks, ribs and chicken wings.

KÁVOVARNA
Map p110   Cafe
☎ 296 236 233; Pasáž Lucerna, Svtěpánská 61; ⏰ 8am-midnight; Ⓜ Můstek

One of the few decent cafes in the region of Wenceslas Square, this retro-styled place has bentwood chairs and curved wooden benches in the smoky, dimly lit front room (there's a nonsmoking room beyond the bar), with exhibitions of arty black-and-white photography on the walls. The coffee is good and reasonably priced, and there's an extensive menu of flavoured and iced coffees, hot chocolates, soda and granitas.

BOKOVKA
Map p110   Wine Bar
☎ 721 262 503; Pštrossova 8; ⏰ 4pm-1am Sun-Thu, 4pm-3am Fri & Sat; Ⓜ Karlovo Náměstí

Owned by a syndicate of oenophiles who include film directors Jan Hřebejk and David Ondříček, this quaint little bar is named after the movie *Sideways* (*bokovka* in Czech), which was set in the California vineyards (the bar makes an appearance in Hřebejk's 2007 film *Medvídek*). The main attraction (other than the chance of being served drinks by a famous film director – they occasionally work behind the bar) is the extensive menu of top-notch Moravian wines – we can recommend the 2006 Sonberk Rýnský Ryzlink (590Kč a bottle).

VINOHRADY & VRŠOVICE

It may lack some of Žižkov's authentic grit, but Vinohrady is a great area for bar- and cafe-hopping. Check out the streets surrounding Peace Square (náměstí Míru), particularly along Americká, as well as Mánesova and those around the big park, Riegrovy sady, which has either Prague's best or second-best open-air beer garden (depending on whom you ask or where you live). With its big-screen TV, it's a popular place to gather for international sporting matches, like the World Cup.

CLUB STELLA
Map p125   Bar
☎ 224 257 869; Lužická 10, Vinohrady; ⏰ 8pm-5am; 🚊 4, 22

Club Stella is an intimate, candlelit cafe-bar that seems to be the first place everyone recommends when you ask about gay and lesbian bars in Prague. There's a long, narrow bar where you can just squeeze onto a bar stool, an armchair-filled lounge that looks like somebody's living room, and a welcoming crowd of locals. Ring the doorbell to get in.

POPO CAFÉ PETL Map p125   Bar
☎ 777 944 672; Italská 18, Vinohrady; ⏰ 10am-1am Mon-Fri, 4pm-1am Sat & Sun; 🚃 11
A popular student dive, usually packed to the rafters and hopelessly smoky, but loads of fun at the same time. Staropramen is on tap. If that doesn't appeal, there's tons of cheap wine on offer and tables filled with drunken members of the opposite sex. It doesn't get any better.

RIEGROVY SADY Map p125   Beer Garden
☎ 222 717 247; Riegrovy sady, Vinohrady; ⏰ noon-1am (summer only); 🚃 11 or Ⓜ Jiřího z Poděbrad (plus walk)
There's a good-natured rivalry between this beer garden and the one across the river at Letná as to which one is best. The answer depends on where you live, and on summer nights the folks in Vinohrady can be counted on to come out and enforce their claim. Order drinks at the bar and carry them to one of dozens of picnic tables. The big-screen TV takes away from the atmosphere, but is a welcome addition during the Euro or World Cup football matches, when the tables are lined elbow to elbow. The easiest way to get here is from Polská, turn up Chopínova, and then enter the park across from Na Švíhance. The beer garden is 30m up the path.

AL CAFETERO Map p125   Cafe
☎ 777 061 161; Blanická 24, Vinohrady; ⏰ 8.30am-9.30pm; Ⓜ Náměstí Míru or Muzeum, 🚃 11
Quirky little cafe and wine bar, just between Vinohradská and náměstí Míru, has several things going for it, including arguably the best coffee drinks in Prague, an excellent wine selection and a rigorously enforced nonsmoking policy, which makes it comfortable for lingering over the newspaper. There are also sweets on hand and savoury snacks like salads and sandwiches.

BLATOUCH Map p125   Cafe
☎ 222 328 643; Americká 17, Vinohrady; ⏰ 10am-11pm; Ⓜ Náměstí Míru; 🛜
When the legendary student cafe Blatouch shut down a couple of years ago in the Old Town, it was viewed as just another casualty of progress. The good news is that Blatouch has reopened here in Vinohrady,

with the same old sign out the front and the same mix of laid-back service and good-natured student clientele. Excellent coffee is served with light eats like salads and sandwiches to go along with the ultra-relaxed vibe. Just what the neighbourhood needed.

CAFÉ CELEBRITY Map p125   Cafe
☎ 222 511 343; Vinohradská 40, Vinohrady; ⏰ 10am-11pm; Ⓜ Náměstí Míru
This gay-friendly cafe is part of the cluster of gay-friendly joints that are part of the old Radio Palác building on Vinohradská. There's nothing special here except a welcoming atmosphere, lots of good-natured people-watching, and decent coffee, beer and wine.

CAFFÉ KAABA Map p125   Cafe
☎ 222 254 021; Mánesova 20, Vinohrady; ⏰ 8am-10pm; 🚃 11; 🛜
Caffé Kaaba is a stylish little architect-designed cafe-bar with retro furniture and pastel-coloured decor that comes straight out of the 1959 Ideal Homes Exhibition. It serves up excellent coffee (made with freshly ground imported beans), offers an extensive list of Czech and imported wines (the house wine is only 30Kč a glass), and also has an in-house news and tobacco counter.

DOBRÁ TRAFIKA Map p125   Cafe
☎ 222 510 261; Korunní 42, Vinohrady; ⏰ 7am-11pm; Ⓜ Náměstí Míru or 🚃 10, 16
From the outside, you'd never know there was a cute little coffee shop tucked behind this tobacconist on busy Korunní. The tobacco shop is interesting in its own right – not just pipes, loose tobacco, cigars and cigarettes, but also excellent teas, sweets and gifts. It feels a bit like a step back in time. At the back there's a small room for drinking coffee (nonsmoking) and a larger garden for just hanging out (smoking). Popular with students.

KAVÁRNA MEDÚZA Map p125   Cafe
☎ 222 515 107; Belgická 17, Vinohrady; ⏰ 10am-1am Mon-Fri, noon-1am Sat & Sun; Ⓜ Náměstí Míru
The perfect Prague coffee house, Medúza is an oasis of old, worn furniture, dark wood and local artworks, with an antique sugar bowl on every table and an atmosphere that invites you to sink into a novel or indulge in a conversation on the nature of

GRAND CAFES

Prague's cafe society flourished from the late 19th century until the 1930s, when the city's coffee houses provided a meeting place for artists, writers, journalists, activists and political dissidents. Many fell into disrepair following WWII, but half a dozen or so have survived or been restored to their former glory.

Café Imperial (Map p108; ☎ 246 011 440; Na Poříčí 15, Nové Město; ☑ 7am-11pm; Ⓜ Náměstí Republiky) First opened in 1914, and given a complete facelift in 2007, the Imperial is a tour de force of art nouveau tiling – the walls and ceiling are covered in original ceramic tiles, mosaics, sculptured panels and bas-reliefs, with period light fittings and bronzes scattered about. The coffee is good, there are cocktails in the evening, and the cafe menu offers all-day English and American breakfasts, as well as excellent eggs Benedict.

Café Savoy (Map p78; ☎ 257 311 562; Vítězná 5, Malá Strana; ☑ 8am-10.30pm Mon-Fri, 9am-10.30pm Sat & Sun; 🚋 6, 9, 22; 🛜) Established in 1893 and restored in 2004, the Savoy fairly glows with belle époque splendour, its colourful, ornately decorated ceiling decked with crystal chandeliers (grab a table on the mezzanine for a closer view) and its waiting staff dressed in matching red waistcoats and ties. Great coffee and hot chocolate, and a decent wine list too.

Grand Café Orient (Map p90; ☎ 224 224 240; Ovocný trh 19, Staré Město; ☑ 9am-10pm Mon-Fri, 10am-10pm Sat & Sun; Ⓜ Náměstí Republiky) Prague's only cubist cafe, the Orient was designed by Josef Gočár and is cubist down to the smallest detail, including the lampshades and coat-hooks. It was restored and reopened in 2005, having been closed since 1920. Decent coffee and inexpensive cocktails.

Kavárna Lucerna (Map p110; ☎ 224 215 495; Palác Lucerna, Štěpánská 61, Nové Město; ☑ 10am-1am Mon-Sat, to 11pm Sun; 🚋 3, 9, 14, 24; 🛜) The least touristy of the cafes listed here, the Lucerna is part of an art nouveau shopping arcade designed by the grandfather of ex-president Václav Havel. Filled with faux marble, ornamental metalwork and glittering crystal lanterns (*lucerna* is Czech for lantern), this 1920s gem has arched windows overlooking David Cerný's famous *Horse* sculpture hanging beneath the glass-domed atrium.

Kavárna Obecní dům (Map p90; ☎ 222 002 763; náměstí Republiky 5, Staré Město; ☑ 7.30am-11pm; Ⓜ Náměstí Republiky) The spectacular cafe in Prague's opulent Municipal House (Obecní dům) offers the opportunity to sip your cappuccino amid an orgy of art nouveau splendour. Also worth a look is the neat little American Bar in the basement of the building, all polished wood, stained glass and gleaming copper.

Kavárna Evropa (Map p110; ☎ 224 228 117; Václavské náměstí 25, Nové Město; ☑ 9.30am-11pm; Ⓜ Můstek) The Grand Hotel Evropa sports the most atmospheric cafe on Wenceslas Square, a fading museum of over-the-top art nouveau. Sadly, it has long since become a tourist trap, with second-rate cakes and coffee and rip-off prices, but it's still well worth a quick look inside.

Kavárna Slavia (Map p90; ☎ 224 220 957; Národní třída 1, Nové Město; ☑ 8am-midnight Mon-Fri, 9am-midnight Sat & Sun; Ⓜ Národní Třída) The Slavia is the most famous of Prague's old cafes, a cherrywood-and-onyx shrine to art deco elegance, with polished limestone-topped tables and big windows overlooking the river. It has been a celebrated literary meeting place since the early 20th century – Rainer Maria Rilke and Franz Kafka hung out here, and it was frequented by Václav Havel and other dissidents in the 1970s and '80s.

self. Coffee, tea, hot chocolate, beer, wine and even nonalcoholic cocktails are all on the menu, along with pancakes, nachos and banana splits.

KAVÁRNA ZANZIBAR
Map p125   Cafe

☎ 222 520 315; Americká 15, Vinohrady; ☑ 8am-11pm Mon-Fri, 10am-11pm Sat & Sun; Ⓜ Náměstí Míru

Zanzibar started out years ago as a *trafika*, a place to buy newspapers and tobacco products. Over the years it's evolved into a homey space that defies easy description. It's not quite a cafe (though coffee is probably the most popular beverage), not quite a bar (though there's beer on tap and a place to sit up front) and not quite a res-

taurant (though the food it serves is pretty good). Treat it as a great place to meet up for whatever mood you're in. The terrace out front is pleasant in nice weather.

RYBA NA RUBY Map p125   Cafe

☎ 731 570 704; Mánesova 87, Vinohrady; ☑ 10am-11pm Mon-Sat; Ⓜ Náměstí Jiřího z Poděbrad

Ryba na Ruby is something different for upmarket Vinohrady: an ecofriendly tea and gift shop on the ground floor with a laidback bar/club downstairs. This is a great place to stock up on things like fair-trade teas and coffees, plus organic foodstuffs like nuts, spices, cocoa, jams and oils. The below-ground club is a relaxed space for a beer or a coffee.

SAHARA CAFÉ Map p125 — Cafe

☎ 222 514 987; náměstí Míru 6, Vinohrady;
🕙 9am-11pm; Ⓜ Náměstí Míru

The beautifully minimalist Morocco-inspired interior sets a design standard that few places can match; unfortunately, the food doesn't always live up to the decor. Still, if it's just a cup of coffee or a glass of wine you're after, you can hardly do flashier in this neighbourhood. The convenient location makes it a good meet-up spot for a drink before heading elsewhere.

BAR & BOOKS MÁNESOVA

Map p125 — Cocktail Bar
☎ 222 724 581; Mánesova 64, Vinohrady; 🕙 5pm-3am; 🚊 11

This upmarket New York–style cocktail and cigar bar occupies a former rugby pub and couldn't be more different in terms of atmosphere. It's been given a bad rap for its cocktail prices, but the truth is if you stick to the basics, they're not much higher here than elsewhere; a Cosmo, for example, costs 145Kč, about the same as in the city centre. There are some lighter food options like sandwiches, cheese platters and fondues. There's also a pool table in the back and live music after 9pm Wednesdays.

SCHEISSE KATZE Map p125 — Cocktail Bar

☎ 737 111 097; Chodská 18, Vinohrady; 🕙 5pm-2am; Ⓜ Jiřího z Poděbrad

This popular cocktail bar in the middle of residential Vinohrady draws a mostly younger, neighbourhood clientele, who come for professionally mixed cocktails and the groovy vibe. The late closing hour makes it a nice stop for a nightcap on the way back to the hotel.

SOKOLOVNA Map p125 — Pub

☎ 222 524 525; Slezská 22, Vinohrady; 🕙 11am-11pm; Ⓜ Náměstí Míru

It might be a little unfair to consign Sokolovna to the 'pub' category. After all, it's also a pretty good restaurant in its own right, serving very good traditional Czech food, including a daily luncheon special that usually stays south of 100Kč. But it's also an excellent beer joint, with *tankové pivo* (unpasteurised Pilsner Urquell) on tap and a dignified 1930s interior that feels much more adult than all the cookie-cutter Pilsner Urquell franchise pubs springing up around town.

VINIČNÍ ALTÁN Map p125 — Wine Bar

☎ 224 262 861; Havlíčkovy sady 1369, Vršovice; 🕙 11am-11pm; 🚊 6, 7, 24 (stop Otakarova plus uphill walk), 4, 22 (stop Jana Masaryka plus walk)

Prague's nicest open-air wine garden claims to be its oldest as well – apparently established by Emperor Charles IV himself. Enjoy a glass of locally made white or red on a refurbished wooden gazebo overlooking the vineyards and the Nusle valley. There's no easy way to get here; try cutting through Vinohrady, following Americká and then continuing through Havlíčkovy sady. There are minimal but decent food offerings, including salads and sausages.

ŽIŽKOV & KARLÍN

Žižkov is famous for having more pubs per head of population than any other city district in Europe, and – depending on your tastes – offers the most authentic or the most terrifying pub-crawling experience in Prague. Be prepared for smoke, sticky floors, wall-to-wall noise and some heroically drunk companions.

BUKOWSKI'S Map p130 — Cocktail Bar

☎ 222 212 676; Bořivojova 86; 🕙 6pm-2am; 🚊 5, 9, 26

Like most of the drinking dens that are popular among expats, Bukowski's – the city's latest barfly magnet – is more a cocktail dive than a cocktail bar. Named after hard-drinking American writer Charles Bukowski, it cultivates a dark and slightly debauched atmosphere – the decor is self-consciously 'interesting' (when you can see it through the smoke-befogged candle-light) – but it peddles quality cocktails and cigars, and has friendly bartenders and cool tunes.

PIVOVARSKÝ KLUB

Map p130 — Pub
☎ 222 315 777; Křižíkova 17; 🕙 11am-11.30pm; Ⓜ Florenc

This bar is to beer what the Bodleian Library is to books – the wall-to-wall shelves are lined with myriad varieties of bottled beer from all over the world, and there are six guest beers on tap (the fresh and hoppy Štěpán *ležák* and the citrusy Primátor yeast beer are both excellent). Perch on a bar stool or head downstairs to the snug cellar

BREWERY TOURS

The Staropramen Brewery in the Prague suburb of Smíchov offers tours to visitors; there are also several other breweries within reach of the capital:

Budweiser Budvar Brewery (off Map p58; ☎ 387 705 341; www.budvar.cz; cnr Pražská & K Světlé, České Budějovice; tour 100Kč; ☉ 9am-5pm, closed Sun & Mon in Jan & Feb) Has one-hour tours for a minimum of eight persons; must be booked in advance. České Budějovice is 160km south of Prague.

Pilsner Urquell Brewery (off Map p58; ☎ 377 062 888; www.beerworld.cz; U Prazdroje 7, Plzeň; tour 150Kč; ☉ 8.30am-6pm Apr-Sep, to 5pm Oct-Mar) Has 1½-hour guided tours (with beer-tasting). Tours in English begin at 12.45pm, 2.15pm and 4.15pm daily; no advance booking needed. Plzeň is 80km west of Prague.

Staropramen Brewery (Map p143; ☎ 257 191 300; www.staropramen.com; Nádražní 84, Smíchov; tour 100Kč; ☉ 9am-5pm) One-hour tours by appointment only; also has an excellent bar and restaurant, Na Verandách (p178).

Velké Popovice Brewery (off Map p58; ☎ 323 683 425; www.kozel.cz; Ringhofferova 1, Velké Popovice; tour 100Kč; ☉ 10am-6pm Apr-Sep, to 4pm Oct-Mar) Has 90-minute tours for individuals in English at noon and 2pm in summer, noon only in winter. Velké Popovice is just 20km southeast of Prague.

(the pub is entirely nonsmoking) and order some of the pub's excellent grub to soak up the beer (authentic *guláš* with bacon dumplings for 185Kč).

U SLOVANSKÉ LÍPY

Map p130   Pub

☎ 222 780 563; Tachovské náměstí 6; ☉ 4-11pm; 🚊 133, 207

Another classic Žižkov pub, plain and unassuming outside and in, 'At the Linden Trees' (the linden is a Czech and Slovak national emblem) has become something of a place of pilgrimage for beer lovers since being popularised in the Pivní Filosof blog (see the boxed text, p193). The reason is its range of beers from the Kout na Šumavě brewery, including a superb *světlý ležák* (26Kč for 0.5L), and the dark and powerful *tmavý speciál*, which weighs in at a head-spinning 18°.

U VYSTŘELENÉHO OKA

Map p130   Pub

☎ 222 540 465; U Božích Bojovníků 3; ☉ 4.30pm-1am Mon-Sat; 🚊 133, 207

You've got to love a pub that has vinyl pads on the wall above the gents' urinals to rest your forehead on. 'The Shot-Out Eye' – the name pays homage to the one-eyed Hussite hero atop the hill behind the pub (see National Monument, p132) – is a bohemian (with a small 'b') hostelry with a raucous Friday-night atmosphere where the cheap Pilsner Urquell (29Kč for 0.5L) pulls in a typically heterogeneous Žižkov crowd. There's no need to worry about the language barrier – everyone here speaks the international language of booze.

HOLEŠOVICE, BUBENEČ & DEJVICE

Working-class Holešovice has always had its share of old-man's pubs, but only relatively recently has the neighbourhood exploded with nicer drinking options, including several new cafes. Most of the better places are clustered around Letenské náměstí in Bubeneč. Look particularly down the street Šmeralová. If you can't find something that suits your fancy, walk to the corner at Keramícká and then on to Čechova. There are at least half a dozen bars and watering holes around here, all offering pretty much the same mix of cheapish beer and tables filled with students and local residents knocking one back.

FRAKTAL Map p136   Bar

☎ 777 794 094; Šmeralová 1, Bubeneč; ☉ 11am-midnight; 🚊 1, 8, 15, 25, 26

This subterranean space under a corner house near Letenské náměstí is easily the friendliest bar this side of the Vltava. This is especially true for English speakers, as Fraktal serves as a kind of unofficial expat watering hole. It serves the Pilsner Urquell family of beers, including popular 10° Gambrinus. There's also good bar fare like burgers and surprisingly decent steaks on hand for spacing the beers. The only drawback is the early closing time. Last orders are at 11.30pm, and every year they seem to bring it forward another 30 minutes.

LA BODEGA FLAMENCA Map p136   Bar

☎ 233 374 075; Šmeralová 5, Bubeneč; ☉ 4pm-1am Sun-Thu, to 3am Fri & Sat; 🚊 1, 8, 15, 25, 26

La Bodega is an atmospheric, red-brick cellar, painted and plastered to look like an adobe shack. With the Latin music turned down low, the buzz of conversation and the flickering candlelight, the crowd seems a bit more reflective (well, at least compared with the crew at Fraktal next door). Most people come for the sangria or the beer, but there's also a nice selection of tapas on hand, including *tortilla español*, *chorizo al vino tinto* (chorizo sausage stewed in red wine) and *gambas pil-pil* (prawns in garlic and chilli). There's also live music and dance some nights.

STROMOFFKA Map p136   Bar
☎ 777 564 918; Kamenická 54, Holešovice; ◷ 5pm-2am Mon-Sat; ⓡ 1, 8, 15, 25, 26
This popular student bar, with occasional DJs and dancing downstairs, draws a local, early-20ish crowd, but is large enough to be welcoming to newcomers. It tends to get packed out late on Fridays and Saturdays, when the lower-level bar is three-deep in drink orders and sweaty bodies are pounding out the beat behind.

ZTRACENÝ RÁJ Map p136   Bar
☎ 774 350 400; Čechova 9, Bubeneč; ◷ 10am-1am; ⓡ 1, 8, 15, 25, 26
One of several mostly student-oriented cafes and bars on this leafy street just off Letenské náměstí. Not much to lure you here aside from decent Pilsner Urquell on tap at nontouristy prices, a general convivial vibe and some scruffy picnic tables out front that feel just right on a warm evening.

LETENSKÝ ZÁMEČEK
Map p136   Beer Garden
☎ 233 378 208; Letenský sady 341, Bubeneč; ◷ 11am-11pm (summer only); ⓡ 1, 8, 15, 25, 26
No accounting of watering holes in the Holešovice area would be complete without a nod towards the city's best beer garden, situated at the eastern end of Letná park. If it's beer you're after, you have two choices: one, known euphemistically as 'business class', is to pull up a chair at the grill–garden restaurant towards the left, where you can get a half-litre Pilsner Urquell for around 30Kč a glass, plus pretty good pizzas and burritos. The other option – 'coach' – is to line up at the beer window and get a 28Kč half-litre in a plastic cup and sit at the picnic tables along the ridge with a gorgeous view

over the Old Town below. Though it's open only in nice weather, it's the best game in town on a warm summer evening.

ALCHYMISTA Map p136   Cafe
☎ 233 370 359; Jana Zajívce 7, Bubeneč; ◷ 10.30am-7.30pm (later in summer); ⓡ 1, 8, 15, 25, 26 (stop: Sparta)
This old-fashioned coffee house with an adjacent art gallery is an oasis in the culturally barren neighbourhood behind Sparta stadium. Freshly ground coffees, a serious selection of teas (no Lipton in a bag here), and freshly made cakes and strudels draw a mostly neighbourhood crowd. In nice weather ask to take your coffee in the back garden. Nonsmoking throughout.

ARTESA Map p136   Cafe
☎ 224 318 625; Dejvická 33, Dejvice; ◷ 8.30am-9pm Mon-Fri, noon-7pm Sat & Sun; Ⓜ Dejvická or ⓡ 2, 8, 20, 26
Retro is big these days, and this tiny coffee joint, just off Vítězné náměstí, evokes the futurism of the 1950s and '60s with its modular chairs, pinkish walls and groovy, hanging cylinder lamps. Customers run the gamut from old ladies to supermodels – all there for the very good coffee as well as cakes, sweets and rolls. The front room is nonsmoking; the back, smoking.

BIO OKO Map p136   Cafe
☎ 233 382 606; Františka Křížka 15, Holešovice; ◷ 3pm-2am; ⓡ 1, 8, 15, 25, 26
The cafe and bar in the repertory cinema Bio Oko (p205) is a gem. It's classically retro as befits a cinema that regularly shows arty faves from the 1950s and '60s. Serving good espresso-based drinks as well as beer and cocktails, it's a nice choice for before or after the show.

ERHARTOVA CUKRÁRNA
Map p136   Cafe
☎ 233 312 148; Milady Horákové 56, Holešovice; ◷ 10am-7pm; ⓡ 1, 8, 15, 25, 26
This stylish 1930s-era cafe and sweetshop in a refurbished functionalist building is adjacent to the local branch of the public library. It draws a mix of mothers with strollers, students and old folks, attracted mainly by the local varieties of biscuits, doughnuts and cinnamon rolls in the glass case, and ice cream in hot weather. Nonsmoking throughout.

KABINET Map p136   Cafe

☎ 233 326 668; Terronská 25, Dejvice; ◷ 11am-11pm Mon-Fri, 3-11pm Sat & Sun; Ⓜ Dejvická or 🚊 8

A retro 1920s-style coffee house, slightly reminiscent of a cabaret, Kabinet is situated in a cool rondocubist building in a pleasantly residential part of Dejvice. Old cameras, posters and photographs emphasise the throwback feel. The name of the cafe, for Czechs, recalls early school days – a *kabinet* being a teacher's office – to add to the nostalgic feel. A perfect spot for a quiet conversation or for relaxing over a coffee and a good book.

KAVÁRNA ALIBI
Map p136   Cafe

☎ no phone; Svatovítská 6, Dejvice; ◷ noon-midnight Mon-Fri, 4pm-midnight Sat & Sun; Ⓜ Dejvická or 🚊 2, 8, 20, 26

Lively, smoky coffee house that is usually packed with students. It's a perfect spot to curl up with a coffee or a beer, write some postcards, consult your Lonely Planet guide or have a heart-to-heart chat with your travelling companion. Free and dependable wi-fi connection on the premises. About a 10-minute hike from the metro stop.

KUMBAL Map p136   Cafe

☎ 777 559 842; Heřmanová 12, Holešovice; ◷ 9am-8pm; 🚊 1, 5, 8, 12, 14, 15, 17, 25, 26

Another stylish coffee bar in a 1930s functionalist building that manages to be both hip and comfortable at the same time. There's good coffee and tea drinks, though not much on the menu aside from a few simple sandwiches and a daily soup (usually vegetarian). It's nonsmoking throughout, which attracts the stroller crowd in the afternoon and makes a pleasant place to linger (maybe that's why there's rarely a free table). Free wi-fi.

LONG TALE CAFÉ
Map p136   Cafe

☎ 266 310 701; Osadní 25, Holešovice; ◷ 9am-7pm; 🚊 1, 3, 12, 14, 25

Inviting, smoke-free cafe that draws a pleasing mix of office workers, mothers with strollers and the occasional freelance writer, who come for the excellent coffee drinks, relaxed vibe and very good and reasonably priced salads and sandwiches. Free and reliable wi-fi on hand.

OUKY DOUKY Map p136   Cafe

☎ 266 711 531; Janovského 14, Holešovice; ◷ 8am-midnight; 🚊 1, 5, 8, 12, 14, 15, 17, 25, 26

This was the original home of the Globe Bookstore & Café (née Coffeehouse) in the 1990s, and a kind of eclectic, San Francisco funkiness lingers. Today it houses a used bookstore with a worn-out selection of Czech-language books and an inviting cafe filled with students, housewives from the neighbourhood, a few bohemian types and a wandering expat or two. The light menu features mostly toasts, sandwiches and salads. Free wi-fi.

TĚSNĚ VEDLE BURUNDI
Map p136   Cafe

☎ 777 170 803; Sládkova 4, Bubeneč; ◷ 10am-10pm; 🚊 1, 8, 15, 25, 26

A curious pub–coffee house hybrid that draws a mix of intellectuals, students, ageing rockers, and garden-variety neighbourhood drinkers. It has a vaguely old-school dissident whiff about the place, making it a more satisfying spot to linger than the swish bars in the city centre. Limited food options include a couple of salads and toasts.

ANDALUSKÝ PES Map p136   Cocktail Bar

☎ 773 026 584; Korunovační 4, Bubeneč; ◷ 7pm-3am; 🚊 1, 8, 15, 25, 26

'Le Chien Andalou' is an after-hours cocktail bar with retro flair. The inviting front room, sporting red-velvet bar stools and purple glitter walls, attracts a kind of Edward Hopper 'Nighthawks' crowd after Fraktal closes and the night-time crowd moves in. The back rooms have a more risqué feel, dark and crowded some nights, with faces recognisable only by the glow of their cigarettes. It tends to close early on quiet nights, so take the official opening hours with a grain of salt.

POSTEL Map p136   Cocktail Bar

☎ 220 874 797; Veletržní 14, Holešovice; ◷ 5pm-2am Mon-Sat; 🚊 1, 5, 8, 12, 14, 15, 17, 25, 26

The name means 'bed', and that's obviously the goal at this flash meat-market–cocktail bar not far from Strossmayerovo náměstí. Fans of the film *Cocktail* will delight at the bartenders' juggling skills. Others will marvel at the attractive clientele. All in all, not a bad place to while away a couple of hours before, well, bed.

MOVE OVER WITTGENSTEIN, MAKE WAY FOR THE 'BEER PHILOSOPHER'

In a country that once had a philosopher president in Václav Havel, it's only fitting it now has a self-proclaimed *pivní filosof* – a beer philosopher. Argentinean expat Max Bahnson first came to Prague eight years ago as a stopover on a holiday trip to Egypt and he never left. Today, he's one of the country's leading *pivo* enthusiasts and through his popular beer blog (www.pivni-filosof.com) is heading the resurgence in interest in regional and microbrews. We caught up with Max on a wintry afternoon to discuss beer trends and get his reasoned recommendation on the Czech Republic's best pint.

The beer in Prague is great, but not every pub and every pint is of the same high quality. How do you know for sure that you're in a place that serves good beer? That's true. They say 50% of a beer's quality is who makes it and the other 50% is who taps it. A pub's pipes have to be clean and there's got to be sufficient rotation, since once a keg's tapped, it's a race against time. If you walk into a place and 40 people are sitting there drinking beer, it's almost always going to be good since that means they're tapping a new keg once every hour or so.

The Czech beer market is dominated by big brewers like Pilsner Urquell and Staropramen, often backed by big foreign multinationals. In fact, in most Prague pubs, that's all you can find. Do these beers still stack up? What's the best 'big-name' beer? Pilsner Urquell's (SABMiller) standard 12° lager is still an excellent beer, particularly the unpasteurised version (served at selected pubs in Prague marked with '*tankové pivo*'). The beer is tapped from sealed bags in huge tanks brought in from the brewery. The beer never comes into contact with gases, giving it a fuller taste. Foreign ownership has been a mixed bag. Heineken's takeover of Krušovice has actually helped improve the beer's quality.

The good news is that it seems like regional beers are getting a bit easier to find in Prague pubs. So, what's your favourite smaller beer around town? Svijany. It's a northern Bohemian brewery that still keeps to the traditional brewing methods. It's unpasteurised and has become relatively easy to find in Prague. You can even buy it bottled in some supermarkets. Czechs are very loyal to their brands and the big brewers traditionally benefited because their quality was reliable. Now the smaller brewers are really improving.

Okay. Here's the big question. Forget about whether you can find it or not, but if you could choose just one beer in the Czech Republic… the best one they make … what would it be? That would be Kout na Šumavě. It's the best lager on the market, hands down. It's brewed near the Šumava (in the southwestern part of the country), but you can actually find it at two places in Prague. One is a dirty, smoky pub in Žižkov called U Slovanské lípy (p190); the other is one of the fanciest restaurants in town: Céleste (p169), in the 'Fred & Ginger' building (Dancing Building) in Nové Město.
An interview with Max Bahnson by Mark Baker.

AKÁDEMIE Map p136   Pub
☎ 233 375 236; Šmeralová 5, Bubeneč; ☺ 4pm-4am; ◉ 1, 8, 15, 25, 26

This cavernous pub has several pool tables and dartboards to amuse in case you tire of sitting around chewing the fat (quite literally given the menu options). The game of choice here is eight ball; the tables are large and well maintained. Waiters bring your beers to the table, and everything is toted up – billiards included – at the end. Late opening hours make this a good place to wrap up.

BUDVARKÁ Map p136   Pub
☎ 222 960 820; Wuchterlova 22, Dejvice; ☺ 11am-11pm; Ⓜ Dejvická or ◉ 2, 8, 20, 26

Handsome Czech pub owned and operated by the Budvar brewery. You'll find the complete 'Budweiser' family of beers here, including the hard-to-find yeast and dark varieties. There's also excellent Czech pub food served in what looks to be a pretty accurate rendition of a 19th-century taproom. There's a smoking room out the front and a large and well-lit nonsmoking area in the back.

KLÁŠTERNÍ PIVNICE (ŠUMAVAN)
Map p136   Pub
☎ 233 376 150; Ovenecká 15, Bubeneč; ☺ 9.30am-10pm; ◉ 1, 8, 15, 25, 26

It's a shame to blow the cover of the secret haunt of Prague's beer bloggers, but beer lovers deserve to know about this modest little old-man's joint near Letná. The house beer is an 11° lager from the highly respected Klášter brewery, but the barman likes to mix it up every once in a while by offering speciality brews on tap from around the country. The early opening hours invite decadence. There's only around a dozen tables here, so this is better suited to small groups of quiet drinkers.

NA SLAMNÍKU
Map p136　　　　　　　　　　　　　　　Pub

☎ 233 322 594; Wolkerova 12, Bubeneč; ◷ 11am-11pm; ◉ 1, 8, 15, 25, 26 (plus walk)

A great traditional Czech pub and beer garden dating from the 19th century, Na Slamníku is tucked away in a small valley in Bubeneč in the neighbourhood just behind the sprawling Russian embassy. There are three separate spaces: on the left side is an old-school tavern with cheap and decent Czech dishes, the right side is more a raucous pub, and in summer you can eat and drink outside under the trees. It's hard to find, so bring a map or take a taxi.

NA STARÉ KOVÁRNĚ
Map p136　　　　　　　　　　　　　　　Pub

☎ 233 371 099; Kamenická 17, Holešovice; ◷ 11am-1am; ◉ 1, 8, 15, 25, 26

The motorcycle hanging from the ceiling sets a rakish tone for one of the most popular Czech pubs in the neighbourhood. The food is at least two notches above standard *hospoda* fare – and has even garnered raves from local critics – but few people actually come just for the food. It's a shot and a beer joint in the best sense of the term.

POTREFENÁ HUSA
Map p136　　　　　　　　　　　　　　　Pub

☎ 233 341 022; Verdunská 23, Dejvice; ◷ 11am-1am Mon-Fri, noon-1am Sat & Sun; Ⓜ Dejvická or ◉ 2, 8, 20, 26

The Dejvice branch of the Potrefená husa chain is a pleasant alternative to most of the grotty local joints that still predominate in this part of town. There's a full complement of high-quality pub food, TVs on the wall, and a well-heeled crowd that keeps things interesting.

SVIJANSKÝ RYTÍŘ
Map p136　　　　　　　　　　　　　　　Pub

☎ 233 378 342; Jirečkova 13, Bubeneč; ◷ 11am-11pm Mon-Fri; ◉ 1, 8, 15, 25, 26

Inviting Czech pub that serves authentic and very good Czech cuisine – heavy

on staples like pork and chicken schnitzels – but the real drawcard here is the availability of nearly the entire family of highly regarded Svijany beers, both light and dark, including the flagship 12° Rytíř and the stronger but even more fabled 13° Kníže. Why not try them all? Service is attentive and friendly, though English-language help is in short supply. Closed weekends.

U SV ANTONÍĆKA
Map p136　　　　　　　　　　　　　　　Pub

☎ 220 879 428; Podplukovníka Sochora 20, Holešovice; ◷ 11am-11pm; ◉ 1, 5, 8, 12, 14, 15, 17, 25, 26

A relative rarity these days close to the centre: a fully unreconstructed Czech pub and all that that entails, including cantankerous locals, an occasional hygiene issue with the glassware, layers of smoke, and toilets that will have to be buried in a nuclear landfill someday. Yet it has a certain charm. If you're curious about how things used to be, or long for a drink far from the tour coaches, this is your place. Not for the faint-hearted.

SMÍCHOV

Smíchov continues to surprise. Every year brings at least one or two new bar and cafe openings. Most of the action is clustered near the Anděl metro station, anchored by the enormous Nový Smíchov shopping centre. The Staropramen brewery is located near here, but alas the funky bar inside the brewery has been replaced by yet another branch of the cookie-cutter, Staropramen-owned Potrefená husa restaurant chain. The beer's still fresh, though, and brewed on-site.

BACK DOORS
Map p143　　　　　　　　　　　　　　　Bar

☎ 257 315 827; Na Bělidle 30; ◷ 11am-1am; Ⓜ Anděl or ◉ 4, 6, 7, 9, 10, 14, 20

The owners say this upmarket cellar-bar-restaurant-club is inspired by similar spaces in New York and Amsterdam (though the subterranean Gothic cellar look could really only be Prague). It offers decent Czech DJs and a relaxed vibe most nights, though it can get stuffy on a crowded weekend night. If you're hungry, there's a full menu of well-done international dishes.

DOG'S BOLLOCKS
Map p143   Bar
☎ 775 736 030; Nádražní 82; ☉ 5pm-midnight
Mon, 5pm-3am Tue-Sat; Ⓜ Anděl
This run-of-the-mill bar and nightspot is
next door to the Staropramen Brewery and
is a decent choice if you're staying in the
area and don't want to go too far for your
fun. In spite of the English-friendly name,
it draws mostly Czech students and young
professionals. Open late.

HELLS BELLS
Map p143   Bar
☎ 723 184 760; Na Bělidle 30; ☉ 3pm-3am;
Ⓜ Anděl
Despite all the new, glitzy office towers,
Smíchov is still a down and dirty kind of
place, and this metal bar is where the locals
let it all hang out. Loud, crowded and fun –
the late closing time makes it a perfect
ticket for that last drink of the night. You'll
find it just across the street from Back
Doors, inside a small courtyard.

KÁVA KÁVA KÁVA
Map p143   Cafe
☎ 257 314 277; Lidická 42; mains 70-120Kč;
☉ 7am-10pm; Ⓜ Anděl
The Smíchov branch of the popular internet
cafe in Staré Město (see the boxed text,
p165) is bigger and brighter than the original, with Etruscan orange walls, terracotta
floor tiles and modern art. There's a more
extensive menu too – you can snack on salads, sandwiches, quiche or nachos, or tuck
into more substantial chicken gyros, Mexican chilli or homemade soup of the day.

WASH CAFÉ
Map p143   Cafe
☎ 608 703 805; Nádražní 66; ☉ 9am-midnight;
🚋 12, 14, 20
This whacky combination of a self-serve
laundromat and cafe sports 70s-era thrift-
shop furniture (think velveteen lounge
chairs) and a laid-back vibe. Not worth
making a special trip out this far for, but if
you happen to be in the 'hood, it's easily
the coolest spot around for coffee. Also
serves beer, wine, mixed drinks and snacks.

LOKAL BLOK
Map p143   Pub
☎ 251 511 490; náměstí 14.října 10; ☉ noon-1am
Mon-Fri, 4pm-1am Sat & Sun; Ⓜ Anděl
The perfect Prague combination: a raucous
pub and a state-of-the-art climbing wall
(though presumably you're supposed to
boulder before you drink and not vice
versa). Most nights there's a lively crowd,
fuelled by Pilsner Urquell on tap and some
good Mexican eats, such as nachos and
quesadillas. Highly recommended.

NA VERANDÁCH
Map p143   Pub
☎ 257 191 200; Nádražní 84; ☉ 11am-midnight
Mon-Thu, to 1am Fri & Sat, to 11pm Sun; Ⓜ Anděl
This pub and restaurant, managed by the
Potrefená husa local restaurant chain, is
inside the Staropramen Brewery, and while
lots of people come here to eat, it's perfectly
fine to come in just for a super-fresh beer
(there are seven varieties on tap). The menu
is basically the same as at other branches of
Potrefená husa. It's high-tone fast food: ribs,
burgers, chicken breasts and the lot. Sit on
the verandah in the back in nice weather, or
up front by the bar on a chilly night.

ENTERTAINMENT

top picks

What's your recommendation? www.lonelyplanet.com/prague

ENTERTAINMENT

Across the spectrum, from ballet to blues, jazz to rock, theatre to film, there's a bewildering range of entertainment on offer in this eclectic city. Prague is now as much a European centre for jazz, rock and hip hop as it is for classical music. The biggest draw, however, is still the Prague Spring festival of classical music and opera.

For reviews, day-by-day listings and a directory of venues, consult the 'Night & Day' section of the weekly *Prague Post* (www.praguepost.com). Monthly listings booklets include *Culture in Prague* and the Czech-language *Přehled*, available from PIS offices (see p263 for contact details).

Check out the online magazine *Provokátor* (www.provokator.org), dedicated to art, music, culture and politics, with listings of upcoming cultural events. There is also *Metropolis*, a free weekly booklet with film, theatre and music listings, available in cinemas, pubs and clubs (it's in Czech only, but the listings are easily deciphered).

For web-based entertainment listings, check out www.prague.tv/events, www.heartofeurope.cz and www.pis.cz/en/prague/events.

NIGHTLIFE

If discussing Kafka over a coffee or analysing last night's hockey match over a glass of Pilsner seems too tame, Prague offers plenty of places for night owls to party on into the small hours. From traditional jazz joints in smoky cellars to innovative live-music venues, cool cocktail clubs and even an underground nuclear bunker, you'll find a place worth staying up late for.

CLUBBING

Prague's club scene is nothing to rave about. With few exceptions, the city's dance clubs cater to crowds of partying teenagers and tourists weaned on MTV Europe – if you want to dance to anything other than '80s hits or happy house, you'll have to look long and hard. Prague's main strengths are its alternative music clubs, DJ bars, 'experimental' venues such as Palác Akropolis and the Roxy

and places that are just plain weird, like Bunkr Parukářka.

Refreshingly, dress codes don't seem to have reached Prague yet, and it's unlikely you'll be knocked back anywhere unless you're stark naked. And there are even a few places that would probably be OK with that…

Check out www.prague.tv, www.techno.cz/party or www.hip-hop.cz for up-to-date club listings (the latter two are in Czech, but you can work out what's going on).

BUNKR PARUKÁŘKA Map p130

☎ 603 423 140; www.parukarka.eu; Na Kříže, Olšanské náměstí, Žižkov; admission free-50Kč; ⊗ vary – check listings on website; 🚊 5, 9, 26

Only in Prague… A graffiti-covered steel door in the hillside at the west end of Parukářka park leads unexpectedly to a vast circular staircase that descends 15m underground into a 1950s nuclear bunker where a makeshift bar serves cheap beer in plastic glasses. This is the unlikely setting for one of Prague's most unusual clubs, a claustrophobic shrine to electropunk, industrial, psytrance-electro-acid and any other weird and wonderful avant-garde electronic music genre you can think of (winners of the most eccentric label so far are Vložte Kočku, whose music is promoted as 'psy-countryemotriphoprap'). See the website for what's on when you're in town.

CROSS CLUB Map p136

☎ 736 535 053; http://crossclub.cz; Plynární 23, Holešovice; admission free-120Kč; ⊗ cafe noon-2am, club 6pm-4am; Ⓜ Nádraží Holešovice

---

top picks

GAY & LESBIAN PRAGUE

- Castle Steps (p219)
- Club Stella (p186)
- Friends (p184)
- Pension Arco (p226)
- Termix (p200)
- Café Celebrity (p187)

BUYING TICKETS

The 'wholesalers' with the largest agency networks are Bohemia Ticket International (BTI), FOK and Ticketpro; the others probably get their tickets from them.

Bohemia Ticket International (BTI; Map p90; ☎ 224 227 832; www.ticketsbti.cz; Malé náměstí 13, Staré Město; ⏰ 9am-5pm Mon-Fri) BTI provides tickets for all kinds of events. There's another branch (Map p110; ☎ 224 215 031; Na Příkopě 16, Nové Město; ⏰ 10am-7pm Mon-Fri, 10am-5pm Sat, 10am-3pm Sun) near the Municipal House.

FOK Box Office (Map p90; ☎ 222 002 336; www.fok.cz; U Obecního Domu 2, Staré Město; ⏰ 10am-6pm Mon-Fri) Prague Symphony Orchestra box office, for classical concert tickets; also open for one hour before performance begins.

Ticketcentrum (Map p90; ☎ 296 333 333; Rytířská 31, Staré Město; ⏰ 9am-12.30pm & 1-5pm Mon-Fri) Walk-in centre for all kinds of tickets; branch of Ticketpro.

Ticketpro (Map p110; www.ticketpro.cz; Pasáž Lucerna, Vodičkova 36, Nové Město; ⏰ noon-4pm & 4.30-8.30pm Mon-Fri) Tickets are available here for all kinds of events. There are Ticketpro branches in PIS offices (see p263) and many other places.

Ticketstream (www.ticketstream.cz) Internet-based booking agency that covers events in Prague and all over the Czech Republic.

This is an industrial club in every sense of the word: the setting in an industrial zone in Holešovice, the thumplng music (with both DJs and live acts) and the interior, an absolute must-see jumble of gadgets, shafts, cranks and pipes, many of which move and pulsate with light to the music. The program includes occasional cabaret nights, theatre performances and art happenings. There's drinking on two levels, plus a cafe and few picnic tables outside. It's easy to find despite the location: after exiting Nádraží Holešovice metro station, walk 100m to the east along Plynární street. You've arrived once you see the enormous industrial sculpture out the front.

FUTURUM
Map p143

☎ 257 328 571; www.musicbar.cz; Zborovská 7, Smíchov; admission 90-120Kč; ⏰ 7pm-2am; 🚊 7, 9, 12, 14

Futurum is a cross-fertilisation of alternative and mainstream, with a bizarre decor that looks like a cross between an art deco ballroom and Flash Gordon's spaceship. Midweek nights see occasional live performances of jazz and soul, indie bands and record launches, but what really pulls in the crowds is the regular Friday- and Saturday-night '80s and '90s Video Party, with local DJs blasting out everything from REM and Nirvana to Bon Jovi and the Village People.

KLUB 007 STRAHOV Map p78

☎ 257 211 439; www.klub007strahov.cz; Block 7, Chaloupeckého 7; admission 50-250Kč; ⏰ 7pm-midnight Sun-Thu, 7pm-1am Fri & Sat; 🚌 143, 176, 217

Klub 007 is one of several grungy student clubs in the basements of the big college dormitory blocks in Strahov. The legendary 007 has been around since 1987, when it was a focus for underground music, and is now famed for its devotion to hardcore, punk, ska, ragga, jungle, ambient and other alternative sounds.

LE CLAN Map p125

www.leclan.cz; Balbínova 23, Vinohrady; admission 50-160Kč; ⏰ 2am-10am Wed-Sun; Ⓜ Muzeum

A popular French-accented after-party club, with DJs on two floors, lots of bars, cosy armchairs and myriad rooms stuffed with people who want to party until dawn. It's usually got a good, decadent vibe, and tends to get more, not less, crowded as the night wears on.

MECCA Map p136

☎ 602 711 225; www.mecca.cz; U Průhonu 3, Holešovice; admission 39-200Kč (women frequently admitted free until midnight); ⏰ 10pm-6am Wed-Sat; 🚊 5, 12, 15

This former warehouse in Holešovice has been going strong for more than a decade and is still one of the best of the city's ultrafashionable dance clubs. Its industrial red brick and right angles are softened by rounded shapes, floaty drapes and futuristic curvy couches. Mecca is a magnet for models, film stars and fashionistas, and for the legion of clubbers who come for the huge, DJ-dominated dance floor and pumping sound system.

RADOST FX Map p125

☎ 224 254 776; www.radostfx.cz; Bělehradská 120, Vinohrady; admission 100-250Kč; ☼ 10pm-6am; Ⓜ IP Pavlova

Though not quite as trendy as it once was, slick and shiny Radost is still capable of pulling in the crowds, especially for its Thursday hip hop night, FXbounce (www .fxbounce.com, women enter free). The place has a chilled-out, bohemian atmosphere, with an excellent lounge and vegetarian restaurant that keeps serving into the small hours (see Café FX, p173). Gay friendly, though the crowd is normally mixed, straight and gay.

ROXY Map p90

☎ 224 826 296; www.roxy.cz; Dlouhá 33, Staré Město; admission free-250Kč Fri & Sat; ☼ 7pm-midnight Mon-Thu, 7pm-6am Fri & Sat; 🚊 5, 8, 14

Set in the ramshackle shell of an art deco cinema, the legendary Roxy has nurtured the more independent and innovative end of Prague's club spectrum since 1987 – this is the place to see the Czech Republic's top DJs. On the 1st floor is NoD, an 'experimental space' that stages drama, dance, performance art, cinema and live music; events here usually begin earlier in the evening before the nightclub kicks off at around midnight. Best nightspot in Staré Město.

SASAZU Map p136

☎ 284 097 455; www.sasazu.cz; Bubenské nábřeží 306 (inside the Holešovice market), Holešovice; admission 100-1000Kč; ☼ 9pm-5am; Ⓜ Vltavská and 🚊 1, 3, 5, 25

Currently the reigning dance club among the city's fashionable elite. If you're into beautiful people, big dance floors and long lines at the door (hint: go early), this is your place. Check the website or posters around town for occasional big-name live events (such as Kool & the Gang, Fun Lovin' Criminals and Nina Hagen, among others), though ticket prices for these tend to shoot through the roof. SaSaZu also boasts

Holešovice's best restaurant, a high-quality Asian affair that's worth a trip out here in its own right (p176).

SEDM VLKŮ Map p130

☎ 222 711 725; www.sedmvlku.cz; Vlkova 7, Žižkov; admission free; ☼ 5pm-3am Mon-Sat; 🚊 5, 9, 26

'Seven Wolves' is a two-level, art-studenty cafe/bar and club. At street level there's candlelight, friendly staff, weird wrought-iron work and funky murals, and music low enough to have a conversation; down in the darkened cellar, DJs pump out techno, breakbeat, drum 'n' bass, jungle and reggae from 9pm on Friday and Saturday nights.

TECHTLE MECHTLE (BOMBA BAR) Map p125

☎ 222 250 143; www.techtle-mechtle.cz; Vinohradská 47, Vinohrady; ☼ 5pm-4am Mon-Sat; Ⓜ Muzeum or Ⓜ Jiřího z Poděbrad, 🚊 11

A popular cellar dance bar and watering hole right on Vinohrady's main drag. The name translates roughly to 'hanky panky' in Czech and that's what most of the swank, good-looking people who come here are after. In addition to a well-tended cocktail bar, you'll find a decent restaurant and dance floor and occasional special events like 'yoghurt battles', where attractive women in T-shirts wrestle each other to the ground in big vats of yoghurt. Arrive early to get a good table, especially on weekends.

TERMIX Map p125

☎ 222 710 462; www.club-termix.cz; Třebízckého 4a, Vinohrady; admission free; ☼ 8pm-5am Wed-Sun; Ⓜ Jiřího z Poděbrad

Termix is one of Prague's most popular gay and lesbian dance clubs, with an industrial-high-tech vibe (lots of shiny steel and glass and plush sofas) and a young crowd that contains as many tourists as locals. The smallish dance floor fills up fast during Thursday's best of the '80s and '90s party, when you may have to queue to get in.

WAKATA Map p136

☎ 233 370 518; www.wakata.cz; Malířská 14, Holešovice; admission free; ☼ 5pm-3am Mon-Thu, to 5am Fri & Sat, 6pm-3am Sun; 🚊 1, 8, 15, 25, 26

There's no designer chic or style statements in this small, unpretentious, laid-back DJ lounge, a house-free zone where you can enjoy inexpensive beers and cocktails among the scuffed and mismatched furniture while you bop along to a soundtrack of funk, Latin, dub, ambient, jungle, reggae or hip hop.

XT3 Map p130

☎ 222 783 463; www.xt3.cz; Rokycanova 29, Žižkov; admission free; ☉ bar 11am-3am Mon-Fri, 2pm-3am Sat & Sun, club 6pm-3am Sun-Thu, 6pm-5am Fri & Sat; ☐ 5, 9, 26
This is the essential Žižkov club – scruffy, laid-back, eclectic and great fun. There's a lively bar at street level, all red-brick arches and wood-and-leather booths, plus a cavern-like club venue that hosts local DJs and live music (from hardcore rock to acoustic singer-songwriters).

JAZZ CLUBS

Prague has lots of good jazz clubs, many of which have been around for decades. Most have a cover charge of around 100Kč to 300Kč.

AGHARTA JAZZ CENTRUM Map p90

☎ 222 211 275; www.agharta.cz; Železná 16, Staré Město; admission 250Kč; ☉ 7pm-1am, music 9pm-midnight; Ⓜ Můstek
Agharta has been staging top-notch modern Czech jazz, blues, funk and fusion since 1991, but moved into this very central Old Town venue only in 2004. A typical jazz cellar with red-brick vaults and a cosy bar and cafe, the centre also has a music shop (open 7pm to midnight), which sells CDs, T-shirts and coffee mugs. As well as hosting local musicians, the centre occasionally stages gigs by leading international artists – you can buy e-tickets direct from the website.

BLUES SKLEP Map p90

☎ 221 466 138; www.bluessklep.cz; Liliová 10, Staré Město; admission 100-120Kč; ☉ bar 7pm-2.30am, music 9pm-midnight; Ⓜ Staroměstská
One of the city's newer jazz clubs, the Blues Sklep (*sklep* means 'cellar') is a typical Old Town basement with dark, Gothic-vaulted rooms that provide an atmospheric setting for regular nightly jazz sessions. Bands play anything from trad New Orleans jazz to bebop, blues, funk and soul.

JAZZDOCK Map p143

☎ 774 058 838; www.jazzdock.cz; Janáčkovo nábřeží 2, Smíchov; admission 90-150Kč; ☉ 3pm-4am; Ⓜ Anděl; ☐ 7, 9, 12, 14

Most of Prague's jazz clubs are smoky cellar affairs. This relatively new club (opened in 2009) is a definite step up, with a clean, modern decor and a smart riverside location (with a decidedly romantic view out over the Vltava). Draws some of the best local talent and occasional international acts. The food is as good as the music, though (as with other Prague jazz clubs) the sightlines to the stage are partially obstructed. Go early or book to get a good table. Shows normally begin at 10pm (on nights when there are two shows, start times are 7pm and 10pm). Bring along a good map or take a taxi.

REDUTA JAZZ CLUB
Map p110

☎ 224 933 487; www.redutajazzclub.cz; Národní třída 20, Nové Město; admission 300Kč; ☉ 9pm-3am; Ⓜ Národní Třída
The Reduta is Prague's oldest jazz club, founded in 1958 during the communist era – it was here in 1994 that former US president Bill Clinton famously jammed on a new saxophone presented to him by Václav Havel. It has an intimate setting, with smartly dressed patrons squeezing into tiered seats and lounges to soak up the big-band, swing and Dixieland atmosphere. Book a few hours ahead at the box office (open from 5pm Monday to Friday and from 7pm Saturday and Sunday), or through Ticketpro.

U MALÉHO GLENA Map p78

☎ 257 531 717; www.malyglen.cz; Karmelitská 23, Malá Strana; admission 200Kč; ☉ 10am-2am, music from 9.30pm Sun-Thu, from 10pm Fri & Sat; ☐ 12, 20, 22
'Little Glen's' is a lively American-owned bar and restaurant where hard-swinging local jazz or blues bands play every night in the cramped and steamy stone-vaulted cellar. There are regular jam sessions where amateurs are welcome (as long as you're good!) – it's a small venue, so get here early if you want to see, as well as hear, the band.

USP JAZZ LOUNGE
Map p90

☎ 734 335 233; www.jazzlounge.cz; Michalská 9, Staré Město; admission 200-250Kč; ☉ 7pm-2am, music 9pm-midnight; Ⓜ Můstek
Located in the basement of the Hotel U Staré Paní, this long-established jazz club

caters to all levels of musical appreciation. There's a varied program of modern jazz, soul, blues and Latin rhythms, and a nightly DJ spot from midnight onwards.

LIVE MUSIC

Prague has a high-energy live-music scene, with rock, metal, punk, electro, industrial, hip hop and newer sounds at a score of DJ and live-music venues; most have a cover charge of around 50Kč to 200Kč. As well as the venues listed here, clubs such as Futurum, Klub 007 Strahov, Palác Akropolis and Roxy (see under Clubbing, p198) also host live rock bands.

For current listings and reviews check out the media listed at the start of this chapter, and keep an eye on flyers that are posted around town.

BATALION
Map p90

☎ 220 108 147; www.batalion.cz; 28.října 3, Staré Město; ⏰ bar 24hr, music from 9pm; Ⓜ Můstek; 🛜

Batalion is a delightfully grungy bar with a basement music club offering anything from rock and jazz to punk and death metal performed by up-and-coming Czech bands (plus DJ-fronted dance parties on Friday and Saturday). Despite a location in the midst of the tourist hordes, it pulls in a young, mainly local crowd.

BUNKR KLUB
Map p143

☎ 722 657 632; www.bunkr-club.net; Nádražní 76, Smíchov; admission 100-200Kč; ⏰ 6pm-3am; Ⓜ Anděl, 🚋 12, 14, 20

The most-recent reincarnation of the legendary Bunkr Klub of the 1990s recaptures the original's energy and overall grottiness. The new location, in an industrial part of Smíchov, suits the post-punk, hard-rock mood perfectly. The club occupies an old brick-lined cellar with two rooms. Bands play in a relatively cramped and narrow back room that quickly fills with smoke, sweat and noise. The front room, with a bar and a few tables, is bigger and quieter.

LA FABRIKA
Map p136

☎ no phone; www.lafabrika.cz; Komunardů 30, Holešovice; admission free-100Kč; ⏰ vary depending on events; Ⓜ Nádraží Holešovice plus 🚋 5, 12 or Ⓜ Vltavská plus 🚋 1, 3, 5, 25

The name refers to a 'factory', but this is actually a former paint warehouse that's been converted into an experimental performance space. Depending on the night, come here to catch live music (jazz or cabaret), theatre, dance or film. Summers are usually slow, but the season picks up again in autumn. Consult the website for the latest program. The ticket office and bar open about an hour before the event starts.

LUCERNA MUSIC BAR Map p110

☎ 224 217 108; http://musicbar.iquest .cz; Vodičkova 36, Nové Město; ⏰ 8pm-4am; Ⓜ Můstek

Nostalgia reigns supreme at this atmospheric old theatre, now looking a little dog-eared, with anything from Beatles tribute bands to mainly Czech artists playing jazz, blues, pop, rock and more on midweek nights. But the most popular event – don't ask us why – is the regular 1980s and '90s video party held every Friday and Saturday night, which pulls in huge crowds of young locals bopping along to Duran Duran and Gary Numan.

MALOSTRANSKÁ BESEDA Map p78

☎ restaurant 257 409 112; www.malostranska -beseda.cz; Malostranské náměstí 21, Malá Strana; shows 150-250Kč; ⏰ box office 3pm-10pm Mon-Sat, 3pm-8pm Sun, restaurant 11am-11pm, cafe 8am-10pm; 🚋 12, 20, 22

Malá Strana's four-storey pleasure palace reopened in 2010 after a five-year reconstruction hiatus. The fabled music club on the 2nd floor is back and better than ever, with a lively roster of cabaret acts, jazz and old Czech rockers. There's now an art gallery on the top floor and a big beer hall in the basement. The ground floor offers an inviting – if a bit too small – cafe on one side and a decent Pilsner Urquell–concept restaurant on the other.

PALÁC AKROPOLIS Map p130

☎ 296 330 911; www.palacakropolis.cz; Kubelíkova 27, Žižkov; admission free-50Kč; ⏰ club 7pm-5am; 🚋 5, 9, 26

The Akropolis is a Prague institution, a labyrinthine, sticky-floored shrine to alternative music and drama. Its various performance spaces host a smorgasbord of musical and cultural events, from DJs to string quartets to Macedonian Roma bands to local rock gods to visiting talent – Marianne Faithfull, the Flaming Lips and the Strokes have all played here. DJs do their stuff in the Theatre Bar (Divadelní Bar) and Small Hall (Malá Scéna), spinning everything from dub-step to hip hop, and reggae to nu-jazz.

ROCK CAFÉ Map p110

☎ 224 933 947; http://rockcafe.cz; Národní třída 20, Nové Město; admission free-150Kč; ☺ 10am-3am Mon-Fri, 5pm-3am Sat, 5pm-1am Sun, music from 7.30pm; Ⓜ Národní Třída

Not to be confused with the Hard Rock Café, this multifunction club next door to the Reduta Jazz Club is the offspring of the influential Nový Horizont art movement of the 1990s. It sports a stage for DJs and live rock bands, a funkily decorated 'rock cafe', a cinema, a theatre, an art gallery and a CD shop. Live bands are mostly local, ranging from nu-metal to folk rock to Doors and Sex Pistols tribute bands, and the arts program leans towards the avant-garde and the just plain weird. Problems with noise mean that live bands have to finish by 10pm, but renovation work may solve this problem in the near future.

VAGON Map p90

☎ 733 737 301; www.vagon.cz; Palác Metro, Národní třída 25; gigs 100Kč, admission free after 11pm; ☺ 7pm-5am, gigs 9pm-midnight; Ⓜ Národní or Ⓣ 6, 9, 18, 22

With its entrance tucked away in a shopping arcade, Vagon is more like a student union bar than a club as such, but it always has a friendly, chilled-out atmosphere. There's live music pretty much every night, from local blues artists, through Pink Floyd and Led Zep tribute bands, to classic Czech rock bands, including regular performances by Plastic People of the Universe. From midnight into the small hours the dancing continues as a DJ-hosted 'rockothèque'.

THE ARTS

For classical music, opera, ballet, theatre and some rock concerts – even with the most thoroughly 'sold-out' events – you can often find a ticket or two on sale at the theatre's box office a half-hour or so before show time.

If you want to be sure of a seat, Prague is awash with ticket agencies (see the boxed text, p199). Their advantage is convenience: most are computerised, fast and accept credit cards. Their drawback is a probable 8% to 15% mark-up.

Many venues have discounts for students and sometimes for the disabled. Most performances have a certain number of tickets set aside for foreigners. For rock and jazz clubs you can turn up at the door, but advance bookings are recommended for big names.

CLASSICAL MUSIC, OPERA & BALLET

There are half a dozen concerts of one kind or another almost every day during the summer, making a fine soundtrack to accompany the city's visual delights. Many of these are chamber concerts performed by aspiring musicians in the city's churches – gorgeous but chilly (take an extra layer, even on a summer day) and not always with the finest of acoustics. However, a good number of concerts, especially those promoted by people handing out flyers in the street, are second-rate, despite the premium prices that foreigners pay. If you want to be sure of quality, go for a performance by one of the city's professional orchestras.

In addition to the hours indicated here in the individual reviews, box offices are also open from 30 minutes to one hour before the start of a performance. For classical music, opera and ballet listings, check out www.heartofeurope.cz and www.czechopera.cz.

DVOŘÁK HALL Map p90

Dvořákova síň; ☎ 227 059 227; www.ceskafilharmonie.cz; náměstí Jana Palacha 1, Staré Město; tickets 200-600Kč; ☺ box office 10am-12.30pm & 1.30-6pm Mon-Fri; Ⓜ Staroměstská

Dvořák Hall in the neo-Renaissance Rudolfinum is home to the world-renowned Czech Philharmonic Orchestra (Česká filharmonie). Sit back and be impressed by some of the best classical musicians in Prague.

DVOŘÁK MUSEUM Map p108

Muzeum Antonína Dvořáka; ☎ 224 918 013; Ke Karlovu 20, Nové Město; tickets 700Kč; ☺ concerts 8pm Tue & Fri Apr-Oct; Ⓜ IP Pavlova

The pretty little Vila Amerika was built in 1717 as a count's immodest summer retreat. These days it's home to the Dvořák Museum (p117), and stages performances of Dvořák's vocal and instrumental works by the Original Music Theatre of Prague (www.musictheatre.cz), complete with period costume. Tickets are available through BTI (see the boxed text, p199).

OTHER CONCERT VENUES

Numerous churches and baroque palaces also serve as concert venues, staging anything from choral performances and organ recitals to string quartets, brass ensembles and occasionally full orchestras. You can get comprehensive details of these concerts from PIS offices (see p263). We've listed here a selection of the more popular venues around town.

Hradčany & Malá Strana

Basilica of St George (Bazilika sv Jiří; Map p62; Jiřské náměstí, Prague Castle) The Czech Republic's best-preserved Romanesque church. See also p66.

Liechtenstein Palace (Lichtenštejnský palác; Map p78; Malostranské náměstí, Malá Strana; ⓡ 12, 20, 22) Home to the Music Faculty of the Prague Academy of Performing Arts (Hudební fakulta AMU; www.hamu.cz).

St Nicholas Church (Kostel sv Mikuláše; Map p78; Malostranská náměstí 38, Malá Strana; Ⓜ Malostranská or ⓡ 12, 20, 22) Mozart himself tickled the ivories on the 2500-pipe organ here in 1787. See also p77.

St Vitus Cathedral (Katedrála sv Víta; Map p62; Pražský hrad, III. nádvoří; Prague Castle, Hradčany; Ⓜ Malostranská) The nave of Prague's cathedral is flooded with colour from beautiful stained-glass windows, and the acoustics are just as impressive. See also p65.

Strahov Monastery (Strahovský klášter; Map p70; Strahovské I.nádvoří, Hradčany; ⓡ 22) Mozart is said to have played the organ here as well. See also p69.

Staré Město

Bethlehem Chapel (Betlémská kaple; Map p90; Betlémské náměstí 3; ⓡ 6, 9, 18, 21, 22) This 14th-century chapel was torn down during the 18th century and painstakingly reconstructed between 1948 and 1954. See also p104.

Chapel of Mirrors (Zrcadlová kaple; Map p90; Klementinum, Mariánské náměstí; ⓡ 17, 18, 53) Ornately decorated chapel dating from the 1720s. See also p101.

Church of St Francis (Kostel sv Františka; Map p90; Křížovnické náměstí; ⓡ 5, 8, 14) Alongside the complex of the Convent of St Agnes (p97).

Church of St Nicholas (Kostel sv Mikuláše; Map p90; Staroměstské náměstí; Ⓜ Staroměstská) Built in the 1730s by Kilian Dientzenhofer. See also p94.

Convent of St Agnes (Klášter sv Anežky; Map p90; U Milosrdných 17; ⓡ 5, 8, 14) Prague's oldest surviving Gothic building. See also p97.

Nové Město

National Museum (Národní muzeum; Map p110; Václavské náměstí 68; Ⓜ Muzeum) Chamber music and operatic duets performed on the grand staircase in the museum's main hall at 6pm most evenings. See also p115.

Take care when buying tickets through people who hand out flyers in the street – some of these concerts are OK, but some may turn out to be a disappointment. Make sure you know exactly where the concert will be held – if you are told just 'the Municipal House', don't expect the magnificent Smetana Hall, as it may well be in one of the smaller concert halls.

ESTATES THEATRE Map p90

Stavovské divadlo; ☎ 224 902 322; www.narod ni-divadlo.cz; Ovocný trh 1, Staré Město; tickets 30-1200Kč; ⏱ box office 10am-6pm; Ⓜ Můstek; ♿ The Estates Theatre (p103) is the oldest theatre in Prague, famed as the place where Mozart conducted the premiere of *Don Giovanni* on 29 October 1787. Mozartissimo – a medley of highlights from several of Mo-zart's operas, including *Don Giovanni* – is performed here several times a week in summer (see www.bmart.cz); the rest of the year sees various opera, ballet and drama productions. The theatre is equipped for the hearing-impaired and has wheelchair access (wheelchair bookings can be made up to five days in advance); you can buy tickets from any National Theatre box office.

NATIONAL THEATRE Map p110

Národní divadlo; ☎ 224 901 377; www.narodni
-divadlo.cz; Národní třída 2, Nové Město; tickets 30-
1000Kč; ☒ box offices 10am-6pm; Ⓜ Národní Třída
The glorious, golden-roofed centrepiece of
the Czech National Revival, the much-loved
National Theatre provided a stage for the
re-emergence of Czech culture in the late
19th and early 20th centuries. Today you'll
find traditional opera, drama and ballet
by the likes of Smetana, Shakespeare and
Tchaikovsky sharing the program, alongside more modern works by composers and
playwrights such as Philip Glass and John
Osborne. The box offices are in the Nový
síň building next door, and in the Kolowrat
Palace (opposite the Estates Theatre).

PRAGUE STATE OPERA Map p110

Státní opera Praha; ☎ 224 227 266; www.opera
.cz; Wilsonova 4, Nové Město; opera tickets 100-
1150Kč, ballet tickets 100-800Kč; ☒ box office
10am-5.30pm Mon-Fri, 10am-noon & 1-5.30pm Sat
& Sun; Ⓜ Muzeum
The impressive neo-rococo home of the
Prague State Opera provides a glorious
setting for performances of opera and
ballet. An annual Verdi festival takes place
here in August and September, and less
conventional shows, such as Leoncavallo's
rarely staged version of La Bohème, are also
performed here.

SMETANA HALL Map p90

Smetanova síň; ☎ 220 002 101; www.obecnidum
.cz; náměstí Republiky 5, Staré Město; tickets
250-600Kč; ☒ box office 10am-6pm; Ⓜ Náměstí
Republiky
Smetana Hall, centrepiece of the stunning
Municipal House (Obecní dům; p102), is the
city's largest concert hall, with seating for
1200. This is the home venue of the Prague
Symphony Orchestra (Symfonický orchestr
hlavního města Prahy), and also stages
performances of folk dance and music.

FILM

Prague has more than 30 cinemas, some
showing first-run Western films, some showing Czech films, and including several excellent art-house cinemas. For cinema listings
check the 'Night & Day' section of the *Prague
Post* or www.prague.tv.

Most films are screened in their original
language with Czech subtitles (*české titulky*),
but Hollywood blockbusters are often dubbed

into Czech (*dabing*); look for the labels 'tit'
or 'dab' on cinema listings. Czech-language
films with English subtitles are listed as having
anglický titulky.

Movies are normally screened twice in the
evening, around 7pm and 9pm, though mul-
tiplexes show films all day long. Most cinemas
screen matinees on weekends.

BIO OKO Map p136

Oko Cinema; ☎ ticket reservations 608 330 088;
www.biooko.net; Františka Křížka 15, Holešovice;
tickets 100Kč; ☒ 1, 5, 8, 12, 14, 15, 17, 25, 26
This repertory cinema shows a varied program of underground films, selections from
film festivals, documentaries, big-budget
movies, and classics from around the world.
Most films are shown in the original language (not necessarily English), with Czech
subtitles. Check the website for the latest
film showings.

KINO AERO Map p130

☎ 271 771 349; www.kinoaero.cz; Biskupcova 31,
Žižkov; tickets 60-100Kč; ☒ 5, 9, 10, 16, 19
The Aero is Prague's best-loved art-house
cinema, with themed programs, retrospec-
tives and unusual films, often in English
or with English subtitles. This is the place
to catch reruns of classics from *Smrt v
Benátkách* (Death in Venice) to *Život Briana*
(The Life of Brian). The same managers run a
similar venue in the city centre, *Kino Světozor*,
and have recently taken over *Bio Oko*, too.

KINO SVĚTOZOR Map p110

☎ 224 946 824; www.kinosvetozor.cz; Vodičkova
41, Nové Město; tickets 60-120Kč; Ⓜ Můstek
The Světozor is under the same management as Kino Aero but is more central, and
has the same emphasis on classic cinema
and art-house films screened in their original language – everything from *Battleship
Potemkin* and *Casablanca* to *Annie Hall* and
Motorcycle Diaries.

PALACE CINEMAS Map p110

☎ 257 181 212; www.palacecinemas.cz; Slovanský
dům, Na Příkopě 22, Nové Město; tickets 169Kč;
Ⓜ Náměstí Republiky
Housed in the posh Slovanský dům shopping centre, this is central Prague's main
popcorn palace – a modern 10-screen
multiplex showing first-run Hollywood films
(mostly in English). There's also a 12-screen
multiplex on the top floor of the huge Nový
Smíchov (p157) shopping centre.

THEATRE

Most Czech drama is, not surprisingly, performed in Czech, which rather diminishes its appeal to non–Czech speakers. However, there are some English-language productions, and many predominantly visual shows at which language is not a barrier. There's also the Prague Fringe Festival (p17), which offers plenty of English-language theatre.

Prague is famous for its black-light theatre – occasionally called just 'black theatre' – a hybrid of mime, drama, dance and special effects in which live actors wearing fluorescent costumes do their thing in front of a black backdrop lit only by ultraviolet light (it's a growth industry in Prague, with at least half a dozen venues). An even older Czech tradition is puppetry, and the city has several marionette shows on offer.

ALFRED VE DVOŘE Map p136

☎ 257 318 666; www.alfredvedvore.cz; Františka Křížka 36, Holešovice; tickets 100-150Kč; ☺ box office 5.30pm-11pm Mon-Fri, 1.30pm-11pm Sat & Sun at the nearby Bio Oko (p205); ® 1, 5, 8, 12, 14, 15, 17, 25, 26

An artistic treasure in an unlikely section of Holešovice, the Alfred regularly stages demanding works of drama, dance, cabaret and movement theatre, including occasional performances in English. Check the website for details.

ARCHA THEATRE Map p108

Divadlo Archa; ☎ 221 716 333; www.archatheatre .cz; Na poříčí, Nové Město; tickets 200-700Kč; ☺ box office 10am-6pm Mon-Fri; ® 5, 8, 14

The Archa (Ark) has been described as Prague's alternative National Theatre, a multifunctional venue for the avant garde and the experimental. As well as contemporary drama (occasionally in English) – Václav Havel's *Leaving* has been performed here – dance and performance art, the theatre also stages live music, from Indian classical to industrial noise.

CELETNÁ THEATRE Map p90

Divadlo v Celetné; ☎ 222 326 843; www.divadlo vceletne.cz; Celetná 17, Staré Město; tickets 120-450Kč; ☺ box office 10am-7.30pm Mon-Fri, 2-7.30pm Sat & Sun; Ⓜ Náměstí Republiky

The Divadlo v Celetné, in a courtyard between Celetná and Štupartská, stages mainly Czech drama, both old and new, some foreign plays (including Shakespeare and Tom Stoppard) translated into Czech, and the occasional opera production by the students of the Prague Conservatory.

IMAGE THEATRE Map p90

Divadlo Image; ☎ 222 314 448; www.image theatre.cz; Pařížská 4, Staré Město; tickets 480Kč; ☺ box office 9am-8pm; Ⓜ Staroměstská

Founded in 1989, this company uses creative black-light theatre along with pantomime, modern dance and video – not to mention liberal doses of slapstick – to tell its stories. The staging can be very effective, but the atmosphere is often dictated by audience reaction.

LATERNA MAGIKA Map p110

☎ 224 931 482; www.laterna.cz; Nová Scéna, Národní třída 4, Nové Město; tickets 250-650Kč; ☺ box office 10am-6pm; Ⓜ Národní Třída

Laterna Magika has been wowing audiences, both at home and abroad, ever since its first cutting-edge multimedia show caused a stir at the 1958 Brussels World Fair. Its imaginative blend of live dance, opera, music and projected images continues to pull in the crowds. Nová Scena, the

---

PRAGUE SPRING

First held in 1946, the Prague Spring (Pražské jaro) international music festival is the Czech Republic's best-known annual cultural event. It begins on 12 May, the anniversary of composer Bedřich Smetana's death, with a procession from his grave at Vyšehrad (p120) to the Municipal House (p102), and a performance there of his patriotic song cycle *Má vlast* (My Homeland). The festival runs until 3 June, and the beautiful concert venues are as big a drawcard as the music.

Tickets can be obtained through the official Prague Spring Box Office (Map p90; ☎ 227 059 234; www.prague -spring.net; náměstí Jana Palacha, Staré Město; ☺ 10am-6pm Mon-Fri; ® 17, 18) in the Rudolfinum, or from any branch of Ticketpro (see the boxed text, p199).

If you want a guaranteed seat at a Prague Spring concert try to book it by mid-March at the latest, though a few seats may still be available as late as the end of May.

futuristic glass-block building next to the National Theatre, has been home to Laterna Magika since it moved here from its birthplace in the basement of the Adria Palace in the mid-1970s.

MINOR THEATRE Map p110
Divadlo Minor; ☎ 222 231 351; www.minor.cz; Vodičkova 6, Nové Město; tickets 80-150Kč; ⏲ box office 10am-1.30pm & 2.30-8pm Mon-Fri, 11am-6pm Sat & Sun; Ⓜ Karlovo Náměstí; ♿
Divadlo Minor is a wheelchair-accessible children's theatre that offers a fun mix of puppets, clown shows and pantomime. There are performances (in Czech) at 3pm Saturday and Sunday and at 6pm or 7.30pm Tuesday to Thursday, and you can usually get a ticket at the door before the show.

NATIONAL MARIONETTE THEATRE
Map p90
Národní divadlo marionet; ☎ 224 819 323; www.mozart.cz; Žatecká 1, Staré Město; tickets adult/child 590/490Kč; ⏲ box office 10am-8pm; Ⓜ Staroměstská
Loudly touted as the longest-running classical marionette show in the city – it has been performed almost continuously since 1991 (a fact, some say, that is reflected in the enthusiasm of the performances) – Don Giovanni is a life-sized puppet version of the Mozart opera that has spawned several imitations around town. Younger kids' attention might begin to wander fairly early on during this two-hour show.

REDUTA THEATRE Map p110
Divadlo Reduta; ☎ 257 921 835; www.black theatresrnec.cz; Národní třída 20, Nové Město; tickets adult/child 590/490Kč; ⏲ box office 3-7pm Mon-Fri; Ⓜ Národní Třída
The Reduta Theatre is home to the Black Theatre of Jiří Srnec, which was a founding member of Prague's original black-light theatre back in the early 1960s. Today the company's productions include versions of Alice in Wonderland and Peter Pan, and a compilation of the best of black-light theatre from the early days.

SPEJBL & HURVÍNEK THEATRE Map p136
Divadlo Spejbla a Hurvínka; ☎ 224 316 784; www.spejbl-hurvinek.cz; Dejvická 38, Dejvice; tickets 80-120Kč; ⏲ box office 10am-2pm & 3-6pm Tue-Fri, 1-5pm Sat & Sun; Ⓜ Dejvická

Created in 1930 by puppeteer Josef Skupa, Spejbl and Hurvínek are the Czech marionette equivalents of Punch and Judy, although they are father and son rather than husband and wife. The shows are in the Czech language, but most can be followed whatever language you speak.

ŠVANDOVO DIVADLO NA SMÍCHOVĚ
Map p143
Šandovo Theatre in Smíchov; ☎ 257 318 666; www.svandovodivadlo.cz; Stefaníkova 57; tickets 150-300Kč; ⏲ box office 11am-7pm Mon-Fri (30-minute lunch break at 2pm), 5-7pm Sat & Sun; 🚋 6, 9, 12, 20
This experimental theatre space, performing Czech and international dramatic works, is admired for its commitment to staging 'English-friendly' performances, by which it means English-language theatre or with English subtitles. It also hosts occasional live music and dance, as well as regular 'Stage Talks', unscripted discussions with noted personalities. A few years ago, one legendary one featured Václav Havel and Lou Reed.

TA FANTASTIKA
Map p90
☎ 222 221 366; www.tafantastika.cz; Karlova 8, Staré Město; tickets 680Kč; ⏲ box office 11am-9.30pm Mon-Fri; Ⓜ Staroměstská
Established in New York in 1981 by Czech émigré Petr Kratochvil, Ta Fantastika moved to Prague in 1989. The theatre produces black light theatre based on classic literature and legends such as Excalibur, The Picture of Dorian Gray and Joan of Arc. The most popular show is Aspects of Alice, based on Alice in Wonderland.

THEATRE ON THE BALUSTRADE
Map p90
Divadlo Na Zábradlí; ☎ 222 868 868; www.nazabradli.cz; Anenské náměstí 5, Staré Město; tickets 100-325Kč; ⏲ box office 2-8pm Mon-Fri, 2hr before show starts Sat & Sun; 🚋 17, 18
The theatre where Václav Havel honed his skills as a playwright four decades ago is now the city's main venue for serious Czech-language drama, including works by a range of foreign playwrights translated into Czech. There are also regular performances in English with Czech subtitles.

SPORTS & ACTIVITIES

top picks

The Czechs have always been keen on sports and outdoor activities, and Prague's extensive green spaces – from the former royal hunting grounds of Stromovka to the riverside parks and islands strung along the Vltava – offer plenty of opportunity for exercise. Although hiking, swimming and ice hockey are the traditional favourites, recent years have seen a steady increase in the numbers of cyclists in the city as bike lanes and dedicated cycle trails have been introduced.

Golf was never a high priority during the communist era, but the emergence of a class of young professionals with money to burn has seen a growth of interest in more exclusive outdoor pursuits, including the construction of a championship golf course at Karlštejn.

HEALTH & FITNESS

There has been a move away from the sweaty gyms and weights rooms of the past towards a new generation of spas and health clubs, where the goal is pampering rather than fitness. Most are associated with top-end hotels – check out http://prague.tv/prague/health/spas for a list.

GYMS & SPAS

CYBEX HEALTH CLUB & SPA Map p130
☎ 224 842 375; www.cybex-fitness.cz; Pobřežní 1, Nové Město; ☯ 6am-10pm Mon-Fri, 7am-10pm Sat & Sun; Ⓜ Florenc
The luxurious spa in the Hilton Hotel charges 900Kč for a day pass, which gives access to the gym, squash courts, pool, sauna, Jacuzzi and steam room, and 1200Kč for a half-hour massage.

HOLMES PLACE Map p143
☎ 221 420 800; Nádražní 32, Smíchov; gym 150Kč (140Kč off-peak 9am-4pm Mon-Fri, all day Sat & Sun); ☯ 6am-10pm; Ⓜ Smíchovské Nádraží
One of the largest and best-equipped gyms in the country, with an enormous cardio and workout room, plus the usual offering of pool, sauna, spa and massage. The only drawback is the location, in a forgotten corner of Smíchov, though the proximity of the metro makes it accessible from other parts of the city.

ACTIVITIES

Summer or winter, rain or shine, Prague is packed with places where you can work off the beer-and-dumpling calorie rush – from hiking and biking trails to swimming pools, skate parks and ice rinks.

HIKING

The Czech Republic is covered with a network of waymarked hiking trails, colour-coded and clearly marked on a range of excellent 1:50,000 and 1:25,000 hiking maps (turistické mapy). Prague has its share of trails – the Klub Českých Turistů (Czech Hiking Club) 1:50,000 map sheet 36, Okolí Prahy-západ (Prague & Around, West) covers the best in and around the city, including Beroun and Karlštejn.

For easy walks of an hour or two, you can head for the big parks and nature reserves – Stromovka in the north (see Letná & Stromovka Walking Tour Walking Tour, p139), Prokopské údolí in the southwest, and Michelský les and Kunratický les in the southeast – or follow the riverbank trails north from Prague Zoo to the little ferry at Roztoky, and return to the city by train.

A more challenging day hike, which takes in a visit to Karlštejn Castle (p234), begins at the town of Beroun to the southwest of the city. From Beroun train station follow a red-marked trail east for 6km to the Monastery of St John under the Rock (Klášter sv Jan pod Skálou), situated in a spectacular limestone gorge. From here, continue on the red trail through wooded hills for another 8km to Karlštejn, where you can catch another train back to the city centre. Allow five hours from Beroun to Karlštejn.

CYCLING

Prague has a long way to go before it's a cycling town comparable with big cities in Germany, or even Vienna. Nevertheless, there's a group of hard-core cyclists at work promoting things like commuter cycling, extending bike paths and raising driver awareness. Their efforts are starting to bear fruit. Prague now has a relatively complete, if disjointed, network of bike paths – signposted in yellow – that criss-cross the city centre and fan out in all directions. Recreational cyclists will probably be content just to putz around on one of the tours offered by the bike-rental companies (p259). More serious cyclists should consider buying a good map, hiring a bike and hitting the outlying trails for a day or two.

Arguably the best cycling trails lead off to the north following the Vltava River in the direction of Germany. Someday, the Prague–Dresden run will be the stuff of cycling legend, but for now there are still significant gaps in the route. That said, the path northward along the river is nearly complete as far as the town of Kralupy nad Vltavou (20km from Prague; it's possible to return by rail), from where you can continue on back roads to Mělník (p238). There are plenty of bridges and ferries to take you back and forth across the river, and some really great trails leading inland along the way. From the centre of Prague, start off at Čechův most (the bridge over the Vltava by the InterContinental Hotel), ride across the bridge and up the hill to Letná. From there, follow the signs to Stromovka and on to Prague Zoo. The riverside trail continues northward from the zoo.

Most large bookstores stock cycling maps (cycloturisticka mapa). One of the best maps to look out for is the 2008 edition Freytag & Berndt Praha a Okoli (Prague & Surroundings; 1:75,000), which costs about 149Kč. Another good choice for the northwestern section of the city is Z prahy na kole, Severozapad (Around Prague by Bike, Northwest, 1:65,000) for about 75Kč. Remember to pack water and sunscreen and always watch out for cars. Czech drivers, inexplicably, are rabidly anticyclist.

There are several useful websites:

Cyklojizdy (www.cyklojizdy.cz) Mostly in Czech, with an English summary – portal that organises the twice-yearly (spring and autumn) Critical Mass rides to raise cycling awareness.

Grant's Prague Bike Blog (http://praguebikeblog .blogspot.com) An American expat's cycling exploits, with great ride ideas, maps and photos.

Greenways (www.pragueviennagreenways.org) Details of a 250-mile cycle trail linking Prague and Vienna.

Prague City Hall (http://doprava.praha-mesto.cz) The city's public transport portal with a nice section in English on bike trails and rules for cyclists.

Hire

City Bike (Map p90; ☎ 776 180 284; www.citybike -prague.com; Králodvorská 5, Staré Město; 4/8hr 400/500Kč; ⏰ 9am-7pm Apr-Oct; Ⓜ Náměstí Republiky) Rental includes helmet, padlock and map; good-quality Trek mountain bikes are available for 700Kč for 24 hours. Guided bike tours from 540Kč.

Praha Bike (Map p90; ☎ 732 388 880; www.prahabike .cz; Dlouhá 24, Staré Město; 4/8hr 360/500Kč; ⏰ 9am-8pm; 🚇 5, 8, 14) Hires out good, new bikes with lock, helmet and map, plus free luggage storage. Also offers student discounts and group bike tours (see also p259).

GOLF

The Czech Republic is one of the undiscovered gems of European golf, with new, quality courses springing up all over the place – the country has gone from having three 18-hole courses in 1990 to no fewer than 70 in 2008. There are a couple of nine-hole courses within the city boundary, but the nearest championship course is at Karlštejn. For more information, see www.czechgolf guide.com.

GOLF CLUB PRAHA Map p58

☎ 257 216 584; www.gcp.cz; Plzeňská 401/2, Motol; green fees (nine holes) Mon-Fri 490-600Kč, Sat, Sun & holidays 750Kč; ⏰ 7am-dusk; 🚇 7, 9, 10 Duffers will be happy to know that Prague has a nine-hole golf course, complete with driving range and chipping and putting greens, behind the Hotel Golf in the western suburbs; you can hire a set of clubs for 500Kč. Take tram 7, 9 or 10 west to the Hotel Golf stop, and follow the trail across the course to the clubhouse.

GOLF & COUNTRY CLUB
off Map p58

☎ 244 460 435; www.hodkovicky.cz; Vltavanů 982, Hodkovičky; green fees (nine holes) Mon-Fri 600Kč, Sat & Sun 800Kč, driving range per 50 balls 100Kč; ⏰ golf course 8am-7pm, driving range 7am-9pm; 🚇 3, 17, 21 Way out on the southern edge of the city, this place offers a nine-hole course, a driving range and chipping and putting greens. Take tram 3, 17 or 21 south to the Černý kůň stop, and walk west towards the river on V Náklích for 100m (follow the signs for Hostel Boathouse), then turn down the first right immediately after passing under the railway bridge.

KARLŠTEJN GOLF COURSE

☎ 311 604 999; www.karlstejn-golf.cz; Běleč 272, Líteň; green fees Mon-Fri 2000Kč, Sat, Sun & holidays 3000Kč; ☺ 7am-9pm May-Aug, 8am-7pm Sep, 8am-6pm Apr & Oct

The closest 18-hole facility to Prague is this prestigious championship course overlooking Karlštejn Castle (p234), southwest of the city. It's 4km south of Karlštejn village, on the southern side of the Berounka River.

RUNNING

The Prague International Marathon (Pražský mezinárodní maraton; ☎ 224 919 209; www.praguemarathon .com; Záhořanského 3, 120 00 Praha 2), established in 1989, is held annually in mid- to late May. It's considered to be one of the world's top 10 city marathons, and attracted 4919 entrants in 2009. There's also a half-marathon, held in late March. If you'd like to compete, you can register online or obtain entry forms from the website. The registration fee is €55 to €100, depending how early you register.

SKATING

With ice hockey probably the country's most popular spectator sport, it's no surprise that the Czechs are skate-mad. In winter, when the mercury drops below zero, sections of parks are sprayed with water and turned into makeshift ice rinks. In summer, ice skates are replaced with in-line skates and street hockey takes over, while the park trails and riverside cycle tracks are taken over by whole families of rollerbladers.

PŮJČOVNA BRUSLÍ MIAMI Map p136

Miami Skate Rental; ☎ 731 281 571; Nad Štolou 1, Holešovice; skate rental per hr 80Kč plus deposit; ☺ 9am-9pm May-Sep, noon-9pm Oct, 2-8pm Apr; ▣ 1, 8, 15, 25, 26

A great way to spend a summer's day: you can rent in-line skates from this place (staff speak a bit of English), which is close to the National Technical Museum, then head off to explore the extensive skating trails in Letná Gardens before enjoying a cold one at the Letná beer garden (see Letenský zámeček; p191).

ŠTVANICE STADIUM Map p136

Zimní stadion Štvanice; ☎ 233 378 327; Ostrov Štvanice 1125, Holešovice; adult/child under 7yr 80/20Kč; ☺ public skating 10am-noon & 3pm-5.30pm Mon-Fri (plus some evenings), 9am-noon & 2-5pm Sat & Sun; ▣ 3, 26

This is the oldest ice-hockey stadium in Central Europe – Czechoslovakia's first ice-hockey match on artificial ice was played here in 1931. It provides public skating sessions as well as hosting ice-hockey games in season. Skate hire costs 160Kč per pair, plus deposit. Situated on Štvanice island (Chase Island; entry from the Nové Město side).

SWIMMING

DIVOKÁ ŠÁRKA Map p58

Evropská; ▣ 20, 26

Prague summers can be hot, and at weekends many locals escape the heat by heading for the open-air swimming at Divoká Šárka (see also p134). There's a large lake with a sandy beach and grassy area for sunbathing, plus volleyball and table-tennis facilities (admission 70Kč). Further down the valley you'll find a stream-fed open-air swimming pool (admission 50Kč); both lake and pool can be a bit chilly, even in high summer.

PODOLÍ SWIMMING POOL Map p58

Plavecký stadión Podolí; ☎ 241 433 952; Podolská 74, Podolí; admission per 1½/3hr 80/125Kč, child under 13yr half-price; ☺ 6am-9.45pm; ▣ 3, 16, 17, 21

There are more swimming and tanning opportunities at this huge swimming complex with Olympic-sized pools, both indoor and outdoor, and plenty of sunbathing space (best to bring footwear for the grotty showers, though). To get here, take the tram to the Kublov stop; from there it's a further five-minute walk south.

SPECTATOR SPORT

Those widescreen TVs perched ubiquitously on pub walls and newsstands groaning under the weight of sports magazines give the game away: the Czechs are avid sports fans. From soccer to ice hockey, rarely a weekend goes by without some sporting showdown providing fertile ground for an in-depth, post-match analysis – in the pub, of course.

FOOTBALL

Football is a national passion in the Czech Republic. The national team performs well in international competitions, having won the European Championship in 1976 (as Czechoslovakia), and reached the final in 1996 and the semifinal in 2004. Sadly, it crashed out in the first round of the 2006 World Cup in Germany, but bounced back to be ranked sixth in the world by FIFA in the run-up to Euro 2008, a ranking that seemed over-optimistic when the Czechs failed to reach the quarter-finals, and then failed to qualify for the 2010 World Cup. Home international matches are played at Slavia Praha's 21,000-seat Eden stadium (aka Synot Tip Aréna) in eastern Prague, which opened in May 2008.

Prague's two big football clubs, SK Slavia Praha and AC Sparta Praha, are both leading contenders in the national *fotbal* (football) league. Two other Prague-based teams – FC Bohemians (Map p58; ☎ 271 721 459; www.bohemians1905 .cz; Vršovická 31, Vinohrady; ⊠ 4, 22) and FK Viktoria Žižkov (Map p130; ☎ 221 423 427; www.fkvz.cz; Seifertova, Žižkov; ⊠ 5, 9, 26) – attract fervent local support. The season runs from August to December and February to June, and matches are mostly played on Wednesday, Saturday and Sunday afternoons.

GENERALI ARÉNA (SPARTA STADIUM) Map p136

☎ 296 111 400; www.sparta.cz; Milady Horákové 98, Bubeneč; match tickets 100–360Kč; box office ⊗ 9am-noon Mon-Fri & 1-5.30pm Mon-Thu, to 4pm Fri; ⊠ 1, 8, 15, 25, 26

The all-seater Generali Aréna, with a capacity of more than 20,000, is the home ground of Sparta Praha – winner of the Czech football league in 2001, 2003, 2005 and 2007, and of the Czech National Cup in 2004, 2006 and 2007. The club was founded in 1893. Tickets are available at the box office (entrance No 1) during the week or just before matches. The season runs from mid-summer to the following spring. The stadium's sponsors (and the name) change from year to year, so do like the locals and simply refer to it as 'Sparta stadium'.

SYNOT TIP ARÉNA (SK SLAVIA OR 'EDEN' STADIUM) Map p125

☎ 731 126 104; www.slavia.cz; www.synottip arena.cz; Vladivostocká, Vršovice; match tickets 150–400Kč; ⊠ 6, 7, 22, 24

This stadium is home to SK Slavia Praha, founded in 1892 – one of the oldest sporting clubs in continental Europe and an honorary member of England's Football Association. Czech National Cup winner in 1997, 1999 and 2002, Slavia holds an

unusual record – the design of its distinctive red-and-white strip has remained unchanged since 1896. Purchase tickets online or at the stadium ticket office before matches.

ICE HOCKEY

It's a toss-up whether football or ice hockey inspires more passion in the hearts of Prague sports fans, but hockey probably wins. The Czech national team has been rampant in the last decade, winning the World Championship three years running (1999 to 2001) and taking the title again in 2005 and 2010; it reached the final in 2006 but lost to Sweden. It also won Olympic gold in 1998 by defeating the mighty Russians in the final.

Prague's two big hockey teams are HC Sparta Praha and HC Slavia Praha, both of which compete in the 14-team national league. Promising young players are often lured away by the promise of big money in North America's National Hockey League, and there is a sizeable Czech contingent in the NHL.

Sparta plays at the huge, slightly run-down Tesla Aréna (formerly T-Mobile Aréna or Sportovní hala) at the Výstaviště exhibition grounds in Holešovice, and Slavia Praha at O2 Arena (formerly known as Sazka Aréna); games are fast and furious, and the atmosphere can be electrifying – it's well worth making the effort to see a game. The season runs from September to early April.

O2 ARENA (SAZKA ARÉNA) Map p58

☎ 266 212 111; www.sazkaarena.com, www.hc -slavia.cz; Ocelářská 2, Vysočany; buy tickets online at www.sazkaticket.cz; match tickets 220–300Kč; Ⓜ Českomoravská

The O2 Arena is Prague's biggest multipurpose venue, and home rink of HC Slavia Praha, Czech Extraliga champions in 2008. It can accommodate up to 18,000 spectators, and is used to host sporting events, rock concerts, exhibitions and other major events as well as hockey games.

TESLA ARÉNA (SPORTOVNÍ HALA) Map p136

☎ 266 727 443; www.hcsparta.cz; Za Elektrámou 419, Výstaviště, Holešovice; buy tickets online at www.sazkaticket.cz or www.ticketportal.cz; ⊠ 5, 12, 14, 15, 17

You can see HC Sparta Praha – Czech Extraliga champions in 2006 and 2007 and in the hunt for another championship as this book was being researched – play at the 13,000-capacity Tesla Aréna beside the exhibition grounds in Holešovice. Buy tickets online or at the stadium box office before matches.

TENNIS

Tennis is another sport in which the Czechs have excelled, having produced world-class players such as Jan Kodeš, Ivan Lendl, Petr Korda, Hana Mandlikova, Jana Novotna, Cyril Suk and up-and-coming star Tomáš Berdych. Plus, of course, very probably the finest female tennis player ever, Martina Navratilova.

In summer the 8000-seat centre court at the Czech Lawn Tennis Club on Štvanice island normally hosts the Prague Open (www .pragueopen.cz), a WTA competition that was established in the 1990s in the hope of luring international tennis talent to the Czech capital (note that the tournament is not held every year).

CZECH LAWN TENNIS CLUB Map p136
Český Lawn-Tennis Klub; ☎ 222 316 317; www .cltk.cz; Ostrov Štvanice 38, Holešovice; match tickets 100-150Kč; 🚊 3, 26
Founded in 1893, this is the oldest and most prestigious tennis club in the country (despite the name, all its courts are clay!), and it was here that Ivan Lendl and Martina Navratilova learned their craft.

HORSE RACING
PRAGUE RACECOURSE off Map p58
Velká Chuchle závodiště Praha; ☎ 242 447 032; www.velka-chuchle.cz; Radotínská 69, Velká Chuchle; adult/child under 18yr 120Kč/free; 🚌 129, 172, 243, 244, 255
If you fancy a flutter on the ponies, check out the *dostihy* (horse racing) scene at this racecourse on the southern edge of the city. There are races run every Sunday from April to October – check the website for more information and the full racing calendar. You can get to the racecourse by taking the bus from Smíchovské Nádraží metro station.

SLEEPING

top picks

- Absolutum Hotel (p227)
- Angelo Hotel (p230)
- Castle Steps (p219)
- Czech Inn (p225)
- Hotel Aria (p218)
- Hotel Josef (p221)
- Golden Well Hotel (p219)
- Icon Hotel (p222)
- Mandarin Oriental (p218)

SLEEPING

A 2007 headline in the *Mlada Fronta Dnes* newspaper said it all – 'More hotels than streets'. According to the article, there were 286 named streets in the Prague 1 postal district (the city centre, including Staré Město and Malá Strana), and no fewer than 320 hotels; by the end of 2009, there were more than 600 hotels in central Prague.

Prague offers a wide range of accommodation options, from cosy, romantic hotels set in historic town houses to luxurious international chain hotels, and from budget hostels and pensions to a new generation of sharply styled boutique hotels.

There was a huge boom in hotel building from 2000 to 2009, especially in the four- and five-star sectors. The Hotel Josef led the way for boutique hotels in 2002, though it took a few more years before the design hotel concept really began to take off in Prague, with a flurry of new places opening from 2005 on, notably the Yasmin and the Icon.

Five-star hotels also popped up all over the place – the long-established Four Seasons in Staré Město and the newer Mandarin Oriental in Malá Strana were joined in 2009 by no fewer than 10 luxury hotels, including offerings from Kempinksi, Rocco Forte and Le Méridien.

But the recession hit Prague's hotel sector hard, and oversupply at the top end of the market resulted in falling occupancy rates. Many places have dropped their prices in an attempt to attract business, and as this book was going to press the city was once more considered a bargain destination, with average accommodation prices for UK travellers down 38% on 2009. It's well worth shopping around and looking for special offers on hotel websites.

An increasing number of Prague hotels provide specially adapted rooms and facilities for wheelchair users; we have noted these facilities in the individual listings. Although smoking is banned in public places, hotels are not covered by this law, and many still accommodate smokers; the reviews here include a no-smoking icon if nonsmoking rooms are available. Air-conditioning is standard in midrange and top-end places, but not in budget options.

Accommodation listings in this book are broken down first by neighbourhood, then by budget, from most to least expensive.

LONGER-TERM RENTALS

More and more travellers are discovering the pleasures of renting an apartment in Prague, and more and more hoteliers are offering 'aparthotels', a collection of serviced apartments with a hotel-style reception desk. The cost of a short-term stay in a self-catering flat is now comparable with a midrange hotel room, and means minimal transport costs, access to cheap local food, and the freedom to come and go as you like.

Many Prague agencies will find a flat for you (see the boxed text, p218). Typical rates for a modern two-person apartment with living room/bedroom, bathroom, TV and kitchenette range from around 1800Kč per night for a place in the outer suburbs, to around 3000Kč or 4000Kč for a flat near Old Town Square; longer stays can knock the price down to as little as 20,000Kč for a month in a two-person flat in Žižkov. All short-term rental apartments are fully furnished and serviced, meaning that utilities (gas, water, electricity) and bedlinen are included in the price, and staff will clean up and change the beds at least weekly.

The real-estate section of the weekly Prague Post (www.praguepost.com) newspaper also lists agencies and private individuals with apartments to rent by the month.

RESERVATIONS

Booking your accommodation in advance is strongly recommended (especially if you want to stay in or near the centre), and there are dozens of agencies that will help you find a place to stay; some are better than others. The places listed in the boxed text (p218) are reli-

PRICE GUIDE

The categories used in this chapter indicate the cost per night of a standard double room in high season.

€€€	more than 4000Kč (more than €160)
€€	2000Kč to 4000Kč (€80 to €160)
€	less than 2000Kč (less than €80)

able, and even if you turn up in peak periods without a booking, these agencies should be able to find you a bed.

Hotels usually require you to check out on the day of departure between 10am and noon. As to check-in times, there are no hard-and-fast rules, but if you're going to arrive late in the evening, it's best to mention this when you book your room.

ROOM RATES

A double room in a midrange hotel in central Prague will cost around 4000Kč (€160) in high season; outside the centre, this might fall to around 3000Kč, though with special offers you can often snag one for 2500Kč or less. Top-range hotels cost from 4000Kč and up, with the best luxury hotels charging 6000Kč and more. The budget options listed in this chapter charge less than 2000Kč for a double room.

Note that some midrange and top-end hotels quote rates in euros, and a few quote in US dollars. At these hotels you can pay cash in Czech crowns if you like, but the price will depend on the exchange rate on the day you settle the bill.

The rates quoted in this chapter are for the high season, which generally covers April to June, September and October, and the Christmas/New Year holidays. July and August are midseason, and the rest of the year is low season, when rates can drop by 30% or 40%.

Even high-season rates can be inflated by up to 15% on certain dates, notably at New Year, Easter, during the Prague Spring festival, and at weekends (Thursday to Sunday) in May, June and September. On the other hand, you can often find much lower rates from January to March and there are often good internet booking deals from June to August; during research we found excellent rooms on offer for 1800Kč to 2600Kč a double.

Most hostel, pension and budget-hotel rates do not include breakfast; most midrange and top-end hotel rates do.

HRADČANY

Hradčany is the place to stay if you're looking for peace and quiet. You'll be within a short walk of the castle, but when the crowds ebb away at the end of the day the streets are almost deserted.

DOMUS HENRICI Map p70   Hotel €€€
☎ 220 511 369; www.domus-henrici.cz; Loretánská 11; s/d from 3985/4370Kč; 🛏 22; 🖳 🛜
This historic building in a quiet corner of Hradčany is intentionally nondescript out front, hinting that peace and privacy are top priorities here. There are eight spacious and stylish rooms, half with private fax, scanner/copier and internet access (via an ethernet port), and all with polished wood floors, large bathrooms, comfy beds and fluffy bathrobes. Service is impeccable, and there's an attractive guest lounge as well as a sunny outdoor terrace with gorgeous views over the city. Free internet and wi-fi in the hotel lobby.

HOTEL U KRÁLE KARLA Map p70   Hotel €€
☎ 257 531 211; www.romantichotels.cz; Úvoz 4; s/d 3500/4000Kč; 🛏 12, 20, 22; 🅿
The 'King Charles' is a cosy, romantic hotel set in a lovely, 'baroquefied' Gothic building, with rooms set on landings around an impressive central atrium with a stained-glass ceiling. The atmosphere here leans towards a sort of medieval–fairy tale look, with studded wood-and-leather antique furniture, painted timber ceilings, murals, stained-glass windows and statues of old Czech kings and queens. The rooms are filled with dark polished-wood furniture, Persian rugs, swagged velvet drapes and ostentatious fireplaces – charming, if you like that sort of thing. The bathrooms, however, though reasonably sized, are beige and forgettable. There's also a restaurant on site with room service and a sauna for guest use. The hotel vies with Hotel Neruda (p219) for the title of closest hotel to the castle; it's just a few minutes' walk to the main gate.

ROMANTIK HOTEL U RAKA
Map p70   Hotel €€
☎ 220 511 100; www.romantikhotel-uraka.cz; Černínská 10; s/d from 2500/3750Kč; 🛏 22
Concealed in a manicured rock garden in a quiet corner of Hradčany, the historic Hotel U Raka is an atmospheric, late-18th-century timber cottage with just six elegant, low-ceilinged doubles, complete with timber beams, wooden floors and red-brick fireplaces. With its cosy bedrooms, attentive staff, artistic decor and farmhouse kitchen-style breakfast room, it's ideal for a romantic getaway, and the castle is less than 10 minutes' walk away. Be sure to book at least a few months ahead.

ACCOMMODATION AGENCIES

- **Alfa Tourist Service** (Map p108; ☎ 224 230 037; www.alfatourist.cz; Opletalova 38, Nové Město; 9am-5pm Mon-Fri) Can provide accommodation in student hostels, pensions, hotels and private rooms.
- **AVE Travel** (☎ 251 551 011; www.praguehotellocator.com) A 24-hour call centre and web-based accommodation agency with a huge range of hotels and apartments on offer.
- **Happy House Rentals** (Map p110; ☎ 224 946 890; www.happyhouserentals.com; Jungmannova 30, Nové Město; 9am-5pm Mon-Fri) Specialises in rental apartments, both short- and long-term.
- **Hostel.cz** (☎ 415 658 580; www.hostel.cz) Website database of hostels and budget hotels, with a secure online booking system.
- **Mary's Travel & Tourist Service** (Map p125; ☎ 222 253 510, in UK 020 7558 8130; www.marys.cz; Italská 31, Vinohrady; 9am-9pm) Friendly, efficient agency offering private rooms, hostels, pensions, apartments and hotels in all price ranges in Prague and surrounding areas.
- **Prague Apartments** (☎ 604 168 756; www.prague-apartment.com) Web-based service with range of comfortable, IKEA-furnished flats. Availability of apartments displayed online.
- **Stop City** (Map p125; ☎ 222 521 233; www.stopcity.com; Vinohradská 24, Vinohrady; 10am-8pm) Specialises in apartments, private rooms and pensions in the city centre, Vinohrady and Žižkov areas.
- **Travel.cz** (Map p90; ☎ 224 990 990; www.travel.cz; Divadelní 24, Staré Město; 8am-8pm) Long-established specialist in holiday apartments near the city centre.

HOTEL MONASTERY Map p70   Hotel €€
☎ 233 090 200; www.hotelmonastery.cz; Strahovské nádvoří 13; s/d 2475/2900Kč; 22;

Ancient meets modern at this small hotel in the peaceful courtyard of Strahov Monastery, where the only noise likely to disturb you is the occasional tolling of a church bell. The 12 quirkily shaped rooms in this 17th-century building have been given a bright, IKEA-style modern makeover with polished wood floors, plain white walls hung with photos of Prague, and a splash of colour from the bedspread and sofa. (Two of the rooms are also wheelchair-accessible.) And it's all just a five-minute walk away from the castle.

MALÁ STRANA

Lots of Malá Strana's lovely old Renaissance and baroque buildings have been converted into hotels and apartments, making this a good district to stay in if you're looking for a romantic atmosphere. You'll also be within walking distance of Charles Bridge and surrounded by lots of good restaurants and bars.

HOTEL ARIA Map p78   Boutique Hotel €€€
☎ 225 334 111; www.ariahotel.net; Tržiště 9; d from 8100Kč; 12, 20, 22;
The Aria offers five-star luxury with a musical theme – each of the four floors is dedicated to a musical genre (jazz, opera, classical and contemporary), and

each room celebrates a particular artist or musician and contains a selection of their music that you can enjoy on the in-room hi-fi system. Service is professional and efficient, and the rooms are furnished with crisp bedlinen, plump continental quilts, Molton Brown toiletries and complimentary chocolates. Other facilities include a music and movie library, screening room, fitness centre and steam room. The location is very central, a few minutes' walk from Charles Bridge, and just around the corner from a major tram stop.

MANDARIN ORIENTAL
Map p78   Boutique Hotel €€€
☎ 233 088 888; www.mandarinoriental.com/prague; Nebovidská 1; r from 7000Kč, ste from 16,850Kč; 12, 20, 22;
One of Prague's most talked-about hotels, the Mandarin occupies the converted premises of a 17th-century Dominican monastery. The main talking point – other than the celeb guestlist, including Madonna and the Dalai Lama – is the sumptuous hotel spa, built inside a Renaissance chapel with the remains of a 14th-century church preserved beneath a glass floor, but the rooms are pretty special too. The interiors were designed by the same team who did the Burj Al Arab in Dubai. Some rooms have antique parquet floors, some have vaulted ceilings, others are completely modern; the most appealing are the garden rooms dotted around the old cloister gardens.

GOLDEN WELL HOTEL

Map p78   Hotel €€€

☎ 257 011 213; www.goldenwell.cz; U Zlaté
Studně 4; d from 6800Kč, ste from 18,000Kč;
Ⓜ Malostranská; 💻
The Golden Well is one of Malá Strana's
hidden secrets, tucked away at the end of a
cobbled cul-de-sac – a Renaissance house
that once belonged to Emperor Rudolf II
(and was once inhabited by astronomer
Tycho Brahe), with an unbeatable location
perched on the southern slope of the castle
hill. The rooms (five twins, 12 doubles and
two luxury suites) are quiet and spacious,
with polished wood floors, reproduction period furniture, and blue-and-white
bathrooms with underfloor heating and
whirlpool baths; many have views over
the Palace Gardens below. The hotel has
an excellent restaurant (see Terasa U Zlaté
Studně; p164) and a terrace with a superb
outlook over the city.

HOTEL NERUDA Map p78   Boutique Hotel €€

☎ 257 535 557; www.hotelneruda.cz; Nerudova
44; r from 2950Kč; 💺 12, 20, 22; 💻 🛜
Set in a tastefully renovated Gothic house
dating from 1348 and extending into the
neighbouring building, the Neruda offers a
refreshingly modern and stylish alternative
to the sometimes-tacky so-called 'historic'
hotels, which are all too common in Malá
Strana. The decor is chic and minimalist in
neutral tones enlivened by the odd splash
of colour, with a lovely glass-roofed atrium
that houses the hotel cafe, and a sunny
roof terrace. The comfortable bedrooms
share the modern, minimalist decor and are
mostly reasonably sized, but be aware that
some of the rooms in the top of the building are a bit on the cramped side – ask for
one on the 1st or 2nd floor. The staff are
friendly and unfailingly helpful, and the
breakfasts are excellent (and served until
11am if you fancy a long lie-in).

HUNGER WALL RESIDENCE

Map p78   Apartments €€

☎ 257 404 040; www.hungerwall.eu; Plaská 8; apt
from 2650Kč; 💺 6, 9, 12, 20; 🛜
A welcome addition to Malá Strana's accommodation scene, the Hunger Wall
offers bright, stylish, modernised apartments at very reasonable rates. From the
smiling welcome at reception to the spotlessly clean rooms, the atmosphere here is
resolutely 'new Prague', with facilities that
include a cafe, a conference room and a
tiny gym. Located in the quieter southern
part of Malá Strana, you're only two tram
stops south of Malostranské náměstí and
Charles Bridge.

PENSION DIENTZENHOFER

Map p78   Pension €€

☎ 257 311 319; www.dientzenhofer.cz; Nosticova
2; s/d 1900/2600Kč; 💺 12, 20, 22
Take a room in this homely pension and
you're rubbing shoulders with famous
figures from the past – this lovely old
16th-century house was once the home
of the Dientzenhofer family of architects
who designed many of Prague's most
famous baroque landmarks (see p48). Set in
a peaceful park but only five minutes' walk
from Charles Bridge, the house has seven
plain but comfortable rooms and a couple
of good-value suites that sleep up to five
(3900Kč). The owner is friendly and helpful,
and will even collect you from the airport.

CASTLE STEPS Map p78   Apartments €€

☎ 257 216 337; www.castlesteps.com; Nerudova 7;
d 1430-2260Kč, 2-person apt 2830-4500Kč; 💺 12,
20, 22; 💻
The name applies to a collection of private rooms and apartments spread across
several buildings on Nerudova and further
uphill on Úvoz. Management is laid-back,
helpful, gay-friendly and decidedly informal – don't expect porters and room service! (By the way, there are no lifts either.)
The various 16th- and 17th-century buildings have been converted into apartments
and suites sleeping from two to eight, and
offer remarkable value in a great location. All have been beautifully renovated
and equipped to a high standard, and are
furnished with antiques, oil paintings and
pot plants. There is free internet access at
the reception office at Nerudova 7; ring
the doorbell labelled Castle Steps. (At the
time of research Castle Steps was for sale,
but expects to continue in business along
much the same lines.)

CHARLES BRIDGE B&B

Map p78   Pension €€

☎ 257 218 103; www.charlesbridgebb.com;
Dražického náměstí 5; s/d 2200/2400Kč, apt 3200-
3500Kč; 💺 12, 20, 22; 🅿 💻 🛜
Location, location, location – those three
little words that mean so much when it
comes to property. It would be hard to

beat this quaint little pension for location – any closer to Charles Bridge and you'd be on it. The rooms are nothing to write home about, with cheap beds and plain decor tastefully brightened up with colourful curtains, dried flowers and a painting or two; for families, there are two apartments with kitchen facilities. There's free internet access at reception and wi-fi in the rooms; the parking space outside must be booked in advance.

DESIGN HOTEL SAX
Map p78   Hotel €€
☎ 257 531 268; www.hotelsax.cz; Jánský vršek 3; r from 2500Kč; 🚋 12, 20, 22; 🖳 🛜
Set in a quiet corner of Malá Strana, amid embassies and monastery gardens, the Sax is refreshingly different. The building is 18th-century on the outside, but the interior has been remodelled with classic furniture and design from the 1950s, '60s and '70s; with a dramatic glass-roofed atrium where the courtyard used to be, bold and colourful retro decor, stylish, uncluttered bedrooms, and impeccable service. The rates are very reasonable considering its peaceful and central location – less than 10-minutes' walk from the castle's main gate.

STARÉ MĚSTO
Staré Město offers a wide range of accommodation, from backpacker hostels to some of the city's most luxurious hotels, with everything in between. Be aware that a lot of pensions and midrange hotels have been squeezed into historic old buildings with no room for a lift – be prepared for a bit of stair climbing.

RESIDENCE KAROLINA
Map p90   Apartments €€€
☎ 224 990 990; www.residence-karolina.com; Karoliny Světlé 4; 2-/4-person apt 4050/6250Kč; 🚋 6, 9, 19, 21, 22; 🖳 🛜
We're going to have to invent a new category of accommodation – boutique apartments – to cover this array of 20 beautifully furnished flats. Offering one- or two-bedroom options, all apartments have spacious seating areas with comfy sofas and flat-screen TVs, sleek modern kitchens and dining areas. The location is good too, set back on a quiet street but close to a major tram stop, across the street from the National Theatre, and just two blocks from

the Tesco supermarket for your self-catering supplies. There's a daily maid service, elevator, and cable or wi-fi broadband in all apartments.

SAVIC HOTEL
Map p90   Hotel €€€
☎ 224 248 555; www.savic.eu; Jilská 7; s/d 3875/4395Kč; Ⓜ Národní Třída; ⨯ 🖳 🛜
From the complimentary glass of wine when you arrive to the comfy king-size beds, the Savic certainly knows how to make you feel welcome. Housed in the former monastery of St Giles, the hotel is bursting with character and full of delightful period details including old stone fireplaces, beautiful painted timber ceilings and fragments of frescoes. The bedrooms are furnished in antique style with parquet floors, dark wooden furniture, wingback armchairs and plush sofas, while the bathrooms are lined with polished marble. And it's barely two minutes' walk from the Astronomical Clock on Old Town Square.

GRAND HOTEL PRAHA
Map p90   Apartments €€
☎ 221 632 556; www.grandhotelpraha.cz; Staroměstské náměstí 22-25; s/d from 3350/3650Kč, apt from 8800Kč; Ⓜ Staroměstská; 🖳 🛜
Three lovely baroque buildings on Old Town Square have been converted into a luxury hotel with large, well-appointed rooms filled with heavy antique furniture and rugs, paintings, wooden floors and chandeliers. Some have the additional charm of painted wooden-beamed ceilings. The most luxurious rooms are in the 'Apostolic Residence' at No 25, which also boasts a magnificent attic apartment (sleeps four), with spiral staircase and massive timber beams. The unique selling point, though, is its location – you can hang out your window and watch the Astronomical Clock do its thing. You'll pay extra for a room with a view of Old Town Square, but for this level of quality, it's still reasonable value compared with many top-end hotels around town.

HOTEL U MEDVÍDKŮ
Map p90   Pension €€
☎ 224 211 916; www.umedvidku.cz; Na Perštýně 7; s/d/tr 2300/3500/4500Kč; Ⓜ Národní Třída; 🖳 🛜
Cosy and centrally located, 'At the Little Bear' is a traditional beer hall (see the boxed text, p183) on the southern edge of the Old Town, about 10 minutes' walk from

Old Town Square. The rooms have polished hardwood floors and dark wooden furniture, with good-sized bathrooms (and good water pressure in the showers). Some of the 1st-floor rooms have Renaissance painted wooden ceilings, and a few are almost big enough to be called a suite (the 'historic' rooms, which have a bit of character, cost 10% more than the ordinary ones, which have less atmosphere but are similar in size). For a romantic splurge, choose one of the attic rooms – No 33 is the best in the house, spacious and atmospheric, with a big pine bed and huge exposed roof beams.

HOTEL JOSEF Map p90   Boutique Hotel €€
☎ 221 700 111; www.hoteljosef.com; Rybná 20; r from 3350Kč; Ⓜ Náměstí Republiky; Ⓟ ⓧ 🖵 📶 ♿

Designed by London-based Czech architect Eva Jiřičná, the Josef is one of Prague's most stylish contemporary hotels. As soon as you step through the doors into the stark, white, minimalist lobby with its glass spiral staircase you get the impression that it's designed to impress you with how exceedingly cool and trendy it all is. But it's tastefully done, and staff are welcoming and helpful. The minimalist design is continued in the bedrooms, where things are kept clean and simple with plenty of subtle neutral tones in the bedlinen and furniture. The glass-walled en suites are especially attractive, boasting extra-large 'rainfall' shower heads and modish glass bowl basins. There are two wheelchair-accessible rooms and a stylish bar and business lounge.

HOTEL ANTIK Map p90   Hotel €€
☎ 222 322 288; www.hotelantik.cz; Dlouhá 22; s/d 2590/2990Kč; Ⓜ Náměstí Republiky; 🖵 📶

Although the name suggests antique, a recent remodelling has left this hotel with a clean, modern vibe, relieved here and there by the odd exposed roof beam and idiosyncratic room layouts. But the location is ideal, right in the heart of the Old Town and close to lots of good restaurants and bars. The cosy rooms have been thoroughly modernised and are perfectly comfortable though a little lacking in character – ask for one with a balcony overlooking the courtyard, to avoid any noise from night-time revellers in the street. Breakfast is served in the lovely atrium-courtyard at the back.

PERLA HOTEL Map p90   Boutique Hotel €€
☎ 221 667 707; www.perlahotel.cz; Perlová 1; s/d from 2350/2950Kč; Ⓜ Můstek; ♿

The 'Pearl' on Pearl St is typical of the brand of slinky, appealing designer hotels that have sprung up all over central Prague. Here the designer has picked a – surprise, surprise – pearl motif that extends from the giant pearls that form the reception desk to the silky, lustrous bedspreads and huge screen prints on the bedroom walls. The rooms are on the small side, but the decor is sleek and modern with muted colours offset by bright-red lacquered chairs and glossy black-tiled bathrooms. The whole building is wheelchair-accessible, and one room is specially designed for wheelchair users.

U ZELENÉHO VĚNCE Map p90   Pension €€
☎ 222 220 178; www.uzv.cz; Řetězová 10; s/d/tr 1700/2200/2800Kč; Ⓜ Staroměstská; 🖵 📶

Located on a quiet side street, but only a few minutes' stroll from Old Town Square, the Green Garland is a surprisingly peaceful and rustic retreat right in the heart of the city. Set in a restored 14th-century building, it takes its name from the house-sign above the door. The bedrooms vary in size – some cramped and some relatively spacious – but all are spotlessly clean and simply but appealingly decorated, with exposed medieval roof beams in the attic rooms, and the English-speaking owner is unfailingly polite and helpful.

OLD PRAGUE HOSTEL
Map p90   Hostel €
☎ 224 829 058; www.oldpraguehostel.com; Benediktská 2; dm from 375Kč, s/d 1000/1200Kč; Ⓜ Náměstí Republiky; ⓧ 🖵 📶

Cheerful and welcoming with colourful homemade murals brightening the walls, this is one of Prague's most appealing and sociable hostels, with a good mix of people from backpackers to families. Facilities are good, with lockers in the dorms, free breakfast and nonsmoking rooms, though the mattresses on the bunks are a bit on the thin side. The staff are very helpful (there's 24-hour reception) and the location could hardly be more central, just five minutes' walk east of Old Town Square and two minutes from tram and metro. There are two PCs with free internet access (often busy) and wi-fi throughout the hostel (though the signal is a bit spotty).

NOVÉ MĚSTO & VYŠEHRAD

Although there are one or two grand old luxury hotels here, Nové Město's accommodation is mostly in modern chain hotels and upgraded 1930s establishments. What they might lack in historical atmosphere and romantic appeal they make up for in spaciousness and facilities. Those on Wenceslas Square are right in the thick of things, but there are quiet corners to be found as well, especially in southern Nové Město (ie Charles Square and its surrounds).

HOTEL YASMIN
Map p110   Boutique Hotel €€€

☎ 234 100 100; www.hotel-yasmin.cz; Politických Věžňů 12, Nové Město; r from 6500Kč; Ⓜ Můstek; Ⓟ ⊠ 🖥 📶

This designer hotel, a block east of Wenceslas Square, is very cutting edge, a blend of space age and organic. The public areas are covered in motifs in the shape of jasmine blossoms (from small white petals on the black granite floors to giant leaf prints on the walls), and decorated with birch-twig arrangements and chrome balls. The spacious bedrooms have a neutral palette of white, beige and tan, the clean lines set off by plants, flowers or a curved edge; the bathrooms are in black tile and chrome. The hotel is entirely nonsmoking.

RADISSON BLU ALCRON HOTEL
Map p110   Hotel €€€

☎ 222 820 000; www.radissonblu.com/hotel-prague; Štěpánská 40, Nové Město; r from 3600Kč; Ⓜ Můstek; Ⓟ ⊠ 🖥 📶 ♿

Located just a few minutes' walk from Wenceslas Square, the five-star Radisson is the modern reincarnation of the 1930s Alcron Hotel, long favoured by celebrities and diplomats. Many of the original art deco marble-and-glass fittings have been preserved, including in the beautiful La Rotonde restaurant, and the 206 rooms have been far more tastefully renovated than in many other refurbished Prague hotels. The rooms have pleasant soft furnishings, retro prints and chic marble bathrooms, while mod cons such as free wi-fi, video games and minibars add to the comfort and convenience. There are also wheelchair-accessible rooms for guests with disabilities.

SUITEHOME RESIDENCE
Map p110   Hotel Apartments €€

☎ 222 230 833; www.suitehome.cz; Příčná 2, Nové Město; 2-person ste from 3640Kč; Ⓜ Karlovo Náměstí; 🖥 📶

Straddling the divide between apartment and hotel, this place offers the space and convenience of a suite with private bathroom and kitchen along with hotel facilities such as 24-hour reception desk, daily maid service and breakfast room. It's a good choice for families or groups of friends, with suites for up to six; the rooms are pleasantly old-fashioned, and some on the upper floors have good views towards the castle. There's a lift, though it's a bit on the small side – important, as the building has five floors. Check the website for special rates.

ICON HOTEL Map p110   Boutique Hotel €€

☎ 221 634 100; www.iconhotel.eu; V Jámě 6, Nové Město; r from 3380Kč; 🚊 3, 9, 14, 24; 🖥 📶

Staff clothes by Diesel, computers by Apple, beds by Hästens – pretty much everything in this gorgeous boutique hotel has a designer stamp on it. Appearing on Europe's trendiest hotels lists, the Icon's sleekly minimalist rooms are enlivened with a splash of imperial purple from the silky bedspreads, while the curvy, reproduction art deco armchairs are supplied by Modernista (p153). High-tech touches include iPod docks, Skype phones and fingerprint-activated safes, and if your muscles are aching after a hard day's sightseeing, the hotel also boasts one of Prague's best Thai massage studios.

HOTEL UNION Map p120   Hotel €€

☎ 261 214 812; www.hotelunion.cz; Ostrčilovo náměstí 4, Vyšehrad; s/d 2900/3300Kč; 🚊 7, 18, 24; 🖥 📶

A grand old hotel from 1906, the Union was nationalised by the communists in 1958 and returned to the former owner's grandson in 1991. It's still family run, and the staff take great pride in looking after their guests properly. Comfortably renovated, with a few period touches left intact, the hotel is at the foot of the hill below Vyšehrad fortress; Charles Bridge is just 10 minutes away on tram 18. Bedrooms are plain but pleasant, and the double glazing helps to cut down on noise from trams and nearby railway; ask for one of the deluxe corner rooms (4800Kč a double), which are huge and have bay windows with a view of either Vyšehrad or distant Prague Castle.

HOTEL 16 U SV KATEŘINY
Map p108   Hotel €€

☎ 224 920 636; www.hotel16.cz; Kateřinská 16, Nové Město; s/d/tr 2300/2600/3500Kč; Ⓜ Karlovo Náměstí; Ⓟ ⓧ ⌨ 📶

Near the Botanic Gardens and about five minutes' walk from Karlovo Náměstí metro station, Hotel 16 is a friendly, family-run little place with just 14 rooms, tucked away in a very quiet corner of town where you're more likely to hear birdsong than traffic. The rooms vary in size and are simply but smartly furnished; the best, at the back, have views onto the peaceful terraced garden. Buffet breakfast is included in the price, and the hotel is fitted with a lift.

HOTEL U ŠUTERŮ Map p110   Hotel €€

☎ 224 948 235; www.accomprague.com; Palack-ého 4, Nové Město; s/d 1590/2390Kč; 🚊 3, 9, 14, 24 or Ⓜ Můstek; ⌨ 📶

A block west of Wenceslas Square, this small side-street hotel (10 rooms) is very central but away from the worst of the city-centre noise. With their polished wooden floors and plain wooden furniture, the bedrooms have a certain rustic charm; it's worth paying a little extra for one of the deluxe doubles (2590Kč), which have a bit more character. Breakfast is served in the Gothic basement, which doubles as a decent restaurant in the evenings.

MISS SOPHIE'S Map p110   Hostel €

☎ 296 303 530; www.miss-sophies.com; Melou-nova 3, Nové Město; dm 510Kč; s/d 1790/2090Kč, apt 2390Kč; Ⓜ IP Pavlova; ⓧ ⌨ 📶

This hostel in a converted apartment building on the southern edge of the New Town makes a pleasant change from the usual characterless backpacker hive. There's a touch of contemporary style here, with oak-veneer floors and stark, minimalist decor – the main motif is 'distressed' con-crete, along with neutral colours and black metal-framed beds. The place is famous for its 'designer' showers, with autographed glass screens and huge 'rainfall' shower heads. There is a very cool lounge in the basement, with red-brick vaults and black leather sofas, and reception (open 24 hours) is staffed by a young, multilingual crew who are always eager to help.

HOSTEL U MELOUNU
Map p108   Hostel €

☎ 224 918 322; www.hostelumelounu.cz; Ke Karlovu 7, Nové Město; dm 350Kč, s/d 990/1100Kč; Ⓜ IP Pavlova; Ⓟ ⌨ 📶

One of the prettier hostels in town, 'At the Watermelon' is set in a historic building on a quiet backstreet, a short walk from Vinohrady's restaurants and bars (it's a 10-minute walk south of IP Pavlova metro station). The rooms are all on the ground floor and range from basic dorms to self-contained apartments radiating off a large central garden, giving the place a peaceful, cottage feel. Dorms, sleeping between six and 10 people in bunk beds, are the basic, functional spaces you would expect, but they are spotlessly clean and have lockers, and there's the added attraction of that peaceful, sunny garden complete with barbecue.

VINOHRADY & VRŠOVICE

Vinohrady is a great place to stay. Not only is it relatively close to the centre, with good metro connections from Náměstí Míru and Jiřího z Poděbrad stations, but there are lots of pleasant places to stroll around and stop for a beer or bite to eat. One drawback is parking. Vinohrady has now introduced dra-conian street-parking restrictions, leaving the only option in most cases being paid lots that are a good distance from the hotel. Vršovice is a little further out, and not quite as con-veniently connected. Nevertheless, prices are lower here and some attractive new proper-ties have recently opened. On the positive side, free street parking is still available in Vršovice, though with parking restrictions popping up all over town, good luck finding an available space.

LE PALAIS HOTEL
Map p125   Hotel €€€

☎ 234 634 111; www.palaishotel.cz; U Zvonařky 1, Vinohrady; s/d €250/280, ste from €400; 🚊 6, 11; Ⓟ ⓧ ⌨

Le Palais is housed in a gorgeous belle époque building dating from the end of the 19th century that was once home to Czech artist Luděk Marold (1865–98; his former apartment is now rooms 407 to 412). It has been beautifully restored, complete with original floor mosaics, period fireplaces, marble staircases, wrought-iron balustrades, frescoes, painted ceilings and delicate stuccowork. The luxury bedrooms are decorated in warm shades of yellow, pink and ochre, while the various suites – some located in the corner tower, some with a south-facing balcony – make the most of the hotel's superb location perched on top of a bluff with views of Vyšehrad fortress. Within easy walking distance of bars and restaurants in Vinohrady and about 15 minutes by foot from the top of Wenceslas Square.

HOTEL SIEBER
Map p125   Boutique Hotel €€€
☎ 224 250 025; www.sieber.cz; Slezská 55, Vinohrady; s/d/ste 4480/4780/5480Kč; Ⓜ Jiřího z Poděbrad, 🚇 11; ✖ 💻
Popular with business travellers, the Sieber is a small luxury hotel with 13 rooms and seven suites, set in a grand 19th-century apartment building. Stylish decor and attentive service are accompanied by thoughtful little touches such as bathrobes and fresh flowers. The building dates from 1889 and has been restored to its former grandeur after suffering years of neglect under the communist regime, and the rooms are decorated in restful, neutral tones (lots of cream and light wood). Service can't be faulted, and the staff are courteous and very helpful. The hotel is also gay-friendly. Rates are frequently discounted on its website.

AMETYST
Map p125   Boutique Hotel €€€
☎ 222 921 921; www.hotelametyst.cz; Jana Masaryka 11, Vinohrady; s/d from €160/225; Ⓜ Náměstí Míru; Ⓟ ✖ 💻 📶
The polished Ametyst straddles the line between boutique and hotel, with just enough style points in the lobby (nice retro flagstone) and the rooms (hardwood floors, arty lamps and flat-screen TVs) to put it in the boutique camp. All rooms have air-conditioning and wi-fi access, and there are tubs and hair dryers in the bathrooms. There's a cosy coffee bar off the lobby and dozens of places to relax within easy walking distance in one of the nicest parts of leafy Vinohrady. On a negative note, rack rates have risen steeply in the past couple of years, though the hotel does offer frequent steep discounts over its website.

HOTEL CHODSKÁ
Map p125   Hotel, Pension €€
☎ 224 251 460; www.hotelchodska.cz; Chodská 26, Vinohrady; s/d from 1600/3000Kč; Ⓜ Náměstí Míru plus 🚇 10, 16; Ⓟ ✖ 💻 📶
This is a small, family-run hotel on a quiet, elegant street in residential Vinohrady. The rooms are plainly furnished and uninspiring, but everything is clean and well maintained, and the price is reasonable for this location. Facilities include free in-room wi-fi, plus a computer terminal for guests without a laptop or smartphone. As with nearly everywhere in Vinohrady, street parking is restricted, meaning you'll probably have to use paid parking at a lot far from the hotel. Be sure to check in advance, since the hotel shuts down to short-term guests during slow periods.

HOTEL LUNÍK
Map p125   Hotel €€
☎ 224 253 974; www.hotel-lunik.cz; Londýnská 50, Vinohrady; s/d from 2000/2900Kč; Ⓜ Náměstí Míru or IP Pavlova; Ⓟ ✖ 💻
Clean, attractive and smallish, Hotel Luník is on a quiet residential street a block from Peace Square and between the Náměstí Míru and IP Pavlova metro stations. There's been a hotel here since the 1920s, and the lobby and public areas exude a quiet sophistication. The rooms are homey and slightly old-fashioned, with attractive green-tiled bathrooms. There's free internet access in the rooms via LAN connection and a couple of terminals off the lobby. The friendly receptionist is willing to negotiate room rates on slow nights.

ORION
Map p125   Hotel Apartments €€
☎ 222 521 706; www.okhotels.cz; Americká 9, Vinohrady; 2-/4-person apt 2290/2590Kč; Ⓜ Náměstí Míru; Ⓟ ✖ 💻 📶
A good-value hotel in an upmarket section of Vinohrady, within easy walking distance of Náměstí Míru and Havlíčkovy sady. All 26 apartments are equipped with a small kitchen, including fridge and coffee maker. Several apartments have multiple rooms and can accommodate small groups. There's also a Finnish sauna on the premises. The rooms are not much to look at but are clean and comfortable. Ask to see a couple of rooms if possible, since they are all slightly different. Some come with hardwood floors, others with carpets.

HOTEL ANNA

Map p125   Hotel, Pension €€

☎ 222 513 111; www.hotelanna.cz; Budečská 17, Vinohrady; s/d from €70/90, ste from €100; Ⓜ Náměstí Míru; Ⓟ ⊠ ▯ 📶

Hotel Anna is small and friendly, with helpful and knowledgeable employees who speak both English and German. The late-19th-century building retains many of its art nouveau features, and the bedrooms are bright and cheerful with floral bedspreads and arty black-and-white photos of Prague buildings on the walls. There are two small suites on the top floor, one of which has a great view towards the castle. The hotel is tucked away on a quiet backstreet but close to the metro and lots of good restaurants and bars; you can walk to the top end of Wenceslas Square in 10 minutes. Check the website for special offers.

ARKADA

Map p125   Boutique Hotel €€

☎ 242 429 111; www.arkadahotel.cz; Balbínová 8, Vinohrady; s/d from €70/90; Ⓜ Muzeum, 🚋 11; Ⓟ ⊠ ▯

This relatively new hotel in Vinohrady comes highly recommended for offering a great combination of style, comfort and location. The rooms are well appointed, with a retro 1930s feel that fits the style of the building. Rooms have flat-screen TVs, free internet access and minibars. Ask to see a couple before choosing, since the decor differs from room to room. The location is about five minutes by foot to the top of Wenceslas Square and within easy walking distance of some of the best Vinohrady clubs and restaurants.

HOLIDAY HOME
Map p125   Pension €

☎ 222 512 710; www.holidayhome.cz; Americká 37, Vinohrady; s/d from 1480/1800Kč; Ⓜ Náměstí Míru; Ⓟ ⊠ ▯ 📶

This simple family-owned and -operated pension offers good value in one of the city's nicest residential neighbourhoods. Don't expect anything fancy in spite of the elegant town-house setting. The rooms are small and nothing fancy, with tiny beds. On the other hand, the location is ideal and the friendly owners will take good care of you from the moment you arrive. Free wi-fi throughout the hotel and an internet cafe next door. Just a short walk to Náměstí Míru metro stop.

PENSION BEETLE

Map p125   Pension €

☎ 222 515 093; www.pension-beetle.cz; Šmilovského 10, Vinohrady; d from 1700Kč, ste from 1900Kč; 🚋 4, 22; Ⓟ ⊠ ▯

The Beetle occupies a lovely 1910 apartment building in a leafy backstreet, far from the tourist throng. The cheaper rooms are plain but functional, while the larger rooms and 'suites' (like two-room apartments) are more stylishly decorated and furnished, with antique and stripped pine furniture, and equipped with bedside lamps, minibar, table and chairs. A continental breakfast, with all the coffee you can drink, is included in the price. Offers steep out-of-season discounts; check the website.

PENZION MÁNES

Map p125   Pension €

☎ 222 252 180; www.penzionmanes.cz; Mánesova 46, Vinohrady; s/d from 1200/1600Kč; Ⓜ Jiřího z Poděbrad, 🚋 11; ⊠ ▯

It's bare-bones accommodation here, but a great price given the location on handsome Mánesova, close to some of the area's best bars, restaurants and clubs. There are few facilities, but rooms (some with a courtyard view) are comfortable and quiet, and staff are friendly.

CZECH INN

Map p125   Hostel, Hotel €

☎ 267 267 600; www.czech-inn.com; Francouzská 76, Vršovice; dm 285-385Kč, s/d 1320/1540Kč, apt from 1650Kč, 3-room apt from 3300Kč; Ⓜ Náměstí Míru plus 🚋 4, 22; Ⓟ ⊠ ▯ 📶

The Czech Inn calls itself a hostel, but the boutique label wouldn't be out of place. Everything seems sculpted by an industrial designer on Ian Schrager's payroll, from the handcrafted iron beds to the swish brushed-steel flooring and minimalist square sinks – right out of a German design catalogue. The Czech Inn offers a variety of accommodation, from standard hostel dorm rooms to good-value private doubles (with or without attached bathroom), and one-, two- or three-room apartments. The 5th-floor apartments come with a shared rooftop terrace and sleep up to eight. A bank of internet terminals in the lobby and an excellent buffet breakfast in the adjoining bar-cafe round out the charms.

PENSION ARCO

Map p125   Pension, Apartments €

☎ 271 740 734; www.arco-guesthouse.cz; Donská 13, Vršovice; d/apt from €44/54; 🖭 4, 22; ✕ 🖳

The Arco's new location is on a still rough but gentrifying street near the Vršovice-Vinohrady line, not far from the Czech Inn (p225). While the neighbourhood might be a little grotty, rest assured that the pension's accommodation is clean and secure. Arco has carved out a name for itself by promoting a gay-friendly attitude as well as clean, comfortably furnished apartments, sporting laminate floors and IKEA furniture. The location is about five-minute tram ride from the Náměstí Míru metro station. Vinohrady's restaurants, pubs and clubs are just a few blocks away.

ŽIŽKOV & KARLÍN

If you're looking for somewhere inexpensive but not far from the city centre, then Žižkov and Karlín are your best bet. The slightly run-down air of these districts puts a lot of people off, but they are as safe as anywhere else in the city and only a couple of tram stops from Staré Město. Unfortunately a lot of the accommodation here is pretty mediocre, but things are improving all the time – Žižkov is sure to sprout some cool designer hotels in the next few years as rising property prices in neighbouring Vinohrady force developers to look elsewhere.

HOTEL ALWYN Map p130   Boutique Hotel €€

☎ 222 334 200; www.hotelalwyn.cz; Vítkova 26, Karlín; s/d from 2900/3400Kč; 🖭 8, 24; 🖳 📶

The Alwyn is the first of what will probably be many designer hotels to appear in the up-and-coming district of Karlín. Set on a quiet side street only a few tram stops east of Staré Město, the hotel sports deliciously modern decor in shades of chocolate brown, beige and burnt orange, with lots of polished wood and Deco-style sofas in the cocktail bar, and super-comfortable Hästens beds in the rooms. It's designed for both business and pleasure, with broadband ports and free wi-fi, conference room, fitness centre, sauna and massage centre.

AMEDIA HOTEL THEATRINO

Map p130   Hotel €€

☎ 221 422 111; www.amediahotels.com; Bořivojova 53, Žižkov; r from 2000Kč; 🖭 5, 9, 26; 🖳 📶

The design of some boutique hotels could be described as theatrical, but there can't be too many that were actually designed as a theatre. Dating from 1910, the art nouveau building that houses this Austrian-run hotel was originally a cultural centre, Žižkov's equivalent of the Municipal House (p102) – guests here can enjoy an excellent buffet breakfast in what was originally the theatre auditorium. The rooms are plain and modern, but the public areas are filled with beautiful period features, from wrought-iron railings to stained glass windows.

HOSTEL ELF Map p130   Hostel €

☎ 222 540 963; www.hostelelf.com; Husitská 11, Žižkov; dm 290-390Kč; s/d 1200/1400Kč; Ⓜ Florenc; 🖳 📶

Young, hip and sociable, Hostel Elf welcomes a steady stream of party-hearty backpackers from across the globe to its well-maintained dorms, and many end up staying longer than they originally planned. The dorms, sleeping up to 11 people, are immaculately clean and brightly decorated with graffiti art or the odd mural. There's a little beer-garden terrace and cosy lounge, with free tea and coffee and cheap beer, and Žižkov with its many pubs is right on the doorstep; the downside is the noisy train line that runs close by. The hostel is less than 10 minutes' walk from Florenc bus station.

CLOWN & BARD HOSTEL

Map p130   Hostel €

☎ 222 716 453; www.clownandbard.com; Bořivojova 102, Žižkov; dm 250-330Kč, d 1000Kč, tw/tr with private bathroom 1400/1950Kč; 🖭 5, 9, 26; 🅿 🖳 📶

Set in the heart of Žižkov's pub district, the Clown & Bard is a full-on party place – don't come here looking for peace and quiet. This ever-popular hostel has a cafe (with free, vegetarian, all-you-can-eat breakfast from 9am to 1pm), a lively bar, friendly, knowledgeable staff and good tours. As well as dorms and doubles, there are two-, three- and four-person rooms with en suite bathroom. The party crowd gravitates towards the thumping basement bar that stays open till midnight and features regular live acts and DJ nights. Rooms are fairly basic, but clean and perfectly comfortable. There are four computers offering free internet access, and free wi-fi.

HOLEŠOVICE, BUBENEČ & DEJVICE

Don't choose a hotel in the neighbourhoods of Holešovice, Bubeneč or Dejvice if you require niceties like a window view of Prague Castle or the ability to tumble from your hotel door onto the cobblestones of Malá Strana. While these neighbourhoods have their attractive areas too, for the most part they are ordinary workaday parts of Prague. On the plus side, the rates tend to be more reasonable than in the centre, and your bargaining power at the reception desk is greater because the demand for rooms is lower. The districts of Dejvice and Bubeneč in Prague 6, in particular, have two other big advantages: both are within easy reach of the airport, and unlike many other parts of Prague, street parking is not restricted here. The properties around the Nádraží Holešovice train station are convenient if you're arriving by train from Vienna, Budapest or Berlin (many international trains stop here). Metro and tram connections to the centre are generally very good.

HOTEL PRAHA Map p58 — Hotel €€€

☎ 224 343 305; www.htlpraha.cz; Sušická 20, Dejvice; d €220; taxi; Ⓟ ☒ ▯ ♿

The Hotel Praha is one of Prague's more interesting hotels. Hidden away on a hill in Dejvice, surrounded by several hectares of private grounds that were once protected by an electric fence, it's a luxury complex that was built in 1981 for the Communist Party elite. The public areas of the hotel are an intriguing mix of 1970s futuristic (sweeping curves and stainless steel) and 1950s Soviet splendour (polished marble and cut-glass chandeliers). The bedrooms are spacious, with all the luxury you'd expect from a five-star establishment, and many are accessible to wheelchair users. But the hotel's biggest drawcard is the fact that each of its 124 rooms has its own private balcony – the entire southern face of the hotel is a sloping grandstand of stacked balconies, all draped with greenery and commanding a superb view of Prague Castle. Before 1989, such Soviet-era stalwarts as Nicolae Ceauşescu, Erich Honecker and Eduard Shevardnadze all hung their hats here; in recent years, the clientele has shifted from heads of state to Hollywood, with stars such as Tom Cruise, Johnny Depp, Alanis Morissette, Kris Kristofferson and Paul Simon ringing room service in the small hours.

ABSOLUTUM HOTEL

Map p136 — Boutique Hotel €€

☎ 222 541 406; www.absolutumhotel.cz; Jablonského 639/4, Holešovice; s/d 3200/4000Kč; Ⓜ Nádraží Holešovice; Ⓟ ☒ ▯ ⎵

A highly recommended, eye-catching boutique hotel (without a boutique price tag if you manage to snag a deal on the hotel website), the Absolutum is located across from the Nádraží Holešovice train and metro stations. While the neighbourhood wouldn't win a beauty contest, the hotel compensates with a list of amenities almost unheard of at this price point, including big, beautifully designed rooms with exposed brickwork, huge modern bathrooms (many rooms have both a shower and a tub), air-conditioning, an excellent in-house restaurant, a massage and wellness centre next door, and free parking. The friendly receptionist is willing to cut rates if you happen to arrive on a slow night. The hotel restaurant is close enough to Nádraží Holešovice that you could jump over for a quick meal if you have to wait for a train.

SPLENDID Map p136 — Hotel €€

☎ 233 375 940; www.hotelsplendid.cz; Ovenecká 33, Bubeneč; s/d 1900/2600Kč; ▯ 1, 8, 15, 25, 26; ☒ ▯

This hotel-cum-guesthouse, occupying a town house on a beautiful residential street next to Stromovka Park, dates from well before the Velvet Revolution, and there is still a slight communist whiff in the air. Maybe it's the '70s-style black-leatherette stools in the hotel bar or the ultra-spartan rooms, with their tiny, narrow beds and thin mattresses (communists apparently never slept together in the same bed). The Splendid is actually crying out for a thorough upgrade. On the other hand, it's clean and quiet, and the location is superb if you're looking for something green and outside the tourist throng. Note that parking is restricted to residents only. The only internet option is a public terminal near reception.

EXPO PRAGUE Map p136 — Hotel €€

☎ 266 712 470; www.expoprag.cz; Za Elektrárnou 3, Holešovice; s/d from 1800/2600Kč; ▯ 5, 12, 14, 15, 17; Ⓟ ☒ ▯ ⎵

Medium-sized and modern, this hotel was built in the mid-1990s to accommodate trade fair delegations at the nearby Výstaviště exhibition grounds. It lacks atmosphere but would do in a pinch if the nearby (and better) Absolutum Hotel (p227) is not available. It's just one tram stop from the Nádraží Holešovice train station and close to the sports and concert venue Tesla Aréna (Sportovní hala). The rooms are decorated in a bland, contemporary, chain-hotel style, but they're clean, and also have air-conditioning, minibars and safes.

HOTEL DENISA Map p136 · Pension, Hotel €€
☎ 224 318 969; www.hotel-denisa.cz; Narodní Obrany 33, Dejvice; s/d from 1700/1900Kč; Ⓜ Dejvická; Ⓟ ✕ 🖳 📶

This small, family-run hotel in a turn-of-the-century apartment building on a quiet side street was thoroughly renovated in 2008, turning an average hotel into an excellent deal. Rooms have nice thick mattresses, flat-screen TVs, minibars and high-speed wi-fi internet access. The location has always been a plus, just a few minutes' walk to the Dejvická metro station that can whisk you downtown in a few minutes, as well as convenient to the airport. The neighbourhood itself is wonderful for strolling, with lots of cafes and restaurants. Good hot breakfasts.

HOTEL BELVEDERE Map p136 · Hotel €€
☎ 220 106 111; www.hhotels.cz; Milady Horákové 19, Holešovice; s/d from 1600/1800Kč; 🚋 1, 8, 15, 25, 26; Ⓟ ✕

The Belvedere is an old communist-era hotel that has been completely refurbished, and now provides good-value accommodation within easy reach of the city centre. The standard rooms are nothing special, but they're comfortable and spotlessly clean. The 'executive' rooms (from 3000Kč in season) are much more spacious, with soundproofed windows, smart crimson drapes and bedspreads, and huge, white, marble-lined bathrooms. Check the website for occasional steep discounts, especially in mid-summer. The large breakfast room has a slightly institutional feel, but the food is good and there's plenty of it. There's a tram stop right outside the front door, and it's only five minutes to Náměstí Republiky metro station on tram 8.

HOTEL EXTOL INN Map p136 · Hotel €€
☎ 220 876 541; www.extolinn.cz; Přístavní 2, Holešovice; s/d from 1050/1800Kč; 🚋 1, 3, 5, 25; Ⓟ ✕ 🖳 ♿

The bright, modern Extol Inn provides budget accommodation in an up-and-coming neighbourhood within easy reach of the city centre. The cheapest rooms (on the upper floors) are basic, no-frills affairs with shared bathrooms. These are often occupied by groups of high-school students, so if you value your peace and quiet it might be worth paying a bit extra for the more expensive three-star rooms (doubles from 2350Kč), which have private bathroom, TV, minibar and free use of the hotel sauna and spa. There's a public internet terminal in the lobby. The hotel is entirely nonsmoking and wheelchair-accessible. There's a tram stop 100m away, from which it's a 10-minute ride to the city centre.

HOTEL LEON Map p136 · Hostel, Hotel €
☎ 220 941 351; www.leonhotel.eu; Ortenovo náměstí 26, Holešovice; s/d from 900/1400Kč; Ⓜ Nádraží Holešovice or 🚋 5, 12, 15; Ⓟ ✕ 🖳

The Hotel Leon advertises itself as something between a hostel and a small hotel. In truth, it's actually much nicer than a standard hostel and not much more expensive (especially if you share a three- or four-bed room). The rooms are basic, with no TV or much of anything else, but are quiet and clean, with adjoining bathrooms. If noise is an issue, ask for a quieter room overlooking the back garden. There's a common room for TV and a shared computer for internet access. It's one tram stop (Ortenovo náměstí) from the Nádraží Holešovice train and metro station.

PLUS PRAGUE HOSTEL Map p136 · Hostel €
☎ 220 510 046; www.plusprague.com; Přívozní 1, Holešovice; dm 300Kč, s/d 800/1600Kč; Ⓜ Nádraží Holešovice; Ⓟ ✕ 🖳 🎦 📶

The cheerful Plus Prague Hostel is one tram stop from Nádraží Holešovice (take any tram heading east (left) as you exit the station to Ortenovo náměstí). Cheap rates, clean rooms with en-suite bathrooms, friendly staff, free wi-fi *and* an indoor swimming pool and sauna make this a special place. The staff hold special game nights at the in-house bar and conduct regular pub-crawls for the guests. It also offers four-, six- and eight-bed 'girls only' dorm rooms, outfitted with hair dryers and fluffier towels, among other amenities.

ART HOTEL Map p136 · Boutique Hotel €€
☎ 233 101 331; www.arthotel.cz; Nad Královskou Oborou 53, Bubeneč; s/d from €120/140; 🚋 1, 8, 15, 25, 26 (stop Sparta); Ⓟ ✕ 🖳

There are lots of word-of-mouth recommendations for this small hotel hidden away in the peaceful embassy district situated behind Generali Aréna (Sparta stadium). It has sleek modern styling with a display of contemporary Czech art in the lobby, and art photography on the walls of the bedrooms. Room 203 is the best in the house, with a balcony and a view of the sunset; rooms 104 and 106 also have balconies. It may look out of the way on the map, but it's only a few minutes' walk from a tram (8) that will take you to the city centre (Náměstí Republiky) in about 10 minutes.

HOTEL VILLA SCHWAIGER
Map p136   Boutique Hotel €€

☎ 233 320 271; www.villaschwaiger.com; Schwaigerova 59/3, Bubeneč; s/d from €70/110; taxi or Ⓜ Hradčanská (plus bus 131 one stop to Sibirské náměstí); Ⓟ ⊠ ▯ 🖭

This elegant, colonial-style villa in a quiet valley in Bubeneč feels a world away from the bustle of Old Town Square. Great care has gone into designing the 22 rooms, including one – No 102 – done up in 'Chinese' style, with dark hardwoods, dramatic crimson fabrics and Chinese prints on the wall. The 'Zen' bathroom is done in brushed metal with a simple porcelain basin. Ask to see a couple of rooms before choosing. Guests can relax in the back garden, take the hotel's bikes out for a spin in nearby Stromovka, or relax in the private sauna. The public areas are stunning, with white woods, marble floors and comfortable wicker furniture. The hotel is tricky to find, so it's best to take a taxi (at least for the first visit).

PLAZA ALTA HOTEL
Map p136   Hotel €€

☎ 220 407 011; www.plazahotelalta.com; Ortenovo náměstí 22, Holešovice; s/d from €80/100; Ⓜ Nádraží Holešovice or 🚋 5, 12, 15; Ⓟ ⊠ ▯ 🖭

The snazziest hotel in this part of town draws a mostly business clientele and travellers looking for a full-service property within easy reach (one tram stop) of Nádraží Holešovice. The hotel had a complete makeover in 2007, giving the rooms a cleaner look, with thicker mattresses and bold, striped bedspreads. All the rooms have air-conditioning and minibars, and free wi-fi is available throughout. It's great value if you manage to snag a good deal

off the hotel's website. There's a faux Mexican restaurant off the lobby (open until 11pm), which is not a bad option if you're arriving late and don't have the energy to go back out.

HOTEL CROWNE PLAZA
Map p136   Hotel €€

☎ 296 537 111; www.austria-hotels.at; Koulova 15, Dejvice; d from €85; 🚋 8 (stop: Podbaba); Ⓟ ⊠ ▯

Originally called the Hotel International, this stunning socialist realist palace was built in the 1950s in the style of Moscow University, complete with Soviet star atop the tower (the star is now gold, not red). Now modernised, it is comfortable and quiet, tucked away at the end of tram 8. Come here for the decor rather than anything else – although the rooms here are standard chain-hotel style, with all the necessities but not too many luxuries, the building itself is really something special, covered in polished marble, bas-reliefs and frescoes of the noble worker. The deluxe rooms, on the 9th floor and above, are more spacious and have good views over the city.

HOTEL LETNÁ
Map p136   Pension, Hotel €€

☎ 233 374 763; www.prague-hotel-letna.com; Na Výšinách 8, Bubeneč; s/d from €50/60; 🚋 1, 8, 15, 25, 26; Ⓟ ⊠ ▯ 🖭

Pleasant and family-owned, Hotel Letná is in a late-19th-century apartment block on a quiet residential street not far from Sparta Stadium, near Letenské náměstí. Don't be put off by the musty lobby: the rooms have gotten a recent update and are quiet and clean, most with tubs as well as showers, hair dryers and minibars. It's about five minutes by foot to the tram stop, from where it's 10 minutes to the centre. Ask to see several rooms before choosing, since they are all slightly different. Check the website for occasional special offers.

SIR TOBY'S HOSTEL
Map p136   Hostel €

☎ 246 032 610; www.sirtobys.com; Dělnická 24, Holešovice; dm 200-400Kč, s/d 950/1200Kč; 🚋 1, 3, 5, 25; Ⓟ ⊠ ▯ 🖭

Set in a quiet, nicely refurbished apartment building with spacious kitchen and common room, and run by friendly, cheerful staff, Sir Toby's is only 10 minutes north of

WORTH A DETOUR

Travellers rave about Hostel Boathouse (off Map p58; ☎ 241 770 051; www.hostelboathouse.com; Lodnická 1, Braník; dm 350-400Kč; 🚊 3, 17, 21; Ⓟ 🖳), a friendly, popular hostel with a peaceful riverbank setting a few miles south of the city centre, run by the vivacious and unstinting crew of Věra and Helena. Accommodation is in three- to nine-bed rooms, with separate bathroom facilities for men and women, and there's a sunny, outdoor deck in front. A continental breakfast is provided free (you can get a cooked breakfast for 50Kč) and extras available include bike and kayak hire, a minishop and laundry service. Take tram 3, 17 or 21 to the Černý kůň stop, and follow the hostel signs west to the river (it's a five-minute walk).

the city centre by tram. The dorms have between four and eight bunks, and the bigger dorms are some of the cheapest in Prague. The private rooms, meanwhile, are fitted with metal-framed single beds. All rooms are light, clean and spacious, but don't expect anything fancy. The mattresses are a little on the thin side, but all sheets and blankets are provided at no extra cost. There's a communal kitchen for self-caterers to do their thing, a lounge and a relaxing little garden where you can sit back and chat.

A&O HOSTEL Map p136   Hostel €
☎ 220 870 252; www.aohostels.com; U Výstaviště 1/262, Holešovice; dm €12, s/d €15/36; Ⓜ Nádraží Holešovice; ⊠ 🖳

This clean, well-maintained hostel is in a converted apartment building across the street and a short walk down from the Nádraží Holešovice train and metro stations. The rooms are plain with wooden floors and white walls, lending a slightly institutional feel (think small hospital). There are a couple of computers in the lobby to check email and some snacks to buy at the reception desk, but not much else to distract you. The rates fluctuate from day to day, depending on demand. Book in advance to lock in a lower rate. There's a popular lounge/nightclub downstairs so you don't have to go far to party.

SMÍCHOV

A few years ago, the idea of staying in Smíchov would have been laughable, but the area has gone upmarket and now boasts some of the city's nicest hotels. While Smíchov is not within easy walking distance of the centre (despite what hotel brochures might imply), the metro connection from Anděl is excellent and puts you at Můstek, at the foot of Wenceslas Square, in about 10 minutes. If you

have your own wheels, Smíchov is one of the few central districts in Prague where street parking is still unrestricted and it's relatively easy to find a spot.

ANDĚL'S HOTEL PRAGUE
Map p143   Boutique Hotel €€€
☎ 296 889 688; www.andelshotel.com; Stroupežnického 21; s/d from €200/225; Ⓜ Anděl; Ⓟ ⊠ 🖳 🖨 🛜

This sleek designer hotel, all stark contemporary style in white with black and red accents, has floor-to-ceiling windows, DVD and CD players, internet access and modern abstract art in every room, while the bathrooms are a wonderland of polished chrome and frosted glass. Superior 'club rooms' come with pleasurable perks such as bathrobes and slippers, newspapers delivered to your room and free room-service breakfast. The website offers packages with significant discounts from the rack rate. The lobby is a stunning example of modern minimalism.

ANGELO HOTEL
Map p143   Boutique Hotel €€€
☎ 234 801 111; www.angelohotel.com; Radlická 1g; s/d from €200/225; Ⓜ Anděl; Ⓟ ⊠ 🖳

The Angelo is the brighter, more-extravagant cousin of Anděl's Hotel Prague. It has the same slick lobby presentation and high-tech room decor, but instead of the Anděl's muted whites, the Angelo is a riot of rich colour. Both are owned and operated by the same Austrian group, Vienna International, and there's not much difference between the two in terms of price or service. It all boils down to personal taste. The hotels are situated back to back, so if you can't get into one, try around the corner. Be sure to check the hotel website for deals; in mid-summer 2010 the hotel was offering standard doubles booked online for around half the rack rate.

SLEEPING SMÍCHOV

ADMIRÁL BOTEL Map p143 Hotel €€

☎ 257 321 302; www.admiral-botel.cz; Hořejší nábřeží 57; s/d 2980/3130Kč; Ⓜ Anděl; Ⓟ 🖙

If you've ever harboured a desire to sleep in a ship's cabin but would rather do without the seasickness, then climb aboard the Admiral, a permanently berthed riverboat floating quietly off the west bank of the Vltava. The reception area, with its plush leather seating and polished wood and brass, has a smart nautical feel, with narrow corridors leading towards the rooms. These cabins are what you might expect: simple, compact and functional rather than luxurious, with tiny en-suite shower rooms. Rooms facing the river have an attractive outlook, and you can feed the swans from your window. The 'botel' recently added free wi-fi throughout. Check the website for special deals.

HOTEL JULIAN Map p143 Hotel €€

☎ 257 311 150; www.julian.cz; Elišky Peškové 11; s/d from €99/119; 🚋 6, 9, 12, 20; Ⓟ ☒ 🖳 ♿

A deservedly popular small hotel with helpful staff and a quiet location just south of Malá Strana. The smart, well-kept bedrooms are decorated with relaxing pastel shades and pine-topped furniture, and the public areas include a clubbish drawing room with a library, comfy armchairs and an open fire; smokers can get their breakfast here (served till 11am at weekends), and the main breakfast room is smoke-free. If you're travelling with kids or in a group, there are a couple of family rooms that can hold up to six people, and there's also a wheelchair-accessible room. The hotel offers a range of services for guests with impaired mobility. The in-room air-conditioning can be a lifesaver in hot weather.

HOTEL ARBES-MEPRO Map p143 Hotel €€

☎ 257 210 410; www.hotelarbes.cz; Viktora Huga 3; s/d from 1900/2400Kč; Ⓜ Anděl; Ⓟ ☒ 🖳

Clean, quiet and excellent value, the Arbes is a down-to-earth tonic to Anděl's Hotel Prague and Angelo Hotel (both opposite). Viktora Huga is a quiet street, about two blocks from the Anděl metro station and the Nový

Smíchov shopping centre, with excellent connections to the centre. The hotel is family-owned and friendly, and the rooms are basic, with modern furnishings and clean bathrooms. Ask for a courtyard room if noise is an issue. There's a public computer near the lobby to check email. There's limited street parking, but paid parking nearby.

IBIS PRAHA MALÁ STRANA
Map p143 Hotel €€

☎ 221 701 700; www.ibishotel.com; Plzeňská 14; s/d from €69/89; Ⓜ Anděl; Ⓟ ☒ 🖳 🖙

Never mind that it's nowhere near Malá Strana (but hey, a nice try by the marketing department) – Smíchov's IBIS hotel is a great addition to the neighbourhood, offering a little of the splash of Anděl's Hotel Prague and Angelo Hotel (both opposite), but at less than half the price. The rooms are stripped down, pretty much standard issue, but they have air-conditioning and free wi-fi. The building's aggressively modern style actually looks rather good amid the futuristic boxes found around the area of the Anděl metro station. It's also an easy walk to public transport and the shopping centre. Breakfast not included in the price.

ARPACAY HOSTEL Map p143 Hostel €

☎ 251 552 297; www.arpacayhostel.com; Radlická 76; dm 250-320Kč, s/d 1300/1300Kč; Ⓜ Smíchovské Nádraží or 🚋 7; Ⓟ ☒ 🖳 🖙

This clean, colourful hostel is near Smíchovské Nádraží train station and is the best cheap accommodation in the immediate vicinity. Though it is not within walking distance of the centre as the website says, it's not a bad trip with metro line B from the train station (access via a bridge across the tracks) or with tram 7 that leaves practically from the hostel's doorstep. The relatively remote location keeps prices a little lower here than at competing hostels, and forces management to offer things like free wi-fi throughout. Accommodation is in two buildings that straddle a busy road. There's a small terrace out back of the main building for relaxing on warm evenings.

EXCURSIONS

Beyond the serried apartment blocks of Prague's outer suburbs, the city gives way to the surprisingly green hinterland of Central Bohemia, a region of rolling hills, rich farmland and thick forests dotted with castles, chateaux and picturesque medieval towns. Rural and rustic, yet within easy reach of the capital, it has for centuries provided an escape for generations of city dwellers, from the aristocrats and kings who built their country retreats here, to the modern-day Praguers who head out on weekends to hike, bike and canoe on its network of trails and rivers.

This region is rich in castles and chateaux. Popular castles include Karlštejn Castle (below), a fairy-tale fortress built to house Charles IV's royal treasury; Konopiště Chateau (p237), the country retreat of the ill-fated Archduke Franz Ferdinand, whose assassination kicked off WWI; and the Lobkowicz family's chateau at Mělník Chateau (p238), with its tiny but historic vineyard overlooking the confluence of the Labe and Vltava Rivers.

There are also many interesting medieval towns, offering an escape from the crowds that churn through the capital's narrow streets. Litoměřice (p241) has a charming town square lined with lovely Gothic and Renaissance houses, while the tiny old town of Mělník (p238) has peaceful backstreets and a stunning view over the Bohemian countryside. The former silver-mining town of Kutná Hora (p242) boasts a lovely cathedral, a collection of exquisite baroque statues and a picturesque hilltop setting. But the winner of the picture-postcard competition has to be the beautiful South Bohemian town of Český Krumlov (p245).

The region to the north of Prague contains two deeply moving monuments to the suffering of the Czech people in WWII – the village of Lidice (p239), destroyed by the Nazis as an act of vengeance for the assassination of Reichsprotektor Reinhard Heydrich, and Terezín (p239), a former concentration camp through which 150,000 Czech Jews passed on their way to the gas chambers.

There are several sights around Prague that are decidedly out of the ordinary. The Trophy Corridor (p237) and Chamois Room (p237) in Konopiště Chateau, crammed with the antlers, skulls and stuffed heads of thousands of animals, stand as bizarre witness to the hunting obsession of Archduke Franz Ferdinand, while Kutná Hora's Czech Silver Museum (p244) offers the chance to don a miner's helmet and lamp and explore the claustrophobic tunnels of a medieval silver mine beneath the town. Most extraordinary of all is the Sedlec Ossuary (p243) at Kutná Hora, where the bones of 40,000 people have been fashioned into a series of weird and wonderful decorations.

Most destinations covered in this chapter can be easily reached on day trips from Prague. The downside of such convenience is the crowds that throng to these places on summer weekends, but you can avoid them by visiting out of season – Karlštejn under snow is a magical sight – or on weekdays, or better still by staying overnight. As the tour coaches and caravans roll out at nightfall, many of the towns and villages belong once again to the locals.

KARLŠTEJN

Karlštejn Castle (☎ 311 681 617; www.hradkarlstejn.cz; Karlštejn; ⏰ 9am-6pm Tue-Sun Jul & Aug, 9am-5pm Tue-Sun May, Jun & Sep, 9am-4pm Tue-Sun Apr & Oct; see website for limited opening times Nov-Mar), rising above the village of Karlštejn, 30km southwest of Prague, is in such good shape these days that it wouldn't look out of place on Disneyworld's Main St. The crowds come in theme-park proportions as well (it's best to book ahead for the guided tours), but the peaceful surrounding countryside offers views of Karlštejn's stunning exterior that rival anything you'll see on the inside.

Perched high on a crag overlooking the Berounka River, this cluster of turrets, high walls and looming towers is as well maintained as it is powerfully evocative. It's rightly one of the top attractions of the Czech Republic, and the only drawback is its overwhelming popularity: in summer it's literally mobbed with visitors, ice-cream vendors and souvenir stalls.

TRANSPORT: KARLŠTEJN

Distance from Prague 30km

Direction Southwest

Travel time One hour

Train Trains to Beroun from Praha-Smíchov stop at Karlštejn (49Kč, 45 minutes, hourly).

Karlštejn was born of a grand pedigree, starting life in 1348 as a hideaway for the crown jewels and treasury of the Holy Roman Emperor, Charles IV. Run by an appointed burgrave, the castle was surrounded by a network of landowning knight-vassals, who came to the castle's aid whenever enemies moved against it.

Karlštejn again sheltered the Bohemian and the Holy Roman Empire crown jewels during the Hussite Wars of the early 15th century, but fell into disrepair as its defences became outmoded. Considerable restoration work, not least by Josef Mocker in the late 19th century, has returned the castle to its former glory.

There are two tours through the castle. Tour I (adult/concession 250/150Kč, 50 minutes) passes through the Knight's Hall, still daubed with the coats-of-arms and names of the knight-vassals, Charles IV's Bedchamber, the Audience Hall and the Jewel House, which includes treasures from the Chapel of the Holy Cross and a replica of the St Wenceslas Crown.

Tour II (adult/concession 300/200Kč, 70 minutes, June to October only) must be booked in advance and takes in the Great Tower, the highest point of the castle, which includes a museum on Mocker's restoration work, the Marian Tower and the exquisite Chapel of the Holy Cross, with its decorative ceiling.

EATING & SLEEPING

Pension & Restaurant U Janů (☎ 311 681 210; info@ujanu .cz; d/apt 1000/1200Kč, mains 90-180Kč) On the road up to the castle, this atmospheric place has a decent dollop of authentic charm; there are three apartments and one double room.

Penzión U královny Dagmar (☎ 311 681 614; www .penzion-dagmara.cz; d/tr/apt 1000/1200/1500Kč) Closer to the castle and with similar prices, this slick place has all the creature comforts and a top-notch eatery.

KŘIVOKLÁT

Křivoklát is a sleepy village beside the Rakovnický potok River. The main attraction is Křivoklát Castle, but half the pleasure of visiting lies simply in getting there by train up the scenic Berounka Valley.

Once a celebrated hunting lodge, Křivoklát Castle (☎ 313 558 120; www.krivoklat.cz; 9am-6pm Tue-Sun Jul & Aug, 9am-5pm Tue-Sun May-Jun & Sep, 10am-4pm Tue-Sun Apr & Oct, 10am-3pm Sat & Sun Nov-Mar) has

TRANSPORT: KŘIVOKLÁT

Distance from Prague 44km

Direction Southwest

Travel time 1½ hours

Train There are very frequent trains to Beroun from Prague's main train station and Smíchov stations (30 minutes, 49Kč). From Beroun, there are nine trains daily to Křivoklát (43Kč, 50 minutes).

survived several fires and endless renovations as a prettified chateau reflecting the whimsy of 19th-century Romanticism.

Tour I (adult/concession 100/70Kč, with English-language guide 150/105Kč) visits the castle's interiors, including the beautiful chapel with its unaltered late-Gothic decor full of intricate polychrome carvings and an altar decorated with angels carrying instruments of torture – a legacy of the castle's 16th-century role as a political prison. The Knights' Hall features a permanent collection of late-Gothic religious sculpture and painted panels, while the 25m-long King's Hall is the second-biggest Gothic hall in the country, after Vladislav Hall in Prague Castle. There is also a library of 52,000 volumes.

Tour II (adult/concession 80/60Kč, with English-speaking guide 120/85Kč; from April to October) takes in the castle's fortifications, including a strenuous climb to the top of the impressive donjon, the massive round tower that dominates the complex.

The town of Beroun, where you have to change trains on the way to Křivoklát, is worth a stop for a stroll around its expansive town square, and a climb to the top of the Plzeň Gate Tower (adult/concession 20/10Kč; 9am-noon Wed & Sat May-Oct).

The wooded hill to the west of Beroun's old town is home to the Medvědarium (admission free; dawn-dusk), an enclosure inhabited by three brown bears (the symbol of the town's icehockey team and of its brewery). A children's playground remains out of reach of the three bears in their secure enclosure.

EATING & SLEEPING

Pivovar Berounský medvěd (☎ 311 622 566; Tyršova 135, Beroun; www.berounskymedved.com; mains 50-80Kč) It doesn't get more local than this microbrewery and restaurant hidden away amid an engineering yard filled with rusting machinery.

Both the beer (just 20Kč for 0.5L) and the food are very good, and the interior is actually very cosy. Turn left out of Beroun train station, then bear left under the bridge – it's ahead on the right.

Penzion Berona (☎ 311 626 184; www.berona.cz; Havlíčkova 116, Beroun; s/d from 700/1100Kč; 🛜) Spacious and comfortable rooms, satellite TV, and a choice of chef-cooked breakfasts. We can thoroughly recommend the 'Lance Armstrong' breakfast, even if you're not about to ride off on two wheels.

Pension restaurace U Jelena (☎ 313 558 529; www.ujelena.eu; Hradní 53, Křivoklát; d/tr/q 1000/1500/2000Kč; 🛜) Located down the hill from the castle, 'The Stag' is a modern pension with rustic, hunting-lodge decor and a good terrace restaurant with castle and river views.

KONOPIŠTĚ

Archduke Franz Ferdinand d'Este, heir to the Austro-Hungarian throne, is famous for being dead – it was his assassination in 1914 that sparked WWI. But the archduke was an enigmatic figure who avoided the intrigues of the Vienna court and for the last 20 years of his life hid away in what became his ideal country retreat, Konopiště Chateau (☎ 317 721 366; www.zamek-konopiste.cz; Benešov; 🕑 9am-5pm Tue-Sun May-Aug, 9am-4pm Tue-Fri, to 5pm Sat & Sun Sep, 9am-3pm Tue-Fri, to 4pm Sat & Sun Apr & Oct, 9am-3pm Sat & Sun Nov, closed Dec-Mar & noon-1pm year-round).

Konopiště, lying amid extensive grounds 2km west of the town of Benešov, is a testament to the archduke's twin obsessions – hunting and St George. Having renovated the massive Gothic and Renaissance building in the 1890s and installed all the latest technology – including electricity, central heating,

flush toilets, showers and a luxurious lift – Franz Ferdinand decorated his home with his hunting trophies. His game books record that he shot about 300,000 creatures in his lifetime, from foxes and deer to elephants and tigers. About 100,000 animal trophies adorn the walls, each marked with the date and place it met its end – the crowded Trophy Corridor (Tour I and III), with a forest of mounted animal heads, and the antler-clad Chamois Room (Tour III), with its 'chandelier' fashioned from a stuffed condor, are truly bizarre sights.

There are three guided tours available. Tour III is the most interesting, visiting the private apartments used by the archduke and his family, which have remained unchanged since the state took possession of the chateau in 1921. Tour II takes in the Great Armoury, one of the largest and most impressive collections in Europe. Tour I and Tour II in English are adult/child 200/130Kč; Tour III in English is 300/200Kč.

The archduke's collection of art and artefacts relating to St George is no less impressive, amounting to 3750 items, many of which are on show in the St George Museum (Muzeum sv Jiří; adult/child 30/15Kč; 🕑 9am-5pm Tue-Sun May-Aug, 9am-4pm Tue-Fri, to 5pm Sat & Sun Sep, 9am-3pm Tue-Fri, to 4pm Sat & Sun Apr & Oct, 9am-3pm Sat & Sun Nov, closed Dec-Mar & noon-1pm year-round) beneath the terrace at the front of the castle.

EATING & SLEEPING

Stará Myslivna (☎ 728 818 567; mains 110-250Kč) After viewing the castle, come back down the hill to this good Czech restaurant in a character-filled 19th-century building. Lots of period photos set the scene.

TRANSPORT: KONOPIŠTĚ

Distance from Prague 50km

Direction South

Travel time 1¼ hours

Bus There are buses from Prague's Roztyly metro station to Benešov (39Kč, 40 minutes, twice hourly) – their final destination is usually Pelhřimov or Jihlava. There are also buses to Benešov from Prague's Florenc bus station (48Kč, 40 minutes, eight daily).

Train There are frequent direct trains from Prague's Hlavní nádraží to Benešov u Prahy (68Kč, 1¼ hours, hourly). Konopiště is 2km west of Benešov. Local bus 2 (10Kč, six minutes, hourly) runs from a stop on Dukelská, 400m north of the train station (turn left out of the station, take first right on Tyršova and then first left) to the castle car park. If you'd rather walk, turn left out of the train station, go left across the bridge over the railway, and follow Konopišťská street west for 2km.

Hotel Atlas (☎ 317 724 771; www.hotel-atlas.cz; Tyršova 2063, Benešov; s/tw from 810/920Kč) This place is bland and functional, but the rooms are spotless and comfortable. Benešov is located just 2km east of the Konopiště Chateau.

Hotel Nová Myslivna (☎ 317 722 496; www.e-stranka .cz/novamyslivna; Konopiště; r per person from 375Kč; (P)) The sweeping angular roof of this chalet-style hotel clashes somewhat with the softer lines of the castle, but the hotel's location by the Konopiště Chateau car park is unbeatable.

MĚLNÍK

Mělník, an hour's drive north of Prague, sprawls over a rocky promontory surrounded by the flat sweep of the Central Bohemian plain. Staunchly Hussite in its sympathies, the town was flattened by Swedish troops in the Thirty Years' War (1618–48), but the castle was rebuilt as a prettier, less threatening chateau and the centre retains a strong historical identity. Modernity has caught up with the town's trailing edge, bringing a clutch of factories to its outskirts, but views from the castle side are untouched and Mělník remains a good place for a spot of wine-tasting – the town is the focus of Bohemia's modest wine-growing region.

The Renaissance Mělník Chateau (Zámek Mělník; ☎ 315 622 121; www.lobkowicz-melnik.cz; adult/concession 80/60Kč; ☽ 10am-5pm) was acquired by the Lobkowicz family in 1739; the family opened it to the public in 1990. You can wander through the former living quarters, which are crowded with a rich collection of baroque furniture and 17th- and 18th-century paintings, on a self-guided tour with English text. Additional rooms have changing exhibits of modern works and a fabulous collection of 17th-century maps and engravings detailing Europe's great cities. A separate tour descends to the 14th-century wine cellars,

where you can taste the chateau's wines; a shop in the courtyard sells the chateau's own label. Wine-tasting sessions cost from 90Kč to 220Kč.

Next to the chateau is the 15th-century Gothic Church of Sts Peter & Paul (kostel sv Petra a Pavla), with its baroque furnishings and tower. Some remnants of its Romanesque predecessor have been incorporated into the rear of the building. The old crypt is now an ossuary (kostnice; adult/child 30/15Kč; ☽ 9.30am-12.30pm & 1.15-4pm Tue-Fri, 10am-12.30pm & 1.15-4pm Sat & Sun), packed with the bones of around 10,000 people dug up to make room for 16th-century plague victims, arranged in macabre patterns. This crypt is much more visceral – and claustrophobic – than the ossuary at Sedlec (see p243); the floor is of beaten earth and you are literally rubbing shoulders with the stacked bones.

The path between chateau and church leads to a terrace with superb views across the river and the Central Bohemian countryside. The steep slopes beneath the terrace are planted with vines – supposedly descendants of the first vines to be introduced to Bohemia, by Charles IV, back in the 14th century.

INFORMATION

Tourist information office (☎ 315 627 503; www.mel nik.cz; náměstí Míru 11; ☽ 9am-5pm daily May-Sep, Mon-Fri only Oct-Apr) Sells maps and historical guides and can help with accommodation.

EATING & DRINKING

Restaurace sv Václav (☎ 315 622 126; Svatováclavská 22; mains 120-180Kč; ☽ 11am-11pm) Dark wood decor, cigar humidors, red-leather seats and an outdoor terrace that's a lunchtime suntrap conspire to make this one of Mělník's most appealing restaurants.

Kavárna ve Věží (☎ 315 621 954; ulice 5.května; mains 30-70Kč; ☽ 7am-10pm Mon-Fri, 2-10pm Sat & Sun) Set in the medieval tower of the Prague Gate (one of the gates of the old town), this atmospheric cafe and art gallery spreads across three floors linked by creaking wooden stairs, and served by an ingenious dumb waiter: write your order on the note pad, ding the bell, and the tray goes down, returning a few moments later with your order. Choose from a wide range of freshly ground coffees and exotic teas, local wines, beer and *medovina* (mead).

TRANSPORT: MĚLNÍK

Distance from Prague 30km

Direction North

Travel time One hour

Bus On weekdays, buses run to Mělník (46Kč, 45 minutes, every 30 minutes) from stop 10 in the bus station outside Praha–Holešovice train station; buy your ticket from the driver (one-way only, no return tickets).

SLEEPING

Hotel U Rytířů (☎ 315 621 440; www.urytiru.cz; Svatová-clavská 17; d 2100-2700Kč) Located conveniently right next to the castle, this opulent little place has plush, apartment-style rooms with all the trimmings, and a garden restaurant (mains 110Kč to 250Kč; open 8am to 11pm).

Pension Hana (☎ 315 622 485; Fugnerova 714; s 450-600Kč, d 900-1200Kč; 🤶) Run by a friendly family with children who speak excellent English, Pension Hana has 10 spacious rooms, some with a sunny outlook onto a private garden. The old town is a steep 10-minute walk away.

LIDICE, TEREZÍN & LITOMĚŘICE

The Bohemian countryside to the north of Prague contains two villages that provide a sobering reminder of the horrors inflicted on the Czech people during WWII. If you're driving, Lidice and Terezín can be combined in one day; if you want to spend the night, head for the attractive town of Litoměřice, 3km north of Terezín. Using public transport, you'll have to choose; it's only practical to do one or the other in a single day.

LIDICE

When British-trained Czechoslovak para-troops assassinated Reichsprotektor Reinhard Heydrich in June 1942 (see the boxed text, p118), the Nazis took a savage revenge. Picking the mining and foundry village of Lidice, 18km northwest of Prague, apparently at random, they proceeded on 10 June 1942 to obliterate it from the face of the earth. All its men were shot, the women and the older children were shipped to the Ravensbrück concentration camp, and the younger children were farmed out to German foster homes. The village was then systematically burned and bulldozed so that no trace remained. Of its 500 inhabitants, 192 men, 60 women and 88 children eventually died. The atrocity caused shock around the world and triggered a campaign to preserve the village's memory. The site is now a green field, eloquent in its silence, dotted with a few memorials and the reconstructed foundations of a farm where most of the men were murdered.

The on-site **Muzeum Lidice** (www.lidice-memorial .cz; Lidice; adult/concession 80/40Kč; 🕙 9am-6pm Apr-Oct, to 5pm Mar, to 4pm Nov-Feb) re-creates the village in

TRANSPORT: LIDICE

Distance from Prague 18km
Direction Northwest
Travel time 30 minutes
Bus Buses from Prague to Lidice (26Kč, 30 minutes, hourly) depart from the bus stop on Evropská, opposite the Hotel Diplomat, just west of Dejvická metro station (Map p136).

photographs, text and an emotive multimedia exhibition, and also screens chilling SS film footage of its destruction. A new installation opposite the museum shows documentary films in Czech, German and English.

TEREZÍN

A massive bulwark of stone and earth, the fortress of Terezín (Theresienstadt in German) was built in 1780 by Emperor Joseph II with a single purpose in mind: to keep the enemy out. Ironically, it is more notorious for keeping people in – it served as a political prison in the later days of the Habsburg empire. Gavrilo Princip, the assassin who killed Archduke Franz Ferdinand in 1914, was incarcerated here during WWI, and when the Germans took control during WWII the fortress became a grim holding pen for Jews bound for the extermination camps. In contrast to the colourful, baroque face of many Czech towns, Terezín is a stark but profoundly evocative monument to a darker aspect of Europe's past.

The bleakest phase of Terezín's history began in 1940 when the Gestapo established a prison in the Lesser Fortress. Evicting the inhabitants from the Main Fortress the following year, the Nazis transformed the town into a transit camp through which some 150,000 people eventually passed en route to the death camps. For most, conditions were appalling. Between April and September 1942 the ghetto's population increased from 12,968 to 58,491, leaving each prisoner with only 1.65 sq m of space and causing disease and starvation on a terrifying scale. In the same period, there was a 15-fold increase in the number of deaths within the prison walls.

Terezín later became the centrepiece of one of the Nazis' more extraordinary coups of public relations. Official visitors to the fortress, including representatives of the Red Cross, saw a town that was billed as a kind of Jewish 'refuge', with a Jewish administration,

EXCURSIONS LIDICE, TEREZÍN & LITOMĚŘICE

EXCURSIONS TEREZÍN

TEREZÍN

SIGHTS & ACTIVITIES	
Church of the Resurrection.........1	C2
Crematorium..........................2	C4
Former Commandant's Office.....3	C2
Ghetto Museum......................4	B2
Lesser Fortress......................5	E1
Magdeburg Barracks.................6	C3
Main Fortress........................7	B1
National Cemetery...................8	E2
Remains of Railway Siding..........9	B3

EATING 🍴	
Memorial Café & Restaurant......10	B2

TRANSPORT	
Bus Stop............................11	C2

0   500 m
0   0.3 miles

To Prague
(60km)

To Litoměřice
(3km)

Tour Bus
Parking Area

Ohře

Jewish
Cemetery

Revoluční
Pražská
Husova
Fučíkova
5. května
Vodárenská
Tyrsova
Legií
Prokopa
Holého
Palackého
Komenského
Zižkova
Máchová
Dlouhá
Školní
R. Němcové
Havlíčkova
Československé armády
28. října
Dlouhá
Bohušovická brána
náměstí
Československé armády
Post Office
Stadium

banks, shops, cafes, schools and a thriving cultural life – it even had a jazz band – in a charade that twice completely fooled international observers. In reality Terezín was home to a relentlessly increasing population of prisoners, regular trains departing for the gas chambers of Auschwitz, and the death by starvation, disease or suicide of some 35,000 people.

From the ground, the sheer scale of the maze of walls and moats that surrounds the Main Fortress (Hlavní pevnost) is impossible to fathom – mainly because the town is actually inside it. In fact, when you first arrive by bus or car you may be left thinking that the central square looks no different from a hundred other old town centres. Take a peek at the aerial photograph in the Ghetto Museum, or wander past the walls en route to the Lesser Fortress, however, and a very different picture emerges. At the heart of the Main Fortress is the neat grid of streets that makes up the town of Terezín. There's little to look at except the chunky, 19th-century Church of the Resurrection, the arcaded former Commandant's office, the neoclassical administrative buildings on the square and the surrounding grid of houses with their awful secrets. South of the square are the anonymous remains of a railway siding, built by prisoners, via which loads of further prisoners arrived – and departed.

The main sight here is the absorbing Ghetto Museum (Muzeum ghetta; ☎ 416 782 576; www.pamatnik -terezin.cz; Komenského, Terezín; adult/child 160/130Kč; ◷ 9am-6pm Apr-Oct, to 5.30pm Nov-Mar), which has two branches. The main branch explores the rise of Nazism and life in the Terezín ghetto, using period bric-a-brac to startling and evocative effect. Erected in the 19th century to house the local school, the museum building was later used by the Nazis to accommodate the camp's 10- to 15-year-old boys. The haunting images painted by these children still decorate the walls. A newer branch is housed in the former Magdeburg Barracks (Magdeburská kasárna), which served as the seat of the Jewish 'town council'. Here you can visit a reconstructed dormitory, and look at exhibits on the extraordinarily rich cultural life – music, theatre, fine arts and literature – that somehow flourished against this backdrop of fear. There is also a small exhibit in the grim Crematorium (Krematorium; ◷ 10am-6pm Sun-Fri Apr-Oct, to 4pm Sun-Fri Nov-Mar) in the Jewish Cemetery just off Bohušovická brána, about

750m south of the main square. The Ghetto Museum has good multilingual self-guide pamphlets, a large selection of books for sale, and guides (some of them ghetto survivors) to offer assistance.

You can take a self-guided tour of the Lesser Fortress (Malá pevnost; ☎ 416 782 576; www.pamatnik -terezin.cz; Terezín; adult/child 160/130Kč; ◷ 8am-6pm Apr-Oct, to 4.30pm Nov-Mar) through the prison barracks, isolation cells, workshops and morgues, past execution grounds and former mass graves. It would be hard to invent a more menacing location, and it is only while wandering through the seemingly endless tunnels beneath the walls that you begin to fully appreciate the vast dimensions of the fortress. The Nazis' mocking concentration camp slogan, *Arbeit Macht Frei* ('Work Makes You Free'), hangs above the gate. In front of the fortress is a National Cemetery, established in 1945 for those exhumed from the Nazis' mass graves. A combined ticket for both the Ghetto Museum and Lesser Fortress is 200/150Kč.

LITOMĚŘICE

After gritting your teeth through the horrors of Terezín, Litoměřice is your chance to exhale. Although only a few kilometres to the north of the infamous fortress, this quaint riverside town is a million miles away in atmosphere. Pastel-hued facades and intricate gables jostle for dominance on the main square, and the town's lively bars and restaurants play host to some vibrant after-hours action. Once stridently Hussite, much of the Gothic face of Litoměřice was levelled during the Thirty Years' War, and today the town's unassuming castle plays second fiddle to a clutch of effete Renaissance houses and impressive churches (many by esteemed 18th-century architect Ottavio Broggio).

Dominating Mírové náměstí, the town's attractive main square, is the Gothic tower of All Saints Church (kostel Všech svatých), built in the 13th century and 'Broggio-ised' in 1718. Beside it, with multiple gables, pointy arches and a copper-topped tower, is the handsome, Gothic Old Town Hall (Stará radnice), which includes a small town museum. Most striking is the 1560 Renaissance House at the Black Eagle (dům U černého orla), covered in *sgraffito* biblical scenes and housing the Hotel Salva Guarda. A few doors down is the present town hall, in the 1539 House at the Chalice (dům U kalicha), featuring a massive Hussite chalice on the roof. This building also houses the tourist information office. The thin slice of baroque wedding cake at the uphill end of the square is the House of Ottavio Broggio.

Along Michalská at the southwest corner of the square you'll find another house where Broggio left his mark, the excellent North Bohemia Fine Arts Gallery (Severo česká galerie výtvarného umění; ☎ 416 732 382; Michalská 7, Litoměřice; adult/concession 32/16Kč; ☼ 9am-noon & 1-6pm Tue-Sun Apr-Sep, 9am-noon & 1-5pm Tue-Sun Oct-Mar) with the priceless Renaissance panels of the Litoměřice Altarpiece.

Turn left at the end of Michalská and follow Domská towards grassy, tree-lined Domské náměstí on Cathedral Hill, passing pretty St Wenceslas Church (kostel sv Václav), a true baroque gem, along a side street to the right. At the top of the hill is the town's oldest church, St Stephen Cathedral (Chrám sv Štěpán), dating from the 11th century.

Go through the arch to the left of the cathedral and descend a steep, cobbled lane called Máchova. At the foot of the hill turn left then take the first right, up the zigzag steps to the old town walls. You can follow the walls to the right as far as the next street, Jezuitská, where a left turn leads back to the square.

INFORMATION

Tourist information office (☎ 416 732 440; www .litomerice-info.cz; Mírové náměstí 15, Litoměřice; ☼ 9am-6pm May-Sep, 9am-5pm Mon-Thu, 9am-4pm Fri 10am-1pm Sat Oct-Apr)

EATING

Bašta Steakhouse (☎ 608 437 783; Mezibraní 5, Litoměřice; mains 100-450Kč; ☼ 11am-midnight) Housed in a former bastion in the old city walls opposite the train station, this lively restaurant boasts a charcoal grill that turns out everything from buffalo wings to thick T-bone steaks.

Memorial Café & Restaurant (☎ 416 783 082; nám Československé armády, Terezín; meals 130-270Kč) Part of the refurbished Hotel Memorial, it serves hearty Czech meals, pasta and kosher wines on a sunny main square terrace.

SLEEPING

Hotel Salva Guarda (☎ 416 732 506; www.salva-guarda .cz; Mírové náměstí 12, Litoměřice; s/d from 1220/1800Kč; ℗) Litoměřice's top hotel is set in the lovely Renaissance House at the Black Eagle; it also has the best restaurant on the square.

Pension Prislin (☎ 416 735 833; www.prislin.cz; Na Kocandě 12, Litoměřice; s/d 750/1260Kč; ℗) A view across the river and breakfast in the garden are good reasons for choosing the family-friendly Prislin. It's five minutes' walk east of the town square, along the main road.

U svatého Václava (☎ 416 737 500; www.upfront.cz/ penzion; Svatováclavská 12, Litoměřice; s/d 800/1200Kč) Tucked away in the shadow of St Wenceslas Church, this pretty villa houses a tip-top pension with sauna, well-equipped rooms and a homely apron-toting owner who whips up a fine breakfast.

KUTNÁ HORA

Now dwarfed by 21st-century Prague, Kutná Hora once marched in step with the capital and, with a little help from fate, might even have stolen its crown as the heart and soul of Bohemia. Enriched by the silver ore that ran in veins through the surrounding hills, the medieval city once enjoyed explosive growth, becoming the seat of Wenceslas II's royal mint in 1308 and the residence of Wenceslas IV just under 100 years later. The silver *groschen* that were minted here at that time represented the hard currency of Central Europe. But while boom-time Kutná Hora was Prague's undisputed understudy, the town tripped out of history when the silver mines began to splutter and run dry in the 16th century, its demise hastened by the Thirty Years' War and finally certified by a devastating fire in 1770. While the capital continued to expand, its sister city largely vanished from sight.

But that's not to say everyone has forgotten about it. Kutná Hora today is an A-list tourist attraction – it was added to Unesco's

World Heritage list in 1996 – luring visitors with a smorgasbord of historic sights and more than a touch of nostalgic whimsy. Standing on the ramparts surrounding the mighty Cathedral of St Barbara, looking out across rooftops eerily reminiscent of Prague's Malá Strana, it's all too easy to indulge in a spot of melancholic what-might-have-been.

If you arrive by train, a natural first stop is the remarkable 'bone church' of the Sedlec Ossuary (kostnice; ☎ 327 561 143; www.kostnice.cz; Zámecká 127; adult/concession 50/30Kč; ☼ 8am-6pm Apr-Sep, 9am-noon & 1-5pm Mar & Oct, 9am-noon & 1-4pm Nov-Feb), an 800m walk south from Kutná Hora's main train station. When the Schwarzenberg family purchased Sedlec monastery in 1870 they allowed a local woodcarver to get creative with the bones that had been piled in the

crypt for centuries. But this was no piddling little heap of bones: it was the remains of no fewer than 40,000 people. The result was spectacular – garlands of skulls and femurs are strung from the vaulted ceiling like *Addams Family* Christmas decorations, while in the centre dangles a vast chandelier containing at least one of each bone in the human body. Four giant pyramids of stacked bones squat in each of the corner chapels, and crosses, chalices and monstrances of bone adorn the altar. There's even a Schwarzenberg coat-of-arms made from bones – note the crow pecking the eyes from the Turk's head, a grisly motif of the Schwarzenberg family.

From Sedlec it is a 1.5m walk (or a five-minute bus ride) into central Kutná Hora. Palackého náměstí, the main square, is not

KUTNÁ HORA

INFORMATION
Tourist Information Office............1 C2

SIGHTS & ACTIVITIES
Alchemy Museum.....................(see 1)
Cathedral of St Barbara (chrám sv Barbora)................................2 A4
Czech Silver Museum...............(see 3)
Hrádek.......................................3 B3

Italian Court (Vlašský dvůr)........4 C3
Jesuit College............................5 A4
St James Church (Kostel sv Jakuba)................................6 B3

SLEEPING
Hotel U Hrnčíre........................7 B3
Hotel Zlatá Stoupa....................8 D3
Penzión Centrum......................9 B3
Penzión U Kata 10 D2

EATING
Pivnice Dačický........................11 B3
Sole Mio..................................12 B2
U Šneka Pohodáře...................13 C2

DRINKING
Kavárna Mokate.......................14 B3

TRANSPORT
Bus Station..............................15 D1

remarkable; the most interesting part of the old town lies to its south. But first, take a look at the Alchemy Museum (☎ 327 511 259; Palackého náměstí 377; adult/concession 50/30Kč ☺ 10am-5pm Apr-Oct, to 4pm Nov-Mar), in the same building as the tourist information office, complete with basement laboratory, Gothic chapel and mad-scientist curator.

From the upper end of the square a narrow lane called Jakubská leads directly to the huge St James Church (kostel sv Jakuba; 1330). Just east of the church lies the Italian Court (Vlašský dvůr; ☎ 327 512 873; Havlíčkovo náměstí 552; adult/concession 100/60Kč; ☺ 9am-6pm Apr-Sep, 10am-5pm Mar & Oct, 10am-4pm Nov-Feb), the former Royal Mint – it got its name from the master craftsmen from Florence brought in by Wenceslas II to kick-start the business, and who began stamping silver coins here in 1300. The oldest remaining part, the niches in the courtyard (now bricked up), were minters' workshops. The original treasury rooms hold an exhibit on coins and minting. The guided tour (with English text) is worth taking for a look at the few historical rooms open to the public, notably a 15th-century Audience Hall with two impressive 19th-century murals depicting the election of Vladislav Jagiello as king of Bohemia in 1471 (the angry man in white is Matthias Corvinus, the loser), and the Decree of Kutná Hora being proclaimed by Wenceslas IV and Jan Hus in 1409.

From the southern side of St James Church, a narrow cobbled lane (Ruthardská) leads down and then up to the Hrádek (Little Castle). Originally part of the town's fortifications, it was rebuilt in the 15th century as the residence of Jan Smíšek, administrator of the royal mines, who grew rich from silver he illegally mined right under the building. It now houses the Czech Silver Museum (České muzeum

stříbra; ☎ 327 512 159; adult/concession 60/30Kč; ☺ 10am-6pm Jul & Aug, 9am-6pm May, Jun & Sep, 9am-5pm Apr & Oct, closed Nov-Mar & Mon year-round). The exhibits celebrate the mines that made Kutná Hora wealthy, including a huge wooden device once used to lift loads weighing as much as 1000kg from the 200m-deep shafts. You can even don a miner's helmet and lamp and join a 45-minute guided tour (adult/child 110/70Kč) through 500m of medieval mine shafts beneath the town.

Just beyond the Hrádek is the 17th-century former Jesuit College, fronted by a terrace with a row of 13 baroque statues of saints, an arrangement inspired by the statues on Prague's Charles Bridge. All are related to the Jesuits and/or the town; the second statue – the woman holding a chalice, with a stone tower at her side – is St Barbara, the patron saint of miners and therefore of Kutná Hora.

At the far end of the terrace is Kutná Hora's greatest monument, the Gothic Cathedral of St Barbara (Chrám sv Barbora; ☎ 776 393 938; adult/concession 50/30Kč; ☺ 9am-5.30pm Tue-Sun May-Sep, 10am-4pm Tue-Sun Oct-Apr). Rivalling Prague's St Vitus Cathedral in size and magnificence, its soaring nave culminates in elegant, six-petalled ribbed vaulting. Work was started in 1380, interrupted during the Hussite Wars and abandoned in 1558 when the silver began to run out. It was finally completed in neo-Gothic style at the end of the 19th century. The ambulatory chapels preserve some original 15th-century frescoes, some of them showing miners at work. Take a walk around the outside of the church, too; the terrace at the east end enjoys the finest view in town.

INFORMATION

Tourist information office (☎ 327 512 378; www.kh.cz; Palackého náměstí 377; ☺ 9am-6pm Apr-Oct, 9am-5pm Mon-Fri, 10am-4pm Sat & Sun Nov-Mar) Books accommodation, rents bicycles (220Kč per day) and offers internet access (per 1Kč minute, minimum 15Kč).

EATING & DRINKING

U Šneka Pohodáře (☎ 327 515 987; Vladislavova 11; pizzas 90-130Kč) Kutná Hora's best Italian flavours are found at this cosy local favourite that's very popular for takeaway or dine-in pizza and pasta. And no, we don't know why it's called 'The Contented Snail'.

Sole Mio (☎ 327 515 505; Česká 184; mains 90-120Kč; ☺ 11am-10pm Sun-Thu, to 11pm Fri & Sat) Choose from

TRANSPORT: KUTNÁ HORA

Distance from Prague 65km

Direction East

Travel time 1½ hours

Bus There are about six direct buses a day, on weekdays only, from stop 2 at Prague's Florenc bus station to Kutná Hora (68Kc, 1¼ hours).

Train There are direct trains from Prague's main train station to Kutná Hora Hlavní Nádraží (180Kč return, 55 minutes, seven daily).

40 varieties of pizza at this homely little restaurant decorated with – surprise, surprise, considering the name – lots of suns.

Pivnice Dačický (☎ 327 512 248; Rakova 8; mains 110-250Kč; ⏰ 11am-11pm) Get some froth on your moustache at this old-fashioned, wood-panelled Bohemian beer hall, where you can dine on dumplings and choose from five different draught beers, including Pilsner Urquell, Budvar and Primátor yeast beer.

Kavárna Mokate (Barborská 37; ⏰ 8am-10pm Mon-Fri, 10am-10pm Sat, 10am-8pm Sun) This cosy little cafe, with ancient earthenware floor tiles, timber beams, mismatched furniture and oriental rugs, dishes up a wide range of freshly ground coffees and exotic teas, as well as iced tea and coffee in summer.

SLEEPING

Penzión U Kata (☎ 327 515 096; www.ukata.cz; Uhelná 596; s/d/tr 500/760/1140Kč; 🛜) You won't lose your head over the rates at this good-value family hotel called 'The Executioner'. Bikes can be rented for 200Kč per hour, and it's a short stroll from the bus station. Downstairs is a welcoming Czech beer hall and restaurant.

Hotel Zlatá Stoupa (☎ 327 511 540; zlatastoupa@iol.cz; Tylova 426; s/d from 1220/1980Kč; Ⓟ) If you feel like spoiling yourself, the most luxurious place in town is the elegantly furnished 'Golden Mount'. We like a hotel room where the minibar contains full-sized bottles of wine.

Penzión Centrum (☎ 327 514 218; www.sweb.cz/penzion _centrum; Jakubská 57; d/tr 1000/1400Kč; Ⓟ) Tucked away in a quiet, flower-bedecked courtyard off Kutná Hora's main drag, this place offers snug rooms and a sunny garden.

Hotel U Hrnčíře (☎ 327 512 113; www.hoteluhrncire .cz; Barborská 24; s/d/tr 800/1300/1500Kč) This beautifully ornate pink town house has five stylish double rooms (rates depend on season and facilities) and a delightful garden terrace out back.

ČESKÝ KRUMLOV

Český Krumlov, in Bohemia's deep south, is one of the most picturesque towns in Europe; its appearance has remained almost unchanged since the 18th century, and in 1992 it was added to Unesco's World Heritage list. It's a little like Prague in miniature – it has a stunning castle above the Vltava River, an old town square, Renaissance and baroque

TRANSPORT: ČESKÝ KRUMLOV

Distance from Prague 180km

Direction South

Travel time Three hours

Bus Student Agency (www.studentagency.cz) runs seven or eight luxury coaches a day from Prague's Na Knížecí bus station (near Anděl metro station) to Český Krumlov (320Kc return, three hours).

architecture, and hordes of tourists milling through the streets, but all on a smaller scale; you can walk from one side of town to the other in 10 minutes. There are plenty of lively bars and riverside picnic spots – in summer it's a popular hang-out for backpackers. It can be a magical place in winter, though, when the crowds are gone and the castle is blanketed in snow.

The old town, almost encircled by the Vltava River, is watched over by Český Krumlov Castle (☎ 380 704 721; www.castle.ckrumlov.cz; ⏰ 9am-6pm Tue-Sun Jun-Aug, 9am-5pm Apr, May, Sep & Oct), and its ornately decorated Round Tower (adult/concession 50/30Kč). Three different guided tours are on offer: Tour I (adult/concession 240/140Kč in English; one hour) takes in the opulent Renaissance rooms, including the chapel, baroque suite, picture gallery and masquerade hall, while Tour II (180/100Kč; one hour) visits the Schwarzenberg portrait galleries and their apartments used in the 19th century; and the Theatre Tour (adult/concession 380/220Kč; 40 minutes, 10am to 4pm Tuesday to Sunday May to October) explores the chateau's remarkable rococo theatre, complete with original stage machinery. Wandering through the courtyards and gardens is free.

The path beyond the fourth courtyard leads across the spectacular Most ná Plášti to the castle gardens. A ramp to the right leads to the former riding school, now a restaurant. The relief above the door shows cherubs offering the head and boots of a vanquished Turk – a reference to Adolf von Schwarzenberg, who conquered the Turkish fortress of Raab in the 16th century. From here the Italian-style Zámecká zahrada (castle gardens) stretch away towards the Bellarie Summer Pavilion.

Across the river from the castle is the Old Town Square (nám Svornosti), with its 16th-century Town Hall and Marian Plague Column (Mariánský sloupek), from 1716.

ČESKÝ KRUMLOV

0 _____ 200 m
0 _____ 0.1 miles

SIGHTS & ACTIVITIES		EATING 🍴	
Český Krumlov Castle..............1	B3	Cikánská jizba.....................10	B4
Egon Schiele Centrum............2	B4	Krčma v Šatlavské................11	B4
Former Riding School.............3	A3	Laibon...............................12	B4
Maleček..............................4	C4		
Marian Plague Column (Mariánský		DRINKING 🍷	
Sloupek)..........................5	B4	Café Schiele....................(see 2)	
Round Tower.......................6	B3	Hospoda Na Louži...............13	B4
Town Hall...........................7	B4		
		TRANSPORT	
SLEEPING 🛏		Bus Station........................14	D3
Dilettante's Hangout.............8	B5	Spičák Bus Stop..................15	B2
Pension Myší Díra.................9	C4		

Below the square, in a former brewery, is the **Egon Schiele Centrum** (☎ 380 704 011; www.schiele artcentrum.cz; Široká 70-72; adult/concession 120/70Kč; 🕙 10am-6pm Tue-Sun). Established in 1993, this excellent private gallery has a retrospective of the Viennese painter Egon Schiele (1890–1918), who lived briefly in Krumlov in 1911, and raised the ire of the townsfolk by hiring young girls to pose as nude models for his work.

In summer, messing about on the river is a great way to keep cool. You can rent boats from **Maleček** (☎ 380 712 508; http://en.malecek.cz; Rooseveltova 28; 🕙 9am-5pm) – a half-hour splash in a two-person canoe costs 350Kč, or you can rent a canoe for a full-day trip down the river from the town of Rožmberk (850Kč, six to eight hours). Maleček also offers sedate river trips through Český Krumlov on giant wooden rafts seating up to 36 people (45 minutes, 290Kč).

EATING & DRINKING

Laibon (☎ 728 676 654; Parkán 105; mains 100-200Kč; **V**) Candles and vaulted ceilings create a great boho ambience in the best little vegetarian tea house in Bohemia. The riverside setting's pretty fine as well. Order the blueberry dumplings for dessert, and don't miss the special 'yeast beer' from the Bernard brewery.

Cikánská Jizba (☎ 380 717 585; Dlouhá 31; mains 100-240Kč; ☻ 3pm-midnight Mon-Sat) At 'The Gypsy Room' there's live Roma music at the weekends to go with the menu of meaty Czech favourites.

Krčma v Šatlavské (☎ 380 713 344; Horní 157; mains 120-250Kč) Nirvana for meat lovers, this medieval barbecue cellar serves sizzling platters in a funky labyrinth illuminated by candles and the flickering flames of open grills.

Hospoda Na Louži (☎ 380 711 280; Kájovská 66) Nothing's changed in this wood-panelled *pivo* (beer) parlour for almost a century. Locals and tourists pack Na Louži for huge meals and tasty dark beer from the local Eggenberg brewery.

Café Schiele (☎ 380 704 011; Široká 71; ☻ 10am-7pm; ☞) A lovely cafe housed in the art gallery, with ancient oak floorboards, mismatched furniture and a grand piano with sawn-off legs serving as a coffee table. Excellent fair-trade coffee.

SLEEPING

Dilettante's Hangout (☎ 728 280 033; www.dilettantes hangout.com; Plesivecke nám 93; r 790-890Kč) Don't be fooled by the bland exterior – inside this intimate homestay are three romantic and arty rooms decorated with mementos of the artistic owner's global wanderings.

Pension Myší Díra (☎ 380 712 853; www.ceskykrumlov -info.cz; Rooseveltova 28; s/d from 790/990Kč; **P** **☐**) This welcoming pension has a great location over-looking the river, and bright, beautiful rooms with lots of pale wood and quirky handmade furniture. Deluxe rooms and weekends (June to August) are 300Kč extra, but rates fall by 40% in winter. Breakfast is served in your room.

Pension Sebastian (☎ 608 357 581; www.sebastianck .com; 5 Května Ul, Plešivec; s/d/tr 790/990/1490Kč; ☒ ☞ ☝) An excellent option just 10 minutes' walk from the old town, and therefore slightly cheaper. Larger four-bed rooms (1780Kč) are good for families, and there's a garden gazebo for end-of-day drinks and barbecues. Breakfast is included in the room price.

Prague sits at the heart of Europe, and is well served by air, road and rail. The city has an excellent integrated public-transport system with frequent tram, metro and bus services, though the historic central neighbourhoods are small enough to cover easily on foot.

AIR
Airport
Prague Airport (Letiště Praha; off Map p58; flight information ☎ 220 113 314; www.csl.cz), 17km west of the city centre, is the hub for the national carrier Czech Airlines (ČSA; Map p108; ☎ 239 007 007; www.csa .cz; V Celnici 5, Nové Město), which operates direct flights to Prague from many European cities, including London, Dublin, Paris, Rome and Amsterdam, and also from New York and Atlanta.

Prague's airport has two international terminals. Terminal 1 is for flights to/from non–Schengen Zone countries (including the UK, Ireland and countries outside Europe), and Terminal 2 is for flights to/from Schengen Zone countries (most EU nations plus Switzerland, Iceland and Norway).

In both terminals the arrival and departure halls are next to each other on the same level.

The arrival halls have exchange counters, ATMs, accommodation and car-hire agencies, public-transport information desks, taxi services and 24-hour left-luggage counters (per piece per day 120Kč). The departure halls have restaurants and bars, information offices, airline offices, an exchange counter and travel agencies. Once you're through security, there are shops, restaurants, bars, internet access and wi-fi.

There's a post office (⏰ 8am-10pm Mon-Fri, 9am-5pm Sat & Sun) in the connecting building between Terminals 1 and 2.

BICYCLE
Prague is not the best city for getting around by bicycle. The traffic is heavy, tram tracks can be dangerous and there are lots of hills and cobbled streets to navigate. That said, the popularity of cycling is steadily increasing and the city now has about 260km of signposted cycle routes.

Bikes must be equipped with a bell, mudguards, a white reflector and white light up front, a red reflector and flashing red light at the rear, and reflectors on pedals – if not, you can be fined up to 1000Kč. Cyclists up to the age of 15 must wear helmets.

CLIMATE CHANGE & TRAVEL
Climate change is a serious threat to the ecosystems that humans rely upon, and air travel is the fastest-growing contributor to the problem. Lonely Planet regards travel, overall, as a global benefit, but believes we all have a responsibility to limit our personal impact on global warming.

Flying & Climate Change
Pretty much every form of motor transport generates CO_2 (the main cause of human-induced climate change) but planes are far and away the worst offenders, not just because of the sheer distances they allow us to travel, but because they release greenhouse gases high into the atmosphere. The statistics are frightening: two people taking a return flight between Europe and the US will contribute as much to climate change as an average household's gas and electricity consumption over a whole year.

Carbon Offset Schemes
Climatecare.org and other websites use 'carbon calculators' that allow jetsetters to offset the greenhouse gases they are responsible for with contributions to energy-saving projects and other climate-friendly initiatives in the developing world – including projects in India, Honduras, Kazakhstan and Uganda.

Lonely Planet, together with Rough Guides and other concerned partners in the travel industry, supports the carbon offset scheme run by climatecare.org. Lonely Planet offsets all of its staff and author travel.

For more information check out our website: www.lonelyplanet.com.

GETTING INTO TOWN

To get into town, buy a transfer ticket (26Kč) from the public-transport (Praha Dopravní podnik hlavního město Praha; DPP) desk in Arrivals and take bus 119 (20 minutes, every 10 minutes, 4am to midnight) to the end of the line (Dejvická), then continue by metro into the city centre (another 10 to 15 minutes; no new ticket needed). Note that you'll also need a half-fare (13Kč) ticket for your bag or suitcase if it's larger than 25cm x 45cm x 70cm. If you're heading to the western part of the city, take bus 100, which goes to Zličín metro station. There's also the Airport Express bus (50Kč, 35 minutes, every 30 minutes 5am to 10pm) which runs to Praha hlavní nádraží (main train station), where you can connect to metro line C (buy ticket from driver, luggage goes free).

Alternatively, take a Cedaz minibus (☎ 221 111 111; www.cedaz.cz) from outside Arrivals to the Czech Airlines office (Map p108), near náměstí Republiky (120Kč, 20 minutes, every 30 minutes 7.30am to 7pm); buy a ticket from the driver. You can also opt to get off earlier at the Dejvická metro stop (90Kč) instead. Or you can get a Cedaz minibus direct to your hotel or any other address in the city centre (480Kč for one to four people, 680Kč for five to eight) – book and pay at the Cedaz desk in the Arrivals hall. Prague Airport Shuttle (☎ 777 777 237; www.prague-airport-shuttle .cz) operates a similar service.

Airport Cars (☎ 220 113 892; www.airport-cars.cz) operates a 24-hour taxi service, charging around 500 to 650Kč to get to the centre of Prague. Drivers usually speak some English and accept Visa credit cards.

If you're at least 12 years old you can take your bicycle on the metro, but you must place it near the last door of the rear carriage, and only two bikes are allowed per train. Bikes are not permitted if the carriage is full, or if there's already a pram in the carriage.

For more information on cycling and bike hire, see p210.

BOAT

See p259 for details of river transport between Prague city centre and Troja (for Prague Zoo and Troja Chateau; see p145).

BUS

Prague has two main bus stations. All international and long-distance domestic buses (and many regional services) use the renovated and user-friendly Florenc bus station (ÚAN Praha Florenc; Map p130; Křižíkova 4, Karlín), while regional buses to the northeastern Czech Republic (including Mělník, see p238) depart from Holešovice bus station (ÚAN Praha Holešovice; Map p136; Vrbenského, Holešovice).

International bus operators include Eurolines (Map p108; ☎ 245 005 245; www.elines.cz) and the excellent Student Agency (Map p108; ☎ 800 100 300; www .studentagency.cz); both have offices at Florenc bus station, or you can buy tickets online.

You can find local and regional bus timetable info in English at www.vlak-bus.cz and ☎ 900 144 444. On these services you buy your ticket from the driver as you board. For details of city bus services see Public Transport, p250.

CAR & MOTORCYCLE

Driving in Prague is no fun, especially in the narrow, winding streets of the city centre. Trying to find your way around – or to park legally – while coping with trams, buses, other drivers, cyclists and pedestrians can make you wish you'd left the car at home.

Prague information service (PIS; see p263) publishes a *Transport Guide* with many useful tips for drivers, including emergency breakdown services, where to find car-repair shops (by make) and all-important parking tips (see also p250).

Driving

Traffic in the Czech Republic drives on the right. In Prague you may overtake a tram only on the right, and only if it's in motion. You must stop behind any tram taking on or letting off passengers where there's no passenger island. A tram has the right of way when making any signalled turn across your path.

In case of an accident the police should be contacted immediately if repairs are likely to cost over 20,000Kč or if there is an injury. Even if damage is slight, it's a good idea to report the accident as the police will issue an insurance report that will help avoid problems when you take the car out of the country or return it to the rental company.

For emergency breakdowns, the ÚAMK (Central Automobile & Motorcycle Club; Map p58; ☎ 261 104 111; www.uamk.cz; Na Strži 9, Nusle) provides nationwide assistance 24 hours a day – call ☎ 1230 for breakdown assistance (or ☎ +420 21230 if calling from a non-Czech mobile phone). ÚAMK has agreements with national motoring organisations across the world through its affiliations with the Alliance Internationale de Tourisme and the Fédération Internationale de l'Automobile. If you are a member of any of these, ÚAMK will help you on roughly the same terms as your own organisation would. If not, you must pay for all services.

Hire

The major international car-hire chains all have airport pick-up points as well as offices in the city centre. Their rates begin at around 1900/6600Kč per day/week for a Škoda Fabia, including unlimited mileage, collision-damage waiver and value-added tax (VAT; 'DPH' in Czech).

Small local companies such as Secco, Vecar and West Car Praha offer much better rates, but are less likely to have fluent English-speaking staff – it's easier to book through their websites than by phone. Typical rates for a Škoda Fabia start at around 600Kč to 900Kč a day, including unlimited mileage, collision-damage waiver and VAT.

A-Rent Car/Thrifty (Map p110; ☎ 224 233 265; www .arentcar.cz; Washingtonova 9, Nové Město; Ⓜ Muzeum)

Avis (Map p108; ☎ 810 777 810; www.avis.cz; Klimentská 46, Nové Město; Ⓖ 5, 8, 14)

CS-Czechocar (Map p120; ☎ 261 222 079; www .czechocar.cz; Congress Centre, 5.května 65, Vyšehrad; Ⓜ Vyšehrad)

Europcar (Map p90; ☎ 224 811 290; www.europcar.cz; Elišky Krásnohorské 9, Staré Město; Ⓖ 17)

Hertz (☎ 225 345 000; www.hertz.cz; Hotel Diplomat, Evropská 15, Dejvice; Ⓜ Dejvice)

Secco Car (Map p136; ☎ 220 802 361; www.seccocar.cz; Přístavní 39, Holešovice; Ⓖ 1, 3, 12, 15, 25)

Vecar (Map p136; ☎ 603 419 343; www.vecar.cz; Svatovítská 7, Dejvice; Ⓜ Dejvická)

West Car Praha (Map p58; ☎ 235 365 307; www.west carpraha.cz; Veleslavínská 17, Veleslavín; Ⓖ 20, 26)

Parking

Parking in Prague was never easy but in the past couple of years it's become positively mind-boggling. Parking is now regulated by district, meaning that nonresident street parking is all but impossible in the districts of Prague 1 (Staré Město, Malá Strana, Nové Město and Hradčany), Prague 2 (parts of Nové Město, Vyšehrad and Vinohrady), Prague 3 (Žižkov) and Prague 7 (Holešovice and Letná). Visitors and nonresidents can park freely in other areas of the city, but finding a space is practically impossible. In restricted districts, nonresidents are not permitted to park in areas marked by a blue line on the street; paid visitor parking is permitted in areas marked by a white line, though often restricted to between two and six hours maximum.

The situation is particularly dire in Prague 1, where blue (restricted parking) is the overwhelming norm. There are some patches of white (paid) parking along the streets around the InterContinental Hotel, and there are parking garages at the InterContinental and the Kotva department store among other places, though at 100Kč per hour rates can quickly add up. If you're still intent on arriving by car, try arranging parking in advance through your hotel. Most offer some form of parking for an additional fee (200Kč to 300Kč per night). A cheaper alternative is use the 'Park & Ride' (P&R) spaces near metro stations on the outskirts of Prague. The best of these include Skalka (metro line A); Zličín, Nové Butovice, Palmovka, Rajská Zahrada, Černý Most (all line B); and Nádraží Holešovice, Ladví and Opatov (line C).

The fine for illegal parking is normally a clamp on the car wheel or (worse) having the car towed to a police parking compound. Figure on a couple of hours of bureaucracy and fine and fees of about 1500Kc.

PUBLIC TRANSPORT

Prague's excellent public-transport system combines tram, metro and bus services. It's operated by Dopravní podnik hlavního město Prahy (DPP; ☎ 800 19 18 17; www.dpp.cz), which has information desks at Prague Airport (7am to 10pm) and in four metro stations – Muzeum (7am to 9pm), Můstek, Anděl and Nádraží Holešovice (all 7am to 6pm) – where you can get tickets, directions, a multilingual transport-system map, a map of night services *(noční provoz)* and a detailed English-language guide to the whole system.

On metro trains and newer trams and buses, an electronic display shows the route number and the name of the next stop, and a recorded voice announces each station or stop. As the train, tram or bus pulls away, the announcer says *Příští stanice…* (The next station is…) or *Příští zastávka…* (The next stop is…), perhaps noting that it's a *přestupní stanice* (transfer station). At metro stations, signs point you towards the *výstup* (exit) or to a *přestup* (transfer to another line).

The metro's operating hours are from 5am to midnight. There are three lines: line A runs from the northwestern side of the city at Dejvická to the east at Skalka; line B runs from the southwest at Zličín to the northeast at Černý Most; and line C runs from the north at Letňany to the southeast at Háje. Line A intersects line C at Muzeum, line B intersects line C at Florenc, and line A intersects line B at Můstek.

After the metro closes, night trams (51 to 58) and buses (501 to 512) still rumble across the city about every 40 minutes through the night (only 26Kč tickets are valid on these services). If you're planning a late evening, find out if one of these lines passes near where you're staying.

Tickets

You need to buy a ticket before you board a bus, tram or metro. Tickets are sold from machines at metro stations and tram stops, at newsstands, Trafiky snack shops, PNS newspaper kiosks, hotels, PIS tourist information offices (see p263), metro station ticket offices and DPP information offices. Tickets are valid on tram, metro, bus and the Petřín funicular.

A transfer ticket *(přestupní jízdenka)* costs 26/13Kč per adult/child aged six to 15 years; kids under six ride free. You'll also need a 13Kč ticket for each large suitcase or backpack if it's larger than 25cm x 45cm x 70cm. Validate (punch) your ticket by sticking it in the little yellow machine in the metro station lobby or on the bus or tram the first time you board; this stamps the time and date on it. Once validated, transfer tickets remain valid for 75 minutes; within this time period you can make unlimited transfers between all types of public transport (you don't need to punch the ticket again).

There's also a short-hop 18/9Kč ticket, valid for 20 minutes on buses and trams, or for up to five metro stations. No transfers are allowed with these (except between metro lines), and they're not valid on the Petřín funicular or on night trams (51 to 58) or buses (501 to 512).

You can also buy tickets valid for 24 hours (100Kč) and three/five days (330/500Kč); the latter two include one adult and one child aged six to 15 years. Again, these must be validated on first use only; if a ticket is stamped twice, it becomes invalid. With these tickets, you don't need to pay an extra fare for your luggage.

Being caught without a valid ticket entails a 500Kč on-the-spot fine (100Kč for not having a luggage ticket). The plain-clothes inspectors travel incognito, but will show a red-and-gold metal badge when they ask for your ticket. A few may demand a higher fine from foreigners and pocket the difference, so insist on a receipt *(doklad)* before paying.

TAXI

Prague City Council has cracked down on the city's notoriously dishonest taxi drivers by installing a network of taxi stands with red-and-yellow signs quoting the correct fares between various parts of the city. The official rate for licensed cabs is 40Kč flag fall plus 28Kč per kilometre and 6Kč per minute while waiting. On this basis, any trip within the city centre – say, from Wenceslas Square to Malá Strana – should cost around 170Kč. A trip to the suburbs should be around 400Kč to 500Kč, and to the airport between 500Kč and 650Kč. Journeys outside Prague are not regulated; negotiate a fare before you get in.

DON'T BLAME US…

…when it comes to sorting out Prague's ever-changing tram and bus schedules. The construction of the city's ring-road system, particularly around the Hradčanská metro station, has everyone flummoxed, including locals. Trams disappear, others are rerouted and, mercifully, some stay the same – but figuring out which is which is nearly impossible. If it's any consolation, the folks at Prague Public Transport (www.dpp.cz) list changes on their website, but you need to know the system well to get much out of it. If you do find yourself on a tram that zigs when it should have zagged, just settle in and enjoy the ride. *By Mark Baker*

However, hailing a taxi on the street – at least in a tourist zone – still holds the risk of an inflated fare. The usual tactic is to quote a 'maximum' fare for a given destination, then drive around long enough to ensure that the meter clocks up the quoted maximum.

You're much better off calling a radio-taxi than flagging one down, as they're better regulated and more responsible. From our experience the following companies have honest drivers (most of whom speak a little English) and offer 24-hour services.

AAA Radio Taxi (☎ 14014; www.aaaradiotaxi.cz)

Airport Cars (☎ 220 113 892; www.airport-cars.cz)

City Taxi (☎ 257 257 257; www.citytaxi.cz)

ProfiTaxi (☎ 14015; www.profitaxi.cz)

TRAIN

The railway system is operated by the privatised České dráhy (ČD; Czech Railways; www.cd.cz). Timetable information is available online at www.vlak-bus.cz. For details on the city's metro train system, see p250.

Arriving in Prague by Train

Most international trains arrive at Praha hlavní nádraží (Prague main train station; Map p110). Some stop only at Praha-Holešovice (Map p136) in the north of the city (including some trains from Berlin, Vienna and Budapest), or Praha-Smíchov (Map p58) in the south; all three stations have their own metro stops. Masarykovo nádraží (Map p108), two blocks north of the main train station, is the main domestic rail terminus. (Note: Praha hlavní nádraží was still undergoing a major redevelopment at the time of research; until it is completed the layout of the station may be changed.)

On arriving at Praha hlavní nádraží, the underpass from the platforms leads you to level 3 of the four-level station complex. Continue down a short flight of stairs to level 2, the main concourse, where you'll find the PIS tourist information booth (☒ 9am-7pm Mon-Fri, to 5pm Sat & Sun) beside the metro entrance at the southern (left) end.

At the north end of the main concourse is a 24-hour left-luggage office (úschovna; per bag per day 15Kč or 30Kč) and luggage lockers (60Kč) that accept 5Kč, 10Kč and 20Kč coins.

There are four metro station entrances in the concourse – the two nearer the stairs from level 3 lead to the northbound platform (direction Letňany), the two nearer the exits are southbound (direction Háje). Public-transport tickets and information are available at the DPP booths beside the southbound metro entrances. There are taxi ranks at either end of the concourse. To find the nearest tram stop (for trams 5, 9 and 26), exit the main concourse and turn right; the stop is at the far end of the park.

Try not to arrive in the middle of the night – the station closes from 12.40am to 3.40am, and the surrounding area is a magnet for pickpockets and drunks.

YOU'RE GOING WHERE?

Although most staff at the international ticket counters in Prague's main train station speak at least some English, those selling domestic tickets rarely do. In order to speed up the process of buying a ticket, and to avoid misunderstandings, it's often easier to write down what you want on a piece of paper and hand it to the clerk (this works for bus tickets, too).

Write it down like this:

- *z:* departure station, eg PRAHA
- *do:* destination station, eg KARLŠTEJN
- *čas:* departure time using 24-hour clock
- *datum:* date, eg for 2.30pm on 20 May, write '14.30h. 20/05'. Or just *dnes* (today)
- *osoby:* number of passengers
- *jednosměrný* (one way) or *zpáteční* (return).

If you're making a reservation on an EC (international) or IC (domestic) train, you may also want to specify 1. *třída* or 2. *třída* (1st or 2nd class), and whether you want an *okno* (window) or *chodba* (aisle) seat.

One-way domestic train tickets for distances of more than 50km are valid for 24 hours from time of purchase, but for distances under 50km only until 6am the next day. Note that domestic return tickets (about 10% more expensive than singles) are only valid for 48 hours from time of purchase – if you plan to be away for more than two days, buy two one-way tickets instead.

Leaving Prague by Train

You can buy international train tickets in advance from train stations and ČD Travel (Map p110; ☎ 972 243 071; Pasáž Broadway, Na příkopě 31, Nové Město) and Čedok (Map p110; ☎ 221 447 242; www.cedok.com; Na Příkopě 18, Nové Město) travel agencies.

At Prague's main train station, the ticket counters are on the basement level. You can get information on international services from the ticket desks with dark blue signs (at the right-hand end) and at the ČD Travel information centre (at the left). There are interactive electronic timetables here, and timetable information is also available online at www.vlak.cz.

The big electronic display board on the main concourse lists departures with columns marked *vlak* (type of train – EC for international, IC for domestic, etc), *čislo* (train number), *doprav* (carrier) *cilová stanice* (final destination), *směr jízdy* (via), *odjezd* (departure time), *našt* (platform number) and *zpoz'vdení* (delay).

You can buy domestic tickets *(vnitrostátní jízdenky)* at the ticket windows with light-blue signs at the left of the basement concourse; for international advance reservations *(mezínárodní rezervace)* and for international tickets *(mezínárodní jízdenky)* go to the desks with dark blue signs to the right.

BUSINESS HOURS

Shops tend to open from 8am or 8.30am and close anywhere between 5pm and 7pm Monday to Friday, and open from 8.30am to noon or 1pm on Saturday. Department stores close at 8pm Monday to Friday, and at 6pm on Saturday and Sunday. Touristy shops in central Prague are open later at night and all day Saturday and Sunday.

Banks generally open from 8am to 4.30pm Monday to Friday. The city's main post office is open from 7am to 8pm every day, while other post offices open from 8am to 6pm or 7pm Monday to Friday and until noon on Saturday. Restaurants tend to be open between 10am and 11pm (cafes generally open at around 8am), while bars usually open from 11am to midnight (though some in the city centre stay open till 3am or 4am).

Most museums and galleries open from 9am or 10am to 5pm or 6pm year-round. Many are closed on Monday and on the first working day after a holiday. Some of Prague's bigger churches are open similar hours.

Castles, chateaux and other historic monuments outside the city are open from May to September, from 8am or 9am to 5pm or 6pm, except for a lunch break, daily except Monday and the first working day after a holiday. Most shut down from November to March, with some limited to weekends in October and April. If you plan to take a guided tour, remember that ticket offices close an hour or so before the official closing time, depending on the length of the tour.

CHILDREN

Czechs are very family oriented, and there are plenty of activities for children around the city. An increasing number of Prague restaurants cater specifically for children, with play areas and so on, and many offer a children's menu (dětský jídelníček); even if they don't, they can usually provide smaller portions for a lower price.

For outdoor activities, take a walk around Prague Zoo (p145) – if possible, go there by boat (p259) – or hire inline skates at Letná Gardens (p136). Petřín (p85) is a beautiful park on a hill

where parents and kids alike can take a break from sightseeing, and climb up the Petřín Lookout Tower for terrific views over Prague. For an even higher viewpoint, go to the TV Tower (p133) in Žižkov.

March is the time of the St Matthew Fair (p16), when Holešovice's exhibition grounds are full of fairground rides, shooting galleries and candy floss; in summer there are rowing and paddle boats for hire along the Vltava River, as well as river cruises and boat tours (p259).

At weekends and on holidays between April and mid-November, vintage tram cars trundle along a special sightseeing route, No 91, around the city centre (see p260). And don't miss the changing of the guard at Prague Castle (see p63 for details) – but get into position before the crowds do, or the kids won't see a thing.

Museums of possible interest to children include the Toy Museum (p67), though, frustratingly, its many displays are hands off; the Public Transport Museum (p146), where kids can climb on the vintage trams and buses; and the Kbely Aircraft Museum (p145), where they can see Russian MiG fighter planes up close.

There are safe, fenced playgrounds by the entrance to Petřín park on náměstí Kinských (Map p78); at the northern end of Kampa island (Map p78); on Children's Island (p82); at the southern end of Slav Island (p116); and on Vlašská, just west of the German embassy (Map p78).

For more information and inspiration on how to make travelling with children as hassle-free as possible, check out Lonely Planet's *Travel with Children* by Brigitte Barta et al. See also the Top Picks boxed text, p116.

Babysitting

The Prague information service (Pražská informační služba, PIS; ☎ 221 714 444, in English & German; www.prague-info .cz) usually has a list of babysitting (hlídaní dětí) agencies, and most top-end hotels provide a babysitting service; rates are generally around 150Kč per hour. Prague Family (☎ 224 224 044; www.praguefamily.cz) is an agency that can provide English-speaking babysitters.

CLIMATE

Prague has warm, occasionally showery summers and cold, often snowy winters with generally changeable conditions. A typical day in Prague from June to August sees the mercury range from about 12°C to 22°C. Temperatures from December to February push below freezing. Wide variations are common, sometimes surpassing 35°C in summer and -20°C in winter. The summer's long, sunny, hot spells tend to be broken by sudden, heavy thunderstorms. In general, May and September enjoy the most pleasant weather.

See p16 for advice on the best time to visit.

COURSES

Places offering Czech language courses:

Institute for Language & Preparatory Studies (Ústav jazykové a odborné přípravy, ÚJOP; Map p120; ☎ 224 990 420; www.ujop.cuni.cz; Vratislavova 10, Vyšehrad; Ⓜ Vyšehrad) ÚJOP runs six-week Czech language courses for foreigners. No prior knowledge of the Czech language is required. The course fee is €610, not including accommodation. You can also opt for individual lessons (45 minutes) at 620Kč each. Further details and an application form are available on the website.

1to1 Czech (Map p108; ☎ 605 554 117; http://1to1czech .weebly.com; Revoluční 8, Nové Město; Ⓡ 5, 8, 14, 51, 54) Offers Czech lessons for both individuals and groups, including three-week beginner's courses. Individual tuition costs from 400Kč for a 45-minute lesson.

CUSTOMS REGULATIONS

Travelling between the Czech Republic and other EU countries, you can import/export 800 cigarettes, 400 cigarillos, 200 cigars, 1kg of smoking tobacco, 10L of spirits, 20L of fortified wine (eg port or sherry), 90L of wine and 110L of beer, provided the goods are for personal use only (each country sets its own guide levels; these figures are minimums).

Travellers from outside the EU can import or export, duty-free, a maximum of 200 ciga-rettes *or* 100 cigarillos *or* 50 cigars *or* 250g of tobacco; 2L of still table wine; 1L of spirits *or* 2L of fortified wine, sparkling wine or liqueurs; 60mL of perfume; 250mL of eau de toilette; and €175 worth of all other goods (including gifts and souvenirs). Anything over this limit must be declared to customs officers. People under 17 do not get the alcohol and tobacco allowances.

Any goods you buy in the Czech Republic can be taken to any other EU country without paying additional VAT. If you are resident outside the EU, you may be able to reclaim VAT on your purchases (see p150). You're not permitted to export genuine antiques.

There is no limit to the amount of Czech or foreign currency that can be taken in or out of the country, but amounts exceeding 500,000Kč must be declared.

DISCOUNT CARDS

The Prague Card is a combined admission card and public-transport pass. The admission card is valid for one year, but the transport ticket is valid only for one day, allowing unlimited travel on metro, trams and buses. The card provides free or discounted entry to 60 city sights, including Prague Castle, the Old Town Hall, the National Museum, the Petřín Lookout Tower and Vyšehrad. However, it does not include the Prague Jewish Museum.

The pass costs €36/25 (926/643Kč) per adult/child, and can be purchased from all tourist information offices, the audio-guide desk at Prague Castle, Čedok travel agencies and many hotels, as well as online at www .praguecitycard.com.

ELECTRICITY

Electricity in Prague is 230V, 50Hz AC. Outlets have the standard European socket with two small round holes and a protruding earth (ground) pin. If you have a different plug, bring an adaptor (see www.kropla.com for info). North American 110V appliances will also need a transformer if they don't have built-in voltage adjustment.

EMBASSIES & CONSULATES

Australia (Map p108; ☎ 296 578 350; www.dfat.gov.au/ missions/countries/cz.html; 6th fl, Klimentská 10, Nové Město) Honorary consulate for emergency assistance only (eg a stolen passport); the nearest Australian embassy is in Vienna.

Austria (Map p143; ☎ 257 090 511; www.bmeia.gv.at/ botschaft/prag.html, in German & Czech; Viktora Huga 10, Smíchov)

Canada (Map p136; ☎ 272 101 800; www.canada.cz; Muchova 6, Bubeneč)

France (Map p78; ☎ 251 171 711; www.france.cz, in French & Czech; Velkopřerovské náměstí 2, Malá Strana)

Germany (Map p78; ☎ 257 113 111; www.deutschland .cz, in German & Czech; Vlašská 19, Malá Strana)

Ireland (Map p78; ☎ 257 530 061; www.embassyof ireland.cz; Tržiště 13, Malá Strana)

Israel (Map p136; ☎ 233 097 500; http://prague.mfa.gov .il; Badeniho 2, Bubeneč)

Netherlands (Map p136; ☎ 233 015 200; www.nether landsembassy.cz; Gotthardská 6/27, Bubeneč)

New Zealand (Map p125; ☎ 222 514 672; egermayer@ nzconsul.cz; Dykova 19, Vinohrady) Honorary consulate providing emergency assistance only (eg stolen passport); the nearest NZ embassy is in Berlin.

Poland Embassy (Map p78; ☎ 257 099 500; www .prague.polemb.net; Valdštejnská 8, Malá Strana); Consular Department (Map p58; ☎ 224 228 722; konspol@mbox .vol.cz; V úžlabině 14, Strašnice) Come here for visas.

Russia (Map p136; ☎ 233 374 100; www.czech.mid.ru; Pod Kaštany 1, Bubeneč)

Slovakia (Map p136; ☎ 233 113 051; www.mzv.sk/ praha, in Slovak; Pelléova 12, Bubeneč)

South Africa (Map p125; ☎ 267 311 114; saprague@ terminal.cz; Ruská 65, Vršovice)

UK (Map p78; ☎ 257 402 370; www.britain.cz; Thunovská 14, Malá Strana)

USA (Map p78; ☎ 257 022 000; www.usembassy.cz; Tržiště 15, Malá Strana)

EMERGENCY

Ambulance (☎ 155)

Breakdown Assistance for Motorists (ÚAMK; ☎ 1230)

EU-wide emergency hotline (☎ 112) English- and German-speaking operators are available.

Fire (☎ 150)

Municipal Police (☎ 156)

State Police (☎ 158)

GAY & LESBIAN TRAVELLERS

Homosexuality is legal in the Czech Republic (the age of consent is 15), but Czechs are not accustomed to seeing same-sex couples show-ing affection to each other in public; it's best to be discreet. However, Prague is the most liberal place in the country, and has a lively gay scene, with most gay bars and clubs concentrated in the city centre and in the districts of Vinohrady and Žižkov.

The bimonthly gay guide and contact magazine *Amigo* has a few pages in English, but the Gay Guide Prague (http://prague.gayguide.net) and Prague Saints (www.praguesaints.cz) are the most useful sources of information. See also the boxed text, p198, for gay-friendly venues and accommodation options.

HOLIDAYS

Banks, offices, department stores and some shops will be closed on public holidays. Restaurants, museums and tourist attractions tend to stay open, though many may close on the first working day *after* a holiday. See also p16.

New Year's Day 1 January

Easter Monday March/April

Labour Day 1 May

Liberation Day 8 May

Sts Cyril & Methodius Day 5 July

Jan Hus Day 6 July

Czech Statehood Day 28 September

Republic Day 28 October

Struggle for Freedom & Democracy Day 17 November

Christmas Eve (Generous Day) 24 December

Christmas Day 25 December

St Stephen's Day 26 December

INTERNET ACCESS

Many hotels now offer wi-fi connections for guests, though you'll probably have to ask reception for a password. If not, you should be able to log on from your hotel room for the cost of a local call by registering with an internet roaming service such as MaGlobe (www.maglobe.com), which has access numbers for Prague. Most midrange and top-end hotels have telephone jacks, usually US standard (RJ-11), which you can plug your modem cable into, or ethernet ports for sharing the hotel's broadband connection. If you plan to use the phone line, buy a line tester – a gadget that goes between your computer and the phone jack – so that you don't inadvertently fry your modem. For more information on travelling with a laptop check out www.kropla.com.

WI-FI ACCESS

You can search for wi-fi hot spots in Prague (and around the world) at www.jiwire.com. More and more cafes and bars in Prague are advertising free wi-fi for paying customers, but in our experience around half the places boasting this service don't actually have a functioning internet connection ('Sorry, it's not working today'); if it's important, make sure you can connect before buying a drink! We have found the following places, along with all branches of Starbucks, to have reliable, free wi-fi connections:

- Blatouch (p187)
- Krásný Ztráty (p185)
- Café Savoy (p188)
- Caffe Kaaba (p187)
- Grand Café Orient (p188)
- Káva Káva Káva (p185)

For those without a laptop, Prague has dozens of internet cafes. Conveniently located ones include the following:

Bohemia Bagel (Map p90; ☎ 224 812 560; www .bohemiabagel.cz; Masná 2, Staré Město; per min 1.50Kč; ☺ 7am-midnight; Ⓜ Náměstí Republiky)

Globe Bookstore & Café (Map p110; ☎ 224 934 203; www.globebookstore.cz; Pštrossova 6, Nové Město; per min 1Kč; ☺ 10am-midnight; Ⓜ Karlovo Náměstí) No minimum. Also has ethernet ports so you can connect your own laptop (same price; cables provided, 50Kč deposit), and free wi-fi.

Internet Centre (Map p90; Rytířská 18, Staré Město; per 15min 25Kč, per hr 100Kč; ☺ 9am-11pm Mon-Fri, 10am-9pm Sat, 11am-9pm Sun; Ⓜ Můstek) At the back of Au Gourmand cafe; low-cost international phone calls.

Pl@neta (Map p125; ☎ 267 311 182; Řipská 24, Vinohrady; per min 0.44-0.88Kč; ☺ 8am-11pm; Ⓜ Jiřího z Poděbrad) Cheapest place in town, with lowest rates before 10am and after 8pm Monday to Friday, all day Saturday and Sunday; 10Kč minimum.

Spika (Map p110; ☎ 224 211 521; http://netcafe.spika .cz; Dlážděná 4, Nové Město; per 15min Mon-Fri 20Kč, Sat & Sun 16Kč; ☺ 8am-midnight; Ⓜ Náměstí Republiky)

LEGAL MATTERS

If you find yourself under arrest for any reason whatsoever, you are entitled to call your embassy (see p255 for listings). Note that it is technically illegal not to carry some form of identification (normally your passport). If you can't prove your identity, police have the right to detain you for up to 48 hours. Some older police officers retain a communist-era mistrust of foreigners; younger officers are easier to deal with, but almost none speak fluent English.

Penalties for dealing in drugs are harsh and it's unlikely that your embassy can do much to help if you are caught, but laws passed in 2008 have decriminalised the possession of 'a small amount' of drugs, defined as fewer than 20 joints or a gram of hashish.

Drink-driving is strictly illegal; there is a zero blood-alcohol limit for drivers. Traffic fines are generally paid on the spot (ask for a receipt). A smoking ban levies a 1000Kč on-the-spot fine for smoking in public places, including hospitals, libraries, railway stations and public transport – and even at bus and tram stops, even though they are in the open air – but not in restaurants, bars and clubs. (See also the boxed text, p160.)

MAPS

City maps are available at newsagents, bookshops and travel agencies. A detailed plan of the city centre and inner suburbs is Kartografie Praha's *Praha – plán města* (1:10,000). It includes public transport and parking information, an index, a metro map, plans of the castle and Charles Bridge, and a brief description of the major historical sites.

The Prague information service (Pražská informační služba, PIS; ☎ 12444, 221 714 444, in English & German; www.prague-info.cz) stocks a free English-language pamphlet called *Welcome to the Czech Republic*, which is produced by the Ministry of Interior. It features a map of the historical centre, transport routes in the centre, and information such as emergency phone numbers and embassy addresses.

If you are staying in Prague for a significant amount of time, Kartografie Praha's pocket atlas *Praha – plán města – standard* (1:20,000), covering all of Prague, is invaluable.

WHEN YOU'RE LEGAL

The following minimum legal ages apply in the Czech Republic. However, travellers should note that they can be prosecuted under the law of their home country regarding age of consent, even when abroad.

- Drinking alcohol – 18 years
- Driving – 18 years
- Heterosexual/homosexual sex – 15 years
- Smoking – 16 years
- Marriage – 18 years
- Voting – 18 years

A public-transport map showing all day and night services (metro, tram and bus) is available from any of the public information offices of Dopravní podnik hlavního město Prahy (DPP; see p250), the city transport department. There's also a commercial *Praha Městská Doprava* (Prague Public Transport) 1:25,000 map, available from bookshops.

MEDICAL SERVICES

Emergency medical treatment and nonhospital first aid are free for all visitors to the Czech Republic. If you have a serious medical emergency (eg suspected heart attack), call ☎ 112 (English- and German-speaking operators are available).

Citizens of EU countries can obtain a European Health Insurance Card (EHIC); this entitles you to free state-provided medical treatment in the Czech Republic (see www .cmu.cz – click on the UK flag – for information on using the card in the Czech Republic). Non-EU citizens must pay for treatment, and at least some of the fee must be paid upfront. Everyone has to pay for prescribed medications.

Clinics

American Dental Associates (Map p108; ☎ 221 181 121; www.americandental.cz; 2nd fl Atrium, Stará Celnice Bldg, V Celnici 4, Nové Město; Ⓜ Náměstí Republiky) Entirely English-speaking.

Canadian Medical Care (Map p58; ☎ 235 360 133, after hr 724 300 301; www.cmcpraha.cz; Veleslavínská 1, Veleslavín; ☾ 8am-6pm Mon-Fri, to 8pm Tue & Thu; Ⓠ 20, 26 from Ⓜ Dejvická) A pricey but professional private clinic with English-speaking doctors; an initial consultation will cost from 1500Kč to 2500Kč.

Polyclinic at Národní (Poliklinika na Národní; Map p90; ☎ 222 075 120, 24hr emergencies 777 942 270; www .poliklinika.narodni.cz; Národní třída 9, Nové Město; ☾ 8.30am-5pm Mon-Fri; Ⓜ Národní Třída) A central clinic with staff who speak English, German, French and Russian. Expect to pay around 600Kč to 1250Kč for an initial consultation.

Emergency Rooms

Na Homolce Hospital (Map p58; ☎ 257 271 111; www .homolka.cz; 5th fl, Foreign Pavilion, Roentgenova 2, Motol; Ⓠ 167 from Ⓜ Anděl) The best hospital in Prague, equipped and staffed to Western standards, with staff who speak English, French, German and Spanish.

Pharmacies

There are plenty of pharmacies *(lékárna)* in Prague, and most city districts have one that stays open 24 hours. In Nové Město you'll find it at the district clinic (Map p110; ☎ 224 946 982; Palackého 5, Nové Město; ☾ 7am-7pm Mon-Fri, 8am-noon Sat; Ⓜ Národní Třída). In Vinohrady go to Lékárna U sv Ludmily (Map p125; ☎ 222 513 396; Belgická 37, Vinohrady; ☾ 7am-7pm Mon-Fri, 8am-noon Sat; Ⓜ Náměstí Míru).

For emergency service after hours, ring the bell – you'll see a red button with a sign *zvonek lékárna* (pharmacy bell) and/or *první pomoc* (first aid). Some prescription medicines may not be available, so it's wise to bring enough for your trip.

MONEY

The Czech crown (Koruna česká, or Kč) is divided into 100 heller or *haléřů* (h). Banknotes come in denominations of 50, 100, 200, 500, 1000, 2000 and 5000Kč; coins are of one, two, five, 10, 20 and 50Kč.

Keep small change handy for use in public toilets and tram-ticket machines, and try to keep some small-denomination notes for shops, cafes and bars – getting change for the 2000Kč notes that ATMs often spit out can be a problem.

See the inside front cover of this guidebook for the exchange-rates table.

Changing Money

The easiest, cheapest way to carry money is in the form of a debit card from your bank, which you can use to withdraw cash either from an ATM *(bankomat)* or over the counter in a bank. Using an ATM will result in your home bank charging a fee (usually 1.5% to 2.5%), but you'll get a good exchange rate and provided you make withdrawals of at least a couple of thousand crowns at a time, you'll pay less than the assorted commissions on travellers cheques. Check with your bank about transaction fees and withdrawal limits.

Travellers cheques are not much use here, as they are not accepted by shops and restaurants and can be exchanged only at banks and currency exchange counters.

The main banks – Komerční banka, Česká spořitelna, Československá obchodní banka (ČSOB) and UniCredit Bank – are the best places to change cash. They charge 2% commission with a 50Kč minimum (but always check, as commissions can vary from branch to branch). They will also provide a cash advance on Visa or MasterCard without commission.

Hotels charge about 5% to 8% commission, while Čedok travel agencies and post offices charge 2% – similar rates to the banks. Note that Scottish and Northern Irish banknotes are almost impossible to change, and where they are accepted you'll get a worse exchange rate than for Bank of England notes.

Try to avoid the many private exchange booths (*směnárna*) in the main tourist areas. They lure you in with attractive-looking exchange rates that turn out to be 'sell' (*prodej* or *prodajáme*) rates; if you want to change foreign currency into Czech crowns, the 'buy' (*nákup*) rate applies. There is also an even worse rate for transactions under a certain amount, typically around €500. Check the rates carefully, and ask exactly how much you will get before parting with any money.

NEWSPAPERS & MAGAZINES

The kiosks on Wenceslas Square, Na Příkopě and náměstí Republiky, and the Relay newsagencies in central metro stations, sell a wide range of international newspapers and magazines, including British papers such as the *Times, Independent* and *Guardian* (international edition), which are available on the day of publication.

See p53 for more about local newspapers.

ORGANISED TOURS

Various private companies operating from kiosks on Na Příkopě offer three-hour city bus tours for around 650Kč to 700Kč per person. They're OK if your time is short, but the castle and other sights get so crowded that you often can't enjoy the tour; we suggest one of our self-guided walking tours instead. There are also some excellent specialist tours on offer.

Bicycle

City Bike (Map p90; ☎ 776 180 284; www.citybike-prague. com; Královdorská 5, Staré Město; ☼ 9am-7pm Apr-Oct; Ⓜ Náměstí Republiky) has 2½-hour guided tours costing from 540Kc, departing at 11am, 2pm and 5pm May to September, and 11am and 2pm April and October. Tours take in the Old Town, the Vltava River and Letná park, and include a stop at a riverside pub.

Praha Bike (Map p90; ☎ 732 388 880; www.prahabike.cz; Dlouhá 24, Staré Město; ☼ 9am-7pm; Ⓜ Náměstí Republiky) offers a 2½-hour guided cycling tour through the city or an easy evening pedal through the parks (490Kč). Tours depart at 2.30pm mid-March to October and also at 11.30am and 5.30pm May to September. Trips outside the city can also be arranged. Helmets and locks are provided, and bikes are available for private rental (see p211).

AVE Travel (☎ 251 551 011; www.bicycle-tours.cz) operates a full-day guided bicycle tour from Prague to Karlštejn Castle (p234) for 1500Kč per person, including bike hire, lunch at Karlštejn and a train ticket back to the city. It also offers bike trips to Konopiště (p237) and one-week tours through the Czech countryside.

Boat

Evropská Vodní Doprava (EVD; Map p90; ☎ 224 810 030; www.evd.cz; Čechův most, Staré Město; Ⓡ 17) operates large cruise boats based at the quay beside Čech Bridge (Čechův most), and offers a one-hour return cruise departing hourly from 10am to 6pm (220/110Kč per adult/child); a two-hour return cruise including lunch and live music, departing at noon (690/380Kč per adult/child); a two-hour return cruise to Vyšehrad (420/350Kč), departing at 3.30pm; and a three-hour evening return cruise with dinner and music (790/500Kč), departing at 7pm. All cruises run year-round.

Prague Venice (Map p90; ☎ 603 819 947; www.prague -venice.cz; Platnéřská 4, Staré Město; adult/child 290/145Kč; ☼ 10.30am-11pm Jul & Aug, to 8pm Mar-Jun, Sep & Oct, to 6pm Nov-Feb; Ⓡ 17) operates entertaining 45-minute cruises in small boats under the hidden arches of Charles Bridge and along the Čertovka millstream in Kampa. Boats depart every 15 minutes from jetties beneath the eastern end of Charles Bridge (entrance next to the Charles Bridge Museum; Map p90), at the western end of Platnéřská, on the Čertovka stream in Malá Strana (Map p78), and at the western end of Mánes Bridge (Mánesův most; Map p78), near Malostranská metro station.

From April to October, Prague Passenger Shipping (Pražská paroplavební společnost, PPS; Map p110; ☎ 224 930 017; www.paroplavba.cz; Rašínovo nábřeží 2, Nové Město; Ⓜ Karlovo Náměstí) runs cruises along the Vltava, departing from the central quay on Rašínovo nábřeží. Most photogenic is a one-hour jaunt taking in the National Theatre, Střelecký island and Vyšehrad, departing at 11am, 2pm, 4pm, 5pm and 6pm April to September (adult/child 190/90Kč).

At 9am on Saturday and Sunday from May to mid-September, a boat goes 37km south (upstream) through a wild, green landscape to the Slapy Dam at Třebrenice. This fine, all-day escape costs 340/170Kč return, arriving back in the city at 6.30pm.

Boats making the 1¼-hour trip to Troja (near the zoo; 150/80Kč one way) depart at 8.30am on weekdays in May and June only, at 9.30am, 12.30pm and 3.30pm daily May to mid-September, and at weekends and holidays in April and from mid-September to the end of October. Returning boats depart from Troja at 11am, 2pm and 5pm.

Bus & Tram

Nostalgic Tram No 91 (☎ 233 343 349; www.dpp.cz; Public Transport Museum, Patočkova 4, Střešovice; adult/child 35/20Kč; ☉ departs hourly noon-5.30pm Sat, Sun & holidays Mar–mid-Nov) offers vintage tram cars dating from 1908 to 1924, which trundle along a special route, starting at the Public Transport Museum (Map p70) and going via stops at Prague Castle, Malostranské náměstí, the National Theatre, Wenceslas Square, náměstí Republiky and Štefánikův most, to finish at Výstaviště (exhibition grounds). You can get on and off at any stop, and buy tickets on board; ordinary public transport tickets and passes are not valid on this line.

A whole range of outings is offered by Prague Sightseeing Tours (☎ 222 314 661; www.ps tours.cz) – look for the yellow kiosk near the metro entrance on náměstí Republiky (Map p90). The two-hour Informative Prague bus tour (adult/child 450/310Kč, departing 11am and 1.30pm from April to October) takes in all of Prague's important historical sites, and the Grand City tour (730/380Kč, departing 9.30am and 2pm April to October) combines a bus tour of the main sites with a walk through Prague Castle.

Jewish Interest

Precious Legacy Tours (Map p90; ☎ 222 321 954; www.legacy tours.net; Kaprova 13, Staré Město; ☉ tours 10.30am Sun-Fri, also 2pm by arrangement) offers guided tours of places of interest to Jewish visitors, including a three-hour walking tour of Prague's Josefov district (630Kč per person; the fee includes admission to four synagogues, but not the Staronová (Old-New) Synagogue – this is 200Kč extra). There's also a daily six-hour excursion to Terezín (1300Kč per person; departs 10am); for more information on Terezín, see p239. Customised, private tours can be arranged for 1300Kč an hour for two people.

Wittmann Tours (☎ 222 252 472; www.wittmann -tours.com; Novotného lavka 5, Staré Město) offers a three-hour walking tour of Josefov (880Kč per person) that begins at 10.30am daily except Saturday from mid-March to December. Wittmann also runs seven-hour day trips to Terezín (p239) for 1450Kč per person (five people or more). In our opinion, the Wittmann tours are better than the Precious Legacy ones as they feel less rushed and more personal.

Personal Guides

Prague information service (Map p90; ☎ 236 002 562; guides@pis.cz; Old Town Hall, Staroměstské náměstí 1; 3hr tour per person 1000Kč, per 2 persons 1200Kč plus 300Kč per additional person; ☉ 9am-6pm Mon-Fri, to 4pm Sat & Sun) can arrange personal guides fluent in all major European languages. The desk is in the PIS office in the Old Town Hall.

Vintage Car

A couple of businesses offer tours around the city in vintage Czech cars dating from the late 1920s and early 1930s. There are pick-up points at various city centre locations; tours depart as available, or whenever you ask, if it's quiet. Tours last about 40 minutes.

3 Veterans (☎ 603 521 700; www.3veterani.cz; per car 1200Kč; ☉ 9am-6pm) has a small fleet of Praga Piccolos and early Škodas, which are all from the early 1930s. Pick-up points in Staré Město are on Rytířská, in Malé náměstí, and at the junction of Pařížská and Staroměstské náměstí; and on Malostranské náměstí in Malá Strana.

With Old Timer History Trip (☎ 776 829 897; www .historytrip.cz; 1-2 persons 950Kč, 3-6 persons 1300Kč; ☉ 9am-6pm Apr-Nov) you can rattle along the city's cobblestone streets in a 1928 Praga Piccolo or a larger 1929 Praga Alfa. Pick-up points in Staré Město are on Malé náměstí, on Karlova and on Malostranská náměstí in Malá Strana. There's also a two-hour night-time tour (from 1890Kč).

Walking

The corner of Old Town Square outside the Old Town Hall is usually clogged with dozens of people touting for business as walking guides; quality varies, but the best are listed here. Most operators don't have an office – you can join a walk by just turning up at the starting point and paying your money, though it's best to phone ahead to be sure of a place. Most walks begin at the Astronomical Clock (Map p90).

Lots of travellers have recommended George's Guided Walks (☎ 607 820 158; www.ggeorge .info), whose intimate, personalised tours include a four-hour History Walk (up to four persons 2200Kč; if you have been to Prague before, he'll take you off the beaten track); a two-hour Iron Curtain Walk (up to four persons 1400Kč); and a five-hour pub crawl, including dinner in a Czech pub (1400Kč per person). George will meet you at your hotel, or anywhere else that's convenient.

Prague Walks (☎ 222 322 309; www.praguewalks.com; per person 300-1000Kč) runs interesting jaunts with themes such as Prague architecture, Žižkov pubs and the Velvet Revolution. Meet at the Astronomical Clock (Map p90), or you can arrange to be met at your hotel.

POST

The main post office (Map p110; ☎ 221 131 111; www .cpost.cz; Jindřišská 14, Nové Město; ⊗ 2am-midnight; Ⓜ Můstek), just off Wenceslas Square, uses an automatic queuing system. Take a ticket from one of the machines in the entrance corridors – press button No 1 for stamps, letters and parcels, or No 4 for Express Mail Service (EMS). Then watch the display boards in the main hall – when your ticket number appears (flashing), go to the desk number shown. Most of the city's other post offices open from 8am to 6pm or 7pm Monday to Friday and until noon Saturday.

The Czech postal service (Česká Pošta) is fairly efficient. Anything you can't afford to lose, however, should go by registered mail *(doporučený dopis)* or by EMS. A postcard or letter up to 20g costs 17Kč to other European countries and 18Kč for destinations outside Europe. A 2kg parcel by EMS costs 900Kč to Europe, 1200Kč to North America and 1600Kč to Australia. You can buy stamps from street vendors and newspaper kiosks as well as from post offices.

You can pick up poste-restante mail *(výdej listovních zásilek)* at desk Nos 1 and 2 (at the far left) in the main post office from 7am to 8pm Monday to Friday and until noon Saturday. Mail should be addressed to Poste Restante, Hlavní pošta, Jindřišská 14, 110 00 Praha 1, Czech Republic. You must present your passport to claim mail (check under your first name, too). Mail is held for one month.

If you need a professional courier service, DHL (Map p110; ☎ 800 103 000; www.dhl.cz; Václavské

náměstí, 47, Nové Město; ⊗ 8am-6.30pm Mon-Fri, 9am-3pm Sat) has a convenient office just off Wenceslas Square, with English-speaking staff.

RADIO

Radio Prague (www.radio.cz; 92.6MHz FM) broadcasts 15-minute-long programs in English covering Czech news, culture and current affairs at 7.07pm Monday to Thursday. The city's best alternative music station is Radio 1 (91.9MHz FM), though commercial-free Radio Wave (100.7MHz FM) gives it a good run for its money.

The BBC World Service (www.bbc.co.uk/world service) broadcasts both English-language and Czech news and cultural programs locally on 101.1MHz FM, from 11am to 1pm and 4pm to 8am.

SAFETY

Although Prague is as safe as any European capital, the huge influx of money to the city has spawned an epidemic of petty crime. Where tourists are concerned, this mainly means pickpockets. The prime trouble spots are Prague Castle (especially at the changing of the guard), Charles Bridge, Old Town Square (in the crowd watching the Astronomical Clock), the entrance to the Old Jewish Cemetery, Wenceslas Square, the main train station, in the metro (watch your backpack on escalators) and on trams (notably on the crowded lines 9 and 22).

There's no need to be paranoid, but keep valuables well out of reach, and be alert in crowds and on public transport. A classic ruse involves someone asking directions and thrusting a map under your nose, or a woman with a baby hassling you for money – anything to distract your attention – while accomplices delve into your bags and pockets.

Lost or Stolen Belongings

If your passport, wallet or other valuables have been stolen, report the loss to any police station within 24 hours. The easiest place is the Praha 1 police station (Map p110; Jungmannovo náměstí 9; ⊗ 24hr), near the foot of Wenceslas Square. Tell them what language you speak, and they'll give you a standard crime report form *(Policejní zpráva)* to fill out, which they will stamp and return (this is for insurance purposes only; the crime will almost certainly not be investigated). Unless you speak Czech, forget about phoning the police, as you will rarely get through to an English speaker. Once you have a crime report, you can apply to the consular department of your embassy for a replacement passport.

Do likewise if you have lost your wallet or other valuables. For anything except travel documents, you might get lucky at the city's lost & found office (ztráty a nálezy; Map p90; ☎ 224 235 085; Karoliny Světlé 5; ☷ 8am-noon & 12.30-5.30pm Mon & Wed, to 4pm Tue & Thu, to 2pm Fri; ◉ 6, 9, 18, 22, 23). There's another lost & found office (☎ 220 114 283; ☷ 24hr) at the airport.

Racism

You may be surprised at the level of casual prejudice directed against the Roma, whom people are quick to blame for the city's problems. Overt hostility towards tourists is rare, though dark-skinned visitors are occasionally on the receiving end of racist comments.

Scams

Beware of men who claim to be plain-clothes police officers investigating counterfeiting or illegal moneychanging. They approach tourists and ask to see their money, which is returned after being examined. When you check your wallet you'll find that a substantial amount of money has been taken. No genuine police officer has the right to inspect your money.

Another ploy involves a 'lost tourist' asking for directions (usually in halting English). Once you have been in conversation for a few minutes, two of the tourist's 'friends' interrupt, claiming to be plain-clothes policemen and accusing you of changing money illegally. They will demand to see your wallet and passport, but if you hand them over they are likely to run off with them.

TELEPHONE

Most Czech phone numbers have nine digits – you have to dial all nine for any call, local or long distance (there are no area codes). All land-line numbers in Prague begin with a 2; mobile numbers begin with a 6 or 7. Exceptions include emergency numbers, some taxi companies and information lines, some of which have fewer than nine digits. See the inside front cover for useful phone numbers and codes.

There are payphones all over town that can be used to make local, long-distance and international calls. Coin-operated phones accept only 2Kč, 5Kč, 10Kč and 20Kč coins; a more common and convenient alternative is a prepaid calling card, which allows you to make domestic and international calls from any phone or payphone in the Czech Republic.

You can also make international calls from the telephone bureau at the main post office (to the left inside the right-hand entrance) – you simply pay a deposit and make your call in a soundproof booth, where a little meter ticks off the rate.

The telephone bureau has directories for Prague and other major cities. You can also look up business phone numbers online at www.zlatestranky.cz.

Mobile Phones

The Czech Republic uses GSM 900 (now 3G compatible), which is the same as the rest of Europe, Australia and New Zealand but is not compatible with the North American GSM 1900 or the different system in Japan. Some North Americans, however, have dual-band GSM 1900/900 phones that do work here; check with your service provider about using your mobile abroad, and beware of calls being routed internationally (which is very expensive for a 'local' call). The main mobile networks in Prague are Telefonica/O2 (www.cz.o2.com), T-Mobile (www.t-mobile.cz) and Vodafone (www.vodafone.cz).

For iPhone and other smartphone users, Telefonica/O2 operates the largest and most reliable 3G network, though the main competitors are working hard to match it.

If your mobile phone is unlocked, you can buy a Czech SIM card from any mobile-phone shop for around 450Kč (including 300Kč of calling credit) and make local calls at local rates (3Kč to 9Kč a minute). In this case, of course, you can't use your existing mobile number.

Phonecards

Local prepaid cards include Smartcall (www.smartcall.cz) and Karta X Plus – you can buy them from hotels, newspaper kiosks and tourist information offices for 300Kč to 1000Kč. To use one, follow the instructions on the card – dial the access number, then the PIN code beneath the scratch-away panel, then the number you want to call (including any international code). Rates from Prague to the UK, USA and Australia with Smartcall are around 6.6Kč to 10Kč a minute; the more expensive the card, the better the rate.

TIME

The Czech Republic is on Central European Time, ie GMT/UTC plus one hour. Clocks are set to daylight-saving time in summer, that is, forward one hour on the last weekend in March and back one hour on the last weekend in October. Czechs use the 24-hour clock.

TOILETS

Public toilets are free in state-run museums, galleries and concert halls. Elsewhere, such as in train, bus and metro stations, public toilets are staffed by attendants who charge 5Kč to 10Kč for admission. Most places are clean and well kept. Men's are marked *muži* or *páni*, and women's *ženy* or *dámy*.

In the main tourist areas, there are public toilets in Prague Castle; opposite the tram stop on Malostranské náměstí; next to the Goltz-Kinský Palace on Old Town Square; on Templova, just off Celetná close to the Powder Gate; on Uhelný trh in the Old Town; and next to the Laterna Magika on Národní třída.

TOURIST INFORMATION

The Prague information service (Pražská informační služba, PIS; ☎ 221 714 444, in English & German; www.prague-info .cz) is the main provider of tourist information: it has good maps and detailed brochures (including accommodation options and historical monuments), all free. PIS also sells public transport tickets.

There are four PIS offices:

Malá Strana Bridge Tower (Map p78; Charles Bridge; ☽ 10am-6pm Apr-Oct)

Old Town Hall (Map p90; Staroměstské náměstí 5, Staré Město; ☽ 9am-7pm Apr-Oct, 9am-6pm Nov-Mar)

Prague main train station (Praha hlavní nádraží; Map p110; Wilsonova 2, Nové Město; ☽ 9am-7pm Mon-Fri, 9am-4pm Sat & Sun Apr-Oct, 9am-6pm Mon-Fri, 9am-4pm Sat & Sun Nov-Mar)

Rytířská (Map p90; Rytířská 31, Staré Město; ☽ 9am-7pm Apr-Oct, 9am-6pm Nov-Mar)

Overseas Offices

Czech Tourism (www.czechtourism.com) offices around the world provide information about tourism, culture and business in the Czech Republic.

Austria (☎ 01-533 21933; Herrengasse 17, 1010 Vienna)

France (☎ 01 53 73 00 22; rue Bonaparte 18, 75006 Paris)

Germany (☎ 030-204 4770; Wilhelmstrasse 44, 10117 Berlin-Mitte)

Netherlands (☎ 020-575 3015; Strawinskylaan 517, 1077 XX Amsterdam)

Poland (☎ 022-629 2916; Al Róż 16, 00-556 Warsaw)

UK (☎ 020-7631 0427, brochure requests 09063-640641; 13 Harley St, London W1G 9QG)

USA (☎ 212-288 0830; 1109 Madison Ave, New York, NY 10028)

TRAVELLERS WITH DISABILITIES

Increasing, but still limited, attention is being paid to facilities for people with disabilities in Prague. Wheelchair ramps are becoming more common, especially at major street intersections, in newer shopping malls and in top-end hotels (in the Sleeping chapter we identify hotels with facilities for wheelchair users). For people who are blind or vision-impaired, most pedestrian crossings in central Prague have a sound signal to indicate when it's safe to cross. McDonald's and KFC entrances and toilets are wheelchair-friendly.

Much of Prague Castle is wheelchair-accessible, but the cobbled streets, narrow pavements and steep hills of the surrounding Hradčany and Malá Strana districts are not. The Estates Theatre (p204) is equipped for the hearing-impaired, while the Convent of St Agnes (p97) has a ground-floor presentation of medieval sculptures with explanatory text in Braille; these venues and several other theatres are wheelchair-accessible. The monthly what's-on booklet *Přehled* – which is published by PIS in Czech only – indicates venues with wheelchair access. We also note lifts and other accessibility factors in individual listings.

Few buses and no trams have wheelchair access; special wheelchair-accessible buses operate Monday to Friday on bus lines 1 and 3, including between Florenc bus station and náměstí Republiky, and between Holešovice train station and náměstí Republiky (visit the website at www.dpp.cz for more information).

Prague's main train station (Praha hlavní nádraží), Praha-Holešovice train station and a handful of metro stations (Hlavní Nádraží, Hůrka, Luka, Lužiny, Nádraží Holešovice, Stodůlky and Zličín) have self-operating lifts. Other metro stations (Chodov, Dejvická, Florenc C line, Háje, IP Pavlova, Opatov, Pankrác, Roztyly and Skalka) have modified lifts that can be used with the help of station staff. Czech Railways (ČD) claims that every large station in the country has wheelchair ramps and lifts, but in fact the service is poor.

Most international airports (including Prague's) have ramps, lifts and wheelchair-accessible toilets and telephones. Aircraft toilets, on the other hand, present problems for wheelchair users, who should discuss this early on with the airline and/or their doctor.

Some useful organisations include the following:

Czech Blind United (Sjednocená organizace nevidomých a slabozrakých v ČR; Map p110; ☎ 221 462 146; www .braillnet.cz; Krakovská 21, Nové Město) Represents the vision-impaired; provides information but no services.

Prague Wheelchair Users Organisation (Pražská organizace vozíčkářů; Map p90; ☎ 224 827 210; www.pov.cz, in Czech; Benediktská 6, Staré Město) Can organise a guide and transportation at about half the cost of a taxi, and has a CD-ROM guide to barrier-free Prague in Czech, English and German.

VISAS

Everyone is required to have a valid passport (or ID card for EU citizens) to enter the Czech Republic. Citizens of EU and EEA (Europe Economic Area) countries do not need a visa for any type of visit. Citizens of Australia, Canada, Israel, Japan, New Zealand and the USA can stay for up to 90 days without a visa; other nationalities can check their visa requirements on www.mzv.cz (click on Information for Aliens). Visas are not available at border crossings or at Prague Airport; you'll be refused entry if you need one and arrive without one.

Non-EU citizens who want to stay in the Czech Republic for more than 90 days must apply for a long-term visa, employment visa or residency permit; get details from your nearest Czech embassy, and apply at least four months in advance.

The Czech Republic is part of the Schengen Zone (a group of countries that allows passport-free travel within the zone's boundaries); visitors who need a visa can apply for a Schengen Visa, which will allow them to visit other countries in the zone (see http:// ec.europa.eu/youreurope for details – click on Citizens, then Travelling in Europe; or http:// en.wikipedia.org/wiki/Schengen_Area for a clearer, less bureaucratic explanation).

Visa regulations change from time to time, so check with the Ministry of Foreign Affairs (www.mzv.cz).

WOMEN TRAVELLERS

Walking alone on the street is as safe – or as dangerous – as in most large European cities. Avoid the park in front of Prague's main train station after dark, and be aware that the area around the intersection of Wenceslas Square and Na Příkopě is effectively a red-light district at night. The city has developed a burgeoning sex industry, with strip clubs, lap-dancing clubs, brothels and street workers all in evidence, and British stag parties stumbling drunkenly through the streets around Wenceslas Square at weekends.

There are few services for women such as help-lines and refuge or rape crisis centres. The main organisation in Prague is the White Circle of Safety (Bílý kruh bezpečí; Map p143; ☎ 257 317 110; www .bkb.cz; U Trojice 2, Smíchov), which provides help and counselling to victims of crime and violence.

WORK

The unemployment rate in the Czech Republic rose to 10% in early 2010 (the official rate in Prague was around 4%, though probably a bit higher in reality) – and although there are job opportunities for foreigners in English-teaching, IT, finance, real-estate and management firms, competition for jobs is fierce and finding one is increasingly difficult.

EU citizens do not need a work permit to work in the Czech Republic; non-EU citizens do, however. You might be able to find short- or long-term employment teaching English (or other languages) at the numerous language schools in Prague. Alternatively, you might look for jobs with the city's many expat-run restaurants, hostels and bars. Possibilities also exist in foreign-owned businesses. Investment banking, real estate, IT and management firms in particular need experienced staff and often employ non-Czech speakers, but the odds of getting such a job are better if you apply from home rather than waiting until you are in Prague.

You can research the employment market on websites such as www.jobs.cz, www.expats .cz and www.prague.tv and look for jobs in the classified-ad section of the *Prague Post* (www .praguepost.com).

Business Contacts

Czech Chamber of Commerce (Map p58; ☎ 296 646 112; www.komoracz.eu; Freyova 27, Vysočany, 190 00 Prague)

Prague Convention Bureau (☎ 224 235 159; www.prague convention.cz; Rytířská 26, Staré Město, 110 00 Prague)

LANGUAGE

Czech *(Čeština)* is the main language spoken in the Czech Republic. It belongs to the western branch of the Slavic family of Indo-European languages, pushed westward with the Slavic people by the onslaught of the Huns, Avars, Bulgars and Magyars in the 5th and 6th centuries. Czech is also related to Polish, though not as closely as to Slovak – adults in Slovakia and the Czech Republic can generally understand one another, although younger people who have not been exposed to much of the other language may have difficulty in communication.

At tourist-frequented establishments in Prague you should be able to get by with English, but learning even a few basic Czech phrases will enrich your travel experience. You'll also find that locals greatly appreciate travellers trying their language.

If you want to learn more Czech than we've included here, pick up a copy of Lonely Planet's comprehensive and user-friendly *Czech* phrasebook. Czech is also covered in Lonely Planet's *Eastern Europe* phrasebook.

PRONUNCIATION

Many English speakers might flinch when they see written Czech – especially words that have seemingly unpronounceable clusters of consonants. However, with a little practice you'll be speaking Czech words in no time. Unlike English, each Czech letter is always pronounced the same way, so once you're familiar with the Czech alphabet you'll be able to read. Stress is usually on the first syllable of a word.

Vowels

Vowels have long and short variants; they have the same pronunciation, but the long vowels are simply held for longer. The long vowels are indicated by an acute accent (′) above the letter. Czech also has a number of vowel sound combinations (diphthongs).

The following pronunciation examples reflect standard British pronunciation:

a	as the 'u' in 'cut'
á	as the 'a' in 'father'
e	as in 'bet'
é	as the word 'air'
ě	as the 'ye' in 'yet'
i/y	as the 'i' in 'bit'
í/ý	as the 'i' in 'marine'
o	as in 'pot'
ó	as the 'aw' in 'saw'
u	as in 'pull'
ú/ů	as the 'oo' in 'zoo'

VOWEL COMBINATIONS

aj	as the 'i' in 'ice'
áj	as the word 'eye'
au	as the 'ow' in 'how'
ej	as the 'ay' in 'day'
ij/yj	short; as 'iy'
íj/ýj	longer version of ij/yj
oj	as the 'oi' in 'void'
ou	as the 'o' in 'note', though each vowel is more strongly pronounced than in English
uj	as the 'u' in 'pull', followed by the 'y' in 'year'
ůj	longer version of uj

Consonants

c	as the 'ts' in 'lets'
č	as the 'ch' in 'chew'
ch	like 'ch' in Scottish *loch*
j	as the 'y' in 'year'
r	a rolled 'r' (at the tip of the tongue)
ř	no English equivalent; a rolled 'rzh' sound, as in the composer, Dvořák
š	as the 'sh' in 'ship'
ž	a 'zh' sound, as the 's' in 'treasure'
ď, ľ, ť	combined with (′), these are soft d, l and t consonant sounds, pronounced as if followed by 'y' (like the 'ny' in canyon). The same applies to d, n and t when followed by i, í or ě.

All other consonants are similar to their English counterparts, although the letters k, p and t are unaspirated, meaning they are pronounced with no audible puff of breath after them.

SOCIAL
Greetings & Civilities
Hello./Good day.
Dobrý den. (polite)
Ahoj. (informal)
Goodbye.
Na shledanou. (polite)
Ahoj./Čau. (informal)
Yes.
Ano./Jo. (polite/informal)
No.
Ne.
May I? (asking permission)
Dovolte mi?
Sorry./Excuse me. (apologising or seeking assistance)
Promiľte.
Could you help me, please?
Prosím, můžete mi pomoci?
Please.
Prosím.
Thank you (very much).
(Mockrát) děkuji.
You're welcome. (as in 'don't mention it')
Není zač.
Good morning.
Dobré jitro/ráno.
Good afternoon.
Dobré odpoledne.
Good evening.
Dobrý večer.
How are you?
Jak se máte?
Well, thanks.
Děkuji, dobře.

Going Out
What's there to do in the evenings?
Kam se tady dá večer jít?
What's on tonight?
Kde se večer můžeme pobavit?
Is there a local entertainment guide?
Existuje přehled kulturních programů?

I feel like going to a/an/the ...
Mám chuť jít ...

bar	do baru
cafe	do kavárny
cinema	do kina
nightclub	do noční podnik
opera	na operu
restaurant	do restaurace
theatre	do divadla

Are there any good nightclubs?
Jsou tady nějaké dobré noční podniky?

Language Difficulties
Do you speak English?
Mluvíte anglicky?
I understand.
Rozumím.
I don't understand.
Nerozumím.
Could you write it down, please?
Můžete mi to napsat, prosím?

PRACTICAL
Directions

Do you have a local map?	Máte mapu okolí?
Where is ...?	Kde je ...?
Go straight ahead.	Jděte přímo.
Turn left.	Zatočte vlevo.
Turn right.	Zatočte vpravo.
behind	za
in front of	před
far	daleko
near	blízko
opposite	naproti

Numbers
It's quite common for Czechs to say the numbers 21 to 99 in reverse; for example, *dvacet jedna* (21) becomes *jedna dvacet*.

0	nula
1	jedna
2	dva
3	tři
4	čtyři
5	pět
6	šest
7	sedm
8	osm
9	devět
10	deset
11	jedenáct
12	dvanáct
13	třináct
14	čtrnáct
15	patnáct
16	šestnáct
17	sedmnáct
18	osmnáct
19	devatenáct
20	dvacet
21	dvacet jedna
22	dvacet dva
23	dvacet tři
30	třicet

40	čtyřicet
50	padesát
60	šedesát
70	sedmdesát
80	osmdesát
90	devadesát
100	sto
1000	tisíc

Banking
Where's a/the ...?
Kde je ...?

ATM	bankomat
bank	banka
exchange office	směnárna

I want to change (a) ...
Chtěl/Chtěla bych vyměnit ... (m/f)

cash/money	peníze
(travellers)	(cestovní)
cheque	šek

What time does the bank open?
V kolik hodin otevírá banka?

Post Office
Where's a/the post office?
Kde je pošta?

I want to buy ...
Rád/Ráda bych koupil/a ... (m/f)

postcards	pohlednice
stamps	známky

I want to send a ...
Chtěl/Chtěla bych poslat ... (m/f)

letter	dopis
parcel	balík
postcard	pohled

Phones & Mobiles
Where's the nearest public phone?
Kde je nejbližší veřejný telefon?
Could I please use the telephone?
Mohu si zatelefonovat?
I want to call ...
Chci zavolat ...
I want to make a long-distance call to ...
Chtěl/Chtěla bych volat do ... (m/f)
I want to make a reverse-charge/collect call.
Chtěl/Chtěla bych zavolat na účet
  volaného. (m/f)
I want to buy a phonecard.
Chtěl/Chtěla bych koupit telefonní
  karta. (m/f)

Internet
Is there a local internet cafe?
Je tady internet kavárna? (m/f)
I'd like to get internet access.
Chtěl/Chtěla bych se připojit na
  internet. (m/f)
I'd like to check my email.
Chtěl/Chtěla bych si skontrolovat můj
  email. (m/f)

Paperwork
name	jméno
address	adresa
date/place of birth	datum/místo narození
age	věk
sex	pohlaví
nationality	národnost
passport number	číslo pasu
visa	vizum
driving licence	řidičský průkaz

Question Words
Who?	Kdo?
What?	Co?
When?	Kdy?
Where?	Kde?
How?	Jak?

Shopping & Services
Where's (a/the) ...?
Kde je ...?
I'm looking for (a/the) ...
Hledám ...

art gallery	uměleckou galérii
city centre	centrum
embassy	velvyslanectví
main square	hlavní náměstí
market	tržiště
museum	muzeum
public toilet	veřejné záchody
tourist office	turistická informační kancelář

What time does it open?/close?
V kolik hodin otevírají?/zavírají?

Signs
Kouření Zakázáno	No Smoking
Otevřeno	Open
Umývárny/Toalety	Toilets
Páni/Muži	Men
Dámy/Ženy	Women

Vchod	Entrance
Vstup Zakázán	No Entry
Východ	Exit
Zákaz	Prohibited
Zavřeno	Closed

Time & Dates

What time is it?	Kolik je hodin?
in the morning	ráno
in the afternoon	odpoledne
in the evening	večer
today	dnes
now	teď
yesterday	včera
tomorrow	zítra
next week	příští týden
Monday	pondělí
Tuesday	úterý
Wednesday	steda
Thursday	čtvrtek
Friday	pátek
Saturday	sobota
Sunday	neděle
January	leden
February	únor
March	březen
April	duben
May	květen
June	červen
July	červenec
August	srpen
September	září
October	říjen
November	listopad
December	prosinec

Dates in Museums

year	rok
century	století
millennia	milénium/tisíciletí
beginning of ...	začátek ...
first half of ...	první polovina ...
middle of ...	polovina ...
second half of ...	druhá polovina ...
end of ...	konec ...

Transport

What time does the train/bus leave?
V kolik hodin odjíždí vlak/autobus?
What time does the train/bus arrive?
V kolik hodin přijíždí vlak/autobus?
Excuse me, where is the ticket office?
Prosím, kde je pokladna?

I want to go to ...
Chci jet do ...

I'd like ...
Rád/a bych ... (m/f)

a one-way ticket	jednosměrnou jízdenku
a return ticket	zpáteční jízdenku
two tickets	dvě jízdenky

FOOD & DRINK

For more information on food and dining out, see p159.

Vegetarians should note that *Bezmasá jídla* ('meatless dishes') are advertised on many traditional Czech menus, but some of these may be cooked in animal fat or even contain pieces of ham or bacon. If you ask, most chefs can whip up something genuinely vegetarian.

Can you recommend a ...?
Můžete doporučit ...?

cafe	kavárnu
pub	hospodu
restaurant	restauraci

I'd like ..., please.
Chtěl/Chtěla bych ..., prosím. (m/f)
a table for (five)
stůl pro (pět)
the nonsmoking section
nekuřáckou místnost
the smoking section
kuřáckou místnost

Is service included in the bill?
Je to včetně obsluhy?
What's the local speciality?
Co je místní specialita?
What would you recommend?
Co byste doporučil/doporučila? (m/f)
Cheers!
Na zdraví!

I'd like (the) ..., please.
Chtěl/Chtěla bych ..., prosím. (m/f)

bill	účet
drink list	nápojový lístek
menu	jídelní lístek
that dish	ten pokrm

I'm a vegetarian.
Jsem vegetarián/vegetariánka. (m/f)
I don't eat meat/pork/fish/poultry.
Nejím maso/vepřové/ryby/drůbež.

Could you prepare a meal without …?
Mohl/Mohla by jste připravit jídlo
   bez …? (m/f)

I'm allergic to …
Mám alergii na …
  dairy produce   mléčné výrobky
  gluten   lepek
  nuts   ořechy
  seafood   plody moře

snack   občerstvení
breakfast   snídaně
lunch   oběd
dinner   večeře

Common Dishes

bramborový salát – potato salad;
mayonnaise based, with yoghurt, diced
potatoes, carrots, peas, dill pickles, onions
and corn
chlebíčky – open sandwiches on French
bread, with cold meat, eggs, cheese, or
mayonnaise salads like lobster, fish, potato
or ham and peas
ďábelská topinka – a piquant toast with
meat and cheese
guláš – thick, spicy stew, usually made
with beef and potatoes, sometimes with
venison or mushrooms
hranolky – French fries (hot chips)
krokety – deep-fried mashed potato balls;
croquettes
kuře na paprice – chicken boiled in spicy
paprika cream sauce
míchaná vejce s klobásou – scrambled
eggs with sausage
opékané brambory – roasted potatoes
párek v rohlíku – hot dog
Pražská šunka – Prague ham; ham pickled
in brine and spices and smoked over a
beechwood fire
ruská vejce – hard-boiled egg, potato and
salami, with mayonnaise
salát – salad
sendvič – sandwich
smažené žampiony – fried mushrooms
smažený květák – fried cauliflower in
breadcrumbs
smažený sýr – fried cheese in
breadcrumbs
smažený vepřový řízek – fried pork
schnitzel
šopský salát – lettuce, tomato, onion and
cheese salad
vejce se slaninou – bacon and eggs

Food Glossary

ananas   pineapple
arašídy   peanuts
banán   banana
brambor   potato
brokolice   broccoli
česnek   garlic
chléb   bread
cibule   onion
citrón   lemon
čokoláda   chocolate
cuketa   zucchini (courgette)
cukr   sugar
dort   cake
dýně   pumpkin
fazole   bean
hlávkový   lettuce
hořčice   mustard
houba   mushroom
hovězí   beef
hrášek   peas
hruška   pear
jablko   apple
jahoda   strawberry
jehněčí   lamb
jogurt   yoghurt
kapusta   cabbage
kari   curry
knedlíky   dumplings
krůta   turkey
kukuřice   corn
kuře   chicken
květák   cauliflower
kyselá smetana   sour cream
lilek   eggplant (aubergine)
losos   salmon
majonéza   mayonnaise
malina   raspberry
mandle   almond
máslo   butter
maso   meat
med   honey
mrkev   carrot
ocet   vinegar
okurka   cucumber or dill
   pickle
olej   oil
omáčka   sauce
omeleta   omelette
ořechy   nuts
ovoce   fruit
palačinka   crêpe (pancake)
paprika   capsicum (bell
   pepper)
pečivo   bread rolls
pepř   black pepper

plody moře	seafood
polévka	soup
pomeranč	orange
pstruh	trout
rajče	tomato
rozinky	raisins (sultanas)
ryba	fish
rýže	rice
salám	salami
skopové	mutton
slanina	bacon
sleď	herring
šlehačka	whipped cream
smetana	cream
sójová omáčka	soy sauce
sójové mléko	soy milk
sójový tvaroh	tofu
špenát	spinach
sůl	salt
šunka	ham
svíčková	sirloin
sýr	cheese
tatarská omáčka	tartar sauce
telecí	veal
těstovina	pasta
tuňák	tuna
tvaroh	cottage cheese
ústřice	oyster
vanilka	vanilla
vejce	eggs
vepřové	pork
zelenina	vegetables
zelí	cabbage, sauerkraut
zmrzlina	ice cream

Methods of Preparation

čerstvý	fresh
fritovaný	deep-fried
grilovaný	broiled
horký	hot
krvavý	rare (of meat)
míchaný	mixed
na roštu	grilled
pečený	roasted
propečený	well-done (of meat)
se sýrem	with cheese
sladký	sweet
smažený	fried
středně propečený	medium rare (of meat)
studený	cold
teplý	warm
uzený	smoked
vařený	boiled
zmrzlí	frozen

Drinks

čaj	tea
káva	coffee
limonáda	lemonade
mléko	milk
nealkoholický nápoj	soft drink
neperlivá voda	still water
odstředěné mléko	skim milk
perlivá minerálka	carbonated mineral water
pivo	beer
pomerančový džus	orange juice
slivovice	plum brandy
víno	wine
voda	water
bez kofeinu	decaffeinated
bez ledu	without ice
s citrónem	with lemon
s ledem	with ice
s mlékem	with milk
se smetanou	with cream

EMERGENCIES

Help!
Pomoc!
It's an emergency!
To je naléhavý případ!
Could you please help me?
Prosím, můžete mi pomoci?
Call an ambulance!/a doctor!/the police!
Zavolejte sanitku!/doktora!/policii!
Where's the police station?
Kde je policejní stanice?

HEALTH

Where's the …?
Kde je …?

chemist/ pharmacy	lékárna
dentist	zubař
doctor	doktor
hospital	nemocnice

I need a doctor who speaks English.
Potřebuji lékaře, který mluví anglicky.
I'm sick.
Jsem nemocný/nemocná. (m/f)
I have a headache.
Bolí mě hlava.

I have (a) …
Mám …

diarrhoea	průjem
fever	horečku

GLOSSARY

You may encounter these terms and abbreviations while in Prague.

autobus – bus

bankomat(y) – ATM(s)

čajovná – teahouse
ČD – Czech Railways, the state railway company
Čedok – the former state tour operator and travel agency, now privatised
chrám – cathedral
ČSA – Czech Airlines, the national carrier
ČSSD – Social Democratic Party
cukrárna – cake shop

divadlo – theatre
doklad – receipt or document
dům – house or building

galérie – gallery, arcade

hlavní nádraží (hl nád) – main train station
hora – hill, mountain
hospoda – pub
hostinec – pub
hrad – castle
hřbitov – cemetery

jízdenka – ticket

kaple – chapel
katedralá – cathedral
kavárna – café or coffee shop
Kč (Koruna česká) – Czech crown
kino – cinema
kostel – church
koupelna – bathroom
KSČM – Czech Communist Party

lékárna – pharmacy

město – town
most – bridge
muzeum – museum

nábřeží (nábř) – embankment
nádraží – station
náměstí (nám) – square
národní – national

ODS – Civic Democratic Party
ostrov – island

palác – palace
pasáž – passage, shopping arcade
pekárna – bakery
penzión – pension
pivnice – small beer hall
pivo – beer
pivovar – brewery
potraviny – grocery or food shop
Praha – Prague
přestup – transfer or connection

restaurace – restaurant
sad(y) – garden(s), park(s), orchard(s)
sleva – discount
stanice – train stop or station
sv (svatý) – Saint

třída (tř) – avenue
ulice (ul) – street
ulička (ul) – lane

Velvet Divorce – separation of Czechoslovakia into fully independent Czech and Slovak republics in 1993
Velvet Revolution (Sametová revoluce) – bloodless overthrow of Czechoslovakia's communist regime in 1989
věž – tower
vinárna – wine bar/restaurant
vlak – train
výdej listovních zásilek – poste restante mail

zahrada – gardens, park
zámek – chateau
zastávka – bus, tram or train stop

BEHIND THE SCENES

THIS BOOK

This 9th edition of *Prague* was researched and written by Neil Wilson and Mark Baker. Mark and Neil both worked on the 8th edition and Neil also wrote the 5th, 6th and 7th editions, and contributed to the 4th edition. This guidebook was commissioned in Lonely Planet's London office, and produced by the following:

Commissioning Editors Joe Bindloss, Jo Potts

Coordinating Editors Anna Metcalfe, Gina Tsarouhas

Coordinating Cartographer Peter Shields

Coordinating Layout Designer Paul Iacono

Managing Editors Imogen Bannister, Bruce Evans, Annelies Mertens

Managing Cartographers David Connolly, Owen Eszeki, Corey Hutchison, Herman So

Managing Layout Designer Indra Kilfoyle

Assisting Editor Kim Hutchins

Assisting Cartographers Andras Bogdanovits, Csanad Csutoros

Cover Research Naomi Parker, lonelyplanetimages.com

Internal Image Research Aude Vauconsant, lonelyplanetimages.com

Indexer Susan Paterson

Language Content Laura Crawford

Thanks to Lisa Knights, Trent Paton, Kalya Ryan

Cover photographs (top) Charles Bridge, Prague, Czech Republic, Walter Bibikow; (bottom) building detail, Old Town, Prague, Czech Republic, Jon Arnold Images.

Internal photographs All images are copyright of the photographer unless otherwise indicated. Many of the images in this guide are available for licensing from Lonely Planet Images: www.lonelyplanetimages.com.

THANKS
NEIL WILSON

A big thank you to all the bartenders, bookshop owners, baristas and bellhops who helped out with my endless questions about the best places to eat, drink etc. Thanks also to the people along Navrátilova who didn't complain on the nights when I stumbled over the dustbins on the way back to my apartment after a long evening of research… And finally *děkuji mockrát* to Jo Potts at Lonely Planet for inviting me on board yet again, and to coauthor Mark for his good company and sense of humour, and for pointing me towards Kout na Šumavě.

MARK BAKER

I would like to thank my three 'local voices': beer aficionado Max Bahnson, Velvet Revolutionary Anna Siskova and dining critic 'Brewsta'. Lonely Planet commissioning editor Jo Potts gets a big thank you for hiring me in the first place and for being a cheerful, authoritative presence in the background. Finally, I'd like to thank my coauthor Neil for his steady

THE LONELY PLANET STORY

Fresh from an epic journey across Europe, Asia and Australia in 1972, Tony and Maureen Wheeler sat at their kitchen table stapling together notes. The first Lonely Planet guidebook, *Across Asia on the Cheap*, was born.

Travellers snapped up the guides. Inspired by their success, the Wheelers began publishing books to Southeast Asia, India and beyond. Demand was prodigious, and the Wheelers expanded the business rapidly to keep up. Over the years, Lonely Planet extended its coverage to every country and into the virtual world via lonelyplanet.com and the Thorn Tree message board.

As Lonely Planet became a globally loved brand, Tony and Maureen received several offers for the company. But it wasn't until 2007 that they found a partner whom they trusted to remain true to the company's principles of travelling widely, treading lightly and giving sustainably. In October of that year, BBC Worldwide acquired a 75% share in the company, pledging to uphold Lonely Planet's commitment to independent travel, trustworthy advice and editorial independence.

Today, Lonely Planet has offices in Melbourne, London and Oakland, with over 500 staff members and 300 authors. Tony and Maureen are still actively involved with Lonely Planet. They're travelling more often than ever, and they're devoting their spare time to charitable projects. And the company is still driven by the philosophy of *Across Asia on the Cheap*: 'All you've got to do is decide to go and the hardest part is over. So go!'

BEHIND THE SCENES

hand in guiding this edition, his appreciation of Prague's quirkier elements and, naturally, his dogged pursuit of the perfect *pivo*.

OUR READERS

Many thanks to the travellers who used the last edition and wrote to us with helpful hints, useful advice and interesting anecdotes:

Kate Ahmad, Ville Alho, Rupert Allen, Sheila Armstrong, Jan-Benjamin Benej, L Carroll, Paul Croft, Peter Daly, Finette Devrell, Nick Dillen, Bruce Dodson, Sanvila Domic, Dave Dutta, Bradford Elder, Martin Fojtek, Mario Freitas, Suzanne Gardent, Jon Giullian, Christina Gousetis, Michaela Jiroutova, Lucy Johnston, Paul Kail, Jana Kleinova, Roos Korevaar, Marek Kubej, Jesse Ligo, Kim Lockwood, John Lovejoy, Emma Månsson, Chris Mills, Deborah O'Bray, Melissa O'Brien, Jessica Olschowka, Alison O'Neill, Lisa Rehman, Adele Reilly, Keith Resnick, Carolyn Robinson, Judith Schulman, Marsha Stewart, Jan Stojaspal, Lisa Street, David Talacko, Franciska Tillema, Manuele Zunelli, Gabriel Zuri, Jane Zwisohn.

Notes

INDEX

INDEX

MAP LEGEND
ROUTES

Tollway	Mall/Steps
Freeway	Tunnel
Primary	Pedestrian Overpass
Secondary	Walking Tour
Tertiary	Walking Tour Detour
Lane	Walking Trail
Under Construction	Walking Path
One-Way Street	Track

TRANSPORT

Ferry	Rail
Metro	Rail (Underground)
Bus Route	Tram
	Cable Car, Funicular

HYDROGRAPHY

River, Creek	Canal
Swamp	Water

BOUNDARIES

International	Regional, Suburb
State, Provincial	Ancient Wall
Disputed	Cliff

AREA FEATURES

Airport	Land
Area of Interest	Mall
Building	Market
Campus	Park
Cemetery, Christian	Reservation
Cemetery, Other	Sports
Forest	Urban

POPULATION

◎ CAPITAL (NATIONAL)	◉ CAPITAL (STATE)
● Large City	◉ Medium City
● Small City	● Town, Village

SYMBOLS

Information
- 🏦 Bank, ATM
- Embassy/Consulate
- Hospital, Medical
- Information
- Internet Facilities
- Police Station
- Post Office, GPO
- Telephone
- Toilets

Sights
- Castle, Fortress
- Christian
- Islamic
- Jewish
- Monument
- Museum, Gallery
- Point of Interest
- Ruin
- Winery, Vineyard
- Zoo, Bird Sanctuary

Shopping
- Shopping

Eating
- Eating

Entertainment
- Entertainment

Drinking
- Drinking
- Cafe

Arts
- Arts

Sports & Activities
- Pool

Sleeping
- Sleeping
- Camping

Transport
- Airport, Airfield
- Border Crossing
- Bus Station
- Cycling, Bicycle Path
- General Transport
- Parking Area
- Petrol Station
- Taxi Rank

Geographic
- Hazard
- Lighthouse
- Lookout
- Mountain, Volcano
- National Park
- River Flow
- Shelter, Hut
- Waterfall

Published by Lonely Planet Publications Pty Ltd
ABN 36 005 607 983

Australia (Head Office)
Locked Bag 1, Footscray, Victoria 3011,
☎03 8379 8000, fax 03 8379 8111

USA 150 Linden St, Oakland, CA 94607,
☎510 250 6400, toll free 800 275 8555,
fax 510 893 8572

UK 2nd fl, 186 City Rd, London, EC1V 2NT,
☎020 7106 2100, fax 020 7106 2101

Contact talk2us@lonelyplanet.com
lonelyplanet.com/contact

© Lonely Planet 2010
Photographs © as listed (p272) 2010

MIX
Paper from
responsible sources
FSC
www.fsc.org
FSC™ C021741